AF167406

Communications
in Computer and Information Science   **2329**

Series Editors

Gang Li, *School of Information Technology, Deakin University, Burwood, VIC, Australia*
Joaquim Filipe , *Polytechnic Institute of Setúbal, Setúbal, Portugal*
Zhiwei Xu, *Chinese Academy of Sciences, Beijing, China*

Rationale

The CCIS series is devoted to the publication of proceedings of computer science conferences. Its aim is to efficiently disseminate original research results in informatics in printed and electronic form. While the focus is on publication of peer-reviewed full papers presenting mature work, inclusion of reviewed short papers reporting on work in progress is welcome, too. Besides globally relevant meetings with internationally representative program committees guaranteeing a strict peer-reviewing and paper selection process, conferences run by societies or of high regional or national relevance are also considered for publication.

Topics

The topical scope of CCIS spans the entire spectrum of informatics ranging from foundational topics in the theory of computing to information and communications science and technology and a broad variety of interdisciplinary application fields.

Information for Volume Editors and Authors

Publication in CCIS is free of charge. No royalties are paid, however, we offer registered conference participants temporary free access to the online version of the conference proceedings on SpringerLink (http://link.springer.com) by means of an http referrer from the conference website and/or a number of complimentary printed copies, as specified in the official acceptance email of the event.

CCIS proceedings can be published in time for distribution at conferences or as post-proceedings, and delivered in the form of printed books and/or electronically as USBs and/or e-content licenses for accessing proceedings at SpringerLink. Furthermore, CCIS proceedings are included in the CCIS electronic book series hosted in the SpringerLink digital library at http://link.springer.com/bookseries/7899. Conferences publishing in CCIS are allowed to use Online Conference Service (OCS) for managing the whole proceedings lifecycle (from submission and reviewing to preparing for publication) free of charge.

Publication process

The language of publication is exclusively English. Authors publishing in CCIS have to sign the Springer CCIS copyright transfer form, however, they are free to use their material published in CCIS for substantially changed, more elaborate subsequent publications elsewhere. For the preparation of the camera-ready papers/files, authors have to strictly adhere to the Springer CCIS Authors' Instructions and are strongly encouraged to use the CCIS LaTeX style files or templates.

Abstracting/Indexing

CCIS is abstracted/indexed in DBLP, Google Scholar, EI-Compendex, Mathematical Reviews, SCImago, Scopus. CCIS volumes are also submitted for the inclusion in ISI Proceedings.

How to start

To start the evaluation of your proposal for inclusion in the CCIS series, please send an e-mail to ccis@springer.com.

Safaa O. Al-Mamory · Ali Al-Sherbaz ·
Triantafyllos Kanakis · Ahmed S. Albahri ·
Wesam S. Bhaya · Eman S. Alshamery ·
Alharith A. Abdullah · Ahmed Al-Ajeli ·
Sura Zaki Alrashid
Editors

Innovations of Intelligent Informatics, Networking, and Cybersecurity

Second International Conference, 3INC 2024
Babylon, Iraq, October 15–16, 2024
Proceedings

 Springer

Editors
Safaa O. Al-Mamory ⓘ
University of Babylon
Hillah, Iraq

Triantafyllos Kanakis ⓘ
University of Northampton
Northampton, UK

Wesam S. Bhaya ⓘ
University of Babylon
Hillah, Iraq

Alharith A. Abdullah ⓘ
University of Babylon
Hillah, Iraq

Sura Zaki Alrashid ⓘ
University of Babylon
Hillah, Iraq

Ali Al-Sherbaz ⓘ
University of Cambridge
Cambridge, UK

Ahmed S. Albahri ⓘ
University of Information Technology
and Communications
Baghdad, Iraq

Eman S. Alshamery ⓘ
University of Babylon
Hillah, Iraq

Ahmed Al-Ajeli ⓘ
University of Babylon
Hillah, Iraq

ISSN 1865-0929   ISSN 1865-0937 (electronic)
Communications in Computer and Information Science
ISBN 978-3-031-81064-0   ISBN 978-3-031-81065-7 (eBook)
https://doi.org/10.1007/978-3-031-81065-7

This Springer imprint is published by the registered company Springer Nature Switzerland AG
The registered company address is: Gewerbestrasse 11, 6330 Cham, Switzerland

If disposing of this product, please recycle the paper.

Preface

The 2nd International Conference on Innovations of Intelligent Informatics, Networking, and Cybersecurity (3INC 2024), held in Babylone, Iraq, on October 15–16, 2024, was hosted and organized by the College of Information Technology at the University of Babylon. It was an international conference focusing on specific topics in Intelligent Informatics, Information Networking, and Cybersecurity.

The 3INC 2024 conference aimed to establish a meeting for advance discussion of the accepted papers for evolving applications of computer methodologies to be used to understand cognition in the fields of Intelligent Informatics, Information Networking, and Cybersecurity. Hence, researchers and participants were invited to submit their high-quality research in such fields. The conference supported researchers and experts together to share novel outcomes and practical findings in the above-mentioned topics. One of the 3INC 2024 conference aims was to enhance scientific research development in Iraq.

From a total of 80 local and international submitted manuscripts, 11 papers were screened out for several reasons like being out of scope or unqualified. Only 15 (with about 22% as an acceptance rate) manuscripts were accepted from the remaining 69 short and long papers. They were delegated to in-depth review by peer reviewers based on their academic interests. The review process was rigorous to ensure selection of the best-quality submissions, with each manuscript being reviewed by at least three reviewers through a double-blind peer-review process. The accepted manuscripts were distributed into three tracks encompassing Information Systems, Computing Methodologies, and Security and Privacy.

Our great gratitude goes to the conference Committee members and all reviewers for their valuable feedback and time during the reviewing process. This high-quality conference would not have been possible without the effort and expertise of the Program Committee members. All submissions were reviewed within the reviewing period and this should be greatly admired.

We would also like to thank the keynote speakers for their time and their excellent speeches. Our great thanks go to the authors for giving us the opportunity to read their great work. It is expected that the accepted papers in this volume will inspire readers and researchers and open the door for further research. It is hoped that readers will find much of interest in these proceedings. The submissions were managed using the Conference Management Toolkit (CMT), which is sponsored by Microsoft Research. We thank the

College of Information Technology at the University of Babylon for supporting this Conference.

October 2024

Safaa O. Al-Mamory
Ali Al-Sherbaz
Triantafyllos Kanakis
Ahmed S. Albahri
Wesam S. Bhaya
Eman S. Alshamery
Alharith A. Abdullah
Ahmed Al-Ajeli
Sura Zaki Alrashid

Organization

General Chair

Wesam Bhaya   University of Babylon, Iraq

Program Committee Chairs

Safaa O. Al-Mamory	University of Babylon, Iraq
Ali Al-Sherbaz	University of Cambridge, UK
Triantafyllos Kanakis	University of Northampton, UK
Ahmed S. Albahri	University of Information Technology and Communications, Iraq
Wesam Bhaya	University of Babylon, Iraq
Eman S. Alshamery	University of Babylon, Iraq
Alharith A. Abdullah	University of Babylon, Iraq
Ahmed Al-Ajeli	University of Babylon, Iraq
Sura Zaki Alrashid	University of Babylon, Iraq

Steering Committee

Ameer Al-Haq Alshamery	University of Babylon, Iraq
May A. Salih	University of Babylon, Iraq
Ameer Kadhim Hadi	University of Babylon, Iraq
Ahmed M. Al-Salih	University of Babylon, Iraq
Nawfal Turki Obeis	University of Babylon, Iraq
Aladdin A. Abdulhassan	University of Babylon, Iraq
Wadhah R. Baiee	University of Babylon, Iraq
Hasanein Alharbi	University of Babylon, Iraq
Hayder Kadhim Zghair	University of Babylon, Iraq
George Ajam	University of Babylon, Iraq
Mohammed Ibrahim Kareem	University of Babylon, Iraq
Mohammad Jawad Kadhim Abood	University of Babylon, Iraq
Hassan H. Alrehamy	University of Babylon, Iraq

Program Committee

Abdelnaser Omran	Bright Star University, Libya
Ahmad Al Smadi	Zarqa University, Jordan
Ahmed Al-Ajeli	University of Babylon, Iraq
Ahmed Al-Azawei	University of Babylon, Iraq
Ahmed Hussein Ali	University of Al-Iraqia, Iraq
Ahmed Mahdi Al-Salih	University of Babylon, Iraq
Ahmed Saad Hussein	UOITC, Iraq
Ahmed Saleem Abbas	University of Babylon, Iraq
Aini Syuhada Md Zain	Universiti Malaysia Perlis, Malaysia
Akhil Mittal	Black Duck, USA
Alaa Al Jarah	University of Babylon, Iraq
Alaa Fareed Abdulateef	Universiti Utara Malaysia, Malaysia
Alaa Shawqi Jaber	University of Babylon, Iraq
Aladdin A. Alsharify	University of Babylon, Iraq
Alejandro Zunino	UNCPBA & CONICET, Argentina
Alharith A. Abdullah	University of Babylon, Iraq
Ali Alnooh	UOITC, Iraq
Ali Al-Bayatti	De Montfort University, UK
Ali Al-Sherbaz	University of Cambridge, UK
Ali Jaddoa	Canterbury Christ Church University, UK
Ali N. Al-Shuwaili	UOITC, Iraq
Ali Saeed Alowayr	Albaha University, Saudi Arabia
Ali Saleem Haleem	Al-Mustaqbal University College, Iraq
Ameer Kadhim Hadi	University of Babylon, Iraq
Ameer A. Alshamery	University of Babylon, Iraq
Amera W. Al-funjan	University of Babylon, Iraq
Angela Amphawan	Sunway University, Malaysia
Asaad Hashim	University of Kufa, Iraq
Ashraf AbdelRaouf	Misr International University, Egypt
Athraa Jani	Al-Nahrain University, Iraq
Aws Yonis	Ninevah University, Iraq
Azhar F. Al-zubidi	Al-Nahrain University, Iraq
Bahaa Al-Musawi	University of Kufa, Iraq
Balqees Talal Hasan	Ninevah University, Iraq
Daniela Litan	Hyperion University, Romania
Ehsan Ali Kareem	University of Kufa, Iraq
Elham M. T. A. Alsaadi	University of Kerbala, Iraq
Emad Ahmed Mohammed	North Technical University, Iraq
Eman S. Alshamery	University of Babylon, Iraq
Hadab Khalid Obayes	University of Babylon, Iraq

Haider M. Al-Mashhadi	University of Basrah, Iraq
Hanaa Mohsin Ali	University of Babylon, Iraq
Haneen Ahmed	University of Baghdad, Iraq
Hasan S. M. Al-Khaffaf	University of Duhok, Iraq
Hassan H. Alrehamy	University of Babylon, Iraq
Haydar Al-Tamimi	University of Technology, Iraq
Hayder Kadhim Zghair	University of Babylon, Iraq
Hiba Ameer Jabir	University of Babylon, Iraq
Hiba Mohammed Al-Khafaji	University of Babylon, Iraq
Hilal Mohammed Yousif Albayatti	Applied Science University, Bahrain
Hind Salim Ghazi	UOITC, Iraq
Hiva Aleqabie	University of Kerbala, Iraq
Huda N. Nawaf	University of Babylon, Iraq
Hussein Alkhazraji	University of Northampton, UK
Iman Kadhim Abood	University of Babylon, Iraq
Iman Qays Abduljaleel	University of Basrah, Iraq
Intisar Shadeed Al-Mejibli	UOITC, Iraq
Jyoti Prakash Singh	University of Calcutta, India
Kadhim B. Swadi	Esraa University, Iraq
Khaldoon Dhou	Texas A&M University, USA
Khaldoon Hasan	University of Babylon, Iraq
Khitam Abdulnabi Salman	University of Technology, Iraq
Ku Ruhana Ku-Mahamud	Universiti Utara Malaysia, Malaysia
Layla H. Abood	University of Technology, Iraq
Daniela Litan	Hyperion University, Romania
Maad M. Mijwil	Baghdad College of Economic Sciences University, Iraq
Mahmood Ahmadi	Razi University, Iran
Mahmood Khalsan	University of Northampton, UK
Manar Hamza Bashaa	Karbalaa University, Iraq
Mark Lochrie	University of Central Lancashire, UK
Marwah Nihad	University of Kirkuk, Iraq
Marwah Kamil Hussein	University of Basra, Iraq
Maryam Abo-Tabik	University of Central Lancashire, UK
Matheel Emad Abdulmunim	University of Technology, Iraq
Mehdi Ebady Manaa	Al-Mustaqbal University, Iraq
Michael Opoku Agyeman	University of Northampton, UK
Mohammad Alhisnawi	University of Babylon, Iraq
Mohammad R. Kadhum	University of Karbala, Iraq
Mohammed Al Jameel	University of Northampton, UK
Mohammed Al-khafajiy	University of Lincoln, UK
Mohammed Al-Neama	University of Mosul, Iraq

Mohammed Ibrahim Kareem	University of Babylon, Iraq
Mohammed Rashad Baker	University of Kirkuk, Iraq
Mohannad M. Al-Yasiry	University of Babylon, Iraq
Muhammad Raheel Mohyuddin	Al Ain University, UAE
Muthana Salih Mahdi	Mustansiriyah University, Iraq
Nadia F. Al Bakri	Al Nahrain University, Iraq
Nashwan D. Zaki	UOITC, Iraq
Nor S. Sani	Universiti Kebangsaan, Malaysia
Kiran Sree Pokkuluri	Shri Vishnu Engineering College for Women, Bhimavaram, India
Qabeela Thabit	Ministry of Education, Iraq
Qaysar S. Mahdi	Tishk International University, Iraq
Rabab Farhan Abbas	University of Technology, Iraq
Rana Hameed Hussain	University of Thi-Qar, Iraq
Ruslan Al-Nuaimi	Al-Nahrain University, Iraq
Saba Ayad Tuama	UOITC, Iraq
Saba Talib Hamada	UOITC, Iraq
Safa S. Abdul-Jabbar	University of Baghdad, Iraq
Safa Saad Abbas	University of Babylon, Iraq
Safaa Hatem	Al Muthanna University, Iraq
Safaa O. Al-Mamory	University of Babylon, Iraq
Sahad Ahmed Hussein	University of Babylon, Iraq
Samar Taha Taha	UOITC, Iraq
Sanjay Poddar	Federation University Australia, Australia
Sarmad K. Ibrahim	Mustansiriyah University, Iraq
Scott Turner	Canterbury Christ Church University, UK
Shayma Nourildean	University of Technology, Iraq
Shaymah Akram Yasear	Al-Qasim Green University, Iraq
Shelan Khasro Tawfeeq	University of Baghdad, Iraq
Soheir Noori	University of Kerbala, Iraq
Suad Abdulelah Alasadi	University of Babylon, Iraq
Suadad Safaa Mahdi	University of Babylon, Iraq
Sumaya Hamad	University of Anbar, Iraq
Sura Zaki Alrashid	University of Babylon, Iraq
Suroor M. Dawood	University of Basrah for Oil and Gas, Iraq
Susan M. A. Saleh	University of Babylon, Iraq
Thar Baker Shamsa	University of Brighton, UK
Triantafyllos Kanakis	University of Northampton, UK
Venkatesh Ramalingam	PSNA College of Engineering and Technology, India
Vijay G. Kumar	PBR Visvodaya Institute of Technology and Science, India

Vijay Kumar	Osmania University, India
Wadhah Razooqi Baiee	University of Babylon, Iraq
Wesam S. Bhaya	University of Babylon, Iraq
Yaseen Ismael	Mosul University, Iraq
Yaseen N. Jurn	UOITC, Iraq
Yasmin Mohialden	Mustansiriyah University, Iraq
Yousif A. Hamad	University of Kirkuk, Iraq
Yousra Fadil	University of Diyala, Iraq
Yusra Faisal al-Irhayim	University of Mosul, Iraq
Zahraa Kadhim Al-Sindy	University of Kerbala, Iraq
Zaineb M Alhakeem	University of Basrah for Oil and Gas, Iraq
Ziad Al-Abbasi	Middle Technical University, Iraq

Contents

Security and Privacy

Information System

Localization in WSNs Based on Machine Learning Approach

Muhammed A. Mahdi$^{(\boxtimes)}$, Ali Y. Yousif, and Mahdi Abed Salman

University of Babylon, Babil, Iraq
{wsci.muhammed.a,wsci.ali.yakoob,mahdi.salman}@uobabylon.edu.iq

Abstract. Several researchers have paid attention on locating coordinates of sensors due to its importance for many applications in Wireless Sensor Networks (WSNs). Usually WSNs consist of a number of small, limited energy and low processing capabilities sensors. These sensors can communicate with each other to carry out a specific task according to the application they have been designed for. Using GPS embedded with each sensor may be expensive in terms of cost and consumed energy. So the attention is focused toward designing localization algorithms without using more GPSs. In this paper, machine-learning approach has been proposed to estimate the position of each unknown node in WSNs. It is based on signal strength and positions of three anchors (sensors know their positions). K-Nearest Neighbours KNN and Neural Network (perceptron back propagation) are used in the proposed model to estimate the coordinates of unknown sensors based on data collected from simulation. The main idea of this paper is motivated by a hypothesis which assumes that the position of sensor has a strong correlation with the signal intensity of other nearby sensors. The results emphasise a good accuracy obtained using the model comparing with some related works. Indeed, the average of difference in distances between the actual locations and the estimated locations of the sensor nodes is about 0.84 m.

Keywords: KN · Localization · ML · NN · RSSI · WSN

1 Introduction

During the last decade, several researchers have increasingly highlighted the use of Wireless Sensor Networks WSNs [1–3]. WSN consists of a number of sensors or nodes. The main limitation of WSNs is limited energy [4]. The most consumed energy is by communication (sending and receiving messages). Energy consumed by communication is more than energy consumed in processing and sensing tasks [5]. However, WSNs have a good role in controlling and monitoring many environments. In fact, WSNs' applications in dangerous and unreachable environments have solved issues of those environments. However, some of these applications may need positions (x,y) of deployed sensors. Because of the cost of using GPS with every sensor, researchers have been motivated to design algorithms for localization in WSNs. Most of these algorithms are designed to estimate the coordinates of sensors with using as less GPSs as possible [6, 7].

S. O. Al-Mamory et al. (Eds.): 3INC 2024, CCIS 2329, pp. 3–14, 2025.
https://doi.org/10.1007/978-3-031-81065-7_1

In this case a number of sensors may have GPSs called anchors. These anchors may be used to help other unknown sensors to estimate their positions. Due to having or knowing location information, the anchors can send some information such as distances or angles to neighbour nodes or unknown nodes. The latter can use this information to estimate their positions. Nevertheless, these algorithms vary in terms of cost and accuracy.

On the other hand, Machine learning (ML) is a technique of artificial intelligence (AI) which has been used extensively for several tasks including regression, classification, and estimation as this paper suggests. Usually the algorithms of ML are based on computational approach, statistics, mathematical, and neuroscience [8]. This paper is motivated by the following idea. It assumes that using signal intensity of nearby sensors can help to estimate positions.

In this study there is a proposed model based on ML technique to estimate the location of unknown sensors in WSNs. It measures Received Signal Strength Indicator (RSSI) of the signal received from several anchors (three anchors in our model). The model detects the relation between the RSSI and locations of anchors to compute the location of unknown sensors using ML: K-Nearest Neighbours KNN and Neural Network NN (perceptron back propagation). This paper is going to contribute in investigating the ability of KNN and NN to estimate the positions of unknown sensors in WSNs based on data prepared in simulation.

Five sections including the introduction have been organized in this paper. The next section is to survey the related works that have been suggested up to now. The proposed model is highlighted in the third section in detail. The collected data and performance metrics also are mentioned in the third section. The fourth section is dedicated to discuss the results. Conclusions and future works are discussed in the last section.

2 Related Works

Localization in WSN has been increasingly brought to light due to its importance [9]. Authors in [1] used multi-strategy fusion to localize the unknown sensor locations in WSNs. Four optimization techniques have been used to minimize error of estimating the locations of unknown sensors. These are African Buffalo Optimization (ABO), Deterministic Selection Optimization DSA, Elephant Herding Optimization (EHO) and KNN. In [10] a connected network has been achieved using localization model. An arithmetic optimization algorithm is used to localize the nodes. Authors in [11] suggested a localization algorithm depending on RSSI measurement. It adopts maximum likelihood estimation. When the signal strength is received it is transformed into estimator non-conves to localize the target. Authors in [12] used four static anchors at the corners of the field. Range-based Angle of Arrival (AoA) approach is used where each anchor has directional antenna. The unknown nodes estimate its location use information of the anchors. In [13] mobile anchors are used to estimate the unknown location. Hexagonal path based on RSSI and triangulation is used. Information about position and distance is sent by three mobile anchors to the unknown nodes to estimate their locations. Trilateral centroid localization algorithm is used in [14] using RSSI to estimate the unknown nodes based on three steps. (1) Calculate the distance between three anchors and unknown node. (2) The coordinate of unknown node will be estimated. (3) In correction step, the error will be decreased. In [15] a new algorithm has been suggested using trilateration and RSSI to estimate locations of unknown nodes. In [16] there are two phases in the suggested algorithm. (1) Trilateration is used in estimating the coordinates. (2) Fuzzy weighted method is used in centroid techniques. Good accuracy has been achieved in this algorithm by using number of anchors. Authors in [17] used three algorithms to localize the positions of unknown sensors. Distance vector DV hop has good accuracy comparing with range free algorithms but it is less than range- based algorithms. As we compare the results with [1], we also compare the results with [18] in which three mobile anchors are used for localizing the sensors, this method is called Triple Mobile Anchors Localization. TMAL used the Relative Side Coordinates based on three mobile anchors. In Table 1 related works are summarized for comparison.

Table 1. Summary of related works

Ref.	Technique	Type
[1]	Multi strategy fusion, Optimization techniques (ABO, DSA, EHO)	RSSI
[10]	An arithmetic optimization algorithm	RSSI
[11]	Maximum likelihood estimation	RSSI
[12]	Range-based approach	AOA
[13]	Mobile anchors	Hexagonal path based on RSSI
[14]	Trilateral centroid localization algorithm	RSSI
[15]	Trilateration	RSSI
[16]	A modified trilateration algorithm	RSSI
[17]	DV hop algorithm achieves 2D Hyperbolic Algorithm Centroid algorithm	RSSI
[18]	Triple Mobile Anchors for Localization	RSSI
Proposed model	Machine learning	RSSI

3   Machine Learning Model for Localization

Machine learning approaches have been used in our model to estimate the positions of unknown nodes. The signal strength and position information of three anchors have been based in the proposed model. It is well known that a machine can learn from previous observations coded as digital data to be used in the future predications whatever was a behaviour or an output [19, 20]. Hence, there are three phases for building a machine learning based project: Dataset preparing, model training and application. The first two phases are made in the laboratory while the last one is implemented in the field. In the following sections, we present the process of each phase in details.

After training, the model is exploiting indicators of signal strength of nearby anchors which is relative to coordinates of unknown nodes. As a result the model estimates the positions of these unknown nodes.

3.1 Data Set Preparing

The most important attributes which are used to be input of the dataset are coordinates (x,y) of mobile anchors and their RSSI. Another item in the vector is the target (position of sensor) so the vector can be represented as: $\{\{p_1(x_1, y_1), rssi_1\}, \{P_2(x_2, y_2), rssi_2\}, \{p_3(x_3, y_3), rssi_3\}\}$, where: $p_i(x_i, y_i)$ is the coordinate of anchor$_i$ and rssi$_i$ is signal strength indicator of anchor$_i$.

The output data of the model is the estimated coordinates of unknown nodes. It is represented as (x_k, y_k) and $k = 1..N$, where N is the number of unknown nodes sensors so the size of dataset depends on N. The length of pattern vector is 11 features (9 input and 2 target).

To collect data, sensors have been deployed in a grid form also using three anchors to form a triangle. At each grid point, RSSI can be computed to complete the vector. Figure 1 demonstrates the possible positions of both sensors and anchors that are considered in preparing the dataset. The points inside the triangle that are not marked by green colour are not considered since they cannot receive signals from all the three anchors at same time.

3.2 Distance Estimation

For reasons of feasibility, the data is collected by simulation. So the RSSI for each mobile anchor is measured at each sensor point relatively to the distance between them plus minus the variation in the Wi-Fi signal. It is computed through the formula (1). The first term represents the real distance between a mobile anchor and an unknown node, while the second term is a value sampled from Gaussian distribution with range θ.

$$dis_i = \sqrt{(x_s - x_{mi})^2 + (y_s - y_{mi})^2} + \theta \times (0.5 - random(1)) \tag{1}$$

where xs, ys are the position coordinates of unknown sensor, xmi, ymi are the coordinate of the reference or anchor node i, θ is the variation range of the Wi-Fi signal.

For n sensors, the dataset will look like the sample in Table 2. The collected data is often divided into training set and testing set as 80% and 20% respectively.

3.3 Machine Learning Approaches

We have implemented two machine learning approaches; namely: k-nearest neighbours Knn and neural network of type perceptron back propagation. Both models are of type multi-output regression. i. e. they estimate the coordinates of the unknown sensor node based on the coordinates and signal strength indicator of the anchor nodes.

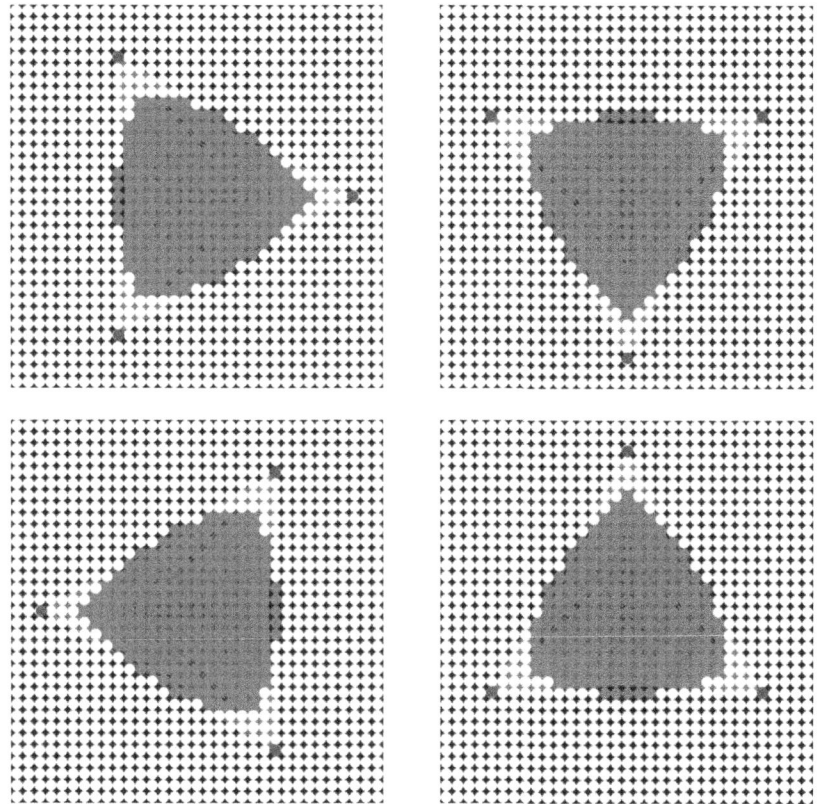

Fig. 1. Candidate locations for anchors and sensors in dataset

Table 2. Dataset sample

Input								Target	
Anchor1(x,y)		$Rssi_1$	Anchor2(x,y)		$Rssi_2$	Anchor3(x,y)		$Rssi_3$	Unknown node(x,y)	
17	23	17	0	5	8	24	0	17	10	14
17	23	18	0	5	20	24	0	6	21	9
17	23	20	0	5	12	24	0	13	13	10
17	23	21	0	5	6	24	0	18	8	13
17	23	5	0	5	17	24	0	22	16	24
17	23	17	0	5	8	24	0	17	10	14

K-Nearest Neighbours KNN

K-Nearest neighbour model is known as lazy machine learning approach since the training dataset is used directly in the application without modification and each data item is previously classified with its class label. For computing the estimated value for new unlabelled item, it is compared with n nearest data points. It is assigned to the class that has most points belonging to it.

Neural network
Neural network NN is a black box model that is trained to learn from data set with known labels to make a decision on classifying new data items.

The most famous type of NN is perceptron neural network, in which the network is composed from three layers: input, hidden and output.

The training process of the neural network uses the Mean Square Error (MSE) performance function to compute the accuracy of training and testing process.

To evaluate the feasibility of the model, the average difference between the actual location of the sensors and the predicted locations is calculated using error formula (2):

$$Error = \frac{\sum_{i=1}^{N} \left(\sqrt{\left(x_{actual} - x_{predected}\right)^2 + \left(y_{actual} - y_{predected}\right)^2} \right)_i}{N} \tag{2}$$

where N is the number of the sensors.

4   Results and Discussions

NetLogo is used to deploy the three anchors and unknown sensors (N). Then each unknown sensor measures RSSI of each anchor node and then the data is collected in a dataset file. An area of deployment is represented by a grid of (33*33) patches (each patch corresponds to one metre square) that are considered as possible locations for unknown sensors. Three locations of anchors are forming a triangle. Then, the dataset is divided into training and testing subsets. After that, training and computing error rate are using MatLab.

4.1   Training the Model

As shown in Fig. 1, three different coordinates for anchors are considered in the proposed model. There are about 240 candidate locations for unknown sensor nodes with each position of the group of anchors. Because of the variation of RSSI some candidate locations do not receive three signals from the anchor nodes at the same time, which makes the size of the obtained dataset 968 vectors.

The dataset obtained from simulation is first normalized. This is a necessary step to scale all attributes to the same range e.g. (0–1). The dataset is split into 677 items for training and 291 items for testing.

For KNN, as it is known, the training dataset is used directly as references vectors. The output is obtained by finding one item of the training set with nearest distance to the input one.

After testing, we obtained that the average of mean squire error MSE equals 0.84. That means the average difference distance between actual locations of the unknown nodes and the estimated locations is 0.84 m, which is acceptable in most applications.

For neural network, the process of training is achieved to have a weight matrix. Here a Three-layer feed forward network is created and trained to estimate the approximate locations using the MSE performance function and regularization value of 0.01.

The input layer contains 9 features vector for each sample, which represent three points positions with X,Y values and the three expected distance with required position. In addition, using one hidden layer with 90 nodes empirically is specified. The output layer contains only two nodes to predict the required location namely x_s,y_s. The data set is divided into three sets where 65% for training, 20% for testing and 15% for validation. The total sample space contains 968 vectors. The obtained average performance measures are:

Network performance = 0.5625
Training Performance = 0.4219
Validation Performance = 0.8963
Testing Performance = 0.6968

The details of each one have been depicted in the following figures. Figure 2 shows the small error range centralized on the fit line for all four measures.

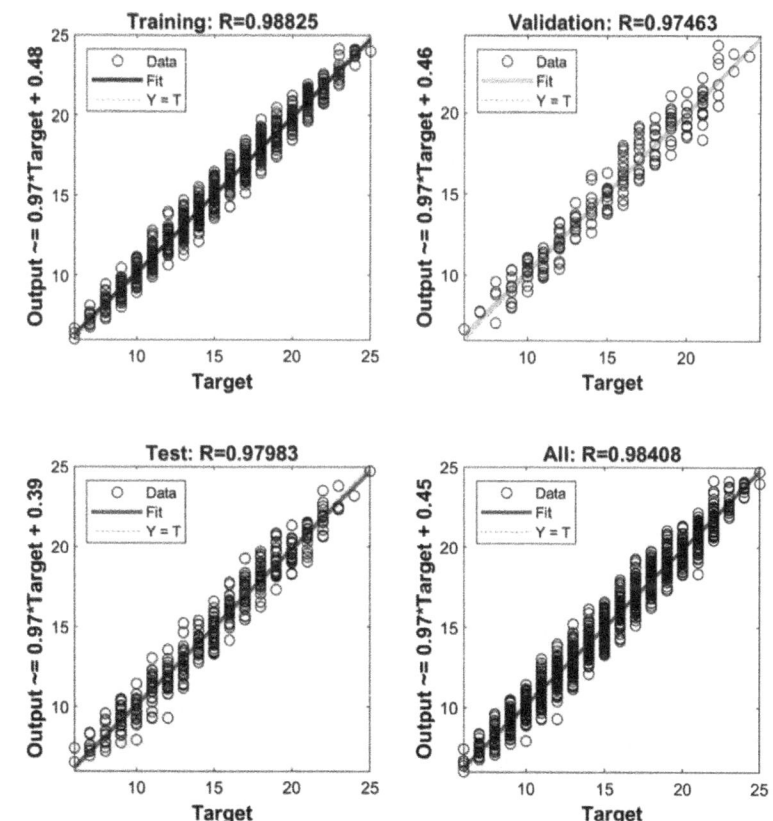

Fig. 2. Performance measures

Figure 3 illustrates the normal distribution of error rate for all data subsets and even for zero error tests. The average error obtaining to the estimated location is:

avgX = 0.5964
avgY = 0.5831

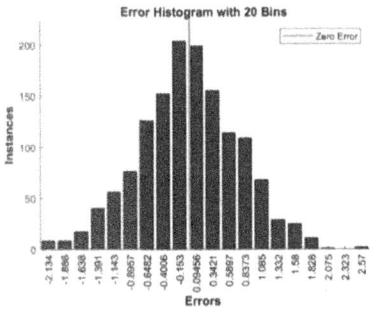

a. overall error histogram

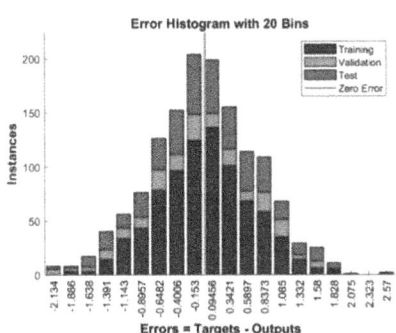

b. detailed error histogram

Fig. 3. Error histogram

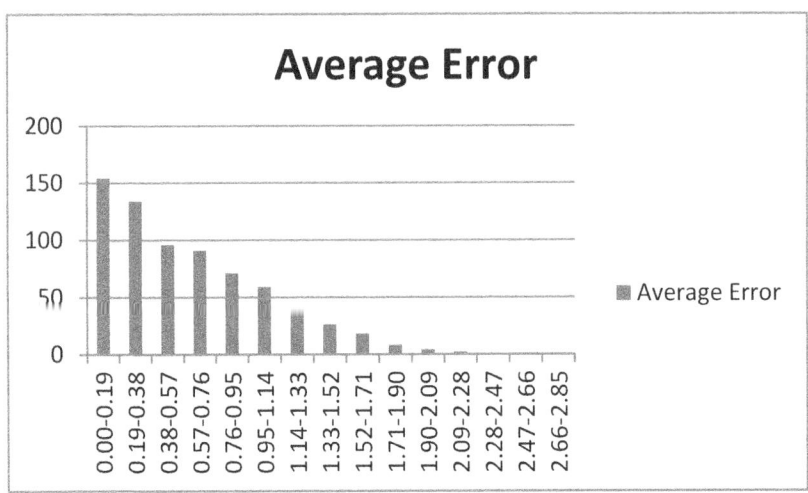

Fig. 4. Final average error between calculated and predicted location

The error histogram is a visual representation of the distribution of errors between the actual and predicted outputs of the network. It is a histogram plot that shows the frequency of occurrence of different error values in the dataset used for training, validation or testing the neural network. The error histogram can help to evaluate the performance of the neural network by visualizing the distribution of errors. It can identify the range of errors, whether they are evenly distributed or skewed towards certain values, and whether there are any outliers in the error distribution. Figure 4 illustrates that only a few sensors have been estimated with relatively high error.

Mean Square Error (MSE) is a commonly used metric for evaluating the performance of a neural network model. MSE measures the average squared difference between the predicted output and the actual output for a set of input data. Figure 5 shows a stable MSE is obtained starting at epoch 6. It indicates that the model is rapidly converging. It also indicates that the data is closely dispersed around its mean (central moment). It gives a good picture which reflects the centralized distribution of the data, in fact it is not skewed, most importantly, it also has fewer errors (errors computed by how dispersion of the data points from the mean).

As shown in Fig. 6 the gradient parameter refers to the gradient of the cost function with respect to the parameters of the model. The gradient is computed during the training of NN, which is used to update the model's parameters in the direction of steepest descent. The gradient parameter is often used as an input to optimization algorithms such as gradient descent or stochastic gradient descent, which are commonly used to minimize the cost function.

In neural networks, momentum is a hyper parameter used in the optimization process to speed up the convergence of the training algorithm. Momentum is used to prevent the optimizer from getting stuck in a local minimum by adding a fraction of the previous weight update to the current update. The value of the momentum parameter typically ranges between 0 and 1, with larger values indicating more momentum.

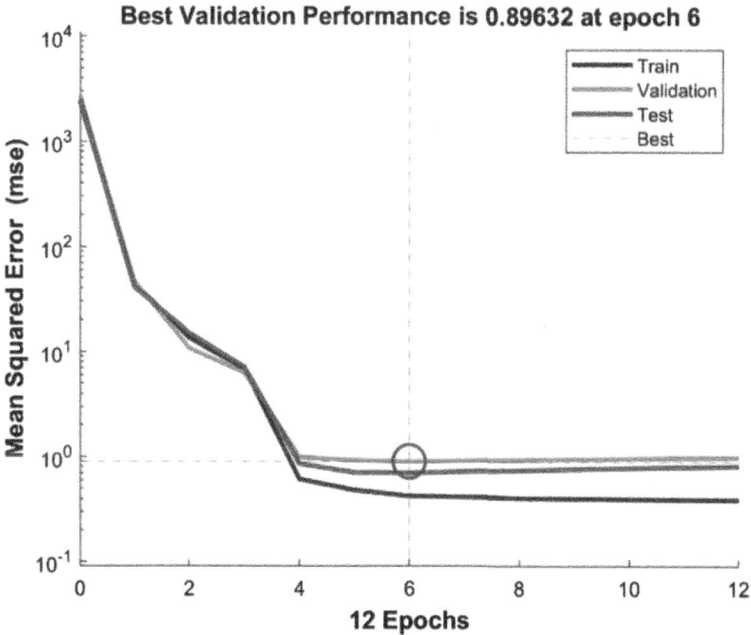

Fig. 5. Performance behaviour of NN after 12 learning epochs

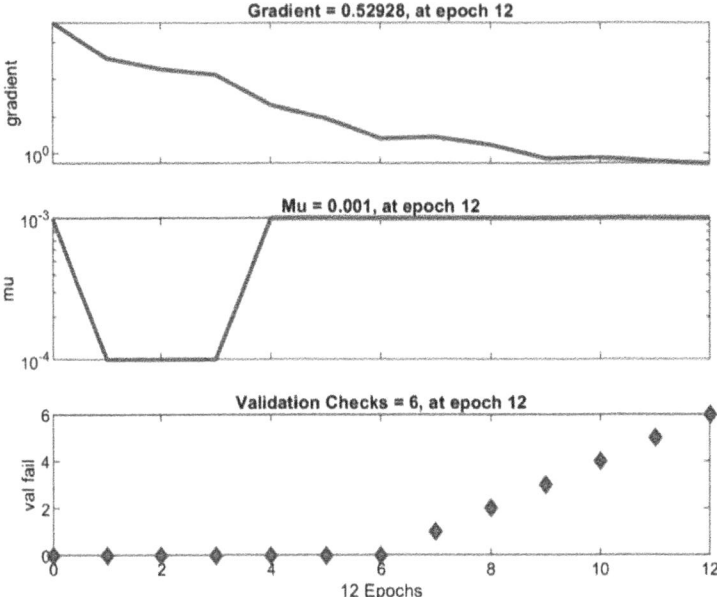

Fig. 6. Network parameters after 12 learning epochs

The validation fail (Val fail) parameter typically refers to the maximum number of validation failures that can occur during training before the training process is stopped. Validation failures occur when the validation error does not decrease for a certain number of epochs during training. The purpose of validation is to ensure that the network does not overfit to the training data and is able to generalize well to new data. If the validation error does not improve after a certain number of epochs (default 6), it is an indication that the network has stopped learning and is overfitting the training data. To prevent overfitting, the validation fail parameter is used to set a limit on the number of consecutive validation failures that are allowed. Once this limit is reached, the training process stops to prevent further overfitting.

4.2 Comparison with Some Related Works

The results are compared with, [1, 21] and [18] in terms of accuracy and energy. The proposed model has better average accuracy than all three models. Although the proposed model has no attention to the consumed energy, it is the same calculated in [18]. The Fig. 7. Shows that our result (average error) is less than others compared.

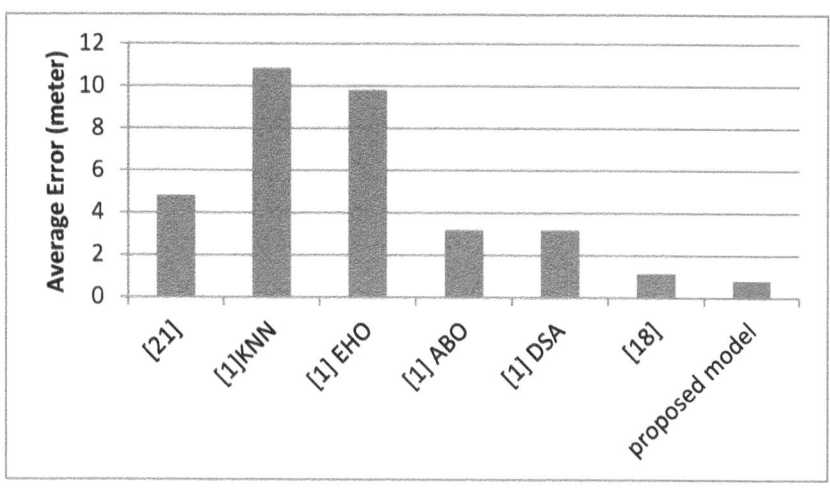

Fig. 7. Comparing results with [1, 21] and [18]

5 Conclusion

Machine learning approach is used to estimate the unknown locations of sensors in WSNs. K-nearest neighbours (KNN) and neural network (perceptron back propagation) are good tools to build the model for locations estimation. The coordinates of unknown sensors based on collected data have been estimated with small error. However NN provides a good accuracy. Average accuracy of the model computed as the distance between actual location and the estimated location is approximately 0.84 m. As a future work, this approach may play an important role if it uses dataset collected from more than three anchor nodes or using different ML techniques.

References

1. Salman, M.A., Mahdi, M.A.: Multi-strategy fusion for enhancing localization in wireless sensor networks (WSNs). Iraqi J. Comp. Sci. Maths. **5**(1), 299–326 (2024)
2. Jutinico, A.L., Rodriguez, G.A., Lopez, J.R.R.C.: Wearable sensor network for lower limb angle estimation in robotics applications. TELKOMNIKA (Telecommunication Computing Electronics and Control) **21**(2), 390–399 (2023)
3. Safiee, R.A., Apandi, N.I.A., Muhammad, N.A., Sheng, W.W., Sarijari, M.A.: Relay node placement in wireless sensor network for manufacturing industry. Bulletin of Electr. Eng. Info. **12**(1), 158–166 (2023)
4. Ullah, A., et al.: A hybrid approach for energy consumption and improvement in sensor network lifespan in wireless sensor networks. Sensors **24**(5), 13–53 (2024)
5. Balachandran Nair Premakumari, S., Mohan, P., Subramanian, K.: An enhanced localization approach for energy conservation in wireless sensor network with Q deep learning algorithm. Symmetry **14**(12), 15–25 (2022)
6. Mahdi, M.A., Hasson, S.T.: A Contribution to the Role of the Wireless Sensors in the IoT Era. J. Telecomm. Electr. Comp. Eng. (JTEC) **9**(2–11), 1–6 (2017)

7. Saeed, R.N., Salman, M.A., Mahdi, M.A.: Data Reduction Based on Adaptive Stream Window Size for IoT Data, pp. 39–44 (2022)
8. Rami Reddy, M., Ravi Chandra, M., Venkatramana, P., Dilli, R.: Energy-efficient cluster head selection in wireless sensor networks using an improved grey wolf optimization algorithm. Computers **12**(2), 35 (2023)
9. Ramalingam, R., Saleena, B., Basheer, S., Balasubramanian, P., Rashid, M., Jayaraman, G.: EECHS-ARO: energy-efficient cluster head selection mechanism for livestock industry using artificial rabbits optimization and wireless sensor networks. Electr. Res. Archi. **31**(6), 3123–3144 (2023)
10. Bhat, S.J., KV, S.: A localization and deployment model for wireless sensor networks using arithmetic optimization algorithm. Peer-to-Peer Networking and Applications **15**(3), 1473–1485 (2022)
11. Ding, W., Zhong, Q., Wang, Y., Guan, C., Fang, B.: Target localization in wireless sensor networks based on received signal strength and convex relaxation. Sensors **22**(3), 733 (2022)
12. Nasipuri, A., Li, K.: A directionality based location discovery scheme for wireless sensor networks, pp. 105–111 (2002)
13. Han, G., Zhang, C., Lloret, J., Shu, L., Rodrigues, J.J.: A mobile anchor assisted localization algorithm based on regular hexagon in wireless sensor networks. The Sci. World J. (2014)
14. Yujun, L., Meng, C.: A trilateral centroid localization and modification algorithm for wireless sensor network. Lecture Notes in Electr. Eng. **355**, 96–97 (2015)
15. Valli, R., Sundhar, A., Vignesh, V., Kotari, S.: Simulation and analysis of rssi based trilateration algorithm for localization in Contiki-Os. ICTACT J. Comm. Technol. **7**(3) (2016)
16. Jyoti, R.Y., Singh, N.: Localization in WSN using modified trilateration based on fuzzy optimization. Int. J. Adv. Res. Comp. Sci. Softw. Eng. **3**(7) (2013)
17. Agarwal, H., Dwivedi, A., Kaur, A.: An improved centroid DV hop based algorithm, pp. 72–75 (2017)
18. Ibrahim, B.K., Mahdi, M.A., Salman, M.A.: Triple Mobile Anchors Approach for Localization in WSN, pp. 174–179 (2020)
19. Humady, Z.A., Mahdi, M.A., Salman, M.A.: Localization in WSN based on area of field and mobility: a survey. J. Kufa for Math. Comp. **10**(1), 72–77 (2023)
20. Alsheikh, M.A., Lin, S., Niyato, D., Tan, H.-P.: Machine learning in wireless sensor networks: Algorithms, strategies, and applications. IEEE Communications Surveys & Tutorials **16**(4), 1996–2018 (2014)
21. Karim, L., Nasser, N., El Salti, T.: RELMA: a range free localization approach using mobile anchor node for wireless sensor networks, pp. 1–5 (2010)

Improved Clustering-Based Feature Selection Using Feature Extraction Based on Principal Component Analysis

Ridho Ananda[1,3]($\boxtimes$) (iD), Dina Rachmawaty[1], Budi Pratikno[2],
Odai Amer Hamid[4], and Maifuza Binti Mohd Amin[3]

[1] Industrial Engineering, Telkom University, Jl. DI. Panjaitan 128, Purwokerto
53147, Jawa Tengah, Indonesia
{ridho,dina}@ittelkom-pwt.ac.id
[2] Universitas Jenderal Soedirman, Banyumas, Jawa Tengah 53122, Indonesia
budi.pratikno@unsoed.ac.id
[3] The National University of Malaysia, 43600 Bangi, Selangor, Malaysia
[4] Northern Technical University, 41001 Mosul City, Iraq
oudayamer@ntu.edu.iq

Abstract. Recently, big data on the phenomenon observed was gained easily. Nevertheless, this data certainly has a high dimensional due to the enormous features involved. Consequently, the accuracy of the analysis is low because of the irrelevant features involved. Besides, the high time complexity will occur. Therefore, several approaches are proposed to overcome it. One of them is feature selection (FS). This study proposed a hybrid model incorporating feature extraction using PCA into clustering for FS termed PCA-clustering, where five algorithms were proposed, namely PCA-KM, PCA-AL, PCA-CL, PCA-WL, and PCA-SL. The UCI dataset was utilized in this study, and three simulation schemes were conducted namely the 75%, 50%, and 25% schemes. The validation used was the goodness-of-fit of proximity matrix (GoFPM), the classification accuracy, the clustering results, and the time complexity. The existing FS algorithms and the performance of non-FS were utilized to evaluate the performance of the proposed algorithms. Generally, PCA-KM outperformed other proposed algorithms. Besides, PCA-KM had better performance in GoFPM, classification, and clustering than the existing algorithms in the particular conditions, especially at the 75% schemes. Meanwhile, in the 50% and 25% schemes, the proposed algorithms were under several existing algorithms. In terms of computational efficiency, the proposed algorithms were efficient, with a time complexity categorized as fair and a low computational time. Those showed that the proposed algorithms are viable for big data analysis.

Keywords: feature selection · principal component analysis · clustering · classification · proximity matrix

S. O. Al-Mamory et al. (Eds.): 3INC 2024, CCIS 2329, pp. 15–38, 2025.
https://doi.org/10.1007/978-3-031-81065-7_2

1   Introduction

In recent years, it has been easy for researchers to get an enormous amount of data related to the phenomenon observed, such as medical detection [1], financial fraud [2], biological systems [3,4], and text classification [5]. It can be known that every minute, millions or even billions of data have been generated. Involving the enormous amount of data in the many features is frequently conducted by researchers to study particular phenomena using data-driven approaches comprehensively. Nevertheless, the large number of features will generate new problems. The accuracy of the analysis will be low because there are repeated or irrelevant features included in the dataset [6,7]. In addition, high dimensional data significantly increases the computational complexity and the complexity of the storage space required [8]. Therefore, data preprocessing can be attempted to reduce its dimension. One of the approaches that can be conducted is dimensionality reduction.

Dimensionality reduction is an attempt to reduce data from high dimensions to low dimensions while retaining as much information as possible in the initial data. There are several advantages of dimensionality reduction, namely (1) reducing storage space, (2) minimizing computing time, (3) eliminating redundant, irrelevant, and noise variables, and (4) increasing the effectiveness and efficiency of the classification process [9]. In general, there are two approaches that can be utilized to conduct dimension reduction, namely feature selection (FS) and feature extraction [10]. FS is a dimensionality reduction approach by selecting some of the features that have the highest relevance to the observed problem and removing other features that are not selected [11,12]. Meanwhile, feature extraction transforms all features in the initial dataset into new features with lower dimensions while maintaining distance among objects and correlation among features in the initial data [13].

The feature extraction outcomes are new features from a linear combination of the initial features. The advantage of this approach is that the compression of new features is more efficient. Nevertheless, the meaning of the initial features is missing because there is no meaning in the new features [14]. FS has addressed this limitation, where this approach can maintain the meaning of the dataset features. Furthermore, FS only selects the important features and removes the others that are indicated as redundant features. Therefore, if the aim is to find out the important features and maintain their meaning, FS is recommended to be utilized [15,16]. These methods have been popularly implemented in various fields, such as disease classification [17,18], gene classification [19,20], water forecasting [21], medical image classification [22], and speech emotion recognition [23].

Algorithms in FS are classified into two groups, namely supervised and unsupervised algorithms. In the supervised algorithm, FS has been conducted by using information gain, ANOVA, tree-based, and recursive feature elimination (RFE) [24–27]. Meanwhile, in the unsupervised algorithms, Procrustes, clustering, B2, and B4 have been proposed to execute the FS process [28–30]. Based on the process, unsupervised algorithms can be more reliable than supervised algorithms because unsupervised algorithms can be implemented on labeled or unlabeled datasets. However, algorithms in unsupervised algorithms still have limitations. Methods B2 and B4 only consider the correlation between the main component of principal component analysis (PCA) and the features in the dataset determined one by one [31]. Consequently, this process is inefficient. The inefficiency process also occurs in Procrustes, where the process is carried out by removing one feature, then using the goodness-of-fit of Procrustes (GoFP) between the initial dataset and the new dataset, where the highest GoFP value indicates that the variable correspondingly is worthy of being selected [28]. Meanwhile, the selection process using clustering is only based on the correlation between features [31]. This means that this process only focuses on features that have a strong influence on each other or are redundant. Features that do not have significant information, such as small variance values, may not be detected and removed in the selection process.

Based on the aforementioned statements, the hybrid model may be able to solve the existing limitation. This is because the particular method has the capability to solve the limitations of the other methods. Therefore, this paper proposed a hybrid model for selecting features by implementing feature extraction based on PCA and FS using clustering. This strategy is proposed to get an efficient process without missing the meaning of features. To measure its performance, the proposed algorithm is compared to the existing algorithm based on the goodness-of-fit of Euclidean distance among objects, the accuracy of classification and clustering, and the complexity time.

This paper was organized as follows. Section 2 discusses the configuration of features based on biplot visualization. Section 3 describes the methods used. Then, Sect. 4 presented the simulation results. Section 5 provides a discussion based on the results obtained. Finally, the conclusion and future work are explained in Sect. 6.

2   Configuration of Features Based on Biplot Visualization

Biplot is a graphical representation of PCA that visualizes objects and features in the low dimensions (two or three dimensions) simultaneously [32]. Gabriel introduced this visualization in 1971. The results of the biplot are object configuration, feature configuration, and the relationship among objects and features. Then, the feature configuration obtained will be leveraged in the FS process. Several steps to obtain the feature configuration from the dataset matrix $\mathbf{X}$ in size $n \times p$ are shown below.

1. Translating $\mathbf{X}$ to its mean value using Eq. 1.

$$\mathbf{X} = \mathbf{X} - \frac{1}{n}\mathbf{1}\mathbf{1}'\mathbf{X} \tag{1}$$

where the vector $\mathbf{1}$ is a unit column vector of size $n \times 1$.

2. By using singular value decomposition (SVD), the factors of $\mathbf{X}$ are obtained using Eq. 2.

$$\mathbf{X} = \mathbf{ULW} = \mathbf{UL}^{\alpha}\mathbf{L}^{1-\alpha}\mathbf{W} \tag{2}$$

where $\alpha \in [0,1]$. $\mathbf{U}$ and $\mathbf{W}$ are matrices in size $n \times r$ and $p \times r$, respectively. Meanwhile, $\mathbf{L} = \mathrm{diag}(\lambda_1, \lambda_2, \ldots, \lambda_r)$ refers to a diagonal matrix in $r \times r$, whose elements are the main component of the dataset.

3. Subsequently, the new matrices are defined by using Eq. 3.

$$_n\mathbf{G}_r = \mathbf{UL}^{\alpha} \text{ and } {}_p\mathbf{H}_r = \mathbf{WL}^{1-\alpha}. \tag{3}$$

If $\alpha = 0$ then $\mathbf{G} = [\mathbf{g}_1^T, \mathbf{g}_2^T, \ldots, \mathbf{g}_n^T] = \mathbf{U}$ and $_p\mathbf{H}_r = [\mathbf{h}_1^T, \mathbf{h}_2^T, \ldots, \mathbf{h}_p^T] = \mathbf{WL}$. Another information from this α value is that the cosine similarity between $\mathbf{h}_i$ and $\mathbf{h}_j$ corresponds to the correlation between the ith and jth features. Meanwhile, the Euclidean distance between $\mathbf{g}_k$ and $\mathbf{g}_l$ indicates the Mahalanobis distance between the kth and lth objects.

4. If we use the principal component in low dimensions ($s \ll r$), it is obtained $_n\mathbf{H}_s$, which is the configuration of features in low dimension (in s).

3   Methods

3.1   The Existing FS Algorithms

The feature selection algorithms are classified into two groups, namely supervised and unsupervised algorithms. Supervised algorithms utilize dataset labels during the selection process to maintain classifier performance. Meanwhile, unsupervised algorithms carry out the selection process without involving data labels, where the distance among objects is maintained in this group. Several FS algorithms included in unsupervised are FS using Procrustes, FS using clustering, B2, and B4. Meanwhile, FS that uses information gain, ANOVA, tree-based, and RFE are in the supervised algorithms. Those algorithms have been utilized to compare with the proposed algorithm. A short description of those algorithms is provided below.

Information Gain (IG). The FS algorithm, which is based on information gain, depends on the entropy value of each class and the conditional probability of the class given a feature. In IG-based FS, the information gain value of each feature is calculated individually, where the average of its information gain value in each class is determined. Features with a high information gain value indicate a strong influence on the classification results [33]. Therefore, those features are suggested to be selected as the FS results. The formula for calculating the information gain value of the X feature is shown in Eq. 4 [34].

$$IG(X) = E(D) - \sum_{i=1}^{n} P(D_i|X)DE(D_i) \tag{4}$$

$$E(D) = -\sum_{i=1}^{n} p(i) \log_2 p(i) \tag{5}$$

where $E(D)$ refers to the general entropy, and n is the number of label classes. Meanwhile, $P(D_i|X)$ indicates the conditional probability of D_i given X. Furthermore, $E(D_i$ is the entropy of the ith feature value determined by separating the dataset based on X. Moreover, p_i denotes the probability of the ith class in the dataset.

ANOVA. The ANOVA-based FS is an algorithm for selecting features by considering the significant differences in mean values across different classes. In this procedure, the statistical approach, i.e., F-score, is utilized. Then, features are selected from the highest F-scores [35]. The F-score formula for the X_j feature are shown in Eq. 6.

$$F\text{-score} = \frac{(N-K)\sum_{k=1}^{K} n_k (\bar{x}_k - \bar{x})^2}{(K-1)\sum_{k=1}^{K} \sum_{i=1}^{n_k} (x_{ik} - \bar{x}_k)^2} \tag{6}$$

where K refers to the number of classes, and N is the total number of samples. Meanwhile, n_k indicates the number of samples in the k class. Furthermore, $\bar{x}_k$, $\bar{x}$, and x_{ik} are the mean of the samples in the k class, the overall mean of all samples, and the ith sample in class k, respectively.

Tree-Based Feature Selection. Tree-based FS has been proposed to identify features from their contribution to the performance of the decision tree. In this approach, features with high-importance values are considered to be selected due to their capability to generalize a model well to new data [33]. The procedure of tree-based FS is provided below.

1. Train the decision tree model using all features.
2. Determine the importance value of each feature from the trained model based on its entropy.
3. Sort features based on their high-importance values.
4. Select k features from the first k highest importance values.

Recursive Feature Elimination (RFE). The RFE-based feature selection refers to a technique to select several features within a dataset based on the rank of the feature. This approach utilizes dependency and collinearity among features. The RFE-based FS constructs the classification model by removing the feature and using the remaining features. This process is conducted recursively until all the features are removed alternately once. The steps of the RFE-based FS are given below [33].

1. Construct the classification model by removing one feature.
2. Calculate the importance value of the removed feature based on the classification results.

3. Repeat the first procedure for the other feature until all features have been removed alternately once.
4. Sort features based on their importance value and select the feature from the high importance value.

Feature Selection Using Clustering. The other approach is cluster-based FS, where the clustering algorithms are leveraged. The main procedure of this approach is clustering the features based on their similarity or proximity measure. Subsequently, one feature is selected from each cluster, and the remaining features are rejected [34]. The clusters can be generated by using the non-hierarchical or hierarchical algorithms, such as k-means, single linkage, complete linkage, average linkage, and ward linkage [36,37]. The general steps of cluster-based FS are listed below.

1. Define the similarity matrix based on the correlation value between features.
2. Construct k clusters by maximizing the similarity value among features in the same cluster and minimizing the similarity value among features in the different cluster.
3. Select one feature with the highest variance on each cluster and then remove the remaining features. The k features are selected.

The B2 and B4 Algorithms. The procedure of the B2 and B4 algorithms was conducted by performing the PCA algorithm only once [28]. The first procedure starts by doing PCA on the dataset and deciding on a number of k features that will be selected. Subsequently, the first k components are chosen. Finally, features are selected based on Eq. 7.

$$Y_j = \operatorname*{argmax}_{Y_j} \rho\left(X_i, Y_j\right) \qquad \forall i \in \{1, 2, \ldots, k\} \tag{7}$$

where Y_j and X_i refer to the jth feature and the ith component, respectively. $\rho\left(X_i, Y_j\right)$ is the person correlation between Y_j and X_i.

Meanwhile, the procedure of the B4 algorithm is backward. When the k features are selected, the $p - k$ components are chosen from the first lowest components. Then, by using Eq. 7, the $p-k$ features are determined and removed from the dataset.

Feature Selection Using Procrustes. In this section, the Procrustes analysis is proposed to solve the FS process. Firstly, the new matrix dataset is generated consecutively by replacing a column of zeros. Subsequently, determining the goodness-of-fit of Procrustes between the new datasets and the initial dataset is calculated. Finally, the k features are selected features corresponding to the first k smallest goodness-of-fit of Procrustes obtained. The condition indicates that the selected features have a high influence on the dataset.

3.2 The PCA-Clustering Algorithm for Selecting Features

This paper proposed a hybrid model for the FS process involving the feature configurations in low dimensions obtained from PCA using biplot visualization. This concept is similar to the concept of feature extraction. However, the main focus of this paper is to obtain the feature configurations by ignoring irrelevant information based on their component values. The minimum value of the cumulative component utilized is 80% [38]. This value means that there is an 80% variance of the initial dataset involved in the feature configuration obtained. This configuration gives an advantage, namely adding criteria to the FS process. Not only the correlation between the features used but also the dominant information of the dataset is considered. Then, several features based on their configurations are selected using the clustering method.

The clustering method has been chosen in the selection process because of its reliability and simplicity. There are two approaches in the clustering method, namely hierarchical and non-hierarchical approaches. In the hierarchical approach, several algorithms that can be leveraged are single linkage, complete linkage, average linkage, and ward linkage. Meanwhile, in the non-hierarchical approach, k-means is the most popular method for clustering dataset objects. Clustering has been implemented in several fields, such as education [39–42], the incomplete data problem [43], and the shape data problem [44].

The procedure of the PCA-clustering algorithm proposed for the proposed FS is listed below.

1. Suppose that $\mathbf{X} = (x_{ij})$, in $n \times p$, is a dataset matrix that has n objects, p features, and r rank.
2. Factorize $\mathbf{X}$ using SVD and define the matrix $_p\mathbf{H}_q$ using Eq. 8.

$$_p\mathbf{H}_q = {}_p\mathbf{W}_q\mathbf{L}_q \tag{8}$$

where, q, the number of the first q principal components, satisfies Eq. 9. This equation is utilized to involve at least 80% initial information into the feature configuration.

$$\frac{\sum_{k=1}^{q} \lambda_k}{\sum_{l=1}^{r} \lambda_l} \geq 0.80 \tag{9}$$

Vector $\mathbf{h}_i \in {}_p\mathbf{H}_q$ is the configuration of the ith feature.
3. Calculate the dissimilarity measure between the ith and the j features, $\forall i, j$ using Eq. 10.

$$d(i, j) = 1 - s(i, j) \tag{10}$$

where $s(i, j)$ is obtained using the cosine similarity formula in Eq. 11.

$$s(i, j) = \frac{\mathbf{h}_i.\mathbf{h}_j}{|\mathbf{h}_i||\mathbf{h}_j|} \tag{11}$$

4. Determine the number of features selected. If k features are selected, then the clustering algorithm will be used to obtain k clusters based on the dissimilarity

measure among features. The high dissimilarity value of the two features indicates that those features are not in the same cluster. Conversely, those features are in the same cluster if their dissimilarity value is low.

5. Choose the feature with the highest variance value in each cluster and then remove the remaining features. The k features are obtained.

Figure 1 presents the illustration of the PCA-clustering process that will help in understanding the step of PCA-clustering. Meanwhile, the proposed algorithms in this study related to the PCA-clustering for processing FS are shown in Table 1.

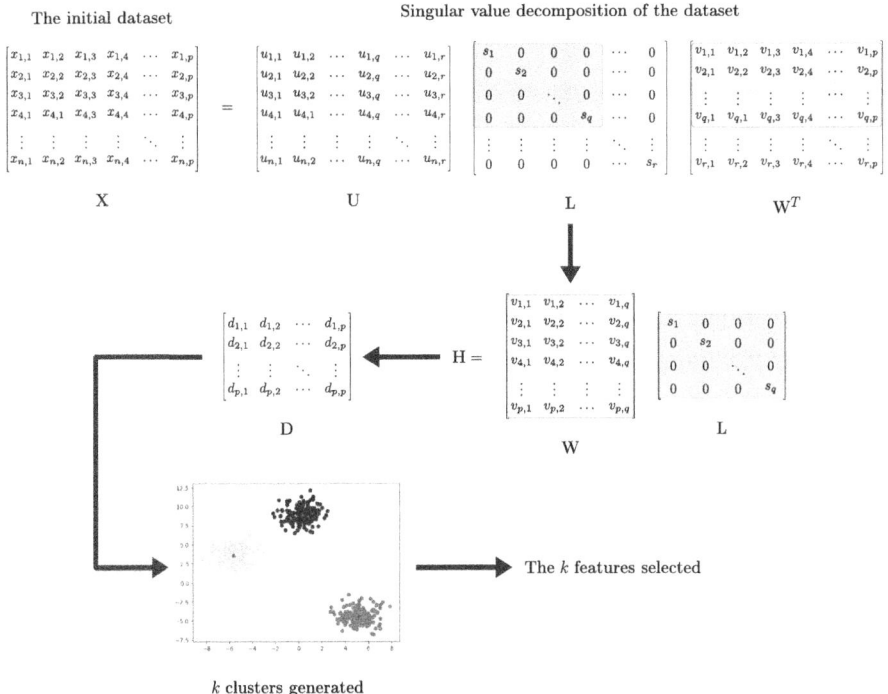

Fig. 1. The illustration of the PCA-clustering process.

3.3   The Validity Used

Comparison activities were carried out to determine the performance of the proposed algorithm. This algorithm was compared with existing algorithms, both supervised and unsupervised, namely clustering, B2, B4, Procrustes, ANOVA, RFE, TREE-based, and information gain. Several validities were used, i.e., the goodness-of-fit (GoF) of the proximity matrix, the classification performance, the clustering results, and the time complexity of the proposed algorithms.

Table 1. The proposed algorithms for feature selection based on PCA and clustering

No	Algorithm	Abbreviation
1	PCA and Hierarchical clustering Kmeans	PCA-KM
2	PCA and Non-hierarchical clustering average linkage	PCA-AL
3	PCA and Non-hierarchical clustering centroid linkage	PCA-CL
4	PCA and Non-hierarchical clustering ward linkage	PCA-WL
5	PCA and Non-hierarchical clustering single linkage	PCA-SL

The GoF of the proximity matrix is obtained by comparing the proximity matrices of the initial dataset ($\mathbf{D}$) and the dataset after the FS procedure ($\bar{\mathbf{D}}$) using the GoF of Procrustes (GoFP) [45], where its formula is presented in Eq. 12 [46].

$$\text{GoFP}(\mathbf{D}, \bar{\mathbf{D}}) = \left(\sum_{i=1}^{r} \sigma_{ii} \right)^2 \tag{12}$$

where r and σ_{ii} are the rank and single values of the matrix in the GoFP procedure, respectively. The GoFP value is expressed in $[0, 1]$, where two matrices have a high goodness-of-fit if the GoFP value is close to 1. On the other hand, those matrices have a low goodness-of-fit if the value is close to 0. The higher the goodness-of-fit of the proximity matrix, the better the performance of the feature selection algorithm will be.

Meanwhile, the classification results are utilized to measure the performance of the feature selection algorithm. It is because one of the goals in feature selection is improving the classification result [47]. In this validity, the k-nearest neighbor (KNN) algorithm is utilized to perform the classification process using the dataset of the feature selection result, where KNN is popular and simple for classification and has been utilized in various fields [48]. Then, the performance of classification based on the accuracy value from FS was compared to the classification results from the initial dataset to know the effect of FS on the classification results. Additionally, the clustering results are also leveraged to identify the performance of the proposed algorithm in clustering. Here, the purity measure was used due to the availability of the initial label. Similar to classification, the clustering results from FS were compared to the results from the initial dataset to recognize the effect of the proposed FS algorithms. Finally, the time complexity is utilized to measure the efficiency of the algorithm.

4   Result

4.1   The Dataset Used

The dataset used in this study is presented in Table 2. Those datasets were obtained from the UCI dataset [49]. Those datasets were selected due to a numerical dataset, where the proposed algorithms work in this type of data. In addition, those datasets have labels. Therefore, the supervised FS algorithms utilized in this study can be implemented.

Table 2. The detail of the dataset used

Symbol	Dataset	n Objects	n Features	n Class
D1	Climate	540	19	2
D2	Cortex Nuclear	552	78	8
D3	E. coli	336	8	8
D4	Ionosphere	351	34	2
D5	Parkinsons	195	17	2
D6	Wine Red	1599	12	6

Three schemes have been utilized in this study,i.e., 75%, 50%, and 25%, which are selecting the number of features in 75%, 50%, and 25%, respectively. The number of features selected in each scheme and each dataset is presented in Table 3.

Table 3. The simulation scheme of the feature selection process in this study

Dataset	n feature	The selected number of feature		
		75% Scheme	50% Scheme	25% Scheme
D1	19	15	9	5
D2	78	59	39	20
D3	8	6	4	2
D4	34	26	17	9
D5	17	13	8	5
D6	12	9	6	3

4.2   Performance of the Proposed Algorithms

In this section, the performance of the proposed algorithms was described after simulation and comparison were conducted. This performance was identified based on its goodness-of-fit of the proximity matrix (GoFPM), accuracy of classification and clustering results, and time complexity. Additionally, the simulation results of each algorithm in each scheme (75%, 50%, 25%) were carried out repeatedly 100 times. The average value of the simulation results of each dataset was presented and described in the subsections below.

Table 4. The GoFP value of each algorithm in the 75% Scheme

No	Algorithm	D1	D2	D3	D4	D5	D6	Avg.
1	PCA-KM	0.696	0.967	0.923	0.868	0.947	0.947	0.891
2	PCA-AL	0.733	0.605	0.916	0.974	0.945	0.022	0.699
3	PCA-CL	0.740	0.624	0.916	0.981	0.945	0.022	0.705
4	PCA-WL	0.740	0.631	0.916	0.986	0.945	0.022	0.707
5	PCA-SL	0.734	0.579	0.916	0.978	0.945	0.022	0.695
6	Clustering	0.710	0.953	0.880	0.848	0.947	0.947	0.881
7	B2	0.706	0.967	0.923	0.875	0.947	0.947	0.894
8	B4	0.711	0.879	0.923	0.846	0.947	0.947	0.876
9	Procrustes	0.705	0.967	0.923	0.877	0.947	0.947	0.894
10	ANOVA	0.724	0.803	0.932	0.865	0.405	0.997	0.788
11	RFE	0.718	0.762	0.932	0.886	0.405	0.481	0.697
12	TREE	0.236	0.742	0.813	0.473	0.949	0.949	0.694
13	IG	0.710	0.668	0.932	0.890	0.966	0.996	0.860
	Max	0.740	0.967	0.932	0.986	0.966	0.997	0.894

Note: The green highlight shows the highest value.

Performance Based on the GoFPM Value. The performance of several algorithms on multiple datasets was presented based on the goodness-of-fit of the proximity matrix under three different schemes. In the 75% schemes as provided by Table 4, PCA-KM achieved higher performance in average value than other proposed algorithms, such as PCA-AL, PCA-CL, PCA-WL, and PCA-SL. In PCA-KM, a high GoFPM value occurred on the Cortex Nuclear (D2), E. coli (D3), Parkinsons (D5), and Wine Red (D6) datasets which were 0.967, 0.923, 0.947, and 0.947 respectively. However, this algorithm was slightly under Procrustes and B2 in terms of the average value obtained. Meanwhile, PCA-AL, PCA-CL, PCA-WL, and PCA-SL were lower performance than PCA-KM and others in their average value. In addition, their performance was poor on the Wine Red (D6) dataset, which was 0.022. Nevertheless, PCA-WL got the highest GoFPM in the Climate (D1) and Ionosphere (D4) datasets, and PCA-CL was highest in the Climate (D1) datasets.

Almost similar conditions to the 75% scheme were found in the 50% scheme in the GoFPM measure as presented in Table 5. However, the performance of all algorithms in this scheme generally decreased compared to the previous scheme. Here, the PCA-KM also got high performance in Cortex Nuclear (D2), E. coli (D3), Parkinsons (D5), and Wine Red (D6), which were 0.970, 0.910, 0.947, and 0.947, respectively. This algorithm outperformed PCA-AL, PCA-CL, PCA-WL, PCA-SL, and several existing algorithms, such as clustering-based FS, B4, ANOVA, RFE, TREE, and IG, in terms of the average value of GoFPM. However, PCA-KM was slightly outperformed by B2 and Procrustes. Furthermore, other proposed algorithms, i.e., PCA-AL, PCA-CL, PCA-WL, and PCA-SL, had

Table 5. The GoFP value of each algorithm in the 50% Scheme

No	Algorithm	D1	D2	D3	D4	D5	D6	Avg.
1	PCA-KM	0.473	0.970	0.910	0.800	0.947	0.947	0.841
2	PCA-AL	0.523	0.583	0.727	0.877	0.275	0.014	0.500
3	PCA-CL	0.524	0.556	0.727	0.904	0.275	0.017	0.500
4	PCA-WL	0.524	0.567	0.727	0.904	0.275	0.014	0.502
5	PCA-SL	0.516	0.577	0.727	0.810	0.275	0.014	0.487
6	Clustering	0.506	0.942	0.697	0.764	0.947	0.993	0.808
7	B2	0.471	0.970	0.943	0.799	0.947	0.947	0.846
8	B4	0.491	0.876	0.939	0.776	0.947	0.947	0.829
9	Procrustes	0.474	0.970	0.881	0.843	0.947	0.947	0.844
10	ANOVA	0.493	0.762	0.856	0.734	0.405	0.949	0.700
11	RFE	0.502	0.722	0.571	0.792	0.008	0.005	0.433
12	TREE	0.236	0.730	0.813	0.568	0.949	0.949	0.708
13	IG	0.462	0.609	0.365	0.761	0.024	0.482	0.451
	Max	0.524	0.970	0.943	0.904	0.949	0.993	0.846

Note: The green highlight shows the highest value.

poor performance in the Parkinsons (D5) and Wine Red (D6) datasets which were around 0.275 and 0.017, respectively.

Also, in the 25% scheme at Table 6, similar conditions to the previous schemes were obtained. However, the performance of the proposed algorithms declined in their GoFPM values. The PCA-KM algorithm slightly underperformed B2 and Procrustes. However, this algorithm was better than the remaining algorithms in the average value. In addition, the PCA-KM got the highest GoFPM value in the Parkinsons (D5) dataset, which was 0.966. Meanwhile, other proposed algorithms generally had poor performance in selecting 25% of the number of existing features.

Performance of Classification. Subsequently, the accuracy results of classification from the proposed FS algorithms were presented in the three schemes (75%, 50%, and 25%) at Table 7, 8, and 9. Here, not only other existing algorithms but also the classification results using the initial dataset (non-FS) were used to identify the effect of FS from the proposed algorithms on the classification performance. In Table 7, where 75% of features were selected, PCA-KM achieved the best classification performance in terms of the average accuracy value, which was 0.880. Meanwhile, PCA-AL, PCA-CL, PCA-WL, and PCA-SL got 0.826, 0.838, 0.838, and 0.830, respectively, indicating their performance was good. Dominantly, those proposed algorithms had a high classification performance in the dataset used, namely more than 0.800, but those algorithms had moderate performance in the Parkinson dataset, i.e., around 0.600. Furthermore, all proposed FS algorithms gave better classification performance than the initial

Table 6. The GoFP value of each algorithm in the 25% Scheme

No	Algorithm	D1	D2	D3	D4	D5	D6	Avg.
1	PCA-KM	0.265	0.979	0.743	0.614	0.966	0.949	0.753
2	PCA-AL	0.238	0.544	0.197	0.773	0.017	0.013	0.297
3	PCA-CL	0.238	0.535	0.197	0.773	0.275	0.013	0.339
4	PCA-WL	0.238	0.544	0.197	0.773	0.275	0.013	0.340
5	PCA-SL	0.240	0.536	0.197	0.768	0.017	0.013	0.295
6	Clustering	0.264	0.932	0.495	0.581	0.947	0.995	0.702
7	B2	0.270	0.980	0.759	0.618	0.947	0.949	0.754
8	B4	0.270	0.871	0.743	0.626	0.947	0.949	0.734
9	Procrustes	0.279	0.977	0.759	0.667	0.947	0.949	0.763
10	ANOVA	0.290	0.734	0.539	0.521	0.405	0.949	0.573
11	RFE	0.281	0.526	0.423	0.557	0.006	0.005	0.300
12	TREE	0.236	0.744	0.813	0.436	0.949	0.949	0.688
13	IG	0.262	0.564	0.052	0.543	0.011	0.042	0.246
	Max	0.290	0.980	0.813	0.773	0.966	0.995	0.763

Note: The green highlight shows the highest value.

dataset. It certainly indicated that they performed well in optimizing the dataset in the classification process by reducing the dimension of data. Compared to the existing FS algorithms, the proposed algorithms had no significant difference in the classification performance.

Meanwhile, in the 50% scheme, the PCA-KM showed a slight decrease compared to the previous scheme and was under the B2 and B4 performance. However, its classification performance was good and outperformed the remaining algorithms, where the average accuracy value was 0.871. Besides, this algorithm got the best accuracy performance in the Cortex Nuclear (D2) dataset, namely 0.996. Then, PCA-KM had successes in increasing the accuracy of the classification process of the initial dataset due to its performance, which was better than the classification Non-FS in all datasets. On the other hand, PCA-AL, PCA-CL, PCA-WL, and PCA-SL performed similarly to each other, and their accuracy was under PCA-KM, clustering, B2, B4, Procrustes, ANOVA, RFE, TREE, IG, and the accuracy result of the non-FS. It indicated that the proposed FS algorithms using hierarchical clustering performed poorly in this scheme because of the decrease in classification accuracy.

Furthermore, in the 25% scheme, as shown in Table 9, it could be known that PCA-KM consistently showed better classification accuracy than other proposed algorithms, such as PCA-AL, PCAL-CL, PCA-WL, and PCA-SL based on its average accuracy value. In addition, this algorithm outperformed clustering, Procrustes, ANOVA, RFE, TREE, IG, and classification non-FS. Furthermore, PCA-KM gained the highest accuracy in several datasets, such as Cortex Nuclear (D2), E. coli (D3), Ionosphere (D4), and Wine Red (D6). On the contrary, other

Table 7. The classification accuracy of each algorithm in the 75% Scheme

No	Algorithm	D1	D2	D3	D4	D5	D6	Avg.
1	PCA-KM	0.931	0.996	0.896	0.855	0.903	0.699	0.880
2	PCA-AL	0.918	0.806	0.894	0.878	0.883	0.579	0.826
3	PCA-CL	0.934	0.827	0.894	0.882	0.891	0.600	0.838
4	PCA-WL	0.934	0.835	0.903	0.878	0.898	0.582	0.838
5	PCA-SL	0.923	0.817	0.903	0.874	0.883	0.578	0.830
6	Clustering	0.928	0.993	0.890	0.858	0.903	0.700	0.879
7	B2	0.920	0.996	0.896	0.858	0.903	0.699	0.879
8	B4	0.915	0.993	0.896	0.858	0.903	0.699	0.877
9	Procrustes	0.935	0.996	0.896	0.846	0.903	0.699	0.879
10	ANOVA	0.944	0.946	0.824	0.859	0.744	0.481	0.800
11	RFE	0.963	0.901	0.824	0.817	0.744	0.441	0.782
12	TREE	0.944	0.973	0.721	0.845	0.872	0.541	0.816
13	IG	0.889	0.730	0.824	0.761	0.821	0.513	0.756
14	Non-FS	0.924	0.889	0.869	0.819	0.815	0.488	0.801
	Max	0.963	0.996	0.903	0.882	0.903	0.700	0.880

Note: The green highlight shows the highest value.

Table 8. The classification accuracy of each algorithm in the 50% Scheme

No	Algorithm	D1	D2	D3	D4	D5	D6	Avg.
1	PCA-KM	0.915	0.996	0.842	0.872	0.903	0.700	0.871
2	PCA-AL	0.918	0.770	0.754	0.870	0.891	0.530	0.789
3	PCA-CL	0.918	0.736	0.763	0.870	0.891	0.504	0.780
4	PCA-WL	0.918	0.788	0.746	0.882	0.854	0.524	0.785
5	PCA-SL	0.921	0.786	0.758	0.886	0.876	0.521	0.791
6	Clustering	0.919	0.993	0.824	0.866	0.903	0.692	0.866
7	B2	0.919	0.996	0.875	0.886	0.903	0.701	0.880
8	B4	0.915	0.993	0.890	0.875	0.903	0.701	0.880
9	Procrustes	0.913	0.996	0.842	0.877	0.903	0.701	0.872
10	ANOVA	0.954	0.964	0.735	0.915	0.744	0.466	0.796
11	RFE	0.954	0.901	0.735	0.859	0.692	0.544	0.781
12	TREE	0.944	0.964	0.721	0.845	0.872	0.541	0.815
13	IG	0.880	0.694	0.662	0.817	0.667	0.444	0.694
14	Non-FS	0.924	0.889	0.869	0.819	0.815	0.488	0.801
	Max	0.954	0.996	0.890	0.915	0.903	0.701	0.880

Note: The green highlight shows the highest value.

proposed algorithms, i.e., PCA-AL, PCAL-CL, PCA-WL, and PCA-SL, predominantly obtained low performance, where their average accuracy performance was worse than other algorithms and the classification non-FS. Nevertheless, in the Ionosphere (D4), Parkinsons (D5), and Wine Red (D6) datasets, those algorithms gave increasing classification accuracy because their accuracy was higher than the classification non-FS.

Table 9. The classification accuracy of each algorithm in the 25% Scheme

No	Algorithm	D1	D2	D3	D4	D5	D6	Avg.
1	PCA-KM	0.915	0.996	0.848	0.892	0.867	0.670	0.865
2	PCA-AL	0.921	0.687	0.534	0.870	0.847	0.491	0.725
3	PCA-CL	0.921	0.693	0.534	0.866	0.869	0.504	0.731
4	PCA-WL	0.918	0.677	0.542	0.866	0.891	0.491	0.731
5	PCA-SL	0.918	0.659	0.551	0.866	0.832	0.492	0.720
6	Clustering	0.924	0.989	0.708	0.860	0.903	0.669	0.842
7	B2	0.915	0.995	0.815	0.889	0.903	0.670	0.865
8	B4	0.915	0.989	0.848	0.883	0.903	0.670	0.868
9	Procrustes	0.911	0.995	0.815	0.892	0.903	0.670	0.864
10	ANOVA	0.963	0.964	0.632	0.873	0.744	0.541	0.786
11	RFE	0.963	0.946	0.588	0.873	0.692	0.556	0.770
12	TREE	0.944	0.973	0.721	0.873	0.872	0.541	0.821
13	IG	0.935	0.568	0.544	0.789	0.590	0.478	0.651
14	Non-FS	0.924	0.889	0.869	0.819	0.815	0.488	0.801
	Max	0.963	0.996	0.848	0.892	0.903	0.670	0.868

Note: The green highlight shows the highest value.

Performance of Clustering. Furthermore, the performance of the proposed FS algorithms has been validated based on their performance in clustering in the 75%, 50%, and 25% schemes. Here, the existing algorithms such as clustering, B2, B4, Procrustes, ANOVA, RFE, TREE, and IG were utilized for comparison, as well as the clustering performance from the initial dataset (non-FS). Because the clustering performance depended heavily on the initial centroid, the clustering performance of each algorithm was obtained from the average of the purity value in 100 times simulation. Here, the k-means algorithm was utilized to obtain the clustering results of each FS algorithm.

In the 75% scheme, as shown in Table 10, the PCA-KM, PCA-CL, and PCA-WL got the same purity value in each dataset used and included in the best results in this scheme due to higher than others. In general, their performance was moderate because the average purity value obtained was 0.674, with high performance only in the Ionosphere and Parkinsons datasets, namely 0.997 and 0.938, respectively. Meanwhile, PCA-AL and PCA-WL had almost the same

Table 10. The clustering performance of each algorithm in the 75% Scheme

No	Algorithm	D1	D2	D3	D4	D5	D6	Avg.
1	PCA-KM	0.587	0.377	0.631	0.997	0.938	0.515	0.674
2	PCA-AL	0.607	0.353	0.741	0.712	0.938	0.440	0.632
3	PCA-CL	0.587	0.377	0.631	0.997	0.938	0.515	0.674
4	PCA-WL	0.624	0.370	0.771	0.704	0.938	0.444	0.642
5	PCA-SL	0.587	0.377	0.631	0.997	0.938	0.515	0.674
6	Clustering	0.587	0.428	0.649	0.997	0.938	0.374	0.662
7	B2	0.565	0.310	0.580	0.670	0.938	0.379	0.574
8	B4	0.587	0.428	0.649	0.997	0.938	0.374	0.662
9	Procrustes	0.591	0.342	0.696	0.709	0.938	0.515	0.632
10	ANOVA	0.565	0.310	0.580	0.670	0.938	0.379	0.574
11	RFE	0.591	0.342	0.696	0.709	0.938	0.515	0.632
12	TREE	0.591	0.342	0.696	0.709	0.938	0.515	0.632
13	IG	0.587	0.428	0.649	0.997	0.938	0.374	0.662
14	Non-FS	0.544	0.403	0.604	0.712	0.811	0.325	0.325
	Max	0.624	0.428	0.771	0.997	0.938	0.515	0.674

Note: The green highlight shows the highest value.

purity value as PCA-KM, PCA-CL, and PCA-WL. Nevertheless, the performance of PCA-AL and PCA-WL was still below. Then, in general, the proposed FS algorithm was able to improve the quality of clustering results. This could be seen from the purity value obtained, which was predominantly higher than the clustering results without FS, namely in the Climate (D1), E. coli (D3), Ionosphere (D4), Parkinsons (D5), and Wine Red (D6) datasets.

Meanwhile, in the 50% scheme, the performance of the proposed algorithms in the clustering performance, as shown in Table 11, showed a low performance. In this scheme, the PCA-KM, PCA-AL, PCA-CL, PCA-WL, and PCA-SL were still under several other comparison algorithms, such as clustering, B2, B4, ANOVA, and Information Gain. Nevertheless, several proposed algorithms still achieved the highest purity value. This can be seen based on the highlighted results on the Climate (D1), E. coli (D3), and Wine Red (D6) datasets. In those datasets, the clustering performance increases compared to the clustering results from other algorithms and non-FS (Table 12).

On the other hand, the decline in performance of the proposed algorithms occurred in the 25% schemes, as shown in Table 11. In this table, the average clustering performance obtained by the proposed algorithm was below the existing algorithms, although it was still above the non-FS clustering performance. In addition, the improvement in the quality of the clustering results was only in the Wine Red (D6) dataset.

Table 11. The clustering performance of each algorithm in the 50% Scheme

No	Algorithm	D1	D2	D3	D4	D5	D6	Avg.
1	PCA-KM	0.543	0.346	0.682	0.712	0.692	0.483	0.576
2	PCA-AL	0.585	0.362	0.595	0.707	0.692	0.370	0.552
3	PCA-CL	0.543	0.346	0.682	0.712	0.692	0.483	0.576
4	PCA-WL	0.587	0.357	0.646	0.712	0.692	0.364	0.560
5	PCA-SL	0.543	0.346	0.682	0.712	0.692	0.483	0.576
6	Clustering	0.539	0.395	0.548	0.704	0.938	0.374	0.583
7	B2	0.546	0.324	0.503	0.980	0.938	0.352	0.607
8	B4	0.539	0.395	0.548	0.704	0.938	0.374	0.583
9	Procrustes	0.585	0.384	0.610	0.707	0.692	0.370	0.558
10	ANOVA	0.546	0.324	0.503	0.980	0.938	0.352	0.607
11	RFE	0.585	0.384	0.610	0.707	0.692	0.370	0.558
12	TREE	0.585	0.384	0.610	0.707	0.692	0.370	0.558
13	IG	0.539	0.395	0.548	0.704	0.938	0.374	0.583
14	Non-FS	0.544	0.403	0.604	0.712	0.811	0.325	0.325
	Max	0.587	0.403	0.682	0.980	0.938	0.483	0.607

Note: The green highlight shows the highest value.

Table 12. The clustering performance of each algorithm in the 25% Scheme

No	Algorithm	D1	D2	D3	D4	D5	D6	Avg.
1	PCA-KM	0.541	0.355	0.482	0.698	0.692	0.348	0.519
2	PCA-AL	0.526	0.348	0.482	0.698	0.810	0.400	0.544
3	PCA-CL	0.541	0.355	0.482	0.698	0.692	0.348	0.519
4	PCA-WL	0.528	0.368	0.482	0.698	0.692	0.364	0.522
5	PCA-SL	0.541	0.355	0.482	0.698	0.692	0.348	0.519
6	Clustering	0.539	0.428	0.554	0.726	0.938	0.374	0.593
7	B2	0.531	0.308	0.479	0.761	0.938	0.415	0.572
8	B4	0.539	0.428	0.554	0.726	0.938	0.374	0.593
9	Procrustes	0.567	0.355	0.470	0.718	0.810	0.373	0.549
10	ANOVA	0.531	0.308	0.479	0.761	0.938	0.415	0.572
11	RFE	0.567	0.355	0.470	0.718	0.810	0.373	0.549
12	TREE	0.567	0.355	0.470	0.718	0.810	0.373	0.549
13	IG	0.539	0.428	0.554	0.726	0.938	0.374	0.593
14	Non-FS	0.544	0.403	0.604	0.712	0.811	0.325	0.325
	Max	0.567	0.428	0.604	0.761	0.938	0.415	0.593

Note: The green highlight shows the highest value.

Performance Based on the Time Complexity. The PCA-clustering algorithms,i.e., PCA-KM, PCA-AL, PCA-CL, PCA-WL, and PCA-SL, have three main parts, namely constructing the feature configuration in the low dimension, calculating the proximity matrix of the features, and conducting the feature selection process based on the clustering approach. The pseudocode of this algorithm was shown in Algorithm 1. This pseudocode provided the time complexity of each part of the PCA-clustering algorithm in Big O notation. Based on the information, the time complexity of each part is shown in the equations below.

Algorithm 1. The PCA-Clustering algorithm

Input: $_n\mathbf{X}_p = \{\mathbf{x}_1^T, \mathbf{x}_2^T, \ldots, \mathbf{x}_n^T\}$ // Dataset with rank r
Output: $_n\mathbf{Y}_k = \{\mathbf{y}_1^T, \mathbf{y}_2^T, \ldots, \mathbf{y}_n^T\}$ // Dataset in the low dimension
Process:

    //Get the feature configuration
    $\mathbf{X}_p \leftarrow \mathbf{X} - \bar{\mathbf{X}}$ // Center the data at its mean $\mathcal{O}(n)$
    $[\mathbf{U}, \mathbf{S}, \mathbf{V}] \leftarrow \mathbf{X}_p$ // factorize $\mathbf{X}_p$ using svd $\mathcal{O}(n.d)$
    $\mathbf{c} \leftarrow$ normalization of $\text{diag}(\mathbf{S}) = [s_1, s_2, \ldots, s_r]$ $\mathcal{O}(n)$
        // $\mathbf{c}$ is the principal component
    $\mathbf{c}_{cumulative} \leftarrow$ cumulative of $\mathbf{c}$ $\mathcal{O}(n)$
    $i \leftarrow$ index where $\mathbf{c}_i \geq 0.8$, $\mathbf{c}_i \in \mathbf{c}_{cumulative}$ $\mathcal{O}(n)$
    $\mathbf{H} \leftarrow {}_{:}V_{1:i} \times {}_{1:i}S_{1:i}$ $\mathcal{O}(n)$

    //Get the proximity matrix of the features $(\mathbf{D})$
    $s_{i,j} \leftarrow$ cosine similarity of $\mathbf{h}_i$ and $\mathbf{h}_j$, where $\mathbf{h}_i, \mathbf{h}_i \in \mathbf{H}, \forall i, j$ $\mathcal{O}(d^2)$
    $d_{i,j} \leftarrow 1 - s_{i,j}$, where $d_{i,j} \in \mathbf{D}, \forall i, j$ $\mathcal{O}(d^2)$

    //Conduct the feature selection process
    Determine k, the number of feature selected $\mathcal{O}(n)$
    $[\text{idx}, \text{centroid}] \leftarrow$ clustering$(\mathbf{D}, k)$ $\mathcal{O}(n.k)$
    $\mathbf{p}_{ik} \leftarrow \text{argmax}_i (\text{Var}(\mathbf{p}_{ik}))$ // $\mathbf{p}_{ik}$ is the ith feature in the kth cluster $\mathcal{O}(d)$
    $_n\mathbf{Y}_k \leftarrow [\mathbf{p}_{i1}, \mathbf{p}_{i2}, \ldots, \mathbf{p}_{ik}]$ $\mathcal{O}(n)$

$$T_1(n) = 5 \times \mathcal{O}(n) + \mathcal{O}(n.d) \tag{13}$$
$$= \mathcal{O}(n.d)$$

$$T_2(n) = 2 \times \mathcal{O}(d^2) \tag{14}$$
$$= \mathcal{O}(d^2)$$

$$T_3(n) = 2 \times \mathcal{O}(n) + \mathcal{O}(n.k) + \mathcal{O}(d) \tag{15}$$
$$= \mathcal{O}(n) + \mathcal{O}(n.k) + \mathcal{O}(d)$$

where $T_1(n)$, $T_2(n)$, and $T_3(n)$ refer to the time complexity of the first, second, and third main parts, respectively.

In many real-world scenarios, the number of features (d) is truly much smaller than the number of objects (n), ($d \leqslant n$). Therefore, simplifying $\mathcal{O}(n.d)$ to $\mathcal{O}(n)$ can be implemented. Likewise, k is also truly much smaller than n. Accordingly, $\mathcal{O}(n.k)$ can also be simplified to $\mathcal{O}(n)$. Based on the dataset and schemes used, it could be known that $d \leqslant n$ and $k \leqslant n$ so that this simplification could be implemented. Consequently, the final time complexity of the PCA-clustering algorithm could be denoted by $T(n)$ and formed in Eq. 16.

$$
\begin{aligned}
T(n) &= T_1(n) + T_2(n) + T_3(n) \\
&= \mathcal{O}(n.d) + \mathcal{O}(d^2) + \mathcal{O}(n) + \mathcal{O}(n.k) + \mathcal{O}(d) \\
&= \mathcal{O}(n)
\end{aligned}
\tag{16}
$$

Based on this analysis, the time complexity of the PCA-Clustering algorithm is generally $\mathcal{O}(n)$. Its time complexity is categorized as fair [50].

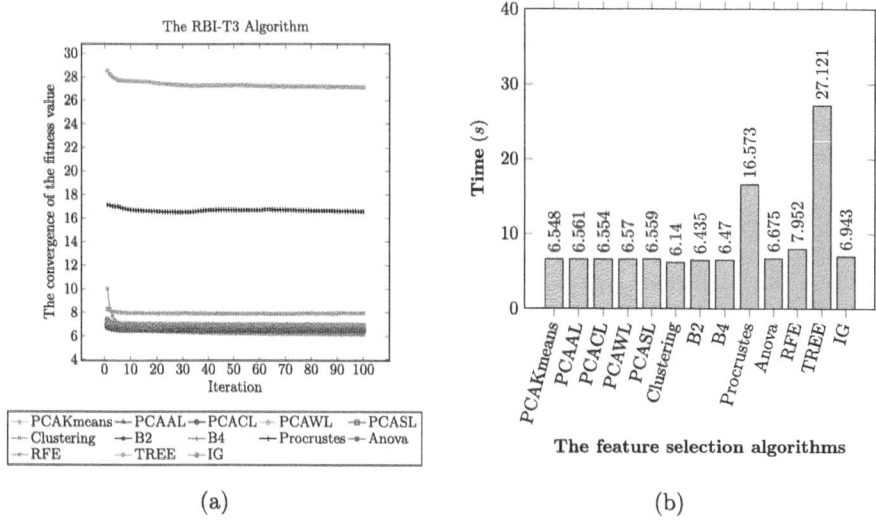

(a)   (b)

Fig. 2. The running time

Meanwhile, to see the efficiency of the PCA-clustering algorithms compared to other algorithms, the required computational time was utilized. Figure 2 presented a comparison of the computational time among the algorithms. Based on this figure, it could be seen that all proposed algorithms had a low computational time, namely under $6.600s$. This value was almost the same as most of the comparison algorithms used. On the other hand, the TREE algorithm had quite a high computational time, followed by Procrustes. This may be because the RFE algorithm involves training the model multiple times, and the Procrustes-based FS requires the calculation of the Procrustes value of all features when selecting one feature.

5   Discussion

This study evaluated the performance of the proposed FS algorithms, namely PCA-KM, PCA-AL, PCA-CL, PCA-WL, and PCA-SL, using datasets from the UCI repository. In the evaluation process, the existing FS algorithms, which were clustering, B2, B4, Procrustes, ANOVA, RFE, TREE, and IG, were utilized for comparison. In addition, in simulation, three schemes were conducted, i.e., selecting 75%. 50%, and 25% of features. The results indicated that PCA-KM generally outperformed other proposed algorithms in terms of GoFPM, classification accuracy, and clustering performance, particularly in the 75% scheme. However, its performance tended to decrease as the number of selected features decreased.

Based on the GoFPM value, PCA-KM presented the highest performance in several datasets, such as Cortex Nuclear (D2), E. coli (D3), Parkinsons (D5), and Wine Red (D6), in all three schemes used. Nevertheless, this algorithm was slightly outperformed by B2 and Procrustes in particular conditions. When it was compared to other proposed algorithms, PCA-KM consistently outperformed PCA-AL, PCA-CL, PCA-WL, and PCA-SL in terms of the average value. On the other hand, the PCA-AL, PCA-CL, PCA-WL, and PCA-SL algorithms had low performance on the particular dataset, especially in the 50% and 25% schemes.

Likewise, in the classification performance, PCA-KM achieved the highest average accuracy across most datasets and schemes. Its performance was high in the 75% scheme, where it outperformed other proposed algorithms, such as PCA-AL, PCA-CL, PCA-WL, and PCA-SL, and several existing algorithms, i.e., ANOVA, RFE, TREE, and IG. However, a slight decline in accuracy occurred in the 50% and 25% schemes, where PCA-KM was slightly under the B2 and B4 algorithms. Nevertheless, the performance of PCA-KM was still good, demonstrating a better accuracy than the classification results from the non-FS. It indicated its effectiveness in optimizing classification performance through feature reduction.

In terms of clustering performance, PCA-KM, PCA-CL, and PCA-WL achieved the highest purity values across multiple datasets in the 75% scheme. However, their performance was generally moderate, where significant improvements were obtained only in the Ionosphere (D4) and Parkinsons (D5) datasets. A decline in the clustering performance of PCA-KM, PCA-CL, and PCA-WL was shown in the 50% and 25% schemes, where they were under several existing algorithms, such as B2, B4, ANOVA, and IG. However, they still outperformed non-FS clustering, suggesting that feature selection by PCA-clustering algorithms has the potential to enhance clustering quality.

Furthermore, the time complexity analysis showed that the proposed PCA-clustering algorithms had a relatively low computational time, typically under 6,600 s. In addition, these algorithms had a fair computational efficiency.

6   Conclusion

The proposed PCA-based feature selection algorithms showed promising results in optimizing the performance of classification and clustering in particular datasets, especially in the 75% scheme. Among the proposed algorithms, PCA-KM got the best performance, consistently achieving higher GoFPM values, better classification accuracy, and good clustering purity compared to PCA-AL, PCA-CL, PCA-WL, and PCA-SL. While PCA-KM was marginally outperformed by some existing methods, such as B2 and Procrustes. In the dominant case in this study, the performance of PCA-KM was better than that of non-FS.

Nevertheless, the study also highlighted that the effectiveness of the proposed algorithms decreased with the reduction in the number of selected features. The PCA-KM, PCA-AL, PCA-CL, PCA-WL, and PCA-SL had low performance in the 50% and 25% schemes on the particular conditions. This suggests that while the proposed algorithms are effective in a moderate number of features, their performance may be limited when feature selection is decreased.

In terms of computational efficiency, the proposed algorithms were efficient, with a time complexity categorized as fair and a low computational time. Those make the proposed algorithms viable for big data analysis and real-world applications where computational resources may be constrained.

Future work could explore further optimization of these algorithms for lower feature selection schemes using the optimization procedure. In addition, GoFPM considerations, the accuracy of classification results, and clustering performance can be involved simultaneously in the selection of features using the PCA-clustering algorithms to get a better FS result. Additionally, integrating these proposed algorithms with other machine-learning techniques could enhance their capability and applicability in complex, high-dimensional data environments.

References

1. Darabi, N., Rezai, A., Hamidpour, S.S.F.: Breast cancer detection using RSFS-based feature selection algorithms in thermal images. Biomed. Eng.: Appl. Basis Commun. **33**, 2150020 (2021)
2. Prabhakaran, N., Nedunchelian, R.: Oppositional cat swarm optimization-based feature selection approach for credit card fraud detection. Comput. Intell. Neurosci. **2023**, 2693022 (2023)
3. Ananda, R., Daud, K.M., Zainudin, S.: Non-dominated sorting differential search algorithm for optimizing regulatory-metabolic networks by using probabilistic approach. In: 2023 International Conference on Electrical Engineering and Informatics (ICEEI), Bandung, Indonesia, p. 1–6. IEEE (2023)
4. Ananda, R., Daud, K.M., Zainudin, S.: A review of advances in integrating gene regulatory networks and metabolic networks for designing strain optimization. J. King Saud Univ. - Comput. Inf. Sci. **36**, 102120 (2024)
5. Asgarnezhad, R., Monadjemi, S.A., Soltanaghaei, M.: An application of MOGW optimization for feature selection in text classification. J. Supercomput. **77**, 5806–5839 (2021)

6. Vandana, C.P., Chikkamannur, A.A.: Feature selection: an empirical study. Int. J. Eng. Trends Technol. **69**, 165–170 (2021)
7. Zhou, H., Wang, X., Zhu, R.: Feature selection based on mutual information with correlation coefficient. Appl. Intell. **52**, 5457–5474 (2022)
8. Liu, H., Motoda, H.: Feature Selection for Knowledge Discovery and Data Mining. Springer, Boston (1998)
9. Zebari, R., Abdulazeez, A., Zeebaree, D., Zebari, D., Saeed, J.: A comprehensive review of dimensionality reduction techniques for feature selection and feature extraction. J. Appl. Sci. Technol. Trends **1**, 56–70 (2020)
10. Salih Hasan, B.M., Abdulazeez, A.M.: A review of principal component analysis algorithm for dimensionality reduction. J. Soft Comput. Data Min. **02** (2021)
11. Ayesha, S., Hanif, M.K., Talib, R.: Overview and comparative study of dimensionality reduction techniques for high dimensional data. Inf. Fusion **59**, 44–58 (2020)
12. Rostami, M., Berahmand, K., Nasiri, E., Forouzandeh, S.: Review of swarm intelligence-based feature selection methods. Eng. Appl. Artif. Intell. **100**, 104210 (2021)
13. Jia, W., Sun, M., Lian, J., Hou, S.: Feature dimensionality reduction: a review. Complex Intell. Syst. **8**, 2663–2693 (2022)
14. Hira, Z.M., Gillies, D.F.: A review of feature selection and feature extraction methods applied on microarray data. Adv. Bioinform. **2015**, 1–13 (2015)
15. Ramachandran, R., Ravichandran, G., Raveendran, A.: Evaluation of dimensionality reduction techniques for big data. In: 2020 Fourth International Conference on Computing Methodologies and Communication (ICCMC), Erode, India, pp. 226–231. IEEE (2020)
16. Ananda, R., Dewi, A.R., Mohd Amin, M.B., Huda, M., Gushelmi, G.: Unsupervised feature selection based on self-configuration approaches using multidimensional scaling. Jambura J. Math. **5**, 351–362 (2023)
17. Wahid, A., et al.: Feature selection and classification for gene expression data using novel correlation based overlapping score method via Chou's 5-steps rule. Chemom. Intell. Lab. Syst. **199**, 103958 (2020)
18. Wang, H., Jing, X., Niu, B.: A discrete bacterial algorithm for feature selection in classification of microarray gene expression cancer data. Knowl.-Based Syst. **126**, 8–19 (2017)
19. Potharaju, S.P., Sreedevi, M.: Distributed feature selection (DFS) strategy for microarray gene expression data to improve the classification performance. Clin. Epidemiol. Glob. Health **7**, 171–176 (2019)
20. Daud, K.M., Ananda, R., Zainudin, S., Howe, C.W.: Optimizing the production of valuable metabolites using a hybrid of constraint-based model and machine learning algorithms: a review. Int. J. Adv. Comput. Sci. Appl. **14**(10) (2023)
21. Moon, S.-H., Kim, Y.-H.: An improved forecast of precipitation type using correlation-based feature selection and multinomial logistic regression. Atmos. Res. **240**, 104928 (2020)
22. Dhal, P., Azad, C.: A novel approach for blood vessel segmentation with exudate detection in diabetic retinopathy. In: 2020 International Conference on Artificial Intelligence and Signal Processing (AISP), pp. 1–6 (2020). ISSN 2640-5768
23. Wu, T., Yang, Y., Wu, Z., Li, D.: MASC: a speech corpus in mandarin for emotion analysis and affective speaker recognition. In: 2006 IEEE Odyssey - The Speaker and Language Recognition Workshop, pp. 1–5 (2006)
24. Li, X., Chong, J., Lu, Y., Li, Z.: Application of information gain in the selection of factors for regional slope stability evaluation. Bull. Eng. Geol. Env. **81**, 470 (2022)

25. Dissanayake, K., Md Johar, M.G.: Comparative study on heart disease prediction using feature selection techniques on classification algorithms. Appl. Comput. Intell. Soft Comput. **2021**, 1–17 (2021)
26. Bashir, S., Khan, Z.S., Hassan Khan, F., Anjum, A., Bashir, K.: Improving heart disease prediction using feature selection approaches. In: 2019 16th International Bhurban Conference on Applied Sciences and Technology (IBCAST), Islamabad, Pakistan, pp. 619–623. IEEE (2019)
27. Bahl, A., Hellack, B., Balas, M., Dinischiotu, A., Wiemann, M., Brinkmann, J., Luch, A., Renard, B.Y., Haase, A.: Recursive feature elimination in random forest classification supports nanomaterial grouping. NanoImpact **15**, 100179 (2019)
28. Siswadi, Muslim, A., Bakhtiar, T.: Variable selection using principal component and procrustes analyses and its application in educational data. J. Asian Sci. Res. **2**, 856–865 (2012)
29. Jolliffe, I.T.: Discarding variables in a principal component analysis. I: artificial data. Appl. Stat. **21**(2), 160 (1972)
30. Jolliffe, I.T.: Discarding variables in a principal component analysis. II: real data. Appl. Stat. **22**(1), 21 (1973)
31. De Oliveira Jr, J.I., Da Rocha, J.C.F., Guimarães, A.M., Da Fonseca, A.F.: A PCA and SPCA based procedure to variable selection in agriculture. Rev. Brasiliera Comput. Aplicada **7**, 30–41 (2015)
32. Nishisato, S., Beh, E.J., Lombardo, R., Clavel, J.G.: History of the biplot. In: Modern Quantification Theory. BQAHB, vol. 8, pp. 167–179. Springer, Singapore (2021). https://doi.org/10.1007/978-981-16-2470-4_9
33. Thakkar, A., Lohiya, R.: Attack classification using feature selection techniques: a comparative study. J. Ambient. Intell. Humaniz. Comput. **12**, 1249–1266 (2021)
34. Kuzudisli, C., Bakir-Gungor, B., Bulut, N., Qaqish, B., Yousef, M.: Review of feature selection approaches based on grouping of features. PeerJ **11**, e15666 (2023)
35. Nasiri, H., Alavi, S.A.: A novel framework based on deep learning and ANOVA feature selection method for diagnosis of COVID-19 cases from chest x-ray images. Comput. Intell. Neurosci. **2022**, 1–11 (2022)
36. Dai, Y., et al.: Feature grouping for no-reference image quality assessment. In: 2022 7th International Conference on Automation, Control and Robotics Engineering (CACRE), pp. 204–208 (2022)
37. Sood, M., Angra, P., Verma, S., Jhanjhi, N.Z.: Efficient Feature Grouping for IDS Using Clustering Algorithms in Detecting Known/Unknown Attacks. CRC Press (2022)
38. Vieira, V.M.N.C.S.: Permutation tests to estimate significances on principal components analysis. Comput. Ecol. Softw. **2**, 103–123 (2012)
39. Ananda, R.: Silhouette density canopy K-means for mapping the quality of education based on the results of the 2019 national exam in Banyumas regency. Khazanah Inform.: J. Ilmu Komputer dan Inform. **5**, 158–168 (2019)
40. Ananda, R., Naf'an, M.Z., Arifa, A.B., Burhanuddin, A.: Recommendation system for specialization selection using K-means density canopy. J. RESTI (Rekayasa Sistem dan Teknol. Inform.) **4**, 172–179 (2020)
41. Adhitama, R., Burhanuddin, A., Ananda, R.: Penentuan jumlah cluster ideal smk di jawa tengah dengan metode x-means clustering dan k-means clustering. JIKO (J. Inform. Komputer) **3**, 1–5 (2020)
42. Ananda, R., Yamani, A.Z.: Determination of initial K-means centroid in the process of clustering data evaluation of teaching lecturers. J. RESTI (Rekayasa Sistem dan Teknol. Inform.) **4**, 544–550 (2020)

43. Ananda, R., Dewi, A.R., Nurlaili, N.: A comparison of clustering by imputation and special clustering algorithms on the real incomplete data. Jurnal Ilmu Komputer dan Inform. **13**, 65–75 (2020)
44. Ananda, R., Prasetiadi, A.: Hierarchical and K-means clustering in the line drawing data shape using procrustes analysis. JOIV: Int. J. Inform. Vis. **5**, 306 (2021)
45. Ananda, R., Siswadi, Bakhtiar, T.: Goodness-of-fit of the imputation data in biplot analysis. Far East J. Math. Sci. (FJMS) **103**, 1839–1849 (2018)
46. Bakhtiar, T., Siswadi, S.: On the symmetrical property of procrustes measure of distance. Int. J. Pure Appl. Math. **99** (2015)
47. Solorio-Fernández, S., Carrasco-Ochoa, J.A., Martínez-Trinidad, J.F.: A review of unsupervised feature selection methods. Artif. Intell. Rev. **53**, 907–948 (2020)
48. Ananda, R., Prasetiadi, A.: Classification based on configuration objects by using procrustes analysis. Jurnal Infotel **13**, 76–83 (2021)
49. UCI Machine Learning Repository
50. Younes, H., Alameh, M., Ibrahim, A., Rizk, M., Valle, M.: Efficient algorithms for embedded tactile data processing. In: Electronic Skin, 1st edn., pp. 113–138. River Publishers, New York (2022)

Computing Methodologies

Real-Time Arabic Speech Recognition from Lips Movement Based on Deep Learning

Ahmed Saud Ketab[1,2]([✉]) [iD] and Nidhal Khdhair El-abbadi[3] [iD]

[1] Faculty of Computer Science and Mathematics, University of Kufa, Najaf, Iraq
ahmedsaudketab@utq.edu.iq
[2] Directorate of Education of Thi Qar, Department of Vocational Education, Thi Qar, Iraq
[3] Computer Engineering Techniques, College of Engineering Techniques, Al-Mustaqbal
University, Babylon, Iraq
Nidhal.Khdhair.Abass@uomus.edu.iq

Abstract. The ability to hear and easily communicate with others is a blessing that some people with hearing impairments lose. Lip-reading may be a solution to this problem. This paper proposes a new lip-reading technique for recognizing Arabic speech. Due to the lack of a public Arabic dataset, a new dataset was created comprising over 2480 videos. The proposed technique includes several stages: face detection, lip alignment, lip region segmentation, and recognition. The initial stage utilizes mediapipe for face detection, followed by proposed lip alignment. Then, accurate delineation of the lip region is performed using a cropping method that removes extraneous elements such as moustaches. Additionally, a new technique selects sixteen different frames and eliminates redundant frames, fusing them into one image. Finally, Modified VGG16 is used to recognize image labels. The proposal's performance was remarkable, with accuracy exceeding 97.45% for words and 98.03% for phrases, surpassing previous Arabic recognition systems.

Keywords: Deep Learning · Hearing Impairment · Visual Speech Recognition

1 Introduction

Speech recognition generally relies on sound, but in some cases, understanding speech solely by sound can be challenging. For instance, in noisy environments like stadiums or when individuals have hearing or speech impairments, lip movements can be used for speech recognition. By observing lip movements, people with hearing or speech difficulties can better understand speech. This relies on analyzing the subtle movements of lips, tongue, and teeth, and converting them into understandable words [1–3].

The global prevalence of hearing loss highlights the critical role of lip reading. Hearing loss is the fourth leading cause of disability worldwide, affecting 1.57 billion people or 20.3% of the global population in 2019. As the population grows and ages, this burden is expected to increase, with nearly 2.5 billion people, or one-fourth of the global population, projected to have hearing loss by 2050. This makes hearing loss a major global health concern [4]. On the other hand, some people may lose the ability

S. O. Al-Mamory et al. (Eds.): 3INC 2024, CCIS 2329, pp. 41–56, 2025.
https://doi.org/10.1007/978-3-031-81065-7_3

to produce clear sounds due to conditions like vocal chord paralysis, laryngeal cancer, spasmodic dysphonia, or dysarthria. These conditions can result in the removal of the larynx and a permanent loss of voice [5].

Visual speech recognition research has indeed predominantly focused on the English language, leaving a gap in research for other languages like Arabic [6]. While advancements have occurred in speech recognition techniques for English, extending these methods to Arabic presents difficulties because of the language's unique attributes. In Arabic, every letter can be articulated in three distinct manners contingent upon its placement within a word. These variations in letter pronunciation are termed phonemes, which phonetics identifies as the smallest individual units that can be discerned in spoken language [7].

Lip-reading emerges as a critical area with potential for effective use in human-computer interaction across various languages. Nevertheless, Arabic still requires extensive research efforts, particularly when compared to English languages [8]. Lip reading for Arabic letters faces many challenges, one of them is related to the similarity of mouth shapes and movements when articulating most Arabic letters, which adds complexity to distinguish between them only based on lip movement. Also, some Arabic script features may not be included in other languages such as some sounds that are not included in other languages, this is another complexity added to the lip reading [9].

Creating a recognition system requires substantial datasets for both training and testing. However, the availability of such datasets is limited, especially when compared to the abundance of audio datasets. Moreover, many of the existing datasets are outdated and characterized by poor video quality. As video standards have improved, these older datasets have become less useful, motivating some researchers to develop new, higher-quality datasets to meet current needs [10].

Therefore, we created an Arabic dataset due to the scarcity of available Arabic datasets in this research. Also, an Arabic lip-reading system proposed aims to improve the communication capabilities of people with hearing or speaking disabilities. The contributions of the current research are first building a new Arabic phrases dataset. The second contribution is to improve the performance of lip-reading for the various Arabic letters.

The rest of the paper is structured as follows: Section 2 focuses on introducing some of the related works. Section 3 presents a comprehensive description and discussion of the suggested technique. The results obtained from implementing the proposed methodology are discussed in Sect. 4. Finally, Sect. 5 concludes the paper by analyzing the findings and summarizing the main points in the paper.

2   Related Works

Most of the research conducted in the field of visual speech recognition has focused on the English language. In this field, research on the Arabic language is much less than English language research. These studies used deep learning (DL) and machine learning (ML) techniques to understand pronounced Arabic words and phrases. ML and DL are powerful technologies that enable us to extract features and make predictions. However, we need to provide them with abundant, high-quality, and diverse data to achieve the best results. From 2019 to the present year 2024, several noteworthy research efforts have emerged, contributing to the advancement of lip-based speech recognition technology in Arabic.

In 2019, Elrefaei, Alhassan, and Omar introduced the Arabic Visual Speech Dataset (AVSD), which comprises 1100 videos spoken by 22 Arabic speakers. AVSD contains 10 words. Initially, they manually cropped and labelled mouth regions. Their model is machine learning-based, where they utilized discrete cosine transform (DCT) for feature extraction and a support vector machine (SVM) for recognition. The accuracy of visual speech recognition reached 70.09% [10]. However, manual cropping of mouth regions can be considered a disadvantage due to the time and effort involved.

In the next year, Mohamad Ezz et al. suggested a hybrid voting framework that operates through lip movement analysis for silent password recognition. The framework combines three feature extraction techniques: Haar-like Features (Haar), Speeded Up Robust Features (SURF), and Histogram of Oriented Gradients (HOG). These features are separately fed into a hidden Markov model (HMM). The results from these three techniques were combined using a voting scheme, achieving an accuracy of 96.2%. The dataset used was self-created and consisted of 2000 videos [11].

Nadia H. Alsulami collected an Arabic visual dataset in 2021. The dataset comprises 2400 videos of Arabic digits and 960 recordings of Arabic phrases. Facial landmark detection from the Dlib toolkit was used to identify faces and crop the mouth regions. These cropped mouth regions were used to produce concatenated frame images (CFI). The CFI is a single image that represents a video of spoken word and includes a specific number of frames. Their model, utilizing VGG19 with batch normalization, attained 94% accuracy for digit recognition and 97% accuracy for phrase recognition [12]. In the same year, Doaa Sami Khafaga introduced a real-time Arabic viseme recognition system using the SAVE dataset for Arabic visemes. The system comprises visual feature extraction and deep CNN classification, achieving the best accuracy of 95.3% [13].

The next year, Dweik et al. proposed a lip-reading system capable of distinguishing ten Arabic words using a dataset of 1051 videos captured from various participants. After preprocessing, the input frames are converted to grayscale. Each of them, the colour and grayscale frames, separately enters three models: CNN, time distributed CNN (TD-CNN) with long short-term memory (LSTM), and TD-CNN with bidirectional LSTM. A voting model combines the results of these models, achieving an accuracy of 82.84% [14].

In the 2023 timeframe, two research efforts emerged. The first one was introduced by N. F. Aljohani and E. S. Jaha. They created a new Arabic lip-reading dataset comprising 10,490 videos, including single letters, disjoined letters and words from the Quran, captured from three different viewpoints. They trained a deep learning CNN model, achieving accuracies of 83.3%, 80.5%, and 77.5% for words, disjoined letters, and single letters, respectively. However, this study has limitations in applying models trained on frontal view data to non-frontal viewpoints [8]. Khalil I. Alsaif et al. utilized a database containing 1080 images from five participants to track the geometrical features of lips for Arabic word utterance recognition [15]. The method calculates various geometric features of the mouth region, but the results lack evaluation criteria.

The latest research conducted this year was by Ali Baaloul et al. in 2024. They created a robust Arabic audio-visual dataset with 1,383 videos of 10 daily communication phrases spoken by 9 native Arabic speakers. Their dataset is publicly available on GitHub. They proposed a CNN model that has been compared with other models. The proposed CNN model achieved a validation accuracy of 90%. When comparing the proposed model with other models, only the Vision Transducer (ViT) achieved a better result, as its accuracy reached about 98% [16].

Research on Arabic speech recognition through lip movement has faced challenges due to the scarcity of available datasets. As a result, most researchers create their own datasets. These datasets include images or videos of isolated mouth regions, as they perform preprocessing. These preprocessed formats of the dataset, although they reduce time and effort for researchers, may cause limitations in their research and make them unable to apply their algorithms. Therefore, formatting the dataset before preprocessing is very important because it allows researchers to perform preprocessing, such as determining the number of frames. The GRID is an example of this format of an English dataset, where participants appear with full faces. To overcome these limitations, our dataset is presented in two versions: the raw version and the pre-processed version. The raw version contains videos of individuals speaking with full faces. While the processed version includes images of isolated mouths. Each image represents a video in the raw dataset. This allows researchers to choose the appropriate version according to their needs. The raw version enables them to apply their algorithms and pre-processing. While the processed version Saves time and effort for researchers.

3 Methodology

This proposal aims to recognize the phrases from lip reading in real-time. Many important stages represent challenges and need to be processed to compromise the proposed method. Figure 1 shows the main stages that contribute to this proposal. The important stages of the current proposal are face detection, lips alignment, lips masking, frame selection, feature extraction, and classification. In the first stage visual data that is not relevant to speech is removed, such as the background, speaker's hair, nose, etc. These elements do not contribute to speech production. However, the mouth is responsible for producing sound and speech, so only this area is cropped. In other words, lips detection aims to remove irrelevant facial features, which helps to identify speech more accurately.

For accurate lips detection, an accurate facial detection algorithm is required. For this purpose, the MediaPipe Face Mesh model is used to predict 468 facial landmarks representing detected face. These facial landmarks include the lip landmarks that are needed to determine the mouth coordinates as shown in Fig. 2. Sometimes, the speaker's head is slightly tilted. The proposed lips alignment algorithm removes this tilt. The alignment process helps to standardize the appearance of the mouth across the dataset, making it easier to extract meaningful features and facilitating accurate analysis and recognition of speech. Alignment also helps in removing variations due to differences in head movements or camera angles, thus improving the robustness of the speech recognition system. Lips alignment is achieved by automatically facing alignment and rotating the image. The lips alignment process aims to correct unintended movements of the speaker.

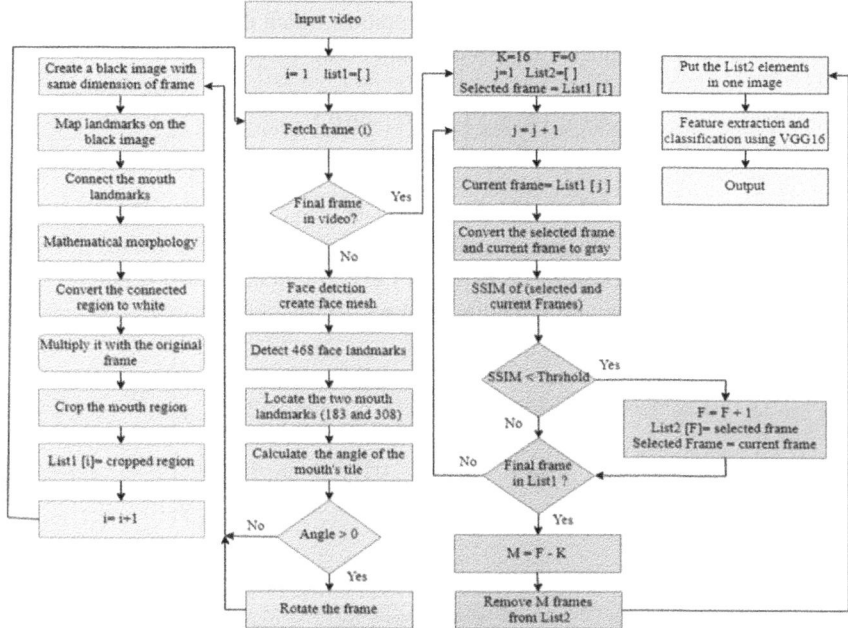

Fig. 1. The block diagram of the proposal method

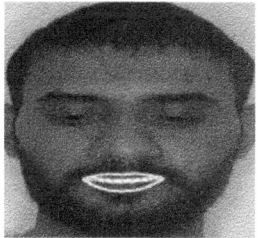

Fig. 2. Detected face with landmark

As mentioned, the face mesh model predicts 468 facial landmarks. The proposed lip alignment algorithm takes advantage of two of them, landmarks 183 and 308. These two landmarks are on either side of the mouth edge. The coordinates (x, y) of the two landmarks are identified. Then the angle (θ) between these two points ($P_1(x_1, y_1)$ and $P_2(x_2, y_2)$) is calculated by (1).

$$\theta = \tan^{-1}(dx/dy) \tag{1}$$

where: $dx = x_2 - x_1$, and $dy = y_2 - y_1$.

Image rotation is different from graphic rotation which depends on (2). Using (2) for image rotation may reduce image quality and produce aliasing.

$$\begin{vmatrix} x^* \\ y^* \end{vmatrix} = \begin{vmatrix} \cos\theta & \sin\theta \\ -\sin\theta & \cos\theta \end{vmatrix} \tag{2}$$

The solution to this problem is to utilize (3) and (4) [17]. Based on the value of the angle (θ), (3) is used for clockwise rotation when a value of (θ) is positive, whereas a negative value of (θ) indicates a counterclockwise rotation, and (4) is employed. No rotation occurs when (θ) equals 0. Figure 3 shows the rotation process.

$$\begin{vmatrix} x^* \\ y^* \end{vmatrix} = \begin{vmatrix} 1 & 0 \\ -\tan(\theta/2) & 1 \end{vmatrix} \begin{vmatrix} 1 & \sin\theta \\ 0 & 1 \end{vmatrix} \begin{vmatrix} 1 & 0 \\ -\tan(\theta/2) & 1 \end{vmatrix} \begin{vmatrix} x \\ y \end{vmatrix} \tag{3}$$

$$\begin{vmatrix} x^* \\ y^* \end{vmatrix} = \begin{vmatrix} 1 & -\tan(\theta/2) \\ 0 & 1 \end{vmatrix} \begin{vmatrix} 1 & 0 \\ \sin\theta & 1 \end{vmatrix} \begin{vmatrix} 1 & -\tan(\theta/2) \\ 0 & 1 \end{vmatrix} \begin{vmatrix} x \\ y \end{vmatrix} \tag{4}$$

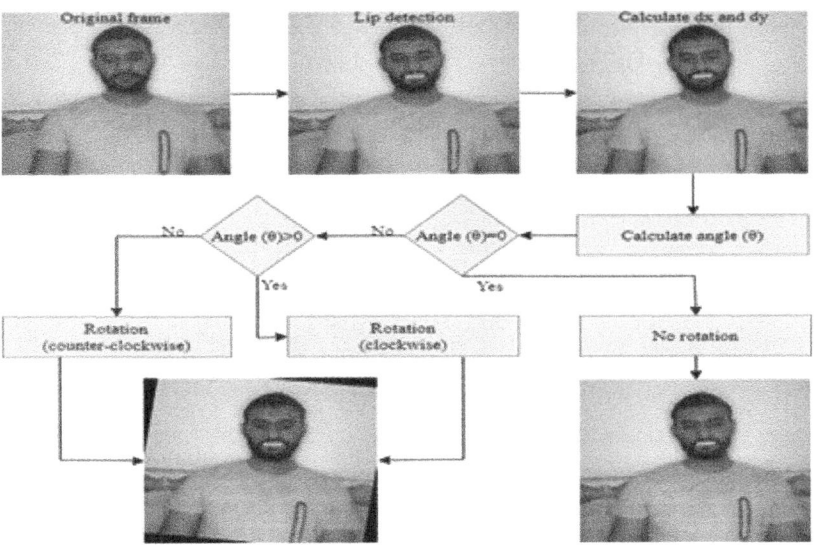

Fig. 3. The block diagram of the rotation process

The accurate delineation of the region of interest (ROI) has a significant impact on the performance of the proposed method. Most research efforts define the ROI as a rectangular area encompassing the mouth region as in Fig. 4 (a). However, this region may also contain extraneous information unrelated to lips, such as facial hair, moustache, and skin tone variations. These factors make the proposal method weak for accurately identifying and interpreting speech cues. Accurately identifying and isolating the lips region is by segmenting the lip region solely as in Fig. 4 (b).

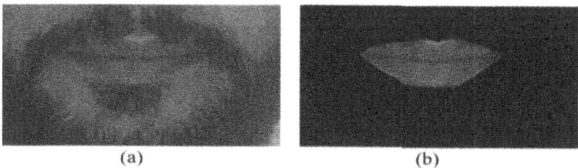

Fig. 4. (a) Traditional cropped ROI (b) proposed cropped ROI

To crop the actual lips (ROI), first create a black image with the same input frame dimension, project all the detected landmarks of the aligned image into the black image, and then connect the lip landmarks, see Fig. 5(a). Next, convert the black image into a binary image and apply the mathematical morphology (opening operation). The open operation removes the small particles and smooths the lip region as in Fig. 5(b).

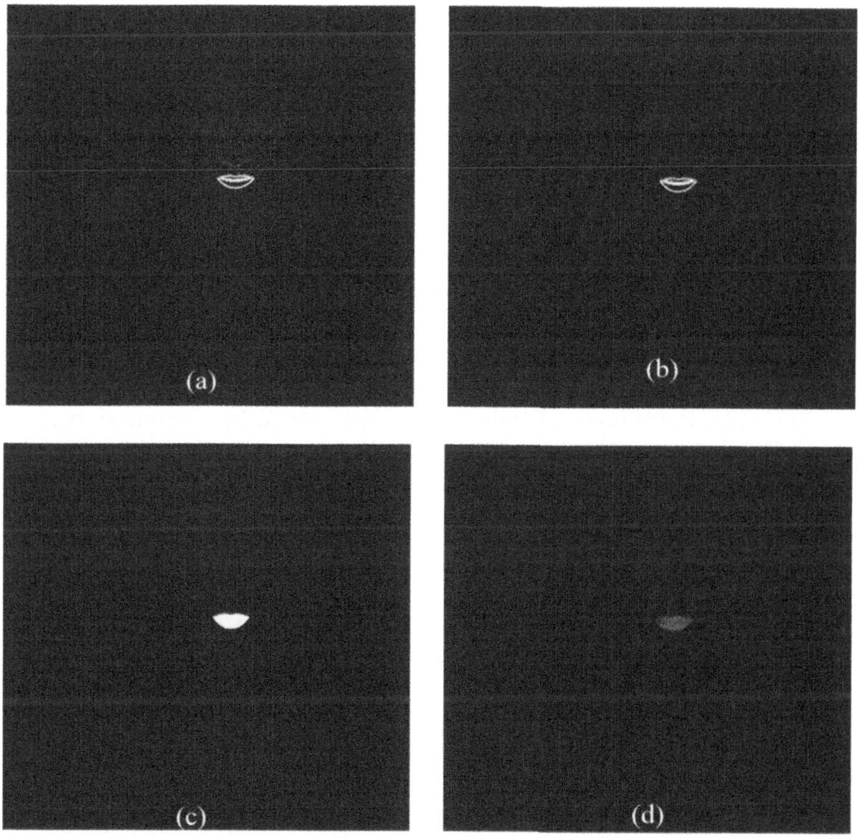

Fig. 5. (a) Black mask with projected landmarks (b) Result of the mathematical open operation (c) The final mask (d) Proposal lip detection

Then convert the connected regions to white to get the final mask. Figure 5(c) illustrates the final mask. The final mask is multiplied by the original image. In this case, the result will include just the ROI of lips, as shown in Fig. 5(d). After the accurate delineation of the lip region, the cropping operation is performed so that the mouth will be in the centre of the cropped box. This process continues until all the frames are done.

The third stage in this proposal is frame selection, which addresses the issue of varying lengths of recorded videos and differences in speaking speed. The Frame Selection algorithm aims to select the most representative frames from the video by eliminating redundant frames. The input to the proposed lip selection algorithm is a video containing many frames, while the output is 16 frames. This process ensures that the model receives a manageable set of frames that accurately represent the video, to improve the accuracy of feature extraction, leading to more reliable speech recognition results. In this proposal, the best frames are selected according to the value of the Structural Similarity Index Measure (SSIM). To compute the SSIM between two frames, x and y, (5) is used [18].

$$SSIM(x, y) = \frac{(2\mu_x\mu_y + c_1)(2\mu_{xy} + c_2)}{(\mu_x^2 + \mu_y^2 + c_1)(\sigma_x^2 + \sigma_y^2 + c_2)} \tag{5}$$

where μ is the average pixel intensities, σ is the variances of pixel intensities, σ_{xy} is the covariance of pixel intensities between frames x and y, c_1 and c_2 are constants.

The proposed frame selection is initiated by selecting the first frame as a selected frame. Then take the next frame as a current frame. Then the SSIM between the selected frame and the current frames is computed. When the SSIM is more than the threshold nothing is done. But if the SSIM is less than the threshold: add one to the counter of the selected frame (F), then the selected frame is saved to the list, and the current frame is updated as a selected frame. Then the process comes back to the step of taking the next frame as the current frame. This process continues until the last frame. Now, F saves the total number of selected frames. In this step, F may be any number of frames, but in the proposal ultimately must select sixteen frames. We found that sixteen frames can give good results. Note that the threshold has been chosen carefully to F not being less than

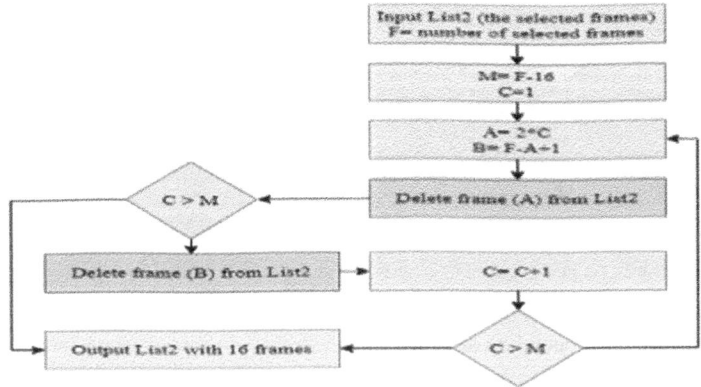

Fig. 6. Block diagram of eliminating M frames

sixteen (the threshold chosen is equal to 0.9). If the F is over sixteen, we must remove the excess frames. Frame removal is not a random process, it is employed according to the suggested rule as in Fig. 6.

After obtaining sixteen frames by proposed frame selection, the generated image looks like a matrix (4 × 4) of lips region, as shown in Fig. 7. Since the dimensions of each cropped frame is 300 × 250, the combined image dimension will be 1200 × 1000. Notice that when loading the dataset to the model resized to 224 × 224.

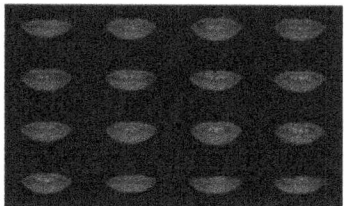

Fig. 7. Combined image

The final stage is the classification stage. In the current proposal, the VGG16 algorithm is suggested to be used for the recognition of phrases. The architecture of VGG16 included 16 layers for convolutional analysis. However, a modification has been applied to the VGG16, where the top fully connected layers of the VGG16 have been removed, and replaced with a flattened layer followed by a batch normalization layer, two dense layers with ReLU activation (512 and 256 units), another batch normalization layer, and a final dense layer with softmax activation. The modified VGG16 architecture is illustrated in Fig. 8.

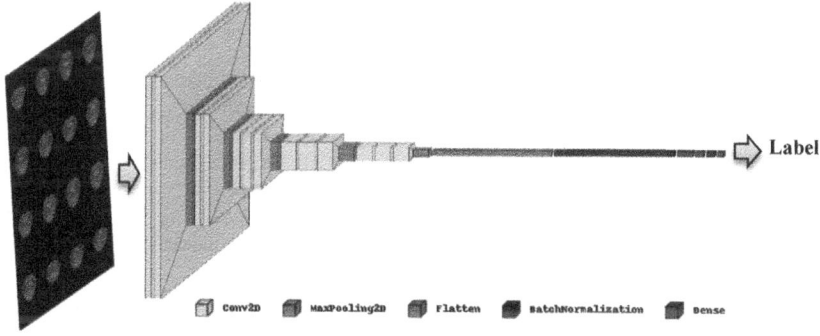

Fig. 8. Modified VGG16 architecture

4   Experimental Results

All the experiments were conducted in the Google Colab Pro environment with 51 GB of RAM, 16 GB of GPU, and 166.8 GB of disk space. The programming language used in this environment is Python. The dataset has been uploaded to Google Drive. Accuracy was used to demonstrate the performance of the proposed system, as defined in (6) [19]. Additionally, precision, recall, and F-score were evaluated of the model's performance, as defined in (7)–(9) [20].

$$\text{Accuracy} = (T_{pos} + T_{neg})/(T_{pos} + F_{pos} + T_{neg} + F_{pos}) \tag{6}$$

$$\text{Precision} = T_{pos}/(T_{pos} + F_{pos}) \tag{7}$$

$$\text{Recall} = T_{pos}/(T_{pos} + F_{neg}) \tag{8}$$

$$\text{F1 - score} = 2(\text{Precision} * \text{Recall})/(\text{Precision} + \text{Recall}) \tag{9}$$

4.1 Dataset Description

Many public visual datasets for the English language such as GRID [21] and OuluVS2 [22] are available but there are so few public Arabic datasets. So, we have created a new Arabic dataset. The dataset consists of 980 videos representing 10 Arabic words and 1524 videos covering 15 Arabic phrases. These phrases and words with their English meaning are listed in Tables 1 and 2.

Table 1. Arabic phrases

ID	Arabic spelling	English meaning
0	احتاج مساعدة.	I need help.
1	أين انت؟	Where are you?
2	الحمد لله.	Praise be to God.
3	انا بخير.	I'm fine.
4	ارجوك سامحني.	Please forgive me.
5	السلام عليكم.	Peace be upon you.
6	ان شاء الله.	If God wills
7	اتصل بالشرطة.	Call the police.
8	في امان الله.	Goodbye.
9	كيف الحال؟	How are you?
10	اطلبوا الاسعاف.	Call for an ambulance.
11	رأسي يؤلمني.	I have a headache.
12	شكرا جزيلا.	Thank you very much.
13	تعالى معي.	Come with me.
14	وعليكم السلام.	Peace be upon you too.

The dataset videos were recorded in several places with different backgrounds and light conditions. The participants are high school students. Their ages were between 17 and 20 years old, and they were of both genders. The male participants were both with and without moustaches/beards. In total, we had 34 participants (16 males and 18 females). Each phrase is repeated three times. This is the raw version of the dataset.

Table 2. Arabic words

ID	Arabic spelling	English meaning
0	أعتذر	I apologize
1	أليوم	Today
2	آسف	Sorry
3	إرجع	Comeback
4	غداً	Tomorrow
5	جميل	Beautiful
6	مرحباً	Hello
7	تفضل	Help yourself
8	تمام	Okay
9	وداعاً	Goodbye

Additionally, there is a processed version. The processed version contains combined images (Fig. 7). Each combined image corresponds to a video in the raw dataset. Despite using dimensions of 224 × 224 in the proposed system, the dataset was introduced with its original dimensions, maintaining the original dimensions of the dataset is crucial to preserve its quality. This ensures that no information is lost or distorted during the combination process, allowing the dataset to remain consistent and reliable for further analysis or use in research. The dataset is publicly available in https://www.kaggle.com/datasets/ahmedsketab/new-arabic-words-and-phrases-dataset.

4.2 Evaluation of Proposed System

The dataset was divided into 90% for training and 10% for testing. The model is trained using the Adam optimizer with the default learning rate and with a batch size of 32. The reported results of the model showcase remarkable performance, with a validation accuracy of 98.03% for Arabic phrases and 97.45% for words. Figures 9 and 10 illustrate the accuracy and loss of the proposed lip-reading system for phrases and words respectively.

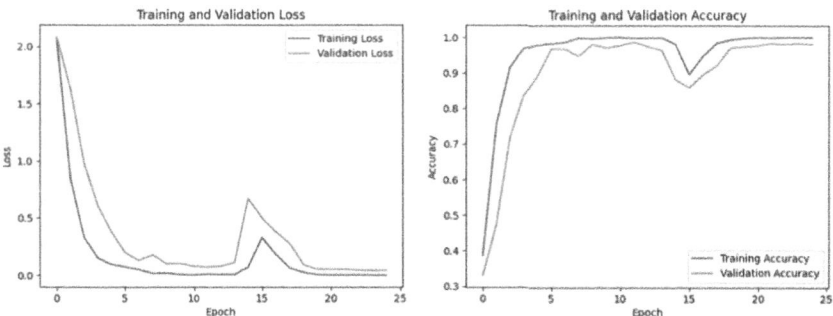

Fig. 9. Accuracy and loss of the proposed system for Arabic phrases

Additionally, Figs. 11 and 12 present the confusion matrices that detail of performance result of the proposed system for the Arabic phrases and words.

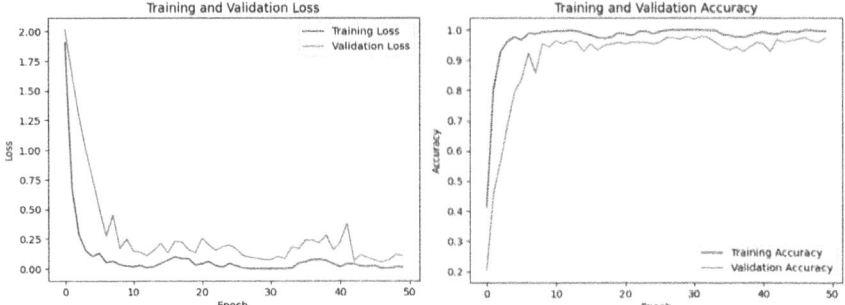

Fig. 10. Accuracy and loss of the proposed system for Arabic words

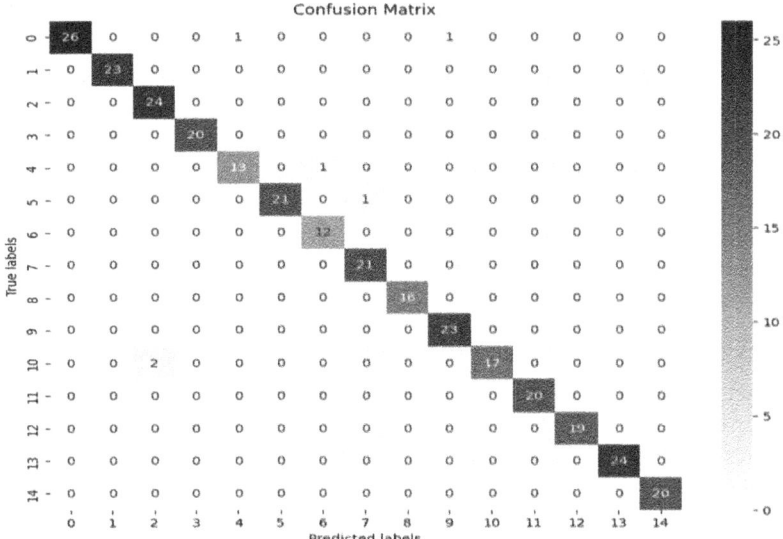

Fig. 11. Confusion matrix of Arabic phrases

Moreover, Figs. 13 and 14 illustrate the classification report of the proposed system's performance. The classification report contains the precision, recall, and F1 score of each class. The model demonstrates high performance overall, with most classes having precision, recall, and F1 scores above 0.9. The average F1 score is high, indicating a good balance between precision and recall across all classes.

The proposal is also compared with other previous works, as shown in Table 3. In comparison with previous works, which identified ten words or phrases, the current method recognizes ten words and fifteen phrases successfully and shows its superior efficiency.

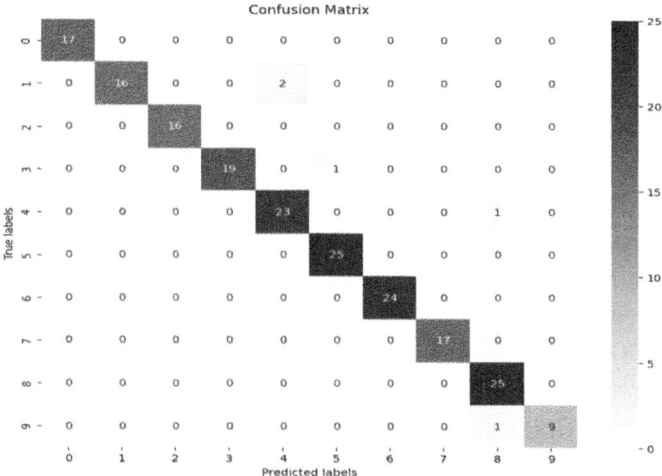

Fig. 12. Confusion matrix of Arabic words

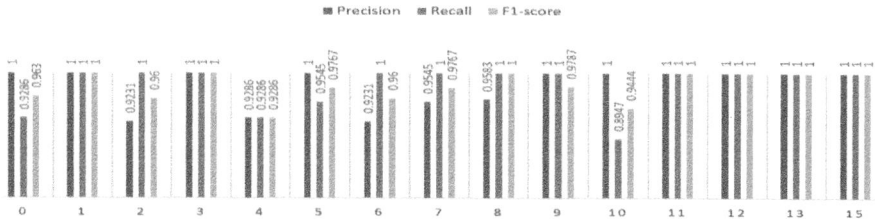

Fig. 13. Classification report of Arabic phrases

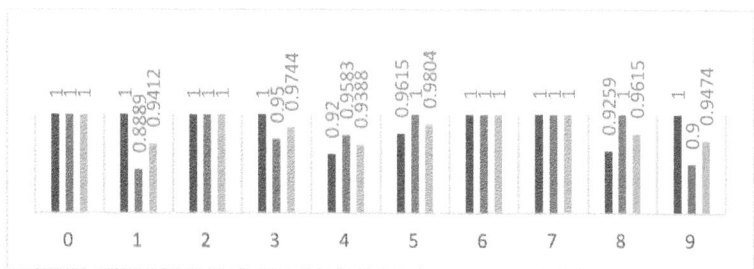

Fig. 14. Classification report of Arabic words

Table 3. Comparison with previous works

Reference	Technique	Class	Accuracy
[16]	CNN + SoftMax	10 Phrases	90%
	ViT		Nearly 98%
[8]	ResNet18 + BiGRU + SoftMax	10 Words	83.3%
[15]	Geometric Features	Words	-
[14]	CNN + TD-CNN + LSTM + BiLSTM + SoftMax + Voting	10 Words	82.84%
[12]	VGG19 + SoftMax + Batch Normalization	10 Digits	94%
		10 Phrases	97%
[11]	SURF + HOG + HAAR + HMM	10 Digits	96.2%
[10]	DCT + SVM	10 Words	70.09%
Proposal	Modified VGG16 + SoftMax	10 Words	97.45%
		15 Phrases	98.03%

5 Conclusion

In this paper, a new technique for real-time Arabic speech recognition from lip reading based on deep learning has been introduced. The suggested technique identified the challenges in recognizing Arabic lip movement, specifically in supporting individuals with hearing impairments, where this field is still in the nascent stage. One of the contributions of this paper is presenting a new mouth alignment approach that eliminates the aliasing problems faced the traditional techniques. The rigorous alignment helps to extract the precise lip region, leading to enhanced feature extraction and accurate detection and tracking of lip movement. Furthermore, the alignment normalizes effectively the lip characteristics for different speakers. In addition, a new method for accurately cropping lip region, which removes non-relevant facial regions like moustaches and part of face skin, has been presented, thereby improving the recognition performance. A new algorithm has been proposed for selecting sixteen different frames that remove redundant data. This approach significantly minimizes computational complexity and provides impressive efficiency, tackles the challenge of varying video lengths and differences in speaking speed. The selected frames are merged into a single image, referred to as the combined image. Finally, the modified VGG16 model performs feature extraction and classifies the label of the combined image.

In response to the lack of Arabic datasets, a new dataset featuring Arabic words and phrases has been developed, providing a valuable resource for future research. The dataset was captured under realistic conditions within different environments and under different lighting conditions. It includes over 2480 videos spoken by 34 Arabic speakers. The other contribution of this method is to achieve recognition of fifteen phrases, surpassing the previous method's performance which typically recognizes fewer words or phrases. In addition to the promised accuracy achieved for both Arabic words and phrases, which reflects the robustness and reliability of this proposal, it proved the out-performance compared with previous methods. For future work, it is encouraged that researchers build upon this study by further advancing Arabic speech recognition using advanced deep learning or hybrid techniques.

References

1. Hao, M., Mamut, M., Yadikar, N., Aysa, A., Ubul, K.: A survey of research on lipreading technology. IEEE Access **8**, 204518–204544 (2020). https://doi.org/10.1109/ACCESS.2020.3036865

2. Aran, L.R., Wong, F., Yi, L.P.: A review on methods and classifiers in lip reading. In: IEEE 2nd International Conference on Automatic Control and Intelligent Systems (I2CACIS), p. 196 (2017). https://doi.org/10.1109/I2CACIS.2017.8239057

3. Wang, H., Pu, G., Chen, T.: A lip reading method based on 3D convolutional vision trans-former. IEEE Access **10**, 77205–77212 (2022). https://doi.org/10.1109/ACCESS.2022.3193231

4. Wang, H., et al.: Estimation and projection of the burden of hearing loss in China: findings from the global burden of disease study 2019. Public Health **228**, 119–127 (2024). https://doi.org/10.1016/j.puhe.2024.01.004

5. Ketab, A.S., El abbadi, N.K.: A survey on speech recognition from lip movement. Sumer Journal for Pure Science **2**(2), 68–87 (2023)

6. Ghadban, N.S., Alkheir, J., Saii, M.: Performance evaluation hybrid visual speech recognition features on Arabic isolated words. Int. J. Comp. Sci. Trends and Technol. (IJCST) **5**(5), 47–50 (2017)

7. Al-Ghanim, A., et al.: I see what you say (ISWYS): Arabic lip-reading system. In: International Conference on Current Trends in Information Technology (CTIT), pp. 11–17. IEEE (2013). https://doi.org/10.1109/CTIT.2013.6749470

8. Faisal Aljohani, N., Sami Jaha, E.: Visual lip-reading for Quranic Arabic alphabets and words using deep learning. Comp. Sys. Sci. Eng. **46**(3), 3037–3058 (2023). https://doi.org/10.32604/csse.2023.037113

9. Altememe, M.S., El Abbadi, N.K.: Alphabets Arabic sign language recognition based on a hybrid model combining linear discrimination analysis and a one-dimensional convolutional neural network. Iraqi Journal of Science **64**(10), 5265–5279 (2023). https://doi.org/10.24996/ijs.2023.64.10.33

10. Elrefaei, L.A., Alhassan, T.Q., Omar, S.S.: An Arabic visual dataset for visual speech recognition. Procedia Comp. Sci. **163**, 400–409 (2019). https://doi.org/10.1016/j.procs.2019.12.122

11. Ezz, M., Mostafa, A.M., Nasr, A.A.: A silent password recognition framework based on lip analysis. IEEE Access **8**, 55354–55371 (2020). https://doi.org/10.1109/ACCESS.2020.2982359

12. Alsulami, N.H., Jamal, A.T., Elrefaei, L.A.: Deep learning-based approach for Arabic visual speech recognition. Computers, Materials & Continua **71**(1), 85–108 (2022). https://doi.org/10.32604/cmc.2022.019450

13. Khafaga, D.S., Mahmoud, H.A.H., Alghamdi, N.S., Albraikan, A.A.: Novel algorithm utiliz-ing deep learning for enhanced Arabic lip-reading recognition. Int. J. Adv. Comp. Sci. Appl. **12**(11) (2021). https://doi.org/10.14569/IJACSA.2021.0121192

14. Dweik, W., Altorman, S., Ashour, S.: Read my lips: artificial intelligence word-level Arabic lipreading system. Egyptian Informatics Journal **23**(4), 1–12 (2022). https://doi.org/10.1016/j.eij.2022.06.001

15. Alsaif, K.I., Salim Allella, N.: Lips reading spoken Arabic word based on the geometric shape features of the lip. Int. J. Sci. Res. Sci. Technol. 624–634 (2023). https://doi.org/10.32628/IJSRST2310164

16. Baaloul, A., Benblidia, N., Reguieg, F.Z., Bouakkaz, M., Felouat, H.: An arabic visual speech recognition framework with cnn and vision transformers for lipreading. Multimedia Tools and Applications 1–35 (2024). https://doi.org/10.1007/s11042-024-18237-5

17. Ghrban, Z.S.A., EL Abbadi, N.K.: Gender classification from face and eyes images using deep learning algorithm. J. Comput. Sci. 19(3), 345–362 (2023). https://doi.org/10.3844/jcssp.2023.345.362

18. Chen, M.-J., Bovik, A.C.: Fast structural similarity index algorithm. J. Real-Time Image Proc. 6(4), 281–287 (2011). https://doi.org/10.1007/s11554-010-0170-9

19. Kadhim, O.N., Abdulameer, M.H.: Biometric identification advances: unimodal to multimodal fusion of face, palm, and iris features. Advances in Electrical & Computer Engineering 24(1) (2024). https://doi.org/10.4316/AECE.2024.01010

20. Kuncan, F., Kaya, Y., Kuncan, M.: A novel approach for activity recognition with downsampling 1D local binary pattern. Adv. Electr. Comp. Eng. 19(1), 35–44 (2019). https://doi.org/10.4316/AECE.2019.01005

21. Cooke, M., Barker, J., Cunningham, S., Shao, X.: An audio-visual corpus for speech perception and automatic speech recognition. The J. Acoustical Soc. America 120(5), 2421–2424 (2006). https://doi.org/10.1121/1.2229005

22. Anina, I., Zhou, Z., Zhao, G., Pietikäinen, M.: Ouluvs2: a multi-view audiovisual database for non-rigid mouth motion analysis. In: 2015 11th IEEE International Conference and Workshops on Automatic Face and Gesture Recognition (FG), pp. 1–5. IEEE (2015). https://doi.org/10.1109/FG.2015.7163155

Parkinson's Disease Prediction and Progression Based on Voice Analysis: A Literature Survey

Huda Jasim[✉] and Noor D. Alshakarchy

Department of Computer Science, College of Computer Science and Information Technology,
University of Kerbala, Karbala, Iraq
huda.jasim@s.uokerbala.edu.iq, noor.d@uokerbala.edu.iq

Abstract. Parkinson's disease (PD) is a worldwide health problem with a wide range of motor symptoms and non-motor symptoms signs caused by the death of dopamine-producing neurons. Voice loss shows up early, which is very helpful for making a quick evaluation. Speech signal processing shows voice as a deep phenotype, which makes it possible for digital measures to speed up evaluations. Traditional testing methods that use neuroimaging and standardized scales have problems, which makes it even more important to come up with new ideas. Using different datasets, machine learning (ML) and deep learning (DL) are revolutionizing how we can predict PD. AI systems improve the accuracy of diagnoses by spotting small patterns. Deep learning, especially convolutional and recurrent neural networks, is very good at catching the complicated voice patterns that come with Parkinson's disease getting worse. There are still problems with using AI to predict PD, such as making sure that data is consistent, models can be understood, and there are social issues to think about. The search for a complete non-invasive clinical screening method goes on, which calls for new tools. This survey reviews recent research findings of artificial intelligence techniques for Parkinson's disease prediction, analyzes the employed methods, techniques, and challenges encountered by researchers, and elucidates their contributions to the field.

Keywords: Parkinson's disease (PD) · Artificial Intelligence (AI) · machine learning (ML) · deep learning (DL) · voice signals

1 Introduction

Parkinson's disease (PD) affects millions worldwide with a complex mix of motor and non-motor symptoms that increasingly impair daily life [1]. That needs complex clinical knowledge to diagnose and treat. Writing, speaking, walking, and other tasks become difficult [2]. Numerous studies have shown that voice impairment is the most common underlying symptom in many Parkinson's disease patients, which can give important information for early diagnosis. By introducing a speech signal processing approach for clinical analysis, the voice is a deep phenotypic feature for PD, which is the 2nd widespread neurodegenerative disease [3]. Voice biomarkers for PD may help detect

© The Author(s), under exclusive license to Springer Nature Switzerland AG 2025
S. O. Al-Mamory et al. (Eds.): 3INC 2024, CCIS 2329, pp. 57–71, 2025.
https://doi.org/10.1007/978-3-031-81065-7_4

signs and severity in daily life. Using established rating scales, neurologists assess the history of medical patients and execute physical examinations, such as the UPDRS to diagnose Parkinson's disease [4]. Neuroimaging, such as dopamine transporter imaging utilizing SPECT or PET, can validate clinical observations [5]. These methods are frequently used, although their early detection and forecasting powers are limited. This emphasizes the need for new methods. It has been demonstrated that deep learning (DL) and machine learning (ML) alter the prediction of PD [6]. Clinical, speech, and imaging data can be analyzed by machine learning techniques to identify patterns and minute characteristics that can point to Parkinson's disease. AI algorithms' integration of motor symptoms and physical activity to identify early-stage Parkinson's disease and the predictive power of AI models demonstrate AI's potential to improve traditional diagnostic methods by making more accurate and timely predictions [7]. Case categorization and prediction depend on selecting appropriate feature extraction and artificial learning methods. Machine learning and deep learning have different decision-making methods. The use of machine learning and deep learning in sickness detection is predicted to grow [8]. Artificial intelligence PD detection methods were developed using Multiple datasets. Traditional machine learning methods, like support vector machines, random forests, K-Nearest Neighbour (KNN), Naïve Bayes, Decision Trees, and Genetic Algorithms, require considerable pre-processing and rely on human-created features [9]. Voice signal measures including MelFrequency Cepstral Coefficients (MFCC), Linear Predictive Coding (LPC), pitch, jitter, and shimmer are used to extract global static features [10]. Then, Minimum Redundancy Maximum Relevance, the Least Absolute Shrinkage Selection Operator (LASSO), Relief, and Local Learning-Base Feature Selection are used to find the better features. Later, methods for reducing dimensional such as LDA and PCA are used to condense a dataset upon a low-dimensional subspace of features. This simplifies models and reduces overfitting [10, 11]. When predicting and evaluating the course of Parkinson's disease using voice datasets, deep learning approaches frequently perform better than conventional machine learning techniques. This is due to unprocessed data auto-extraction of complicated and hierarchical features [12]. Deep neural networks can efficiently record voice signals' complex and non-linear patterns. Due to their outstanding ability to acquire complicated data representations and linkages [13], Deep learning models like convolutional and recurrent neural networks can adapt to Parkinson's disease-related voice pattern changes. These models make more accurate predictions than typical machine learning methods, which may struggle to capture the nuanced and abstract properties needed for accurate diagnosis and monitoring in this area [14]. Many researchers have developed artificial intelligence detection methods for Parkinson's disease that work on various datasets. There are motion sensors, audio signals, brain signals (EEG), and other metrics in databases [15].

2 Parkinson's Disease and Speech Characteristics

Speech factors including phonation, articulation, prosody, and intelligibility can diagnose Parkinson's disease. Parkinson's patients often have dysarthria and dysphagia. Since dysarthria reduces speech intelligibility, it often limits function. This limitation may be due to articulation and phonation issues [16] such as Hypokinetic dysarthria:

reduced vocal harshness and intensity, decreased speech rates with occasional rapid speech, and decreased speech clarity [17]. Parkinson's disease patients often speak softly and monotonously, sometimes with breathiness or roughness. [18]. Phonation characteristics exhibit a strong association with perturbation measures including jitter, shimmer, and Pitch Perturbation Quotient (PPQ) [19]. Statistical hypothesis testing and metrics derived from sustained phoneme recordings—that is, /o/, /i/, /e/, /a/, and /u/—are commonly used to analyse these features. The comparison of speech signals and fundamental frequency during sustained articulation of monophonic /a/ is depicted in Fig. 1. The subjects examined in this comparison include (a) a healthy control (HC) signal, (b) individual diagnosed with PD (b) [10, 20]. The investigation demonstrates that the healthy control (HC) speaker exhibits greater stability compared to that of the individual diagnosed with Parkinson's disease. The assessment of continuous signals from speech additionally entails the articulation characteristic. This is done by calculating content during move (also referred to as start) between unvoiced and voiced clips and during move (from voiced to unvoiced clips) [21]. According to the hypothesis, individuals with Parkinson's disease exhibit atypical production of voiceless sounds and have difficulties in initiating and/or terminating vocal fold oscillation [22]. The frequency content of unvoiced frames and transitions between voiced and unvoiced sounds can be analyzed in speech signals, as demonstrated in previous studies [10]. Numerous research studies have elucidated notable disparities in vocal characteristics between patients diagnosed with Parkinson's disease and individuals without the disease serving as control subjects. Nevertheless, the integration of these discoveries into a comprehensive automated system poses a complex challenge, as indicated by the inconsistent outcomes observed in many research investigations. The investigations have mostly concentrated on parameters that are closely associated with vocal chord vibration deficits. Previous studies thoroughly investigated many metrics related to pitch frequency variation, number of pulses, jitter, shimmer, autocorrelation, and harmonics-to-noise ratio (HNR/NHR) [23–25]. Furthermore, certain studies have utilized machine-based analysis to establish correlations between perceptual variables such as voice quality, loudness, pitch, and resonance. Various acoustic features have been recognized as significant in evaluating the characteristics of the Parkinsonian voice, including vocal strength, jitter, shimmer, harmonics-to-noise ratio (HNR), and fundamental frequency (F0) [24, 26–28]. From a physiological perspective, the characteristics of the glottic source are interconnected with several aspects such as the frequency, amplitude, symmetry, and periodicity of vocal fold vibration. The presence of breathiness in speech among individuals with Parkinson's disease is attributed to the imperfect closure of the vocal folds, which allows air to escape. This phenomenon leads to increased levels of noise in the voice, and lower intensity [29]. Individuals diagnosed with Parkinson's disease commonly demonstrate increased jitter and decreased harmonics-to-noise ratio (HNR), which are suggestive of irregular vocal fold vibration and are subjectively regarded as roughness. Moreover, it has been observed that patients with Parkinson's disease exhibit a tendency towards monotonous linked speech, characterized by diminished variations in pitch and volume [28]. Numerous studies have further explored these factors by integrating thirteen Mel Frequency Cepstral Coefficients (MFCCs), which serve as indicators of energy and articulatory locations [30]. The utilization of fractal dimension (FD) features, which quantify the complexity of signals, was also implemented [28]. In recent times, scholars have discovered the efficacy of multivariate deep features [31] in enhancing comprehension and delineation of the intricacies associated with the Parkinsonian voice.

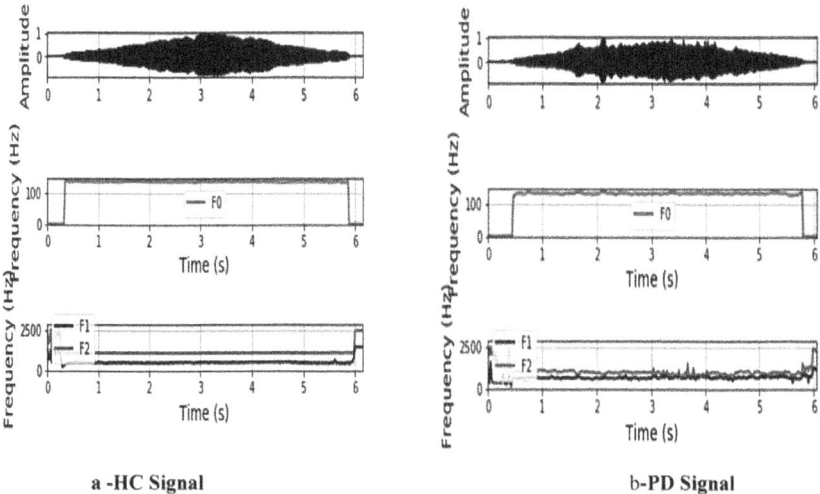

a -HC Signal   b-PD Signal

Fig. 1. The fundamental frequency, energy, and signal of a continuous monophonic /a/ were recorded by a patient with PD (b) and an (a) HC signal [10].

3 Literature Review

This section critically evaluates work that has advanced Parkinson's disease detection from audio data using traditional machine learning and advanced deep learning approaches. The discussion will also cover audio data pre-processing, feature selection, and researcher contributions.

3.1 Machine Learning Approaches

Machine learning (ML) is increasingly used in medical diagnosis, particularly in distinguishing PD patients from healthy controls. However, feature selection and extraction remain issues, requiring further examination. This survey will examine the latest machine learning algorithms related to the dataset and feature selection technique. Almeida et al. [32] investigated Parkinson's disease detection using voice signal processing using multiple classification models. This approach evaluates 18 feature extraction approaches and four machine learning methods (KNN, MLP, OPF, and SVM) for classifying sustained phonation and speech data. Phonation tasks detected diseases better than speech tasks. The AC channel performed well with 94.55% accuracy and 92.94% accuracy. Acoustic voice features in dysphonia speech were used to classify Parkinson's illness by S. Sharanyaa et al. [33]. Their contribution was to predict PD using dysphonia voice features of patients with PD and HC. The voice features dataset is analyzed using parametric and nonparametric methods, evaluating the performance of K-Nearest Neighbours, Random Forest, Naïve Bayes, and Logistic Regression Algorithms to improve Parkinson's disease prediction accuracy using acoustic features. Nonparametric models like Random Forest and K-Nearest Neighbours outperform parametric models with classification accuracy rates of 87.2% and 90.2%, respectively. Sajal and colleagues [34] suggested a novel remote Parkinson's disease (PD) diagnosis approach by combining rest tremor and voice degradation by remote data collection. The primary data collection used cell phones with accelerometers and audio sensors to collect samples from PD patients and healthy people [36]. Newly identified PD suspects gave data to evaluate PD detection techniques. A majority-vote technique from several algorithms connects PD patients with nearby neurologists for consultation. The best offline PD detection accuracy was 98.3% from voice data and 98.5% from tremor data. KNN was more accurate than SVM and NB. Pramanik et al. [35] developed a speech sign data and voice-based Parkinson's disease detection system. This study used the Parkinson's disease Speech dataset, which had high dimensionality but few data points. This study shows how comprehensive data processing improves data quality for Parkinson's disease diagnosis. Additionally, it shows that the suggested model improves classification accuracy. Parkinson's disease was classified using KNN, SVM, RF, logistic regression and AdaBoost. The SVM model provided was successful, with 94.10% accuracy. This performance was 8.00% better than previous testing on the same dataset. Solana-Lavalle et al. [40] found that high-frequency speech content helps diagnose PD in women but not in men. The proposed voice-based detection technique uses feature subset selection and four classifiers: SVM, MLP, KNN, and RF. These classifiers are applied to gender-based, balanced, and unbalanced voice recordings from five datasets. These datasets [37] are based on the largest publicly available voice-based PD dataset. The work shows improved performance and complexity over earlier voice-based PD detection research utilizing the same dataset, the k-nearest neighbour (KNN) classifier algorithm achieves 95.9% accuracy. Zhang et al. [41] detect Parkinson's disease by extracting pathological information from voice signals. Energy direction features based on empirical mode decomposition (EDF-EMD) are used to show how speech signals differ between Parkinson's disease (PD) patients and healthy people. The proposed feature is tested on dataset-Sakar and dataset-CPPDD. SVM and RF classifiers are used in the suggested method. In experiments, SVM had the highest average accuracy of 96.54% on the Sakar dataset [38] and 92.59% on the CPPDD dataset [39]. This study enhances arithmetic speed without losing accuracy discovers the best SVM hyperparameter scheme, and may need to compare with more models for verification results. Ahmed et al. [42]. Six machine learning (ML) algorithms— Stochastic Gradient Descent (SGD), Logistic Regression, Random Forest, Extreme Gradient Boosting (XGB), Decision Tree (DT) and K-Nearest Neighbour (KNN)—are used in this work. These algorithms classify PD using human speech signals [15]. This work extracts voice signal features to simplify the dataset [39]. Voice intensity and spectrum in Parkinson's disease (PD) patients are analyzed using machine learning classifiers. Compared to SGD (91%), XGB (95%), Logistic Regression (91%), KNN (95%), and Decision Tree (95%), the Random Forest Classifier has the highest accuracy (97%). The researchers [43] use machine learning (ML) in telemedicine to identify PD in its early stages, taking into account PD patients' movement and speech problems. The study implements a K-Nearest Neighbours, Support Vector Machine, Logistic Regression and Random Forest. These models are trained using MDVP audio data from 30 PD patients and HC persons. The Random Forest classifier performs well with 91.83% detection accuracy and 0.95 sensitivity. The Support Vector Machine (SVM) model following Principal Component Analysis (PCA) achieved 91.836% accuracy and 0.94 sensitivity in this investigation. SVM and Random Forest models handle outliers well without creating false positive predictions. Automated acoustic analysis was used to characterize the voice signature of early PD and prodromal iRBD patients [44]. Early PD and healthy controls were among 256 French speakers in the study. Speech samples from various microphones were analyzed for prosody, phonation, fluency, and rhythm. These attributes allowed an SVM to diagnose early PD in males with 89% balanced accuracy and females with 70%. The study found that automated voice analysis can reveal sex-dependent early PD speech deficits, supporting its use in prodromal PD diagnosis. The paper [45] can accurately predict PD and be readily included in healthcare diagnoses; it applied ML and DL models including SVM, RF, DT, K-Nearest Neighbour (KNN), and MLP to PD detection. The study uses audio signal characteristics from 195 voice recordings from 31 patients from (UCI) machine learning repository. The best results are from MLP and SVM. Where MLP has 98.31% accuracy, SVM has 95% accuracy. Table 1 below offers a summary of the research's findings.

Table 1. Brief of Machine Learning studies

Author & Ref.	Year	Dataset	Feature methods	ML method	Contributions	Accuracy
Almeida et al. [32]	2019	Private - audio dataset recorded using acoustic cardioid and a smartphone	eighteen feature extraction techniques	KNN, MLP, OPF, and SVM	Use multiple classifiers for detection	The best is 94.55% and 92.94% respectively, on the smartphone dataset
Sharanyaa et al. [33]	2020	UCI-Parkinson's Disease (Neurodegenerative)	parametric and nonparametric methodologies	Naïve Bayes, Logistic Regression, KNN, and Random Forest	predict PD using dysphonia voice features of patients with PD and HC	Random Forest and KNN, demonstrate higher accuracy rates of 87.2% and 90.2% respectively

(continued)

Table 1. (*continued*)

Author & Ref.	Year	Dataset	Feature methods	ML method	Contributions	Accuracy
Sajal et al. [34]	2020	In [36], and from UCI	UPDRS, maximum relevance minimum redundancy (MRMR)	KNN, SVM, and Naïve Bayes	Combine rest tremor and voice degradation by remote data collection	KNN is 98.5%
Pramanik et al. [35]	2021	PD Speech data-set from Istanbul University's Faculty of Medicine, Department of Neurology in Cerrahpa̧ sa	PCA, ICA	KNN, SVM, Random Forest, AdaBoost, and logistic regression	using voice and speech signal data, use using voice and speech signal data, Comparison of five different ML models	SVM 94.1% was the best one
Solana-Lavalle et al. [40]	2021	PD Speech dataset from Istanbul University and it was introduced by Sakar et al. [37]	feature subset selection technique	SVM, MLP, SVM, KNN, RF	achieves better detection performance with low computational complexity,	KKN reached up to 95.9% as the best model
Zhang T et al. [41]	2021	Dataset-Sakar [38] and Dataset-CPPDD [39]	A novel (EDF-EMD)	SVM, RF	enhance arithmetic speed without losing accuracy and discover the best SVM hyperparameter scheme	SVM achieves the highest average accuracy of 96.54% on the Sakar dataset and 92.59% on the CPPDD dataset
Ahmed et al. [42]	2022	voice signal dataset [39]	unsupervised feature selection methods	SGD, XGB, Logistic Regression Classifier, RF, KNN, Decision Tree	using the voices dataset as an input to several ML models	Forest Classifier has the highest level of accuracy, reaching 97%
Govindu and Palwe S. [43]	2022	MDVP dataset	PCA	SVM, RF, KNN, Logistic Regression	Five ML models, various data processing, and accurate comparison are used	RF was the best one reaching 91.83%

(*continued*)

Table 1. (*continued*)

Author & Ref.	Year	Dataset	Feature methods	ML method	Contributions	Accuracy
Jeancolas L. et al. [44]	2022	private	ANOVA	SVM	highlights the value of gender particular automated voice analysis for prodromal screening or PD monitoring	89% in males and 70% in females
Alshammri R. et al. [45]	2023	voice signal features (UCI)	SMOTE, GridSearchCV	SVM, RF, Decision Tree (DT), KNN, MLP	approach can accurately predict PD and be readily included in healthcare diagnosis	MLP was the best model which got 98.31% SVM 95%

3.2 Deep Learning Approaches

Advances in computing power, the capacity of deep learning techniques to the learn automatically from complex representations of raw input, improvements in neural network architectures specifically designed for medical applications, and interdisciplinary collaboration have led to the widespread adoption of deep learning methods for prediction and diagnosis. The section highlights developments in deep learning applications in the field of audio data analysis. Berus et al. [46] use 26 speech samples per participant to predict PD using several feed-forward ANNs. This study demonstrated the importance of feature extraction and neural network architectures' effect on results; this study was however poor in model parameters and structure. Kendall's correlation coefficient-based feature selection produced the most accurate test results, identifying the most relevant speech samples. The project concludes with fine-tuning a neural network to achieve 86.47% test accuracy. Marek W. et al. describe a new Parkinson's disease detection method [47]. The ResNet architecture, originally designed for photo classification and persistent vowel phonation is used in this technique. To reduce overfitting, the dataset was heavily augmented temporally. The PC-GITA database provided 100 individuals for this investigation. These participants included 50 HC and 50 PD. Each participant's data was collected three times. The validation set's accuracy exceeded 90%, matching the most advanced methodologies. The positive outcome shows that natural picture knowledge can be used for artificial speech signal spectrogram images. The Deep MultiVariate Vocal Data Analysis (DMVDA) System [8] incorporates three neural networks: ADNN, ADRNN, and ADCNN. A clever algorithm processes many voice features in the DMVDA system, increasing value. Acoustic data sampling techniques in the DMVDA framework optimize the speech-processing algorithm, maximizing its benefits. ADNN, ADRNN, and ADCNN improve performance by about 3% over current methods. ADNN, ADRNN, and ADCNN have an accuracy of 98.96%, 99.88%, and 99.92%, respectively. Rizvi et al. [48] tested a deep neural network (DNN) and long short-term memory (LSTM) network model for PD prediction utilizing participant speech samples. The researchers optimized the network's performance on the Parkinson's disease dataset by adjusting hyperparameters. The findings show DNN accuracy of 97.12% and LSTM accuracy of 99.03%. Karaman et al. [49] created deep convolutional neural networks (CNN) to automatically diagnose PD using voice signal biomarkers to meet the urgent need for rapid sickness detection. The evaluation and training used mPower Voice datasets. Three architectures—SqueezeNet1_1, ResNet101, and DenseNet161were retrained and tested for frequency-time classification. Study results showed DenseNet-161 design had the highest accuracy. The proposed approach detected Parkinson's disease (PD) with 89.75% accuracy. Quan et al. [10] research focuses on static and dynamic speech factors to improve Parkinson's disease (PD) detection and early management before physical symptoms appear. The authors' unique method captures continuous speech signals' temporal aspects by integrating dynamic articulation transition features with a Bidirectional Long Short-Term Memory (LSTM) model. Applying the Bidirectional LSTM model to brief sentence speech inputs improves classification accuracy. The Bidirectional LSTM model improves CNN accuracy to 84.29% from 83.52%. T. Vital et al. [50] pioneered Parkinson's disease research using a probabilistic neural network (PNN). A sophisticated intelligent system that can effectively diagnose and classify Parkinson's disease is the study's major goal. The study uses 1200 vowel vocalizations ('a', 'e', 'I', 'o', 'u') from 62 PD patients and 51 healthy controls at various time intervals. A projected probabilistic neural network (PNN) model with 7 hidden layer neurons is an effective and cost-efficient technique to early PD diagnosis employing voice signal data. Quan, C et al. [51] developed a DL voice signal analysis algorithm to diagnose Parkinson's. Time-distributed two-dimensional convolutional neural networks extract dynamic properties from time series data. A 1D CNN captures dependencies using these qualities. The model was evaluated on 2 databases. The model outperformed expert-based machine learning models on Database-1, reading a short Chinese word with 75.3% accuracy and sustaining vowel /a/ with 81.6% accuracy. The model read simple (/loslibros/) and complex (/viste/) sentences with up to 92% accuracy on Database-2, which contains Spanish vowels, words, and phrases. Reddy et al. [52] developed a new Parkinson's Disease prediction method. Deep Speech Data Analysis (DSDA) model integrating DNN, DRNN, and DCNN architectures was presented in the study. Using the UCI PD dataset, the researchers compared DSDA to known models and found substantial results. The DSDA model has high accuracy, with the DNN achieving 98.90%, the DRNN 99.21%, and the DCNN 99.91%. Ali et al. [53] introduced the Ensemble model with Optimal Features and Sample Dependant Base Classifiers (EOFSC) to address Parkinson's disease identification problems. The research processes vowel phonations using the suggested integrated method to create base classifiers for different feature subsets [39]. These attributes and sample-dependent base classifiers are then added to the EOFSC model. Finally, the recently implemented ensemble model improves by 6.5% and has a maximum accuracy of 94.5%. Table 2 is the Abstract for the results of the above researches.

Table 2. Abstract for Deep Learning studies

Author & Ref.	Year	Dataset	method	Contributions	Accuracy
Berus et al. [46]	2018	UCI-dataset [39]	ANN	reveals how feature selection and neural network architecture affect categorization results	86.47%
Marek Wodzinski et al. [47]	2019	PC-GITA database	ResNet	Use pre-trained network, power, and easy methodology	90%
Nagasubramanian, G., & Sankayya, M [8]	2020	Private: Telemonitoring dataset(D1), Multi-variate sound record dataset(D2)	ADNN, ADRNN, and ADCNN	Using the DMVDA technique on multiple datasets to increase the model's efficiency	98.96%, 99.88%, and 99.92% correspondingly
Rizvi et al. [48]	2020	Dataset-Sakar [39]	DNN, LSTM	Efficient models experimental and results	97.12% for DNN and 99.03% for LSTM
Karaman et al. [49]	2021	collected by mPower governance allowance	CNN	Powerfully data preprocessing, and using transfer learning technique for CNN model	89.75%
Quan et al. [10]	2021	volunteers at GYENNO SCIENCE PD Research Center	CNN, LSTM	uses (BiLSTM) to obtain voice signal time-series dynamics in a new way	83.52%, 84.29% respectively

(continued)

Table 2. (*continued*)

Author & Ref.	Year	Dataset	method	Contributions	Accuracy
T. Vital et al. [50]	2021	collected 2016–2019 from Andhra Pradesh, India	PNN	excellent suggested PNN model for voice analysis PD identification	100%
Quan, C et al. [51]	2022	Dataset-1: Chinese language, Dataset-2: Spanish	2D-CNN, 1D-CNN	Use multiple datasets and different model structures	2D-CNN 92% on Dataset-2
Reddy et al. [52]	2022	UCI PD dataset	DNN, DRNN, DCNN	Multiple audio samples are examined to produce an integrated data set and a DL model is used to validate performance in the suggested research	98.90%, 99.21%, and 99.91% respectively
Ali, L. et al. [53]	2023	UCI PD dataset, [39]	DNN	good Feature selection of the model input, compare the DNN model with F-DNN	Maximum was 94.5%

4   Discussion

When analyzing these studies, it was diagnosed that there are strengths and weaknesses in both approaches, and the most prominent strengths are the multiplicity of algorithms and models used as well as the diversity of neural network structures, achieving high accuracy in most models, using advanced feature selection techniques for the extracted audio features and their comprehensive analysis, and using applications. The process of remote diagnosis and also cooperation between different specialties. The most notable weaknesses are the limitations imposed when obtaining data for this several studies have addressed concerns regarding overfitting and instability of a few models in performance. The use of complicated models which includes deep neural networks also makes the models difficult to interpret, and such models require extensive computational sources. Heterogeneity of audio data collection sources, which in turn leads to differences in performance and difficulty comparing results.

5 Direction of Research

Despite the fact that most of the present work has advanced significant developments in the topic of Parkinson's Disease Prediction and Progression Based on Voice analysis there are still many potential research avenues based on Voice analysis. A primary hurdle, particularly for deep learning models, is the scarcity of ample and varied datasets for training, particularly for uncommon or intricate medical conditions like PD. Moreover, the reported efficiency of the detection model and the experimental results are highly dependent on the dataset that was used. Therefore, upcoming studies should concentrate on creating algorithms to accurately identify this disease and track how it evolves.

6 Conclusion

Research on PD prediction, and evaluation based on voice analysis is promising but faces difficulties including difficulty in interpretation, finite data, and computational resources. Research should focus on developing algorithms and techniques for accurate diagnosis and progression tracking, improving interpretability, and strengthening collaboration between disciplines. Practical applications like mobile applications and real-time monitoring systems can also contribute to early diagnosis management. The immediate need for non-invasive methods to identify Parkinson's disease early necessitates ongoing efforts towards improving prediction models and guaranteeing data diversity.

References

1. Poewe, W., et al.: Parkinson disease. Nat. Rev. Dis. Primer **3**(1) (2017). https://doi.org/10.1038/nrdp.2017.13
2. Church, F.C.: Treatment options for motor and non-motor symptoms of parkinson's disease. Biomolecules **11**(4), 612 (2021). https://doi.org/10.3390/biom11040612
3. Tracy, J.M., Özkanca, Y., Atkins, D.C., Hosseini Ghomi, R.: Investigating voice as a biomarker: deep phenotyping methods for early detection of Parkinson's disease. J. Biomed. Inform. **104**, 103362 (2020). https://doi.org/10.1016/j.jbi.2019.103362
4. Jankovic, J.: Parkinson's disease: clinical features and diagnosis. J. Neurol. Neurosurg. Psychiatry **79**(4), 368–376 (2008). https://doi.org/10.1136/jnnp.2007.131045
5. Hemmerling, D., Wójcik-Pędziwiatr, M., Jaciów, P., Ziółko, B., Igras-Cybulska, M.: Monitoring of Parkinson's Disease Progression based on Speech Signal. In: 2023 6th International Conference on Information and Computer Technologies (ICICT), pp. 132–137. IEEE, Raleigh, NC, USA (2023). https://doi.org/10.1109/icict58900.2023.00029
6. Wang, W., Lee, J., Harrou, F., Sun, Y.: Early detection of Parkinson's disease using deep learning and machine learning. IEEE Access **8**, 147635–147646 (2020). https://doi.org/10.1109/access.2020.3016062
7. Templeton, J.M., Poellabauer, C., Schneider, S.: Classification of Parkinson's disease and its stages using machine learning. Sci. Rep. **12**(1) (2022). https://doi.org/10.1038/s41598-022-18015-z
8. Nagasubramanian, G., Sankayya, M.: Multi-Variate vocal data analysis for Detection of Parkinson disease using Deep Learning. Neural Comput. Appl. **33**(10), 4849–4864 (2021). https://doi.org/10.1007/s00521-020-05233-7

9. Hoq, M., Uddin, M.N., Park, S.-B.: Vocal feature extraction-based artificial intelligent model for Parkinson's disease detection. Diagnostics **11**(6), 1076 (2021). https://doi.org/10.3390/diagnostics11061076

10. Quan, C., Ren, K., Luo, Z.: A deep learning based method for Parkinson's disease detection using dynamic features of speech. IEEE Access **9**, 10239–10252 (2021). https://doi.org/10.1109/access.2021.3051432

11. Meghraoui, D., Boudraa, B., Merazi-Meksen, T., Gómez Vilda, P.: A novel pre-processing technique in pathologic voice detection: application to Parkinson's disease phonation. Biomed. Signal Process. Control **68**, 102604 (2021). https://doi.org/10.1016/j.bspc.2021.102604

12. Nissar, I., Mir, W.A., Izharuddin, Shaikh, T.A.: Machine learning approaches for detection and diagnosis of Parkinson's disease - a review. In: 2021 7th International Conference on Advanced Computing and Communication Systems (ICACCS). IEEE, Coimbatore, India (2021). https://doi.org/10.1109/icaccs51430.2021.9441885

13. Mehrish, A., Majumder, N., Bhardwaj, R., Mihalcea, R., Poria, S.: A review of deep learning techniques for speech processing. (2023). http://arxiv.org/abs/2305.00359. Accessed: 17 Sep. 2024

14. Ahmed, S.F., et al.: Deep learning modelling techniques: current progress, applications, advantages, and challenges. Artif. Intell. Rev. **56**(11), 13521–13617 (2023). https://doi.org/10.1007/s10462-023-10466-8

15. Alqahtani, E.J., Alshamrani, F.H., Syed, H.F., Olatunji, S.O.: Classification of Parkinson's disease using NNge CLASSIFICATION ALGORITHM. In: 2018 21st Saudi Computer Society National Computer Conference (NCC). IEEE, Riyadh, Saudi Arabia (2018). https://doi.org/10.1109/ncg.2018.8592989

16. Tjaden, K.: Speech and swallowing in Parkinson's disease. Top. Geriatr. Rehabil. **24**(2), 115–126 (2008). https://doi.org/10.1097/01.tgr.0000318899.87690.44

17. Skodda, S., Grönheit, W., Mancinelli, N., Schlegel, U.: Progression of voice and speech impairment in the course of Parkinson's disease: a longitudinal study. Park. Dis. **2013**, 1–8 (2013). https://doi.org/10.1155/2013/389195

18. Gillivan, P., Murphy: Voice tremor in Parkinson's disease (PD) Identification, characterisation and relationship with speech, voice, and disease variables (2013)

19. Orozco-Arroyave, J.R., et al.: NeuroSpeech: an open-source software for Parkinson's speech analysis. Digit. Signal Process. **77**, 207–221 (2018). https://doi.org/10.1016/j.dsp.2017.07.004

20. Orozco-Arroyave, J.R., et al.: Characterization methods for the detection of multiple voice disorders: neurological, functional, and laryngeal diseases. IEEE J. Biomed. Health Inform. **19**(6), 1820–1828 (2015). https://doi.org/10.1109/jbhi.2015.2467375

21. Orozco-Arroyave, J.R., et al.: Automatic detection of Parkinson's disease in running speech spoken in three different languages. J. Acoust. Soc. Am. **139**(1), 481–500 (2016). https://doi.org/10.1121/1.4939739

22. Orozco-Arroyave, J.R.: Analysis of speech of people with Parkinson's disease. In: Studien zur Mustererkennung, no. Band 41. Logos Verlag Berlin GmbH, Berlin (2016)

23. Pah, N.D., Motin, M.A., Kempster, P., Kumar, D.K.: Detecting effect of levodopa in Parkinson's disease patients using sustained phonemes. IEEE J. Transl. Eng. Health Med. **9**, 1–9 (2021). https://doi.org/10.1109/jtehm.2021.3066800

24. Ali, L., Zhu, C., Zhang, Z., Liu, Y.: Automated detection of parkinson's disease based on multiple types of sustained phonations using linear discriminant analysis and genetically optimized neural network. IEEE J. Transl. Eng. Health Med. **7**, 1 (2019). https://doi.org/10.1109/jtehm.2019.2940900

25. Tsanas, A., Little, M.A., McSharry, P.E., Spielman, J., Ramig, L.O.: Novel speech signal processing algorithms for high-accuracy classification of parkinson's disease. IEEE Trans. Biomed. Eng. **59**(5), 1264–1271 (2012). https://doi.org/10.1109/tbme.2012.2183367

26. Sechidis, K., Fusaroli, R., Orozco-Arroyave, J.R., Wolf, D., Zhang, Y.-P.: A machine learning perspective on the emotional content of Parkinsonian speech. Artif. Intell. Med. **115**, 102061 (2021). https://doi.org/10.1016/j.artmed.2021.102061

27. Tsanas, A., Little, M.A., McSharry, P.E., Ramig, L.O.: Accurate telemonitoring of Parkinson's disease progression by noninvasive speech tests. IEEE Trans. Biomed. Eng. **57**(4), 884–893 (2010). https://doi.org/10.1109/TBME.2009.2036000

28. Pah, N.D., Motin, M.A., Kumar, D.K.: Phonemes based detection of parkinson's disease for telehealth applications. Sci. Rep. **12**(1), 9687 (2022). https://doi.org/10.1038/s41598-022-13865-z

29. Yang, S., et al.: The physical significance of acoustic parameters and its clinical significance of dysarthria in Parkinson's disease. Sci. Rep. **10**(1), 11776 (2020). https://doi.org/10.1038/s41598-020-68754-0

30. Viswanathan, R., et al.: Complexity measures of voice recordings as a discriminative tool for Parkinson's disease. Biosensors **10**(1), 1 (2019). https://doi.org/10.3390/bios10010001

31. Khojasteh, P., et al.: Parkinson's disease diagnosis based on multivariate deep features of speech signal. In: 2018 IEEE Life Sciences Conference (LSC), pp. 187–190. IEEE, Montreal, QC (2018). https://doi.org/10.1109/LSC.2018.8572136

32. Almeida, J.S., et al.: Detecting Parkinson's disease with sustained phonation and speech signals using machine learning techniques. Pattern Recognit. Lett. **125**, 55–62 (2019). https://doi.org/10.1016/j.patrec.2019.04.005

33. Sharanyaa, S., Renjith, P.N., Ramesh, K.: Classification of Parkinson's disease using speech attributes with parametric and nonparametric machine learning techniques. In: 2020 3rd International Conference on Intelligent Sustainable Systems (ICISS), pp. 437–442. IEEE, Thoothukudi, India (2020). https://doi.org/10.1109/ICISS49785.2020.9316078

34. Sajal, M., Ehsan, M., Vaidyanathan, R., Wang, S., Aziz, T., Mamun, K.A.A.: Telemonitoring Parkinson's disease using machine learning by combining tremor and voice analysis. Brain Inform. **7**(1), 12 (2020). https://doi.org/10.1186/s40708-020-00113-1

35. Pramanik, A., Sarker, A.: Parkinson's disease detection from voice and speech data using machine learning. In: Uddin, M.S., Bansal, J.C. (eds.) Proceedings of International Joint Conference on Advances in Computational Intelligence, in Algorithms for Intelligent Systems, pp. 445–456. Springer Singapore, Singapore (2021). https://doi.org/10.1007/978-981-16-0586-4_36

36. Vaiciukynas, E., Verikas, A., Gelzinis, A., Bacauskiene, M.: Detecting Parkinson's disease from sustained phonation and speech signals. PLoS ONE **12**(10), e0185613 (2017). https://doi.org/10.1371/journal.pone.0185613

37. Sakar, C.O., et al.: A comparative analysis of speech signal processing algorithms for Parkinson's disease classification and the use of the tunable Q-factor wavelet transform. Appl. Soft Comput. **74**, 255–263 (2019). https://doi.org/10.1016/j.asoc.2018.10.022

38. Sakar, B.E., et al.: Collection and analysis of a parkinson speech dataset with multiple types of sound recordings. IEEE J. Biomed. Health Inform. **17**(4), 828–834 (2013). https://doi.org/10.1109/JBHI.2013.2245674

39. Little, M.A., McSharry, P.E., Roberts, S.J., Costello, D.A., Moroz, I.M.: Exploiting nonlinear recurrence and fractal scaling properties for voice disorder detection. Biomed. Eng. OnLine **6**(1), 23 (2007). https://doi.org/10.1186/1475-925X-6-23

40. Solana-Lavalle, G., Rosas-Romero, R.: Analysis of voice as an assisting tool for detection of Parkinson's disease and its subsequent clinical interpretation. Biomed. Signal Process. Control **66**, 102415 (2021). https://doi.org/10.1016/j.bspc.2021.102415

41. Zhang, T., Zhang, Y., Sun, H., Shan, H.: Parkinson disease detection using energy direction features based on EMD from voice signal. Biocybern. Biomed. Eng. **41**(1), 127–141 (2021). https://doi.org/10.1016/j.bbe.2020.12.009

42. Ahmed, I., Aljahdali, S., Shakeel Khan, M., Kaddoura, S.: Classification of Parkinson disease based on patient's voice signal using machine learning. Intell. Autom. Soft Comput. **32**(2), 705–722 (2022). https://doi.org/10.32604/iasc.2022.022037

43. Govindu, A., Palwe, S.: Early detection of Parkinson's disease using machine learning. Procedia Comput. Sci. **218**, 249–261 (2023). https://doi.org/10.1016/j.procs.2023.01.007

44. Jeancolas, L., et al.: Voice characteristics from isolated rapid eye movement sleep behavior disorder to early Parkinson's disease. Parkinsonism Relat. Disord. **95**, 86–91 (2022). https://doi.org/10.1016/j.parkreldis.2022.01.003

45. Alshammri, R., Alharbi, G., Alharbi, E., Almubark, I.: Machine learning approaches to identify Parkinson's disease using voice signal features. Front. Artif. Intell. **6**, 1084001 (2023). https://doi.org/10.3389/frai.2023.1084001

46. Berus, L., Klancnik, S., Brezocnik, M., Ficko, M.: Classifying Parkinson's disease based on acoustic measures using artificial neural networks. Sensors **19**(1), 16 (2018). https://doi.org/10.3390/s19010016

47. Wodzinski, M., Skalski, A., Hemmerling, D., Orozco-Arroyave, J.R., Noth, E.: 2019 41st Annual International Conference of the IEEE Engineering in Medicine and Biology Society (EMBC): Biomedical Engineering Ranging from Wellness to Intensive Care: 41st EMB Conference. Berlin (2019)

48. Raza Rizvi, D., Nissar, I., Masood, S., Ahmed, M., Ahmad, F.: An LSTM based deep learning model for voice-based detection of Parkinson's disease, vol. 29 (2020)

49. Karaman, O., Çakın, H., Alhudhaif, A., Polat, K.: Robust automated Parkinson disease detection based on voice signals with transfer learning. Expert Syst. Appl. **178**, 115013 (2021). https://doi.org/10.1016/j.eswa.2021.115013

50. Vital, T.P.R., Nayak, J., Naik, B., Jayaram, D.: Probabilistic neural network-based model for identification of Parkinson's disease by using voice profile and personal data. Arab. J. Sci. Eng. **46**(4), 3383–3407 (2021). https://doi.org/10.1007/s13369-020-05080-7

51. Quan, C., Ren, K., Luo, Z., Chen, Z., Ling, Y.: End-to-end deep learning approach for Parkinson's disease detection from speech signals. Biocybern. Biomed. Eng. **42**(2), 556–574 (2022). https://doi.org/10.1016/j.bbe.2022.04.002

52. Reddy, D.S.S., Kumar, R.U.: Voice Data Analysis for Early Detection of Parkinson's Diseaseusing Deep Learning Algorithms Over Big Data, vol. 13 (2022)

53. Ali, L., Chakraborty, C., He, Z., Cao, W., Imrana, Y., Rodrigues, J.J.P.C.: A novel sample and feature dependent ensemble approach for Parkinson's disease detection. Neural Comput. Appl. **35**(22), 15997–16010 (2023). https://doi.org/10.1007/s00521-022-07046-2

BGWO-Based Classification of Parkinson's Disease via MEG Signals

Zahraa Awad Ghani$^{(\boxtimes)}$ and Firas Sabar Miften

College of Education for Pure Sciences, The University of Thi Qar, Thi Qar, Iraq
{zahraaawad.comp,firas}@utq.edu.iq

Abstract. Parkinson's illness is an incurable nervous disorder marked by a fall in dopamine levels in the brain of humans. It ranks as the second most common neurological disorder. Developing tools for early and automated diagnosis of Parkinson's illness is crucial. This study aims to enhance the advance of computerised methods for detecting Parkinson's disease (PD) utilizing Magnetoencephalography (MEG). MEG sub-bands were created using discrete wavelet transform (DWT). Many features were extracted from sub-band decomposed signals, and the Binary grey wolf optimizer (BGWO) was employed to determine the most significant features. Multiple machine learning models were employed, utilizing these crucial properties as input. The proposed methodology is assessed using data obtained from The Swedish National Facility for Magnetoencephalography Parkinson's disease dataset (NatMEG-PD), which comprises a data sample that contains 66 individuals with Parkinson's illness and 68 individuals who do not have the illness. The Random Forest classifier produces accuracy, specificity, sensitivity, precision, and F-Score of 99.46%, 99.60%, 99.30%, 99.53%, and 99.41, respectively. The proposed methodology would benefit neurologists' diagnostic methods and clinical performance.

Keywords: Parkinson's disease (PD) · Discrete wavelet transform (DWT) · Magnetoencephalography (MEG)

1 Introduction

Parkinson's disease (PD) has a global prevalence of 2–3% among individuals aged 65 and above; this neurological ailment is the second most public, behind Alzheimer's disease [1, 2]. With nearly one million instances in only the United States, Parkinson's illness is probable to influence 1.2 million persons by 2030 and increase twofold in prevalence by 2040. Although PD is growing more prevalent, existing methods of diagnosis are still not perfect [3]. Parkinson's illness is an incurable neurological illness that causes a decline in dopamine levels in the human brain. A neurotransmitter called dopamine assists in communicating with the basal ganglia, the area of the brain in charge of controlling movement and coordination. Dopamine production in the basal ganglia depends on cells; levels drop when these cells die or malfunction [4, 5]. Dopamine levels are higher in healthy individuals than in PD patients. The signs and symptoms may be subtle at

© The Author(s), under exclusive license to Springer Nature Switzerland AG 2025
S. O. Al-Mamory et al. (Eds.): 3INC 2024, CCIS 2329, pp. 72–86, 2025.
https://doi.org/10.1007/978-3-031-81065-7_5

first and tricky to observe, but they will become apparent over time. The symptoms of PD encompass both kinetic and non-motor manifestations, such as dyskinesia, syncope, fatigue, tremor, inflexibility, dystonia, hypomimia, constipation, anosmia or hyposmia, and weight loss [6]. The disorder worsens with time. With time, symptoms could worsen, and new ones might appear. The Hoehn and Yahr Measure is used to quantify the five phases of Parkinson's disease (HY) [7]:

stage 1: This is the mildest level, and in some cases, the symptoms might not even be noticeable at this point.
stage 2: It may take several months to reach this stage, during which time patients may have tremors, muscle rigidity, altered facial expressions, and other symptoms. Postural and gait abnormalities also become apparent.
stage 3: Patients' everyday activities become disrupted by the symptoms.
stage 4: Assistance is required to carry out daily tasks.
stage 5: During this phase, patients become completely bedridden.

The Unified Parkinson's Disease Rating Scale, or UPDRS, is another tool for measuring Parkinson's disease. It exhibits symptom intensity and presence and is primarily intended to track the evolution of PD symptoms. The HY rating is solely derived from the present observation of individuals with Parkinson's illness. The UPDRS is widely recognized as the most widely used clinical grading system for PD patients and has undergone extensive validation. The four parts of the UPDRS are UPDRS I, UPDRS II, UPDRS III, and UPDRS IV. These sections assess psychiatric symptoms in Parkinson's illness, activities of everyday living, dependable motor symptoms measured in PD identified by physical examination, and therapy consequences [8].

It is difficult to diagnose Parkinson's illness early for several reasons. Since most patients are over sixty, the diagnosis of this condition is typically made by neurologists and movement order experts only after a comprehensive evaluation of the patient's medical background and several scans, which take time and are inconvenient for the patients. An accurate diagnosis of Parkinson's illness is mainly dependent on the domain expertise of the medical professionals who examine the patient's data and symptoms. Regretfully, nevertheless, in developing nations like Brazil, India, Argentina, etc., there aren't enough medical professionals in the country. Because of this, diagnosing or detecting Parkinson's is a challenging task because professionals are under pressure from their heavy workload [9].

This has prompted us to create a system that supports decisions to help doctors diagnose Parkinson's illness. Because machine learning plays a role, this can lessen the possibility of errors and act as a second assessment for the diagnosis of Parkinson's. To diagnose Parkinson's illness, researchers have employed a variety of techniques, including handwritten images, SPECT scans, MRIs, EEG signals, Freezing of Gait (FoG), EMG signals, and MRI images. MEG is regarded as one of the most crucial instruments for diagnosing Parkinson's disease from brain signals.

There is still a latent potential for MEG, unlike other methods, MEG does not need intrusive procedures to measure the high temporal resolution magnetic fields produced by brain activity. Although MEG is a new technology, its use in diagnosing Parkinson's disease is nascent, with only a small number of research specifically investigating its incorporation into clinical practice. In resource constrained environments, the restricted availability of MEG devices has hindered their extensive use. Additional, MEG poses a significant challenge for physicians because of the multitude of sensors, the intricate pre-processing needed to extract cortical signals, and the expertise necessary to classify the diverse waveforms [10]. Since MEG devices are scarce and expensive, which limits their application for diagnosing Parkinson's disease; however, in recent years, an increasing number of researchers have started studying MEG signals to identify various neurological disorders. Therefore, MEG analysis has previously been used to diagnose several neurological diseases, such as depressive disorder, autism spectrum disorder, epilepsy, Alzheimer's disease, and schizophrenia [10–14].

The present work aims to fill these gaps by:

1- Developing a decision support system based on machine learning to analyse MEG signals for earlier and more accurate diagnoses.
2- A comparative analysis of the most recent studies of EEG signals versus MEG signals in the classification of Parkinson's illness is conducted to illustrate the superior capabilities of MEG in the diagnosis of Parkinson's illness.
3- Propose potential areas of future study that advocate for the progress of MEG technologies and their further integration into clinical practice.
4- Our efforts are focused on augmenting early detection, enhancing the accuracy of patient results, and alleviating the strain on healthcare infrastructures.

The following sections of this paper are structured in the following method:

In Sect. 2, the related works for the diagnosis of Parkinson's illness, the methodology used in this work is defined in Sect. 3, Sect. 4 show the experimental results, Sect. 5 discusses the research results of the present study and also contrasts them with previous studies that utilized EEG signals. Furthermore, Sect. 6 concludes the paper by providing a conclusion of our proposed method and recommendations for future research directions.

2 Related Work

Parkinson's disease has been diagnosed using several AI-based techniques, which are summarized in Table 1.

Karakas et al. [15] presented a novel approach to the analysis of EEG signals from Parkinson's illness patients. They employed several machine learning techniques, including the grey-level co-occurrence matrix method, and found that the SVM classifier performed the best, yielding an accuracy rate of 92.4%.

Rizvi et al. [16] classified EEG signals to PD from the healthy control using a 23-layered convolutional neural network (CNN) with graphs. For the UNM dataset, the model's maximum accuracy was 93.10%.

Anjum et al. [17] created the innovative Linear-predictive-coding EEG Algorithm for Parkinson's disease (LEAPD) index, which reliably and quickly distinguishes between PD patients and controls. With just a few parameters, the LEAPD technique encodes PSD and can potentially produce PD diagnostics or help develop control algorithms for real-time applications, and attained an 85.4% classification accuracy.

Qiu et al. [18] provide a prototype calibration technique and a unique EEG-based PD automatic detection model called MCPNet, which combines prototype learning and multiscale convolutional neural networks. The accuracy of the model is 92.5%.

Sugden et al. [19] utilized a channel-wise convolutional neural network and optimized it using a leave-one-subject-out cross-validation method. The method attained an accuracy of 82.8%.

Chang et al. [20] created an attention-based sparse graph convolutional neural network (ASGCNN) specifically designed to detect and diagnose Parkinson's disease. The accuracy score achieved is 87.67%.

Time-frequency analysis of MEG signals by DWT and a combination of many features allows the current framework to accurately identify PD patients among healthy controls, which is one of its main contributions. Furthermore, the following is a summary of the contributions made by the current work:

- The technique for an automated PD diagnosis system employing DWT is proposed in this paper, along with the best possible input parameter selection to manage the non-stationary nature of MEG signals appropriately.
- Binary Grey Wolf Optimization is used to choose essential features to get an accurate and timely classification with a high diagnostic rate for Parkinson's disease.
- Lastly, it concludes the acceptability of the suggested Random Forest classifier fed with DWT and multiple features that show up as an effective method with the best computational time to guarantee its applicability for real-time use.

Table 1. Summary of methods used in related work

Authors	Feature extraction approaches	Classifiers	Dataset	Accuracy (%)
Karakas et al. [15]	grey-level co-occurrence matrix	SVM	UNM dataset	92.4%
			Iowa dataset	
			Turku dataset	
Rizvi et al. [16]	23-layered of CNN with graphs	CNN	UNM dataset	93.10%
Anjum et al. [17]	LEAPD		UNM dataset	85.4%
Qiu et al. [18]		MCPNet	UNM dataset	92.5%
Sugden et al. [19]		CNN	UNM dataset	82.8%
Chang, et al. [20]	ASGCNN		EEG (auditory oddball)	87.67%

3   Methodology

The suggested approaches for processing MEG signals are covered in this part, along with information on data description, preprocessing, feature extraction, feature selection, and classification algorithms. Figure 2 provides a high-level overview of the various steps of analysis and classification of MEGs from both healthy individuals and Parkinson's patients. After the initial reading of the raw MEG signals, artefacts are eliminated through preprocessing. The cleaned signals are now fed through a band-pass filter to find the necessary frequency range. The filtered MEG signals are then split up into nonoverlapping pieces of the same length. Subsequently, as we will cover later in this section, the DWT technique is used for decomposition. Then, utilizing a variety of metrics, such as statistical features. The PD/HC features are recovered from the decomposed signals. Lastly, many classifiers are used to distinguish between the properties of healthy controls and those of PD patients. These include decision trees (DT), Linear Discriminant Analysis (LDA), random forests (RF), and support vector machines (SVM) (Fig. 1).

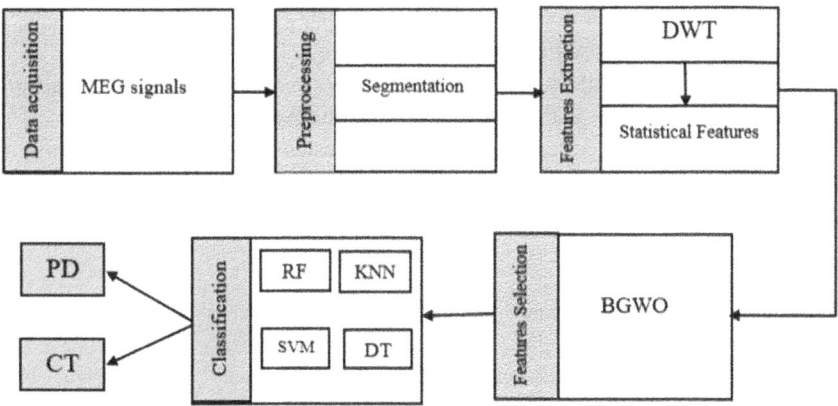

Fig. 1. Block diagram of the suggested classification techniques.

3.1   Data Description and Preprocessing

The data is obtained from the NatMEG-PD, which is The Swedish National Facility for Magnetoencephalography (MEG) dataset [21].

The NatMEG-PD dataset comprises data from a total of 66 individuals diagnosed with Parkinson's disease, ranging in age from 44 to 77 years, with 28 being female. Additionally, the dataset includes data from 68 healthy individuals who were the controls, ranging in age from 46 to 78 years, with 30 being female. The MEG data was obtained using a Neuromag TRIUX 306-channel MEG device. The data was digitized at a rate of 1000 Hz. Recorded concurrently with the MEG, the electrooculogram (EOG), electrocardiogram (ECG), and electromyogram (EMG) from the right forearm, precisely above the flexor carpi radialis, were included. A three-minute session of resting-state magnetoencephalography (MEG) was performed with the participants in a seated position with their eyes closed. The participants were provided with clear instructions to close their eyes, stay still, and relax. Table 2 includes the demographics of the participants and the control health of the patients in this dataset.

The MEG signals are divided into short segments for additional preprocessing. These signals are divided into two seconds of non-overlapping time, with each segment length of 2000.

Table 2. Patient and control participant demographics

Measure	Parkinson's patients (N = 66)	Healthy controls (N = 68)
Sex (F/M)	28/38	30/38
Age (years)	64.4	63.3
Disease duration (years)	4.0	-
LEDD (mg)	512	-
MDS-UPDRS-III	19.3	-

3.2 Discrete Wavelet Transform (DWT)

The discrete wavelet transform (DWT) may examine the properties of a signal in the time and frequency domains by dividing it into many sub-bands [22]. Decomposition of the signal involves combining the detailed (D) and approximate (A) wavelet coefficients that are produced from the wavelet transform linearly. The High Pass filter (HPF) provides the detailed coefficient, whereas the Low Pass filter (LPF) provides an approximate coefficient. Using db4 as the mother wavelet function, 4th-level wavelet decomposition is used in this study. The DWT breaks down each preprocessed-segmented signal from each channel into an approximate coefficient (cA4) and four detail coefficients (cD4, cD3, cD2, and cD1) that represent sub-bands within specific frequency ranges: 0–16 Hz, 16–32 Hz, 32–64 Hz, 64–128 Hz, and 128–256 Hz.

3.3 Feature Extraction

This study identifies 11 distinct types of statistical features [23, 24]. This section offers an elaborate explanation of each of the recommended feature categories that are used to classify MEG data into Parkinson's illness and healthy control groups. The sub-bands of the decomposed MEG signals are utilized to extract statistical features, which are then used to evaluate the irregularity of the signals. The statistical features used to depict MEG data include maximum, median, minimum, range, mean, mode, standard deviation, root mean square value, skewness, variance, and kurtosis. Table 3 presents a brief description of each statistical attribute.

Table 3. Brief Explanation of Statistical Features

No.	Features	Formula
1	Maximum	$X_{Max} = Max[x_n]$
2	Minimum	$X_{Min} = min[x_n]$
3	Range	$X_{Range} = X_{Max} - X_{Min}$
4	standard deviation	$X_{SD} = \sqrt{\sum_{n=1}^{N}(x_n - AM)\frac{2}{n-1}}$
5	Mean	$X_{mean} = \frac{1}{n}\sum_{1}^{n}x_i$
6	Mode	$X_{mod} = L + \left(\frac{f_1 - f_0}{2f_1 - f_2}\right)xh$
7	Median	$X_{median} = \left(\frac{N+1}{2}\right)^{th}$
8	Variance	$X_{var} = \sum_{n=1}^{N}(x_n - AM)\frac{2}{N-1}$
9	Skewness	$X_{Ske} = \sum_{n=1}^{N}(x_n - An)\frac{3}{(N-1)SD^3}$
10	Root mean square	$X_{RMS} = \sqrt{\frac{\sum_{i=1}^{n}x_i^2}{N}}$
11	Kurtosis	$X_{ku} = \sum_{n=1}^{N}(x_n - AM)\frac{4}{(N-1)SD^4}$

3.4 Binary Grey Wolf Optimizer for Feature Selection

The binary grey wolf optimizer (BGWO) is an advanced method used for feature selection. It has proven to be effective in solving the feature selection problem, specifically in EEG data classification [25]. Grey wolves typically reside in packs consisting of 5 to 12 members. The alpha (α) wolf is the dominant leader, followed by the beta (β) and delta (δ) wolves. The others are thought to be omegas, who follow the leaders in the process of seeking and locating prey [26]. The following is a description of how BGWO operates in Algorithm 1.

Algorithm 1: Pseudocode of binary grey wolf optimizer
Input: n Number of grey wolves in the pack. Output: X_α Optimal grey wolf binary position.

Initialize variables: Xi, A, a, C and T_{max}
Xi wolves population (i=1,2,3...n)
$\vec{A} = 2a \cdot \vec{r_1} - a$, where, $\vec{A}$ is a coefficient vector. a is decreasing from 2 to 0 as,
 	
$a = 2 - \dfrac{2.t}{Tmax}$
 	
$\vec{C} = 2 + \vec{r_2}$, where, $\vec{r_2}$ is a random vector in the interval [0,1].
Evaluate the fitness: X_α , X_β and X_δ
While (t < T_{max})
   For each search agent:
 	
$\left\|\vec{D}\right\| = \left\|\vec{C} \cdot \vec{X_{P(t)}} - \vec{X}(t)\right\|$
 	
$\vec{X}(t+1) = \vec{X_{P(t)}} - \vec{A} \cdot \vec{D}$
 	
$\vec{X}(t+1) = \dfrac{\vec{X_1} + \vec{X_2} + \vec{X_3}}{3}$,
 	
where, $\vec{X_1}, \vec{X_2}$ and $\vec{X_3}$ Calculated as,
 	
$\left\|D_\alpha\right\| = \left\|\vec{C}_1 \cdot \vec{X}_\alpha - \vec{X}\right\|$,
$\left\|D_\beta\right\| = \left\|\vec{C}_2 \cdot \vec{X}_\beta - \vec{X}\right\|$,
$\left\|D_\delta\right\| = \left\|\vec{C}_3 \cdot \vec{X}_\delta - \vec{X}\right\|$
$\vec{X_1} = \vec{X_\alpha} - \vec{A}_1 \cdot (\vec{D_\alpha})$,
$\vec{X_2} = \vec{X_\beta} - \vec{A}_2 \cdot (\vec{D_\beta})$,
$\vec{X_3} = \vec{X_\delta} - \vec{A}_3 \cdot (\vec{D_\delta})$
 	
Grey wolf position vectors are updated and then forced into binary using the sigmoid algorithm.
 	
$x_d^{t+1} = \begin{cases} 1 & if\ sigmoid(\dfrac{x1 + x2 + x3}{3}) \geq rand \\ 0 & otherwise \end{cases}$
 	
   End For
Update a, A & C
Compute the fitness of every search agent.
Update X_α, X_β, and X_δ
t=t + 1
End while
Return X_α

3.5 Machine Learning Classifiers

To classify MEG signals, the features extracted are fed into the classification algorithms. The subjects are classified using the random forest (RF), decision tree (DT), support vector machine (SVM), and Linear Discriminant Analysis (LDA) techniques. The approaches listed above are briefly detailed below.

1. LDA is a supervised ML method for classification and data reduction. LDA optimizes class distinction by linearly converting data (features) into a lower-dimensional space [27].
2. DT employs conditional control statements to make predictions about the value of a target variable, taking into account the properties of the data. A decision-making process that can result in a positive conclusion is represented by the branches of a decision tree [28].
3. Random Forest (RF) is an ensemble of decision trees, where each tree is constructed using a random vector that is independently and uniformly sampled from the dataset. The class chosen by the most significant number of trees determines the classification outcome in this procedure. The advantage of this approach is that it exhibits greater resilience to noise [29].
4. SVM is a machine learning algorithm (MLA) that reduces risk by providing several solutions to various linear and nonlinear issues. It can be applied to multiclass classification issues as well as binary classification problems. SVM is separated into two categories based on the condition of the data: linear SVM and nonlinear SVM [15].

3.6 Performance Evaluation

This study employs different ways to assess the performance of the constructed classification models:

Accuracy: Accuracy is the proportion of correctly predicted outcomes from all of the forecasts made.

$$Accuracy = \frac{CorrectPredictions}{TotalPrediction} \times 100\% \qquad (1)$$

Sensitivity: Also referred to as True Positive Rate (TPR) or Recall, sensitivity quantifies a system's capacity for accurate positive prediction-making.

$$TPR = \frac{TruePostive}{TruePositives + FalseNegatives} \times 100\% \qquad (2)$$

Specificity: Specificity, called True Negative Rate (TNR), is a metric to assess how well a system can anticipate negative outcomes.

$$TNR = \frac{TrueNegatives}{TrueNegatives + FalsePositives} \times 100\% \qquad (3)$$

Precision: Also referred to as Positive Prediction Value (PPV), precision measures a system's capacity to generate only relevant outcomes.

$$Precision = \frac{TruePositives}{TruePositives + FalsePositives} \times 100\% \qquad (4)$$

F-score: Since the F-score allows for the integration of sensitivity and precision into a single metric, it is widely used.

$$F-score = 2 \times \frac{Precision - Sensitivity}{Precision + Sensitivity} \times 100\% \qquad (5)$$

4 Experimental Results

This study aimed to use MEG signals to classify PD patients and HC groups. For this, a discrete wavelet transform was applied to extract different features from MEG signals. To discover the most successful performance, these features were input into four different machine learning algorithms. The present study's initial stage was that MEG signals were broken down into sub-bands using discrete wavelet transform to extract properties from each component. The MEG signals were separated into four sub-bands using DWT after various features were extracted from each band in the second stage of the study. The feature selection problem in the classification of MEG data was solved using the binary grey wolf optimizer before the classification process. This method is used to find essential features that will be fed into ML algorithms and are effective at classifying outcomes. Classification was the last phase of the experiment.

The final results were obtained by averaging the performance requirements achieved at each step. The classification procedure involved the selection of four specific machine learning algorithms often utilized in biological research: Random Forest, Support Vector Machine, Linear Discriminant Analysis, and Decision Tree. The classification results were evaluated using performance measures such as Accuracy, Sensitivity, Specificity, Precision, and F-score. The groups were classified as PD - HC using the DWT approach. The classifying procedures of the DWT methodology yielded findings for the PD -HC groups, which are presented in Table 3 and Fig. 2. According to the study's findings, the RF algorithm yielded the most precise classification results for the PD -HC groups (Table 4).

Table 4. Classification results from PD VS HC based on DWT and different classification models

	Accuracy	Sensitivity	Specificity	Precision	F-score
RF	99.46	99.30	99.60	99.53	99.41
LDA	96.88	96.26	99.10	99.06	96.63
DT	94.62	95.40	97.07	94.17	94.89
SVM	71.00	71.42	72.30	67.94	70.88

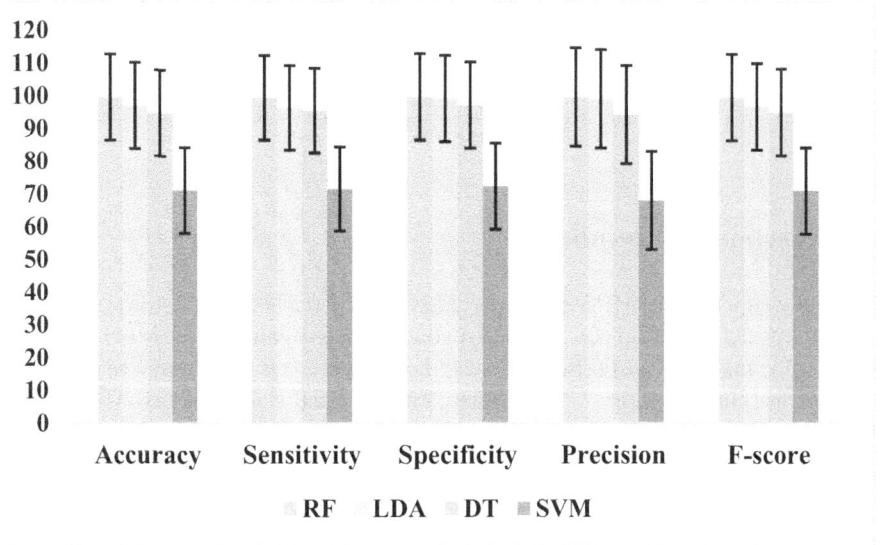

Fig. 2. Performance and Variability Comparison of Machine Learning Models.

5 Discussion

Our study is innovative since it is the first to use multichannel magnetoencephalography (MEG) data to classify Parkinson's disease (PD). We employed the discrete wavelet transform (DWT) and binary grey wolf optimization (BGWO) techniques to extract and choose distinctive characteristics. It is essential to mention that no prior studies have utilized MEG data to classify Parkinson's disease. Previous studies have primarily concentrated on alternative methods like EEG and imaging techniques. Therefore, our methodology is distinctive as it offers a new application and is well-suited to investigate this unexplored field.

MEG and EEG data capture neural oscillations, but MEG has notable advantages, including enhanced spatial resolution and the ability to detect activity in deep brain areas. These qualities enable more accurate localization of brain sources and perhaps more precise detection of biomarkers associated with Parkinson's disease compared to EEG. Although no prior studies have utilized MEG data for the classification of PD, findings from research based on EEG offer a fundamental point of comparison. EEG studies have demonstrated a diagnostic accuracy of over 90% when employing different machine and deep learning approaches, therefore emphasizing the efficacy of neuroimaging methods in diagnosing Parkinson's illness. For instance, a study conducted by Karakas et al. [15] employed the grey-level co-occurrence matrix technique alongside other machine learning methods, resulting in an accuracy rate of 92.4%. However, it is worth noting that this approach is characterized by its time-intensive nature. Increasing the number of windows in the approach reduces the amount of data that needs to be segmented. Anjum et al. [17] A linear predictive coding technique was used to extract spectral markers of Parkinson's disease. They achieved an accuracy of 85.4%. Qiu et al. [18] present a calibration technique prototype that integrates prototype learning and multiscale convolutional neural networks. The model achieves an accuracy of 92.5%. However, the study uses a relatively small sample size. Additionally, this model's computational cost is higher than our proposed approach.

Rizvi et al. [16] employed a 23-layered convolutional neural network (CNN) with graphs, and the model attained a peak accuracy of 93.10. However, the need for interpretability poses a challenge in identifying the most distinguishing EEG signals for classification. Sugden et al. [19] employed a channel-wise convolutional neural network and optimized it using a leave-one-subject-out cross-validation technique. The approach achieved an accuracy of 82.8%. However, the accuracy of the classification is significantly lower when compared to the approach that has been suggested.

Chang et al. [20] created an attention-based sparse graph convolutional neural network (ASGCNN) to diagnose Parkinson's illness. The acquired accuracy score is 87.67%. However, the model explicitly targets brain regions that have been recognized as significant factors in the classification of Parkinson's illness. Nevertheless, this emphasis may overlook the possible contributions of additional cerebral areas.

Our approach utilizes the outcomes of DWT (Discrete Wavelet Transform) and BGWO (Grey Wolf Optimization) by applying them to MEG (Magnetoencephalography) data. The objective is to outperform conventional EEG (Electroencephalography) methods in precision and computational speed.

MEG has significant benefits compared to EEG in measuring brain electrical activity. This is because MEG specifically detects the magnetic fields generated by these electrical currents, offering a non-invasive technique with better spatial and temporal resolution.

The relative advantage of MEG highlights its potential as a viable technique for improving the diagnosis of Parkinson's disease, particularly in situations that necessitate precise spatial data and thorough brain activity mapping.

Although our investigation is innovative, its scope is restricted due to the utilization of a dataset from a solitary source, potentially impeding the applicability of our findings. Future research should focus on validating more extensive and diversified datasets that incorporate MEG and EEG data to clarify shared and unique biomarkers across different measurement methods. Furthermore, investigating the incorporation of supplementary imaging modalities or fine-tuning optimization parameters could augment the dependability and practicality of Parkinson's disease detection by employing our suggested approach (Table 5).

Table 5. Comparison of several related works in terms of performance evaluation.

Authors	Accuracy	Specificity	Sensitivity	Precision	F-Score
Karakas et al. [15]	92.4%	91.85%	92.96%	91.96%	92.96%
Rizvi et al. [16]	93.10%	-	93.18%	93.09%	93.13%
Anjum et al. [17]	85.4%	85.7%	85.7%	-	-

(continued)

Table 5. (*continued*)

Authors	Accuracy	Specificity	Sensitivity	Precision	F-Score
Qiu et al. [18]	92.5%	91.9%	93.1%	-	-
Sugden et al. [19]	82.8%	74.89%	90.71%	-	84.11%
Chang et al. [20]	87.67%	-	90.36%	88.43%	88.41%
Proposed approach	**99.46%**	**99.60%**	**99.30%**	**99.53%**	**99.41%**

6　Conclusion

This work uses the discrete wavelet transform (DWT) technique on magnetoencephalography (MEG) signals to identify Parkinson's illness using machine learning autonomously. This study analyses PD and HC MEG signals using DWT and a binary grey wolf optimizer, which determined the significant features. After that, four machine-learning approaches were used to classify PD groups using the identified characteristics. Comparing four machine-learning models' performance, we found that the Proposed approach could discriminate PD and HC with 99.46% accuracy using RF. Diagnosing PD patients from the dataset takes 5.78 s. A detailed review and comparison with existing studies showed that the Discrete Wavelet Transform (DWT) strategy using multiple Features and a Random Forest (RF) classifier is an emerging method for diagnosing Parkinson's illness using MEG data. We have substantially enhanced accuracy and interpretability, establishing a solid basis for future investigations into individualized diagnosis and monitoring of Parkinson's illness. Validation and expansion of our discoveries in the field of neuroimaging can significantly benefit from collaborative endeavours, leading to enhanced clinical outcomes for people with Parkinson's disease. Neurologists can better detect Parkinson's disease early with this strategy. This technique may be expanded to provide quick and intelligent healthcare monitoring for Parkinson's disease accuracy using cloud computing and the Internet of Things (IoT).

References

1. Skaramagkas, V., Pentari, A., Kefalopoulou, Z., Tsiknakis, M.: Multi-modal deep learning diagnosis of parkinson's disease - a systematic review. IEEE Trans. Neural Syst. Rehabil. Eng. **31**, 2399–2423 (2023). https://doi.org/10.1109/TNSRE.2023.3277749
2. Luna-Ortiz, I., et al.: Parkinson's disease detection from voice recordings using associative memories. Healthcare (Switzerland) **11**(11) (2023). https://doi.org/10.3390/healthcare11111601
3. Kumar, A., Kouznetsova, V.L., Kesari, S., Tsigelny, I.F.: Parkinson's disease diagnosis using miRNA biomarkers and deep learning. Frontiers in Bioscience - Landmark **29**(1) (2024). https://doi.org/10.31083/j.fbl2901004
4. Abdullah, S.M., et al.: Deep transfer learning based Parkinson's disease detection using optimized feature selection. IEEE Access **11**, 3511–3524 (2023). https://doi.org/10.1109/ACCESS.2023.3233969

5. Arora, P., Mishra, A., Malhi, A.: N-semble-based method for identifying Parkinson's disease genes. Neural Comput. Appl. **35**(33), 23829–23839 (2023). https://doi.org/10.1007/s00521-021-05974-z

6. Aljalal, M., Aldosari, S.A., Alsharabi, K., Abdurraqeeb, A.M., Alturki, F.A.: Parkinson's disease detection from resting-state EEG signals using common spatial pattern, entropy, and machine learning techniques. Diagnostics **12**(5) (2022). https://doi.org/10.3390/diagnostics1 2051033

7. Goyal, J., Khandnor, P., Aseri, T.C.: Classification, prediction, and monitoring of parkinson's disease using computer assisted technologies: a comparative analysis. Eng. Appl. Artif. Intell. **96** (2020). https://doi.org/10.1016/j.engappai.2020.103955

8. Nilashi, M., et al.: Predicting Parkinson's disease progression: evaluation of ensemble methods in machine learning. J. Healthc. Eng. 2022 (2022). https://doi.org/10.1155/2022/2793361

9. Lamba, R., Gulati, T., Alharbi, H.F., Jain, A.: A hybrid system for Parkinson's disease diagnosis using machine learning techniques. Int. J. Speech Technol. **25**(3), 583–593 (2022). https://doi.org/10.1007/s10772-021-09837-9

10. Pan, R., Yang, C., Li, Z., Ren, J., Duan, Y.: Magnetoencephalography-based approaches to epilepsy classification. Frontiers in Neuroscience, vol. 17. Frontiers Media SA (2023). https://doi.org/10.3389/fnins.2023.1183391

11. Jiang, H., Dai, Z., Lu, Q., Yao, Z.: Magnetoencephalography resting-state spectral fingerprints distinguish bipolar depression and unipolar depression. Bipolar Disord. **22**(6), 612–620 (2020). https://doi.org/10.1111/bdi.12871

12. Roberts, T.P.L., Kuschner, E.S., Edgar, J.C.: Biomarkers for autism spectrum disorder: opportunities for magnetoencephalography (MEG). Journal of Neurodevelopmental Disorders **13**(1). BioMed Central Ltd. (2021). https://doi.org/10.1186/s11689-021-09385-y

13. Yang, S., et al.: Integrated space–frequency–time domain feature extraction for MEG-based Alzheimer's disease classification. Brain Inform **8**(1) (2021). https://doi.org/10.1186/s40708-021-00145-1

14. Kim, J., et al.: Feature optimization method for machine learning-based diagnosis of schizophrenia using magnetoencephalography. J. Neurosci. Methods **338** (2020). https://doi.org/10.1016/j.jneumeth.2020.108688

15. Karakaş, M.F., Latifoğlu, F.: Distinguishing Parkinson's disease with GLCM features from the hankelization of EEG signals. Diagnostics **13**(10) (2023). https://doi.org/10.3390/diagno stics13101769

16. Rizvi, S.Q.A., Wang, G., Khan, A., Hasan, M.K., Ghazal, T.M., Khan, A.U.R.: Classifying Parkinson's disease using resting state electroencephalogram signals and UEN-PDNet. IEEE Access **11**, 107703–107724 (2023). https://doi.org/10.1109/ACCESS.2023.3319248

17. Anjum, M.F., Dasgupta, S., Mudumbai, R., Singh, A., Cavanagh, J.F., Narayanan, N.S.: Linear predictive coding distinguishes spectral EEG features of Parkinson's disease. Parkinsonism Relat. Disord. **79**, 79–85 (2020). https://doi.org/10.1016/j.parkreldis.2020.08.001

18. Qiu, L., et al.: A novel EEG-based Parkinson's disease detection model using multiscale convolutional prototype networks. IEEE Trans. Instrum. Meas. **73** (2024). https://doi.org/10.1109/TIM.2024.3351248

19. Sugden, R.J., Diamandis, P.: Generalizable electroencephalographic classification of Parkinson's disease using deep learning. Inform Med Unlocked **42** (2023). https://doi.org/10.1016/j.imu.2023.101352

20. Chang, H., Liu, B., Zong, Y., Lu, C., Wang, X.: EEG-based parkinson's disease recognition via attention-based sparse graph convolutional neural network. IEEE J. Biomed. Health Inform. **27**(11), 5216–5224 (2023). https://doi.org/10.1109/JBHI.2023.3292452

21. Vinding, M.C., et al.: The Swedish national facility for magnetoencephalography Parkinson's disease dataset. Sci. Data **11**(1) (2024). https://doi.org/10.1038/s41597-024-02987-w

22. Aksoy, G., Cattan, G., Chakraborty, S., Karabatak, M.: Quantum machine-based decision support system for the detection of schizophrenia from EEG records. J. Med. Syst. **48**(1) (2024). https://doi.org/10.1007/s10916-024-02048-0

23. Diykh, M., Miften, F.S., Abdulla, S., Saleh, K., Green, J.H.: Robust approach to depth of anaesthesia assessment based on hybrid transform and statistical features. IET Sci. Meas. Technol. **14**(1), 128–136 (2020). https://doi.org/10.1049/iet-smt.2018.5393

24. Mohammed, H., Diykh, M.: Improving EEG major depression disorder classification using FBSE coupled with domain adaptation method based machine learning algorithms. Biomed Signal Process Control **85** (2023). https://doi.org/10.1016/j.bspc.2023.104923

25. Yadav, V.P., Sharma, K.K.: Variational mode decomposition and binary grey wolf optimization-based automated epilepsy seizure classification framework. Biomed. Tech. **68**(2), 147–163 (2023). https://doi.org/10.1515/bmt-2022-0098

26. Mirjalili, S., Mirjalili, S.M., Lewis, A.: Grey wolf optimizer. Adv. Eng. Softw. **69**, 46–61 (2014). https://doi.org/10.1016/j.advengsoft.2013.12.007

27. Rahman, A., et al.: Parkinson's disease diagnosis in cepstral domain using MFCC and dimensionality reduction with SVM classifier. Mobile Information Systems **2021** (2021). https://doi.org/10.1155/2021/8822069

28. Kara Gulay, B., Demirel, N., Vahaplar, A., Guducu, C.: A novel feature extraction method using chemosensory EEG for Parkinson's disease classification. Biomed Signal Process Control **79**(2023). https://doi.org/10.1016/j.bspc.2022.104147

29. Coelho, B.F.O., et al.: Parkinson's disease effective biomarkers based on Hjorth features improved by machine learning. Expert Syst. Appl. **212** (2023). https://doi.org/10.1016/j.eswa.2022.118772

Enhancing Twitter Comment Classification Using Convolutional Neural Networks and Support Vector Machines

Noor A. Thwiny[✉] and Kadhim Hasen Alibraheemi

Computer Sciences, University of Thi Qar, Thi Qar, Iraq
{noorabdalwahed.23co2,khalibraheemi}@utq.edu.iq

Abstract. Social media provides a vibrant environment for sharing content and communicating online, allowing users to express themselves freely. Text is one of the most important and widely used types of content on these platforms, and classifying text comments is important for understanding individuals' thoughts and trends. The study aims to develop an effective model for analyzing and classifying comments on social media networks into negative, positive, and neutral comments using natural language processing techniques, deep learning models, and machine learning, with word embedding. Convolutional Neural Networks (CNN) are used to extract information from texts and apply the Support Vector Machine (SVM) model to classification accuracy. Twitter was chosen due to its importance nowadays, as it is considered the most influential and interactive platform on social media. The results showed a high accuracy of up to 98% for this hybrid model compared to the traditional machine learning model on the Twitter datasets available on Kaggle.

Keywords: Convolutional Neural Networks · Support Vector Machine · Twitter

1 Introduction

Humans by nature communicate with each other. Communication has always been a key component of problem-solving and encouraging community involvement. However, today's means of communication have changed radically compared to the means of communication in the old days. Almost every societal group now uses social media, making it a crucial medium for communication [1]. Social media is considered the platform that witnesses many discussions, where individuals can freely express their opinions, but the bias of some people may cause them to abuse this freedom, which makes some people hesitate to participate in online discussions [2]. These comments, about which you may feel positively or negatively about goods or services, are frequently based on user opinions and experiences. Recognizing negative customer reviews is essential to an organization's development since these insights can assist them in making improvements to their goods and services, increasing their revenue. Thus, analyzing customer feedback from websites and social media platforms is crucial [3].

© The Author(s), under exclusive license to Springer Nature Switzerland AG 2025
S. O. Al-Mamory et al. (Eds.): 3INC 2024, CCIS 2329, pp. 87–100, 2025.
https://doi.org/10.1007/978-3-031-81065-7_6

With the increasing use of social media sites, the amount of data generated has increased tremendously daily. Textual content is considered the most common and influential, as it plays an important role in decision-making processes both at the individual and group levels. Texts are often the basis for interpreting individuals' tendencies, making it easier to predict their behaviour [4]. The purpose of this study is to analyze and classify comments on social networking sites into negative, positive, and neutral comments, and enhance classification accuracy, thus being able to detect content types on social media. To classify the comments we are using SVM and the proposed hybrid model CNN-SVM. We are applying them separately and comparing these models to see which fits and works best. Twitter dataset is used to train the model, as Twitter is one of the social networks that has been examined the most among the various social network research. Twitter is used by people, organizations, and groups due to its blog features, which allow users to share content instantly and collaborate on important decisions. Twitter facilitates communication between users and institutions or organizations in this way [5]. The following is a summary of the study's contributions:

1. Develop a hybrid model that combines CNN and SVM, by combining the capabilities of CNN in extracting textual features and the effectiveness of SVM in classification.
2. Address the challenges of short texts and big, diverse, and heterogeneous data in Twitter comments using advanced natural language processing techniques.
3. Use word embedding to generate accurate text representations that take into account context and semantic meanings.

The remainder of the paper is arranged as follows. A few studies linked to the current study are described in Sect. 2. The theoretical background is introduced in Sect. 3. A method of the approach used is provided in Sect. 4. Section 5 presents the experimental results and discusses them. Section 6 provides the conclusion.

2 Related Works

Many previous studies have focused on classification comments on social media sites, including the following:

Monika, et al. [6] use deep learning algorithms to classify tweets of American Airlines flights. Recurrent neural networks (RNNs), long-term memory networks (LSTMs), and word embedding models like Word2Vec and Glove are used to classify sentiment for six different US airlines as positive, negative, or neutral. To improve performance using a bidirectional LSTM model (Bi-LSTM), which produced the best accuracy of 91.78%. Utama et al. [7] examine consumer perceptions of American Airlines through sentiment analysis of Twitter data. It employs a Kaggle-provided dataset and machine learning algorithms that choose to examine features based on mutual information since it is a useful way for determining feature correlation. When choosing features using mutual information, the results show that training data is better than Chi-Square and Annova F, with an accuracy of 76.91%. Jain, et al. [8] present a hybrid CNN-LSTM model with dropout, max pooling, and batch normalization for sentiment analysis of web content on social media sites. When word embedding is used to analyze Twitter sentiment and airline quality datasets, the model outperforms classical machine learning algorithms with 91.3% accuracy on Twitter sentiment.

Tan, et al. [9] present an ensemble hybrid deep learning model that combines GRU, LSTM, BiLSTM, and RoBERTa for sentiment analysis. To handle unbalanced datasets, the model makes use of the advantages of each component and uses data enhancement with GloVe pre-trained word embeddings. Experiments using Sentiment140, Twitter US Airline Sentiment, and IMDb show significantly higher accuracy (89.81%, 91.77%, and 94.9%, respectively). Jasim, et al. [10] analyze Twitter sentiment and classify tweets as positive or negative. Deep learning methodologies use building a recurrent neural network using CNN models, trained on a dataset of the Sentiment140. The hybrid model achieved the best (CNN-LSTM classifier) 93.91% in predicting tweets.

Şengül, et al. [11] explore sentiment analysis on Twitter data using different algorithms, including NB, SVM, LR, LSTM, and CNN. After pre-processing English tweet messages from the Sentiment140 dataset, the LSTM + CNN hybrid approach achieved the highest accuracy of 85%. The evaluation was based on the f1 score, which demonstrates the effectiveness of these methods in classifying emotions on digital social networks. Vidyashree, et al. [12] propose an ensemble classifier combining RF, SVM, and DT to categorize tweets based on polarities like positive and negative. Social media users often share semi-structured data containing valuable patterns and knowledge. NLP and data mining techniques are crucial for sentiment analysis, particularly on Twitter. The public's opinions on particular subjects are determined by independently collecting and analyzing data from the Twitter API. The output from several machine-learning classifiers is combined by the ensemble classifier using Adaptive Boosting (AdaBoost). The experimental results demonstrate that the proposed ensemble classifier outperforms the current Convolutional Bidirectional - Long Short-Term Memory (ConvBiLSTM) classifier and Hybrid Lexicon-Naïve Bayes Classifier (HL-NBC), which yield classification accuracy of 91.53% and 896.61%, respectively. The proposed classifier offers a higher accuracy of 93.42%.

Despite the significant progress in previous classification models, challenges in classification accuracy still exist, especially when dealing with diverse and variable comments. Existing models suffer from high error rates, which limits the effectiveness of the systems and leads to inaccurate results. This study aims to improve classification accuracy by developing a hybrid model that combines CNN and SVM to classify Twitter comments. The proposed model is characterized by its ability to combine the extraction of fine-grained textual features through CNN with the effectiveness of SVM inaccurate classification. It also takes advantage of advanced word embedding techniques to enhance classification accuracy and address the challenges of short and diverse texts, which contributes to bridging the current research gap and providing a more efficient and accurate solution for comment classification.

3 Background

In this part, we explain the methods used to classify text comments.

3.1 Word Embedding

Neural networks can learn from input data by transforming it into a vector representation, where numerical vectors represent the input. This highlights the geometric significance of a word's semantic meaning [13]. The word embedded layer representation was used in this study. It is a neural network consisting of layers to deal with data, uses a corpus of text as input data, and produces a series of vectors as output. Sentence-based word embedding transforms words into low-dimensional scalar (vector) representations. The network can comprehend texts more efficiently because of these vectors, which represent the syntactic and semantic links between words. The model receives the generated numerical vectors. After each word is turned into a vector, the whole sentence is represented by a matrix, whose dimensions are equal to the product of the sentence's word count and vector size. After receiving it, the neural network applies it to several tasks, such as text classification, sentiment analysis, and machine translation [14].

3.2 Bag of Words

The bag of words (BoW) technique is applied to extract features from the text data. Texts can be represented using the BoW representation method, which is a natural language processing methodology that counts the occurrences of each word in a word cloud, regardless of word order or grammar. The process involves segmenting the text into words, creating a dictionary in which the frequency of each word is assigned a value, and creating an illustration of a BoW. It is one of the most widely used methods for classifying texts and items. The BOW technique is simpler than other approaches both theoretically and computationally [15].

3.3 Support Vector Machine

One practical supervised machine learning method for classification is the SVM. This is the most often used algorithm for situations involving regression and classification. SVMs are rapidly replacing other methods in machine learning and data mining because they yield cutting-edge results in practical applications like classifying texts, handwritten character identification, picture classification, bio sequences analysis, etc. Even with tiny datasets, it performs extraordinarily well, and its influence increases with increasing dimensional space [16].

SVM divides the data into classes by drawing a line or a hyperplane. One of the main disadvantages of SVM is its extraordinarily high time complexity. Although SVMs were initially intended to handle binary classification, today we usually have a lot of data to classify. Multiclass classification is the term used to describe classification that has more than two classes [17]. To describe the division of the hyperplane, we use the following linear equation:

$$w^T x + b = 0 \qquad (1)$$

where W is a normal vector that establishes the hyperplane's direction, x is the training sample, and b is a displacement that shows how far the hyperplane is from the origin. Assume that the hyperplane can accurately categorize the training samples, meaning that the training samples satisfy the following formula:

$$w^T x_i + b \geq +1 \qquad (2)$$

$$w^T x_i + b \leq -1 \tag{3}$$

3.4 Convolution Neural Network

CNN is a special kind of neural network used in image processing. The CNN model has shown to be a highly effective tool for text classification, nonetheless. CNNs are suited for the classification of text because they can identify important text features like n-grams and phrases without the need for intricate feature building. A matrix of word embeddings is typically used to represent the input data in a CNN, with each row denoting a single word and each column denoting an embedding feature or dimension [18]. The CNN architecture consists of a series of convolutional layers that use filters to search the input matrix for patterns or features as shown in Fig. 1.

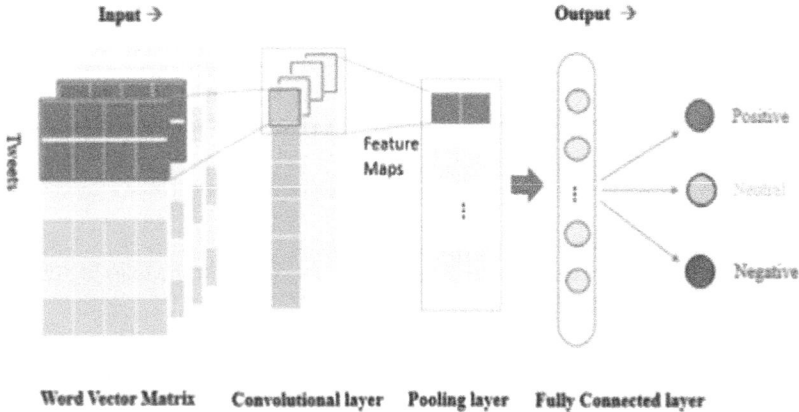

Fig. 1. Stages of CNN network for text classification [11].

The network can pick up patterns at different sizes by applying filters to every potential word window in the input. The output of the convolutional layer is then transmitted via a pooling layer, which gathers the most important data and lowers dimensionality. Finally, the output of the pooling layer is sent through one or more completely linked layers before the final classification decision is made [19].

4   Proposed Method

This section presents the specifics of our models, and the basic steps in this study are depicted in Fig. 2.

4.1   Data Description

In this study, two different datasets from Twitter were used, with the study focusing on text comments. If the comment contained text accompanied by an image or emoji, the image or emoji was ignored and the text alone was used to perform text processing.

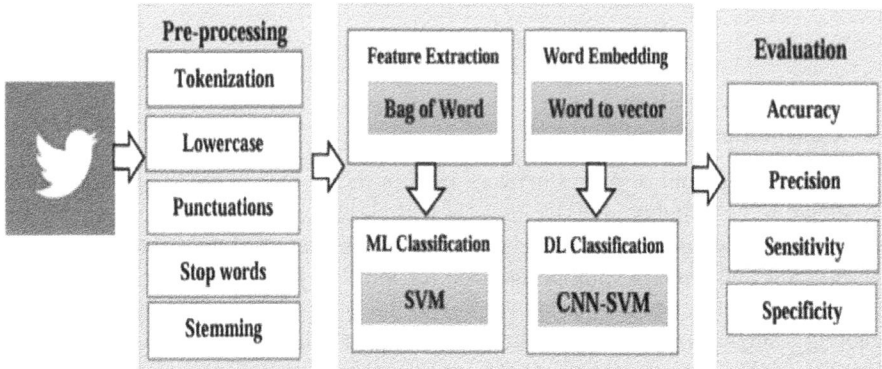

Fig. 2. Framework of comments classification.

- The first "twitter-airline-sentiment" comprises 14,640 comments, obtained through Kaggle [20].
- The second dataset is the "twitter-and-reddit-sentimental-analysis-dataset". Contains 162890 tweets obtained through Kaggle [21]. The positive tweet refers to (1), negative (−1) and neutral (0).

4.2 Pre-Processing

Pre-processing techniques are used to clean up the data to boost the learning efficiency of deep learning models [22]:

Tokenization Is the method of dividing a text into smaller sections referred to as "tokens." Any character, word, or number that accurately represents the data's essential features without affecting its security can be used as a token.

Punctuation Removal: Is the process of eliminating punctuation from comments by utilizing methods from natural language processing. Punctuations are symbols used in sentences and comments to help make them readable and understandable to humans but to enhance the learning process of machine learning algorithms, it must be eliminated because it causes issues [2].

Number Removal: This is the process of eliminating numerical data, which enhances the effectiveness of deep learning algorithms. Numerical data is superfluous and does not aid in the comprehension of text analysis methodologies. Removing the numbers reduces the complexity of the data and improves model efficiency.

Stop Words Removal: Stop words are English terms that don't contribute any meaning to a phrase. Thus, stop-word removal can eliminate these without changing the sense of the phrase. The model performs better and the complexity of the input features is reduced when stop-words are removed.

Stemming: In the text preprocessing module, stemming is a fundamental component. Returning the targeted words to their original form is essentially what stemming is. It removes words from their complicated forms. Data preprocessing is done using a technique called stemming. When a stemmer is used to change a word into its root form, the term stays unique without further processing.

4.3 Hybrid Model

Following pre-processing, which uses the word encoding function to give each word in the tweet a unique encoding, the dataset is organized by applying basic operations before moving on to the next step. If every n-word text is represented as:

$$T = \{w1, w2, ..., wn\} \in R^{n*d} \tag{4}$$

The input text must have a uniform length (l) because it varies in length. It uses a zero-padding technique to cushion its length. Text will be shortened if it is greater than the specified length (l). On the other hand, no padding will be provided to the text if its length is less than l. Consequently, the matrix's dimension is the same for every text. The definition of each text of l dimension is as follows:

$$T = \{w1, w2, ..., wn\} \in R^{l*d} \tag{5}$$

The suggested model uses CNN-SVM. It transforms the unorganized, raw dataset into a structured, functional dataset for further use. Eight layers consist of the CNN-SVM model: four convolutional layers, and four pooling layers. In addition, the activation functions, dropout, batch normalization, and the Adam optimizer are used. The features extracted by CNN are given to SVM for classification. This section explains the CNN-SVM model that has been suggested to classify comments. Figure 3 shows the structure of the hybrid model.

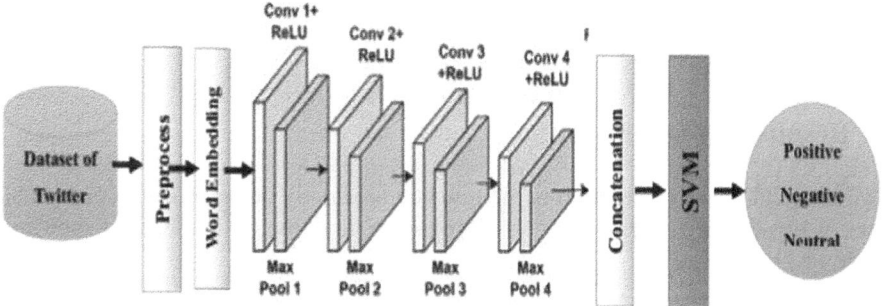

Fig. 3. The architecture of a hybrid model.

Convolution Layer

The convolutional layer extracts features from the input text. The input used by the convolutional layer consists of word embeddings, where each row corresponds to a word vector. The equation is used to embed each word $w_t \in W$ into a word-dimensional vector space given a sequence of T words $\{w_1, w_2, ..., w_t\}$:

$$\phi_\theta(w_t) = Ef_t \tag{6}$$

The matrix $E \in R^{d_{wrd} \times T}$ where $E_{wt} \in R^{d_{wrd}}$ relates to the word w_t embedding.

$$\phi_\theta(w_1, w_2, ..., w_T) = [E_{w1}; E_{w2}; ...; E_{wT}] \in R^{d_{wrd} \times T} \tag{7}$$

The convolutional layer traverses a set of fixed-size filters over the rows of the input matrix to produce a feature map. A collection of feature maps that are correlated to specific filters are generated by convolutional layers. In most cases, word embeddings are represented as vectors of real numbers, some of which may be negative. In case the input value is positive, the ReLU function yields the positive value; if not it returns 0. The representation of this function is:

$$ReLU(x) = \max(0, 1) \tag{8}$$

Global Max Pooling Layer
The output is run via a pooling layer after the activation function, which down-samples the feature maps to lower their dimensionality. Max pooling, the pooling layer uses a fixed window of the feature map to extract the maximum value. The pooling layer's output is forwarded to the subsequent phase.

Concatenation Layer
This layer in a CNN for text classification is used to combine the outputs (features) of several layers, such as convolution and pooling layers at a certain point in the CNN, enabling it to use a wider set of local and global features in classification. This helps improve classification accuracy and enhance the model's ability to recognize complex patterns in texts.

5   Results and Discussion

Two different models were used in the research to classify comments on social media sites of two datasets, where a set of variables was used the CNN model as shown in Table 1.

Table 1. The main parameters of the CNN model.

Parameter name	Value
Embedding dimension	100
Num filter	200

(continued)

Table 1. (*continued*)

Parameter name	Value
Batch size	128
Optimizer	Adam
Epoch	10
Activation function	Relu, Softmax
Dropout	0.2
Split dataset	80% train 20% test
Initial learning rate	0.001

Table 2. The accuracy for all models.

Models	Dataset 1	Dataset 2
SVM	79%	87%
CNN - SVM	95%	98%

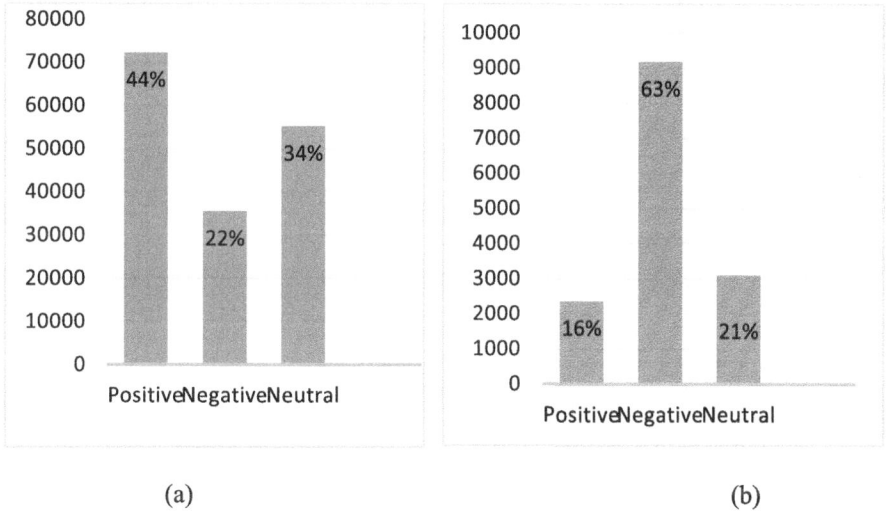

| (a) | (b) |

Fig. 4. Distribution of tweets in datasets 1 (b) and datasets 2 (a).

Table 2 shows the classification accuracy of the two models on two datasets. Experimental results reveal that the hybrid model is better than the single model.

Figure 4(a) and (b) show the distribution of tweets in positive, negative, and neutral in Twitter-airline-sentiment, and Twitter-and-reddit-sentimental-analysis datasets.

The results performance of the comments classification models on the first dataset using the measures of precision, sensitivity, and specificity across the three categories positive, negative, and neutral are shown in Table 3. The hybrid model provides the most balanced and superior performance across all categories and scales. This shows that the CNN + SVM model can classify texts more accurately and reliably compared to other models.

Table 3. Results of SVM and CNN-SVM for dataset (1).

	SVM			CNN-SVM		
	Negative	Neutral	Positive	Negative	Neutral	Positive
Precision	0.88	0.59	0.73	0.97	0.93	0.91
Sensitivity	0.86	0.66	0.69	0.98	0.87	0.94
Specificity	0.80	0.88	0.95	0.94	0.99	0.98

Figure 5 shows the classification results for each model, showing that the hybrid model outperforms the single model in the airline dataset.

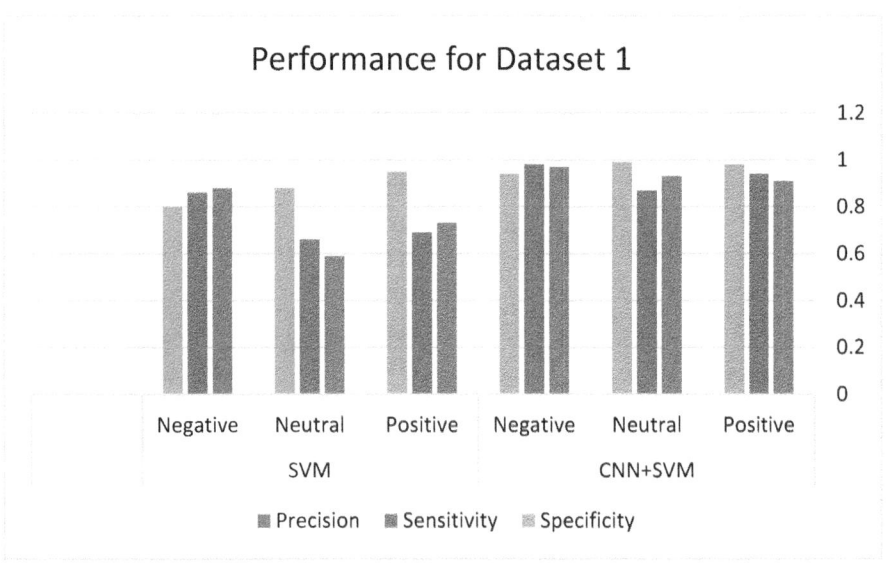

Fig. 5. Comparison of results for dataset 1.

Table 4 demonstrates that the combination of a CNN and SVM model performs exceptionally well when classifying texts. This model performed exceptionally well in terms of specificity, sensitivity, and precision. In the majority of categories, the combined model yielded the highest results, demonstrating its ability to strike a solid compromise between minimizing errors and correctly classifying data. This demonstrates how text classification performance in the second dataset may be greatly enhanced by combining CNN and SVM features.

Table 4. Results of SVM and CNN + SVM for dataset (2).

	SVM			CNN-SVM		
	Negative	Neutral	Positive	Negative	Neutral	Positive
Precision	0.83	0.87	0.88	0.99	0.98	0.96
Sensitivity	0.78	0.91	0.88	0.92	1.00	0.99
Specificity	0.96	0.93	0.91	1.00	0.99	0.97

Figure 6 shows the results of the comparison calculation for classification and the precision, sensitivity, and specificity values for SVM, and CNN + SVM. By comparing the results of the second dataset, it was found that the proposed hybrid model is the best among other models.

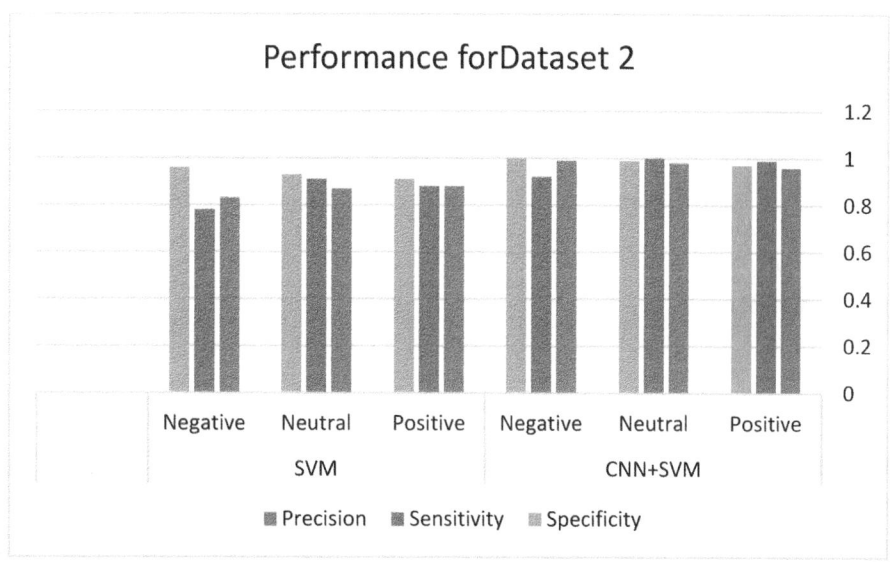

Fig. 6. Comparison of results for dataset 2.

The confusion matrix in Fig. 7 shows the performance of the classification model across different categories: negative, neutral, and positive.

The suggested model outperforms previous models on the two datasets according to a comparison between the proposed system and earlier studies on the same Twitter airline dataset as shown in Table 5, and the Twitter Reddit dataset as shown in Table 6.

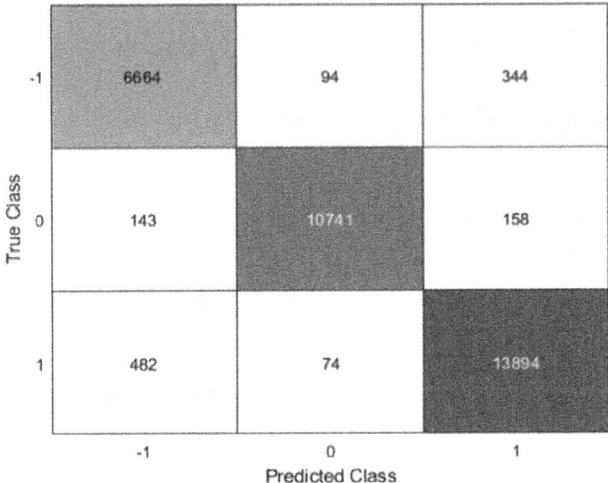

Fig. 7. Confusion metrics of a hybrid.

Table 5. Comparative with related work for airline dataset.

Paper	Accuracy
Monika, et al. [6]	91.78%
Patel, et al. [22]	83%
Rustam, et al. [23]	79%
Hasib, et al. [24]	91%
Kumar, et al. [25]	75.99%
Tan, et al. [9]	91.77
Proposed Model	**95%**

Table 6. Comparative with related work for Twitter and Reddit dataset.

Paper	Accuracy
Swarup, et al. [26]	90%
Kapur, et al. [27]	89%
Proposed Model	**98%**

6 Conclusion

Due to the rapid and widespread expansion in the use of social media, it has become necessary to analyze and classify comments generated by users through these means. In this context, the research proposes the use of a hybrid model consisting of a CNN with

SVM, instead of traditional learning methods. The model includes the use of natural language processing techniques to eliminate noise in comments, which helps speed up model training and improve results. Technologies such as word embedding and BoW are used to extract information from comments. The model was tested on large unbalanced, multi-classify datasets, such as airline Twitter and Reddit Twitter datasets. The study results showed the superiority of the CNN + SVM hybrid model, as it achieved the highest accuracy of 98% compared to 87% for SVM alone. In the future, advanced techniques such as transformation models BERT (Bidirectional Encoder Representations from Transformers) will be used. With its capacity to comprehend context and handle phrases in both directions, BERT is regarded as an advanced model in the field of natural language processing, to gather data and broaden the research to encompass Arabic-language databases.

References

1. Yue, L., Chen, W., Li, X., Zuo, W., Yin, M.: A survey of sentiment analysis in social media. Knowl. Inf. Syst. **60**(2), 617–663 (2019). https://doi.org/10.1007/s10115-018-1236-4
2. Poojitha, K., Charish, A.S., Reddy, M.A.K., Ayyasamy, S.: Classification of social media Toxic comments using Machine learning models (2023). http://arxiv.org/abs/2304.06934
3. Zhu, F., (Michael) Zhang, X.: Impact of online consumer reviews on sales: the moderating role of product and consumer characteristics. J. Mark. **74**(2), 133–148 (2010). https://doi.org/10.1509/jm.74.2.133
4. Jalil, A., Aliwy, A.H.: Classification of Arabic Social Media Texts Based on a Deep Learning Multi-Tasks Model. Al-Bahir J. Eng. Pure Sci. **2**(2) (2023). https://doi.org/10.55810/2313-0083.1030
5. Hemmatian, F.: And sentiment analysis (2017)
6. Monika, R., Deivalakshmi, S., Janet, B.: Sentiment analysis of US airlines tweets using LSTM/RNN. In: 2019 IEEE 9th International Conference on Advanced Computing (IACC), pp. 92–95. IEEE (2019)
7. Utama, H.: Sentiment analysis in airline tweets using mutual information for feature selection. In: 2019 4th international conference on information technology, information systems and electrical engineering (ICITISEE), pp. 295–300. IEEE (2019)
8. Jain, P.K., Saravanan, V., Pamula, R.: A hybrid CNN-LSTM: A deep learning approach for consumer sentiment analysis using qualitative user-generated contents. Trans. Asian Low-Resource Lang. Inf. Process. **20**(5), 1–15 (2021)
9. Tan, K.L., Lee, C.P., Lim, K.M., Anbananthen, K.S.M.: Sentiment analysis with ensemble hybrid deep learning model. IEEE Access **10**(July), 103694–103704 (2022). https://doi.org/10.1109/ACCESS.2022.3210182
10. Jasim, Y.A., Saeed, M.G., Raewf, M.B.: Analyzing social media sentiment: twitter as a case study. Adv. Distrib. Comput. Artif. Intell. J. **11**(4), 427–450 (2022). https://doi.org/10.14201/adcaij.28394
11. Şengül, F., Adem, K., Kavalcı Yılmaz, E.: Sentiment analysis based on machine learning methods on twitter data using oneAPI. no. May, 207–213 (2023). https://doi.org/10.59287/iccar.781
12. Vidyashree, K.P., Rajendra, A.B., Gururaj, H.L., Ravi, V., Krichen, M.: A tweet sentiment classification approach using an ensemble classifier. Int. J. Cogn. Comput. Eng. **5**, 170–177 (2024)

13. Rehman, A.U., Malik, A.K., Raza, B., Ali, W.: A hybrid CNN-LSTM model for improving accuracy of movie reviews sentiment analysis. Multimed. Tools Appl. **78**(18), 26597–26613 (2019). https://doi.org/10.1007/s11042-019-07788-7

14. Pilehvar, M.T., Camacho-Collados, J.: Embeddings in natural language processing: theory and advances in vector representations of meaning. Synth. Lect. Hum. Lang. Technol. **13**(4), 1–175 (2020). https://doi.org/10.2200/S01057ED1V01Y202009HLT047

15. Eshan, S.C., Hasan, M.S.: An application of machine learning to detect abusive Bengali text. 20th Int. Conf. Comput. Inf. Technol. ICCIT 2017, vol. 2018-January, pp. 1–6 (2017). https://doi.org/10.1109/ICCITECHN.2017.8281787

16. Jakkula, V.: Tutorial on Support Vector Machine (SVM). Sch. EECS, Washingt. State Univ., pp. 1–13 (2011). http://www.ccs.neu.edu/course/cs5100f11/resources/jakkula.pdf

17. Gaye, A., Zhang, D., Wulamu, A.: Improvement of support vector machine algorithm in big data background. Math. Probl. Eng. **2021** (2021). https://doi.org/10.1155/2021/5594899

18. Hecht-Nielsen, R.: Theory of the backpropagation neural network. In: Neural networks for perception, pp. 65–93. Elsevier (1992)

19. Chen, Y.: Convolutional Neural Network for Sentence Classification by (2015)

20. Kaggle: Twitter U.S. Airl. Sentim. [Online] Available https://www.kaggle.com/crowdflower/twitter-airline-sentiment

21. Kaggle: https://www.kaggle.com/datasets/cosmos98/twitter-and-reddit-sentimentalanalysis-dataset

22. Patel, A., Oza, P., Agrawal, S.: Sentiment analysis of customer feedback and reviews for airline services using language representation model. Procedia Comput. Sci. **218**, 2459–2467 (2022). https://doi.org/10.1016/j.procs.2023.01.221

23. Rustam, F., Ashraf, I., Mehmood, A., Ullah, S., Choi, G.S.: Tweets classification on the base of sentiments for US airline companies. Entropy **21**(11), 1–22 (2019). https://doi.org/10.3390/e21111078

24. Hasib, K.M., Habib, M.A., Towhid, N.A., Showrov, M.I.H.: A novel deep learning based sentiment analysis of twitter data for us airline service. In: 2021 International Conference on Information and Communication Technology for Sustainable Development (ICICT4SD), pp. 450–455. IEEE (2021)

25. Ravi Kumar, G., Venkata Sheshanna, K., Anjan Babu, G.: Sentiment analysis for airline tweets utilizing machine learning techniques. In: International Conference on Mobile Computing and Sustainable Informatics: ICMCSI 2020, pp. 791–799. Springer (2021)

26. Kumar, J.N.V.R.S., et al.: Sentiment analysis on textual tweets using ensemble classifier (LSTM-GRU). 7th Int. Conf. Commun. Electron. Syst. ICCES 2022 - Proc., no. June, pp. 926–932 (2022). https://doi.org/10.1109/ICCES54183.2022.9835850

27. Reis, A.V.C.: Comparative study of sentiment analysis for multi-sourced social media platforms. Neurosurgery **62**(2), 294–310 (2008)

High-Stakes Deception Detection Leveraging 3D Facial Landmarks

Amira Abbas Hussein[✉] 🆔 and Israa H. Ali 🆔

Software Department, College of Information Technology, University of Babylon, Babylon, Iraq
amiraabbash.sw@student.uobabylon.edu.iq,
israa_hadi@itnet.uobabylon.edu.iq

Abstract. Deception detection is essential for establishing a secure and reliable society. It plays a critical role in high-stakes circumstances like court trials or police interrogations, when the result is greatly impacted by the behaviour of the individual being investigated. Facial expressions can serve as valuable cues for detecting deception, which is a challenging task due to the ability of deceptive individuals to mask their true feelings or intentions. Besides, facial landmarks, essential locations on the face utilized to identify facial muscle movement and shape changes, play an important role in determining deceptive behaviour. Facial landmark detection is crucial in several applications, including facial analysis for 3D reconstruction and expression. It provides a substantial amount of information about an individual. This paper addresses 3D facial landmark extraction, feature selection, and a Bi-directional Long Short-Term Memory (Bi-LSTM) model. Firstly, the Mediapipe framework extracted 478 facial landmarks with coordinates (x, y, z) to enhance the reliability and precision of deception. Next, the 3D facial landmarks most relevant to deception cues were selected using a feature selection-based Pearson correlation coefficient method. Then, 3D facial landmarks are used to train a Bi-LSTM model that predicts deception from truth-tellers using a high-stakes real-life trial dataset. Finally, the model successfully achieved an accuracy of 97%, surpassing other state-of-the-art methods.

Keywords: Deception Detection · 3D Facial Landmarks Extraction · Mediapipe Framework · Feature Selection-based Pearson Correlation Coefficient Method · Bi-directional Long Short-Term Memory (Bi-LSTM) Model

1 Introduction

Lying is intentionally not telling the truth or keeping one's emotions and feelings hidden; human beings have practised it since the earliest times [1]. Detecting deception plays an important role in various domains, including security [2], court trials [3], and healthcare [4]. To detect deception accurately, there are many effective indicators for distinguishing liars from truth-tellers. These can manifest through verbal cues such as voice [5], text analysis, and non-verbal cues such as facial expression and head and body movement [6]. This study focuses on facial expression as a strong source of nonverbal deception cues that provide vital indicators for revealing essential insights about individuals' feelings

© The Author(s), under exclusive license to Springer Nature Switzerland AG 2025
S. O. Al-Mamory et al. (Eds.): 3INC 2024, CCIS 2329, pp. 101–118, 2025.
https://doi.org/10.1007/978-3-031-81065-7_7

[7], psychological alterations, and mental processes. They are important and serve as a direct and genuine means of communication [8], conveying real-time emotions more effectively than language. These facial expressions involve the coordinated movement of multiple facial features [9], which are facial muscles that tighten or loosen up, giving the appearance of altered facial features. These muscular movements correspond to landmarks around specific facial points [10], such as the corner of the eyes and the corner of the lips. Based on their number, the landmarks on the face are categorized into three groups: sparse, moderate, and dense. Sparse models have fewer than 50 landmarks; moderate models have 50–100 landmarks and dense models have over 100 landmarks [11]. Due to the difficulties in detecting deceitful behaviour, this study used dense facial landmarks to capture detailed and subtle facial expressions often indicative of deception. By focusing on 3D facial landmarks, the study aimed to track intricate muscle movements and provide a comprehensive analysis of facial behaviour.

Furthermore, deception can occur in high or low stakes [12]. High-stakes circumstances include defending oneself in court or being questioned by the police; low-stakes circumstances do not involve any risk and are an example of common interpersonal deception [13]. While automatic lie detection may help us understand these features of lying, existing systems remain relatively limited, partly due to a lack of high-stakes datasets [14]. Most deception detection techniques rely on data from subjects who intentionally act in front of the camera after receiving expert training in a laboratory setting, which is not natural. However, participants may not take the experiments seriously due to their lack of motivation or low stakes, resulting in non-realistic data. Therefore, a high-stake, multimodal deception dataset was used in this study to obtain real facial expressions. The contribution of this study includes the following:

1. Proposing a high-stakes deception detection technique using deep learning techniques to extract 478 3D facial landmarks per frame for each video that analyzes and captures a broad spectrum of facial muscle movements reflecting deceitful behaviour.
1. Proposing a robust method that can accurately measure the strength of the linear correlation between facial landmarks to select the most relevant 3D facial landmarks, reducing input complexity and focusing on features most indicative of deception.
2. Proposing a deep learning model that can capture temporal dependencies from past and future contexts, understanding both directions of the sequence data, to accurately predict deceptive tellers from truth-tellers.

This study is organized as follows: Sect. 2 outlines the related work. Section 3 details the methodology, which consists of the dataset preparation, 3D facial landmark extraction, feature selection, prediction using the Bi-LSTM model, evaluation of the Prediction Bi-LSTM model for learning loss, and performance and analyzing results. Section 4 is the Conclusion.

2 Related Work

Deceptive behaviour is a common occurrence in all aspects of daily life [15]. Most of the deception researchers discovered that liars could not control multiple elements of their facial expressions, such as brow movements, pupil dilation, eye tracking, and blinking, which are potentially valuable indicators for differentiating deceivers from truth-tellers in high-stakes circumstances. To capture facial movement associated with deceitful behaviour, they have used a variety of different methodological techniques, including the utilization of models such as studies [16–19] using low-stakes datasets like the Miami University Deception Detection Database (MU3D) and Facial Expression Recognition 2013. The study [16] extracts micro expressions using a custom convolutional neural network (CNN), achieving an accuracy of 74.17%. The study [17] employs a smartwatch to measure pulse rates and utilizes OpenFace deep learning to extract facial features. Applying a random forest (RF) classifier resulted in accuracy and an F1-score ranging from 75% to 80% across participants. Furthermore, [18] developed a self-adaptive population-based firefly algorithm for facial cue detection with 99% accuracy using the long short-term memory (LSTM) model. Another study [19] used Silent Talker and Haar Cascade to extract non-verbal features and employ various classifiers. However, RF produces better results with 78% accuracy using facial micro expressions and eye signals. While studies [20–22] based on human judgment utilize the facial action coding system (FACS), a taxonomy of human facial movements based on their appearance on the face, this system divides the face into many action units (AUs), which are basic movements caused by a single muscle or a group of muscles in response to a facial expression. [20] employed OpenFace to extract facial action units, subsequently feeding them into a Temporal Convolutional Network (TCN). Additionally, it employed a unique attention module to identify specific areas within the video's duration that significantly impacted the model's prediction, resulting in an accuracy of 92.36%. Also, [21] used OpenFace deep learning to extract action units and WEKA to classify videos as either lying or honest, resulting in an accuracy rate exceeding 80%. Meanwhile, [22] used geometry and appearance features to identify the presence or absence of specific action units. On the other hand, [23–28] used a high-stakes dataset. [23] used the multimodal deep neural network FacialCueNet, which employed action units and micro expressions to reveal an individual's intentions and feelings. Additionally, LSTM and convolutional neural networks construct the spatial-temporal attention module. The approach achieved an evaluation accuracy of 88.45%. Both [24] and [25] employ individual modalities and multimodal (audio, video, text) lying detection techniques. [24] Using the visual features provided with the dataset yields the best accuracy of 88% in an individual-level model, and combining features from multiple modalities improves the detection of deceptive behaviours to an accuracy of 97%. In [25], semi-automatic lying detection utilized OpenFace to extract facial action units automatically, and the visual features provided with the dataset achieved a maximum accuracy of 80.97% in the individual model using the nearest neighbour classifier, fully automatic lying detection, which also used OpenFace to extract facial action units automatically, achieved an accuracy of 61.58% in the individual model using a random forest classifier. The final classifier is then obtained by combining the three modalities, achieving an accuracy of

83.02% in detecting deceptions at the level of subjects. Moreover, [26] offers a novel app-roach to deception detection by disentangling facial expression and head pose features using a 2D-to-3D face reconstruction technique with separate CNNs for identity and expression. The system achieves an accuracy of 68% in high-stakes scenarios and 71% in low-stakes scenarios, introducing a new dataset for low-stake deceit detection. [27] presents a well-structured approach that employs hybrid deep neural network (HDNN) models to detect deception. The method reveals promising advances in accuracy and methodology. Nikbin and Qu's research demonstrates that their HDNN model achieves a 91% accuracy rate in detecting fear-related micro-expressions, outperforming tradi-tional CNNs. Another approach [28] uses multiple sets of facial cues, each predicted by its own Convolutional Neural Network (CNN). The method involves CNN models analysing gaze, head pose, and facial emotions, as well as Action Units (AUs), with an early fusion of CNN outputs for deception classification. The research found that the effectiveness of deception detection varies by dataset context, with the best results on high-stake datasets. The research revealed that integrating multiple modalities and classifiers led to an average accuracy of 67% and an F1-score of 0.71.

3   Methodology

Different approaches were used for detecting deception as shown in Fig. 1.

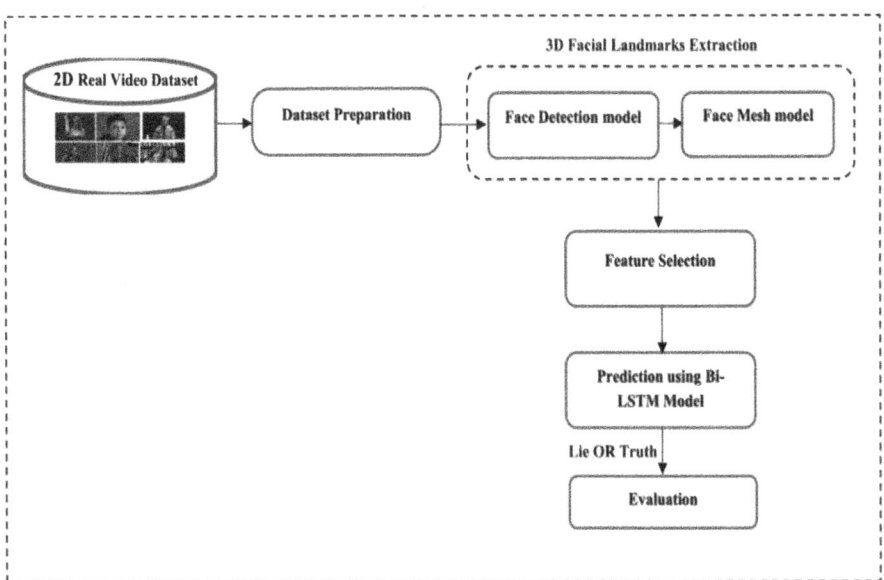

Fig. 1. Proposed system's block diagram

3.1 Dataset Preparation

We employ the high-stakes dataset known as the real-life trial dataset [29], which consists of 121 videos, including 61 deceptive and 60 truthful trial clips from the "Innocence Project", trial court videos, and police interrogations, all available online, as shown in Fig. 2. It consists of 21 unique female and 35 unique male speakers, with ages ranging from 16 to 60, providing a diverse range of behaviours and reactions for analysis.

Researchers have also extracted certain features from the videos. These features include visual features, which are nonverbal, and audio and text features, which are verbal indicators of deceptive behaviour. In this study, one model-based raw video was used to extract the 3D facial landmarks.

Thus, the real-life trial dataset consisted of real-life scenario videos. Therefore, some videos were excluded because they have no visible face, subtitles, or confessions; the confessor only listens to someone else. The study used only videos with high-quality visuals, thereby enhancing the dataset's quality.

Fig. 2. Samples of dataset videos

3.2 3D Facial Landmarks Extraction

Face landmarks are spatial features that represent key critical locations on the face, such as the chin centre, eye corner and nose tip. Facial landmark detection is the process of identifying specific locations (landmarks) around facial features and contours. It plays an important role as an initial step in several other face-related tasks, such as biometric identification and interpretation of mental states [30]. The two main dimensions in which facial landmark detection is performed are two coordinates, which represent height and width (2D), and three coordinates, which represent height, width, and depth (3D). However, there are several challenges to overcome when attempting facial landmark detection, particularly in relation to variations in position and emotion. Despite advancements in 2D face landmark processing, as shown in Fig. 3, it still faces restrictions due to issues including head posture, expression, occlusion, and illumination. Also, the 68 facial landmarks cannot cover many facial movements, which causes a lack of representation of facial expressions. Moreover, the 68 facial landmarks are insufficient for describing delicate shapes [31].

Fig. 3. The map for 2D 68 facial landmarks

Hence, this study utilized the Mediapipe open-source framework [32] to extract the 3D coordinates of 478 face landmarks from a 2D input video. It provides a thorough analysis of facial muscle movements, as shown in Fig. 4. It is an end-to-end deep learning framework that has a set of pre-trained models, which can capture more facial landmarks in different positions, which is important to address the challenges associated with a multimodal, real-life trial dataset used in our study. This dataset was collected under unconstrained circumstances, allowing for variations in poses, lighting, occlusion, and other factors. Moreover, our approach assumes that the chosen high-level representation input to the Bi-LSTM model is more robust than raw videos, which reduces the likelihood that the deception detection model will overfit to background noise and capture unimportant characteristics. Additionally, these dense facial landmarks encompass a wider range of facial muscle movements, which allows for more analysis of the data, and are capable of delicate shape representation. One of them is Mediapipe face landmark detection, which uses a sequence of models to predict facial landmarks; two models were used [33]:

1-Face detection model: This model is used to determine whether a frame contains a face. It is performed by processing each video frame by frame and determining the bounding box to detect and localize faces with main face points such as the left eye, right eye, nose, mouth, right ear, and left ear. The bounding box allows us to obtain the upper, lower, left, and right boundaries of the face, thereby providing us with a comprehensive understanding of the entire face.

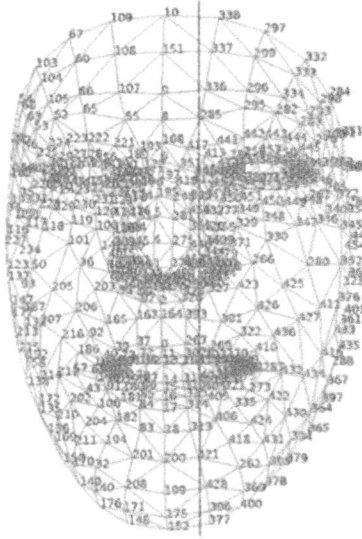

Fig. 4. The map for 3D 478 facial landmarks

2-Face mesh model: It employed transfer learning and trained a network to estimate 478 facial landmarks with three coordinates (x, y, z). It creates a metric 3D space and uses the face landmark screen positions to estimate the face transformation within that space. The face transformation data includes regular 3D primitives such as the face pose transform matrix and the triangular face mesh. See Fig. 5.

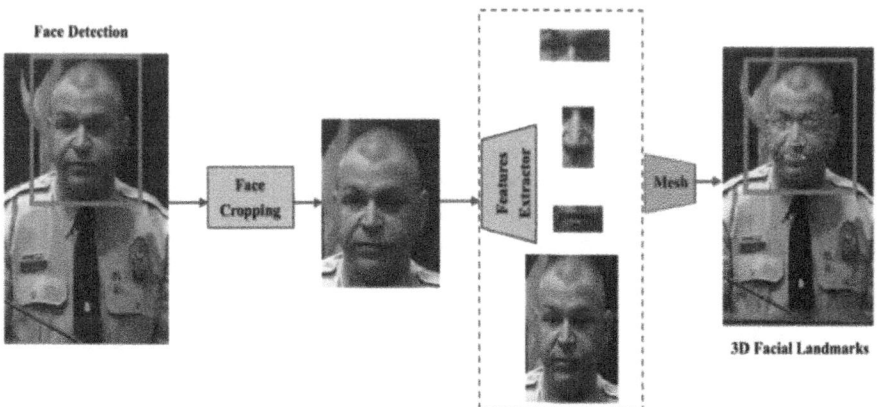

Fig. 5. Mediapipe face landmark detection

Using scaling, rotating, and translating methods, a simple statistical analysis tool known as Procrustes Analysis [34] improves the fit of a 3D shape model to 2D facial landmarks in the background. The alignment process can ensure that the 3D face mesh exactly fits the individual's real facial features. The model was trained using synthetic visualized data and 2D semantic contours from annotated real-world data. The resulting model provided us with reasonable predictions of 3D 478 landmarks, not only on synthetic data but also on real-world data. This combination of data helps the model accurately infer the depth of facial features, resulting in robust 3D landmark detection from 2D inputs. This training enables the model to understand how 2D features map to a 3D face mesh.

3.3 Feature Selection

Feature selection is the process of selecting the most suitable features for the model. This approach may change from one technique to another, but the essential goal is determining which features impact the model most. It is utilized to enhance the accuracy of classification, reduce dimension, evaluate the important degree of features, and remove duplicate information [30]. Feature selection has two types of methods: supervised and unsupervised, illustrated in Fig. 6 with examples. Filter-based feature selection methods utilize statistical measures to evaluate the correlation or dependence between input features, allowing for the selection of the most relevant features [35]. In this paper, the Pearson correlation coefficient method is used, which is a valuable tool for studying the strength of the linear correlation between facial landmarks that represent the features [36]. It has a range of -1 to 1, where a value of -1 means a total negative linear relationship, 0 means no relationship, and $+1$ means a total positive relationship. The following formula computes the Pearson correlation [37]:

$$r = \frac{n \sum xy - (\sum x)(\sum y)}{\sqrt{\left[n \sum x^2 - (\sum x)^2\right]\left[n \sum y^2 - (\sum y)^2\right]}} \tag{1}$$

where (x) represents the independent landmarks, (y) represents the dependent landmarks, and (n) represents the size of samples. A threshold was set to ascertain the degree of correlation between facial landmarks. It allows us to focus on features that have strong correlations above it and weak correlations below it, concentrate on high-correlation facial landmarks, and drop one of them because they are linearly related and have similar impacts. This prevents features from being duplicated and overfitting.

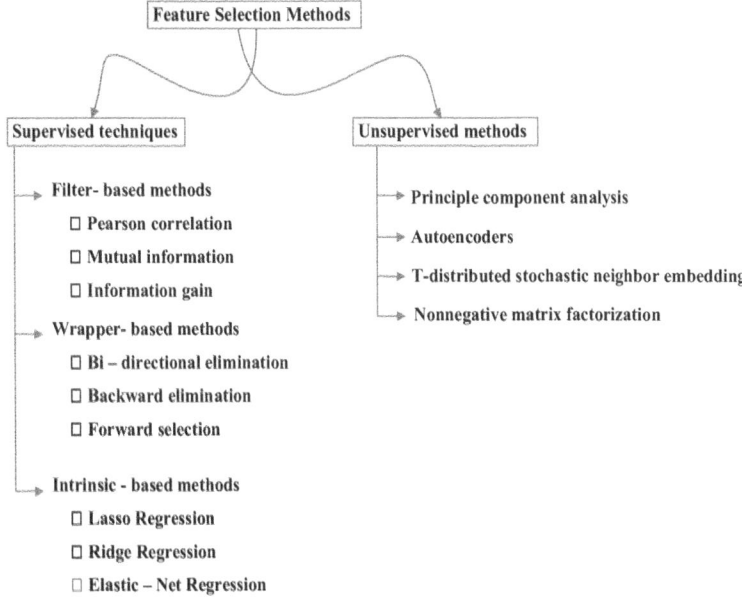

Fig. 6. Types of feature selection methods with examples

The Bi-LSTM model retrained with several threshold values and determined that 0.97 was the optimal threshold. At this threshold, the Pearson correlation coefficient method found 27 facial landmarks that reflect facial muscles having the following indices (0, 1, 2, 5, 11, 20, 23, 26, 32, 44, 56, 65, 98, 110, 113, 119, 122, 131, 143, 146, 167, 176, 197, 251, 254, 368, 446) as shown in Fig. 7, which serve as indicators of deceitful behaviour and have a major impact on the model, resulting in an accuracy of 97%.

Fig. 7. Selected facial landmarks using Pearson correlation coefficient method

3.4   The Prediction Using Bidirectional-Long Short Memory (Bi-LSTM) Model

Bi-LSTM layers consist of two LSTMs: one that processes the input sequence in the forward direction and another that processes it in the backward manner, as shown in Fig. 8. The mathematical equations for forward and backward LSTM are as follows [38]:

$$\overrightarrow{h_r} = \sigma \left(w \rightarrow_{xh} x_r + w \rightarrow_h \rightarrow_h \overrightarrow{h_{r-1}} + b \rightarrow_h \right) \qquad (2)$$

$$\overleftarrow{h_r} = \sigma \left(w \underset{xh}{\leftarrow} x_r + w \underset{h}{\leftarrow} \underset{h}{\leftarrow} \overleftarrow{h_{r-1}} + b \underset{h}{\leftarrow} \right) \qquad (3)$$

$$H_r = \sigma \left(w \rightarrow_{xh} \overrightarrow{h} + w \underset{xh}{\leftarrow} \overleftarrow{h} + b_y \right) \qquad (4)$$

where, $\overrightarrow{h_r}$ is the output of the forward LSTM at time step (r), $\overleftarrow{h_r}$ is the output of the backward LSTM at time step (r), H_r is the combined output, x is the input, and σ is the sigmoid activation function. b_y represents the bias term for output, b_h represents the bias term for hidden state, h_r is the current hidden state at time step (r), h_{r-1} is the previous hidden state at time step (r-1), h_{r+1} is the next hidden state at time step (r + 1), the weights represented by w, y are the output. The training process involves inputting concatenated samples and their labels, selecting facial landmarks, and fine-tuning the weights to reduce the difference between the actual and predicted outputs. This process goes on cyclically until the model reaches a good level of accuracy in predicting truth or lies. The bidirectional technique enables the network to learn dependencies in both past and future contexts, thus providing a more accurate way of making predictions based on sequential data. The Bi-LSTM network is based on the LSTM network, which consists of three gates: these are the input gate, which controls the flow of new information into the cell; the forget gate, which controls the amount and kind of information that is to be overlooked and the output gate which controls the information that is to be allowed out of the cell. These gates will enable the network to regulate the information that is passed through the network in a way that the network can retain important information while avoiding the storage of unnecessary information.

3.5   Evaluation of the Prediction Bi-LSTM Model for Learning Loss

The dataset used is split into training, validation, and test sets randomly, with 70%, 15%, and 15%, respectively. The Bi-LSTM model, trained with strong features, produces a good fit by achieving a balance between overfitting and underfitting. The learning loss in Fig. 9. Shows, initial Phase (Epochs 0–10), the training loss experiences a sharp decline from approximately 0.35 to below 0.15, indicating that the model is effectively minimizing errors on the training data. The validation loss also decreases but with noticeable fluctuations, reflecting the model's ongoing efforts to generalize while still adapting to the validation data. These fluctuations are expected in the early stages of training as the model fine-tunes its learning. Middle Phase (Epochs 10–30), the training loss continues to decrease gradually, flattening out around 0.05, which indicates that the model's

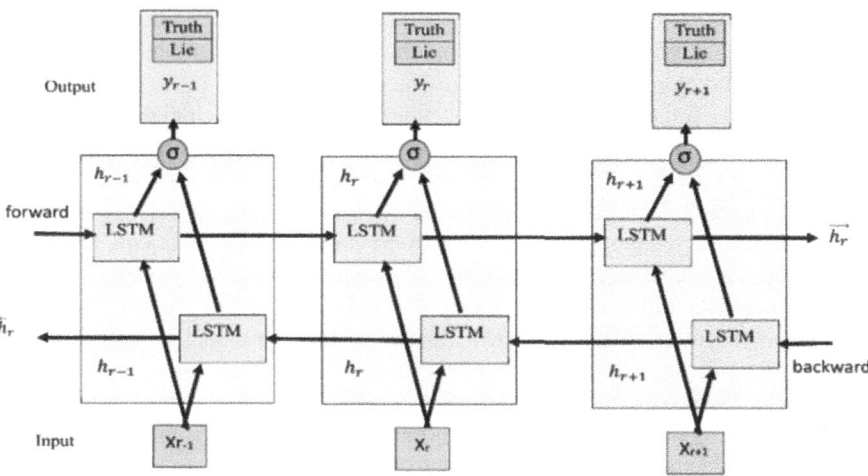

Fig. 8. Structure of prediction using Bi-LSTM model

learning rate has slowed as it approaches convergence. Simultaneously, the validation loss stabilizes with fewer fluctuations, settling at a value close to the training loss. This suggests that the model is maintaining a balance between minimizing training errors and effectively generalizing unseen data, without overfitting.

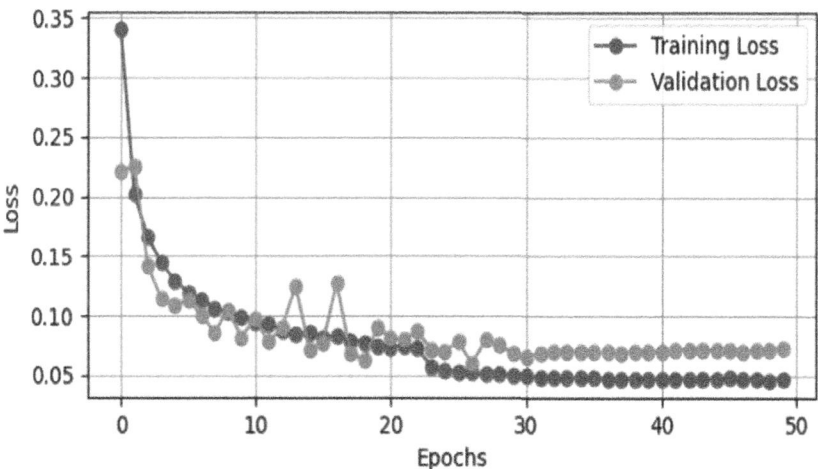

Fig. 9. Loss of training and validation of Bi-LSTM model

Final Phase (Epochs 30–50), both training and validation losses remain steady, with the training loss reaching a minimum of 0.0458 and the validation loss stabilizing at 0.0594. This stability indicates that the model has fully converged, and that further training is unlikely to yield significant improvements. The close alignment of training and validation loss suggests that the model has achieved good generalization capabilities, with minimal signs of overfitting. With a slight generalization gap between the two curves, the loss graph demonstrates that the model offers a good match because the training and validation losses are reduced to the point of stability.

Moreover, the training and validation accuracy in Fig. 10, show initial Phase (Epochs 0–10), the training accuracy shows a rapid increase from approximately 82% to around 92%, demonstrating that the model is quickly learning and effectively recognizing patterns in the training data. The validation accuracy also rises sharply, closely mirroring the training accuracy, although it experiences more pronounced fluctuations. These fluctuations suggest that while the model is quickly adapting, it may be slightly overfitting to the training data during this early stage. Middle Phase (Epochs 10–30), the training accuracy begins to stabilize around 96%, indicating that the model is nearing convergence. Meanwhile, the validation accuracy continues to fluctuate but remains within a narrow range, hovering close to the training accuracy. These fluctuations are typical and suggest that the model is consistently performing well on both the training and validation datasets, reflecting good generalization to unseen data. Final Phase (Epochs 30–50), both the training and validation accuracies stabilize, with the training accuracy peaking at 97.18% and the validation accuracy reaching its maximum at 96.57%. This stabilization indicates that the model has fully converged, with the validation accuracy remaining close to the training accuracy, further confirming that the model is not overfitting and is well-suited to generalize effectively on new data.

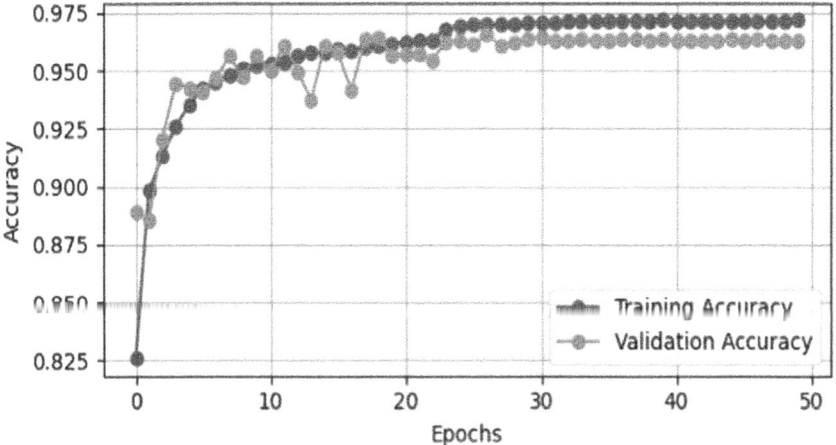

Fig. 10. Accuracy of training and validation of Bi-LSTM model

Furthermore, the confusion matrix [39] was used to assess the effectiveness of a classification algorithm. It allows visualization of an algorithm's performance by comparing the actual and predicted classifications. The matrix consists of four quadrants true positive (TP), true negative (TN), false positive (FP), and false negative (FN).

In our deception detection, the TP and TN stand for the person being genuinely telling deceptive and the model's predict of being deceptive, and the person being genuinely telling truth and the model's predict of being truthful respectively. This illustrates how closely the model's prediction matches reality. FN denotes a missed detection in which the person is telling deceptive, and the model predicts that the person is telling the truthful; FP is a misdetection in which the person is telling truthful, and the model predicts that the person is telling deceptive. The confusion matrix shows the classification model's good performance, as depicted in Table 1., that can concurrently determine the number of correct predictions and errors for both actual deceptive and truthful instances.

Table 1. Confusion matrix of deception detection

			Predictive Label	
			No	Yes
Actual Label	Truthful	No	True Negative 5998	False positive 293
	Deceptive	Yes	False Negative 46	True Positive 6310
			Truthful	Deceptive

Also, confusion matrix provides several key metrics for evaluating a classifier's performance: accuracy, precision, recall, and F1 score as shown in Table 2. Consequently, the Bi-LSTM model has demonstrated its capacity to capture long-term dependencies by preserving information over numerous time steps and from past steps. This is made possible by the fact that they possess an internal memory state. In contrast to feedforward neural networks, which deal with data in an autonomous manner, the Bi-LSTM tracking the movement of facial muscles, capture and analyze temporal dependencies in both forward and backward directions. This bidirectional approach ensures that the model can consider the entire sequence context, making it well-suited for facial expression analysis where past and future frames influence the current state of the facial muscles.

Table 2. Classification report of deception detection

	Precision = TP/(TP + FP)	Recall = TP/(TP + FN)	F1-Score = 2*(Recall*Precision)/ (Recall + Precision)
Truthful Label	99%	96%	97%
Deceptive Label	96%	99%	97%
Accuracy = (TP + TN)/(TP + FP + FN + TN)	97%		

3.6   Comparing Performance and Analyzing Results

A comparison analysis with several state-of-the-art methods was implemented to evaluate the effectiveness of the suggested model, as shown in Table 3. Since our proposed system focuses on facial features, it solely relies on facial features, utilizing raw videos to extract 478 facial landmarks with coordinates (x, y, z) per frame from each video. Thus, we have presented comparative studies using only unimodal accuracy-based facial features.

As shown in Table 3, the comparative studies [20, 24], and [25] used a facial action coding system (FACS) to detect facial expressions. FACS is a well-established method that relies on 2D techniques to identify specific facial action units (AUs) linked to muscle movements. While effective in many contexts, FACS is limited by its focus on predefined AUs and its operation within a 2D plane. This may result in missing fine movements, imprecise rendering of the facial features, and challenges in addressing head movements or different lighting environments. It is also based on human judgments, and this brings in another source of error in the results that are obtained. FACS involves the use of trained coders who have to observe and categorize facial action units (AUs) making it subjective and may contain biases and inter coder variability.

On the other hand, the study [26] automated detect deception, it reconstructs a complete 3D facial model from 2D images using depth and shape estimation through the use of CNNs. This process is able to learn face identity, environmental parameters and facial expressions all at once in order to create a 3D face representation. It is still a computationally intensive process, which takes a lot of computational power and time to generate a complete 3D model of the face from 2D images. This makes it difficult to apply in real time, particularly in situations where timely decisions are necessary. Moreover, introduce unnecessary noise by reconstructing the whole face and the facial features that are not necessarily useful in detecting fake expressions. The reconstruction process is also affected by changes in lighting conditions, viewpoint and occlusions.

Therefore, our approach outperforms the comparative studies with 97% accuracy. By directly and automatically localizing 3D facial landmarks from 2D inputs, cover a large range of facial muscles and pay much attention to the key areas, including eyebrows, eyes, and mouth, which are significant for detecting facial expressions linked with deceit. This kind of approach is less demanding in terms of computational power than the complete reconstructing of the 3D facial structure, which means that it can be used in real time. Additionally, concentrating on particular landmarks helps to minimize noise and exclude nonessential information, which contributes to the enhancement of deception detection since the most important signs of deceitful behaviour. This makes it especially suitable for high stakes situations.

4   Conclusion

The quantitative findings generated by this approach show notable advancements in facial expression-based deception detection accuracy. With an accuracy of 97%, the system made significant progress over earlier study results. This improvement is a good start toward creating more consistent methods of detecting deceit. In this study, the proposed system demonstrated the effectiveness of using 3D facial landmarks, specifically

Table 3. Comparative methods of deception detection

References	Dataset	Feature	Method	Accuracy
[20]	Multimodal real-life trial	Facial action units	OpenFace, Temporal Convolutional Network, Attention module	92.36%
[24]	Multimodal real-life trial	Micro expression provided with the dataset	AdaBoost classifier	88%
[25]	Multimodal real-life trial	Facial action units, visual features provided with the dataset	OpenFace, nearest neighbour classifier, random forest classifier	Semi-automatic deception detection has 80.79%, Fully automatic deception detection has 61.58%
[26]	Multimodal real-life trial	Head pose, facial expression	CNN	68%
Our proposed model	Multimodal real-life trial	3D facial landmarks	Bi-LSTM model	97%

the 478 points extracted by the Face Mesh model, to detect deception through facial expressions. With their three-dimensional coordinates (x, y, z), these landmarks provide a comprehensive view of facial muscle movements, capturing subtle cues that reflect deceptive behaviour. By covering a wider range of facial movements and head poses, the model effectively analyzes facial expressions from various angles, which is crucial given the real-world scenarios reflected in our dataset.

Moreover, the Pearson correlation coefficient method measured the relationships between input features, enhancing the model's performance. This allowed us to select the most relevant landmarks by focusing on those with high correlations while eliminating redundant features that were linearly related. This process prevents feature duplication and reduces the risk of overfitting, ensuring the model remains robust and accurate. Additionally, using a Bi-LSTM model, which excels in capturing temporal dependencies in sequential data, complements the feature selection process. Together, these methods create a powerful and efficient system for detecting deception through facial expressions, with the selected 3D landmarks playing a critical role in identifying subtle and significant facial cues associated with deceptive behaviour.

References

1. Levine, T.R.: Truth-default theory (TDT) a theory of human deception and deception detection. J. Lang. Soc. Psychol. **33**(4), 378–392 (2014). https://doi.org/10.1177/0261927X1453 5916

2. D'Ulizia, A., D'Andrea, A., Grifoni, P., Ferri, F.: Detecting deceptive behaviours through facial cues from videos: a systematic review. Appl. Sci. **13**(16), 9188 (2023). https://doi.org/10.3390/app13169188

3. Ding, M., Zhao, A., Lu, Z., Xiang, T., Wen, J.-R.: Face-focused cross-stream network for deception detection in videos. In: Proceedings of the IEEE/CVF Conference on Computer Vision and Pattern Recognition, pp. 7802–7811 (2019). https://doi.org/10.1109/CVPR.2019.00799

4. Rogers, R., Gillard, N.D.: Assessment of malingering on psychological measures. Psychol. Desk Ref. 53–57 (1998)

5. Vrij, A., Granhag, P.A., Ashkenazi, T., Ganis, G., Leal, S., Fisher, R.P.: Verbal lie detection: its past, present and future. Brain Sci. **12**(12), 1644 (2022). https://doi.org/10.3390/brainsci1 2121644

6. Brennen, T., Magnussen, S.: Research on non-verbal signs of lies and deceit: a blind alley. Front. Psychol. **11**(December), 1–4 (2020). https://doi.org/10.3389/fpsyg.2020.613410

7. Ekman, P., Oster, H.: Facial expressions of emotion. Annu. Rev. Psychol. **30**(1), 527–554 (1979)

8. Gamer, M., Ambach, W.: Basic and applied research on deception and its detection (2014). https://doi.org/10.3389/978-2-Poppe88919-254-0

9. Van der Zee, S., Taylor, R.P.J., Anderson, R.: To freeze or not to freeze: a culture-sensitive motion capture approach to detecting deceit. PLoS One **14**(4) e0215000 (2019). https://doi.org/10.1371/journal.pone.0215000

10. Yue Wu, Q.J.: Facial landmark detection: a literature survey. Int. J. Comp. Vision 115–142 (2018). https://doi.org/10.1007/s11263-018-1097-z

11. Chen, F., Xu, Y., Zhang, D., Chen, K.: 2D facial landmark model design by combining key points and inserted points. Expert Syst. Appl. **42**(21), 7858–7868 (2015). https://doi.org/10.1016/j.eswa.2015.06.015

12. Su, L., Levine, M.D.: High-stakes deception detection based on facial expressions. Proc.-Int. Conf. Pattern Recognit. **1**, 2519–2524 (2014). https://doi.org/10.1109/ICPR.2014.435

13. Azizli, N., et al.: Lies and crimes: Dark Triad, misconduct, and high-stakes deception. Pers. Individ. Dif. **89**, 34–39 (2016). https://doi.org/10.1016/j.paid.2015.09.034

14. Rodriguez-Diaz, N., Aspandi, D., Sukno, F.M., Binefa, X.: Machine learning-based lie detector applied to a novel annotated game dataset. Futur. Internet **14**(1), 2 (2021). https://doi.org/10.3390/fi14010002

15. Chebbi, S., Ben Jebara, S.: Deception detection using multimodal fusion approaches. Multimed. Tools Appl. **82**(9), 13073–13102 (2023). https://doi.org/10.1007/s11042-021-111 48-9

16. Yildirim, S., Chimeumanu, M.S., Rana, Z.A.: The influence of micro-expressions on deception detection. Multimed. Tools Appl. 1–19 (2023). https://doi.org/10.1007/s11042-023-14551-6

17. Tsuchiya, K., Hatano, R., Nishiyama, H.: Detecting deception using machine learning with facial expressions and pulse rate. Artif. Life Robot. 1–11 (2023). https://doi.org/10.1007/s10 015-023-00869-9

18. Alaskar, H.: Hybrid metaheuristics with deep learning enabled automated deception detection and classification of facial expressions. Comput. Mater. Contin. **75**(3) (2023). https://doi.org/10.32604/cmc.2023.035266

19. Khan, W., Crockett, K., O'Shea, J., Hussain, A., Khan, B.M.: Deception in the eyes of deceiver: A computer vision and machine learning based automated deception detection. Expert Syst. Appl. **169**, 114341 (2021). https://doi.org/10.1016/j.eswa.2020.114341
20. Stathopoulos, A., Han, L., Dunbar, N., Burgoon, J.K., Metaxas, D.: Deception detection in videos using robust facial features with attention feedback. In: Handbook of Dynamic Data Driven Applications Systems, Vol. 2, pp. 725–741. Springer (2023). https://doi.org/10.1007/978-3-031-27986-7_27
21. Shen, X., Fan, G., Niu, C., Chen, Z.: Catching a liar through facial expression of fear. Front. Psychol. **12**, 675097 (2021). https://doi.org/10.3389/fpsyg.2021.675097
22. Abd, S.H., Hashim, I.A., Jalal, A.S.: Optimized action units features for efficient design of deception detection system. Iraqi J. Inf. Commun. Technol. **1**(1), 104–111 (2021). https://doi.org/10.31987/ijict.1.1.160
23. Nam, A., et al.: FacialCueNet: unmasking deception-an interpretable model for criminal interrogation using facial expressions. Appl. Intell. **53**(22), 27413–27427 (2023). https://doi.org/10.1007/s10489-023-04968-9
24. Venkatesh, S., Ramachandra, R., Bours, P.: Robust algorithm for multimodal deception detection. In: 2019 IEEE Conference on Multimedia Information Processing and Retrieval (MIPR), pp. 534–537. IEEE (2019). https://doi.org/10.1109/MIPR.2019.00108
25. Sen, M.U., Perez-Rosas, V., Yanikoglu, B., Abouelenien, M., Burzo, M., Mihalcea, R.: Multimodal deception detection using real-life trial data. IEEE Trans. Affect. Comput. **13**(1), 306–319 (2022). https://doi.org/10.1109/TAFFC.2020.3015684
26. Ngo, L.M., et al.: Identity unbiased deception detection by 2d-to-3d face reconstruction. In: Proceedings of the IEEE/CVF Winter Conference on Applications of Computer Vision, pp. 145–154 (2021). https://doi.org/10.1109/WACV48630.2021.00019
27. Nikbin, S., Qu, Y.: A study on the accuracy of micro expression based deception detection with hybrid deep neural network models. European J. Electr. Eng. Comp. Sci. **8**(3), 14–20 (2024). https://doi.org/10.24018/ejece.2024.8.3.610
28. Dinges, L., et al.: Exploring facial cues: automated deception detection using artificial intelligence. Neural Comput. Appl. 1–27 (2024). https://doi.org/10.1007/s00521-024-09811-x
29. Pérez-Rosas, V., et al.: Verbal and nonverbal clues for real-life deception detection. In: Proceedings of the 2015 conference on empirical methods in natural language processing, pp. 2336–2346 (2015). https://doi.org/10.18653/v1/D15-1281
30. Farghaly, H.M., Ali, A.A.: Artificial intelligence and bioinspired computational methods, vol. 1225, no. August. Springer International Publishing (2020). https://doi.org/10.1007/978-3-030-51971-1
31. Jabberi, M., Wali, A., Chaudhuri, B.B., Alimi, A.M.: 68 landmarks are efficient for 3D face alignment?3D face alignment method applied to face recognition. Multimedia Tools and Applications, 41435–41469 (2023). https://doi.org/10.1007/s11042-023-14770-x
32. Li, S.Z., Jain, A.K., Deng, J.: Handbook of face recognition, Vol. 1, p. 699. Springer International Publishing (2024). https://doi.org/10.1007/978-3-031-43567-6
33. Face landmark detection guide | MediaPipe | Google for Developers. https://developers.google.com/mediapipe/solutions/vision/face_landmarker. Accessed 10 June 2024
34. Ye, L., Hunsicker, E., Li, B., Zhou, D.: Procrustes analysis of muscle fascicle shapes based on DTI fibre tracking. In: Annual Conference on Medical Image Understanding and Analysis, pp. 172–186. Springer International Publishing, Cham (2022). https://doi.org/10.1007/978-3-031-12053-4_13
35. Alshamy, R., Ghurab, M.: A review of big data in network intrusion detection system: Challenges, approaches, datasets, and tools. J. Comp. Sci. Eng. **8**(7), 62–74 (2020). https://doi.org/10.26438/ijcse/v8i7.6275

36. Ton, A.H.Z., Cleophas, J.: Bayesian pearson correlation analysis. In: Modern Bayesian Statistics in Clinical Research, Modern Bayesian statistics in clinical research, pp. 111–118 (2018). https://doi.org/10.1007/978-3-319-92747-3_11
37. Zou, H., Tuncali, K., Silverman, S.G.: Correlation and simple linear regression. Radiology **227**(3), 617–628 (2003). https://doi.org/10.1148/radiol.2273011499
38. Anki, P., Bustamam, A.: Measuring the accuracy of LSTM and BiLSTM models in the application of artificial intelligence by applying chatbot programme **23**(1), 197–205 (2021). https://doi.org/10.11591/ijeecs.v23.i1.pp197-205
39. Su, H., Liu, S., Zheng, B., Zhou, X., Zheng, K.: A survey of trajectory distance measures and performance evaluation. The VLDB Journal **29**, 3–32 (2020). https://doi.org/10.1007/s00778-019-00574-9

Enhancement of Low Light Images Using Residual Deep Learning

Anwar Basim$^{(\boxtimes)}$ (iD) and Asmaa Sadiq (iD)

Computer Science Department, Mustansiriyah University, Baghdad, Iraq
{anwar.basim,asmaasadiq}@uomustansiriyah.edu.iq

Abstract. Low-light image enhancement is an essential requirement for various applications in different fields such as image processing and computer vision. In this paper, a new approach to enhance the low-light images has been proposed. The proposed model consists of two main steps: preprocessing of the input images and the CNN model based on residual learning with skip connections. The architecture of the suggested CNN model contains three main residual blocks, each block has groups of convolution layers with activation functions and add operations. In the suggested model, the convolution layers will process the image, and some of these layers' output will be stored in the add operation in order to forward them to the next convolution groups in the networks as input while skipping some connections, this process represents the "residual learning". The proposed approach has been implemented on four datasets (LOL, MEF, NPE, and DICM) and compared with other state-of-the-art methods. The qualitative and quantitative results indicate excellent visual quality enhancement, improving lighting while restoring the actual colour and details of the image. And attains superior results in quality evaluation metrics, where PSNR was 34.86 in the NPE dataset, SSIM was 0.96 in the LOL dataset and NIQE was 3.18 in the MEF dataset.

Keywords: low-illumination · image enhancement · residual learning · convolutional neural network · AI

1 Introduction

High-quality images are necessary for computer vision systems to extract information and achieve reliable performance such as in medical images, autonomous driving, object (face) recognition, and object detection [1, 2]. In the context of low-light images, it will be quite difficult to perform computer vision application tasks and get useful information with low lighting and unclear details. Thus, one of the most crucial issues in the field of image processing to be resolved is how to increase detail and visibility in low light, making images more useful and clearer for correct analysis, safety, and efficient decision-making, such as in astronomy, security, photography, and medical imaging [3, 4]. Depending on the surrounding environments, there are several kinds of low-light images, such as low backlighting, night-time photography, or dimly lit interior situations with shadows [5, 6]. At present, with the rapid development of the use of artificial

© The Author(s), under exclusive license to Springer Nature Switzerland AG 2025
S. O. Al-Mamory et al. (Eds.): 3INC 2024, CCIS 2329, pp. 119–132, 2025.
https://doi.org/10.1007/978-3-031-81065-7_8

intelligence (AI), it has been applied in a variety of applications, such as voice recognition, image processing, autonomous driving, smart homes, security, medicine, and many more [7–9], also most of these applications use the deep learning as a subfield of AI to perform their tasks. In the context of low-light image enhancement, many algorithms have been proposed in the field of image processing with artificial intelligence (AI) [10]. In this paper, a new approach has been introduced based on the CNN network and residual learning in order to enhance the low-light images.

The paper is structured as follows: Sect. 2 illustrates the related works of low-light image enhancement. Section 3 illustrates Residual Learning with Skip Connections. Section 4 illustrates the proposed low-light enhancement algorithm and the network Architecture. Section 5 illustrates the experiment results for the proposed low-light enhancement algorithm compared with State-Of-The-Art algorithms. Finally, in Sect. 6 the conclusion summarizes the proposed low-light enhancement algorithm and its performance.

2   Related Works

Artificial intelligence (AI) especially deep learning has been extensively used to improve low-light images. As an illustration, Liang Shen et al. [11], in 2017, proposed an MSR-net technique using a Deep Convolutional Network and Retinex model showing that MSR is equivalent to a feedforward convolutional neural network with a variety of Gaussian convolution kernels. In response to this discovery, MSR-net, CNN was built with the ability to automatically learn an end-to-end mapping between dark and bright images with the least amount of extra pre- or post-processing. Applying the suggested method to both synthetic and real-world data showed encouraging results, highlighting the algorithm's advantages from both a qualitative and quantitative standpoint. However, significant drawbacks with this method were observed since the model's narrow receptive field occasionally produced a halo effect in exceptionally smooth regions, such as pure sky. In 2019, the Gaussian Process for feature retrieval was proposed by Yuen Peng Loh et al. [12]. It involved using the Gaussian Process to model low-light enhancement as a set of localized functions. The underlying feature information for these functions is learned during runtime using data that was taken from the underlying CNN. Conversely, CNN Large amounts of artificial data were used to train it in order to replicate the brightness distribution found in low-light photos taken in the real environment. The CNN was able to understand the intricate relationship between individual pixels and image characteristics thanks to this training. The Microsoft ExDark and COCO datasets were used to test the suggested technique. The findings show that the suggested framework is a novel strategy that deviates from conventional low-light image enhancement. Xiaomei Feng et al. [13], in 2020, proposed an approach for low-light image enhancement that starts with generating a foggy image and then using a CNN network to process the foggy image. This algorithm has been performed on various datasets and gave a positive result in both quantitative and qualitative comparisons. In 2021, Racherla Balaji Shashipreeth et al. [14] proposed an approach that depends on both Deep Curve Estimation Networks with Pack and UnPack algorithms for low-light image enhancement. The results of this algorithm indicated that it is suitable for use on low-power devices. In the same year, Minglu Zhang et al. [15] proposed the DC-WGAN Algorithm to improve the lighting of images in Space Environment, a deep learning-based technique that blended Wasserstein generative adversarial networks (DC-WGAN) and deep convolutional networks in the CIELAB colour space. First, the dark image was converted from RGB to improve the assessment of illumination and decrease aberrations. After adding DC-WGAN to the generating network, the brightness component was enhanced. The final image was then obtained by transforming the LAB back into the RGB space. The VOC, SID, and LOL datasets were subjected to the suggested methodology. The findings showed positive outcomes in terms of both quantitative and qualitative measures. Manli Wang et al. [16], in 2022, proposed an approach that combines Retinex theory with CNN by performing three models (decomposition, illumination, and reflection model). This algorithm gave a positive result in both quantitative and qualitative comparisons. While Nianzeng Yuan et al. [17], in 2023, proposed an approach that designs a U-shape network for enhancement of the low light image. The network has several numbers of fusion blocks. Every block has a stem of CNN and a transformer, they together work for local and global feature extraction from the image. This algorithm gave a positive result in both quantitative and qualitative comparisons.

3   Residual Learning with Skip Connections

The process of transforming data from one Convolution layer to another through the network by skipping one or more layers is known as the skip connection or shortcut connection. The main advantage of using a skip connection is to improve the training process and accuracy during the testing process. This process is employed for implementing residual learning [18, 19]. ResL (or residual learning) is a technique that aims to combine multiple numbers of Convolution layer outputs in order to generate a stack of convolutional blocks (known as the residual block) and then feed the residual block to other forward Convolution layers as inputs [20, 21]. Residual learning and skip connection work together in the network in order to improve the performance of the trained network by allowing the reuse of the feature maps of previous Convolution layers by the early Convolution layers of the network [21].

4 Methodology

The proposed low-light enhancement algorithm aimed to enhance the low-light images while retaining as much of the critical information as possible. The algorithm starts by preprocessing the input images and next uses the proposed model to improve the images' brightness and restore details with the true colour of the enhanced images. The model structure is reliant on CNN and residual learning with skip connections.

4.1 Preprocessing Phase

In low light image enhancement, it is important to have low illumination data from real scenes but with the lack of real data, the low illumination data is produced by using different methods for low lighting and escalating the noise in the images [22]. In this phase, the input images get prepared before being processed by the model. The preprocessing operations in this study include the conversion of the image from RGB to HVS colour space to control the lighting of images, and adding noise using impulse noise, (see Fig. 1 and Algorithm 1):

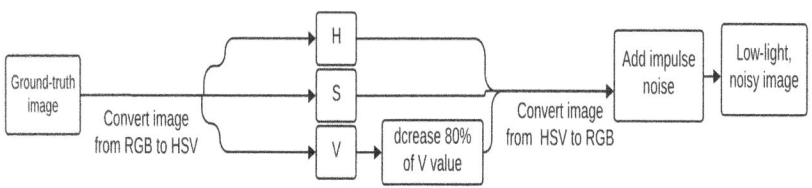

Fig. 1. Preprocessing phase

Algorithm (1) preprocessing phase

Input: ground truth image
Output: low light noisy image
Begin -read RGB image -convert image color space from RGB to HSV - decrease 80% of v value (lighting) - convert HSV image to RGB colour space - add impulse noise using equation (1) - resize image to (500x500) End

The input image is a ground truth image which is an image in normal light and its colour space is RGB. RGB components have a strong colour correlation, changing the brightness will have an impact on the image's colour [23]. To mitigate this correlation, we converted the image colour space to HSV, the HSV colour space consists of three components that are separated and nearly orthogonal. The components of HSV are (hue, Saturation, and value) the hue stands for Chroma, the saturation represents the quantity of white with the colour and the value stands for the brightness of the image [23, 24]. Then, without impacting the other elements, reduce the brightness by 80% to create a low-light image. Since the HSV image is not optimal for display systems, it is then converted back to the RGB space. Next adding the noise, impulse noise is an example of image noise which is often caused by low-quality camera sensors, software, or hardware failures during the image capture, the noise will be as white pixels (salt) and black pixels (pepper) in images. This type of impulse noise is known as salt and pepper noise [25]. Implementing Eq. (1), the impulse noise can sometimes be observed in images, which is correlated to the change in the pixel intensity value of the image [26].

$$P(N) = \begin{cases} 0.5p & pepper\, N = 0 \\ 1 - P & no\, noise\, added \\ 0.5p & salt\, N = L - 1 \end{cases} \tag{1}$$

P(N) represents the distribution (P) of the noise (N). When the noise value is zero a pepper noise is added, the other value is a salt noise. In the case of no change in the intensity value of the pixel, no noise is added. In this study, impulse noise (salt and pepper) will be applied to the raw data in the preprocessing phase to make these image data closer to real-world low-light images. Finally, the images are resized to (500×500). The practical response is that the task's accuracy and processing time may be impacted by the image's size [27].

4.2 Network Architecture

The proposed model of low-light image enhancement consists of four Residual blocks, each block has several numbers of convolution layers with their ReLU activation function, arranged in groups. The model also contains of addition operation to merge the output of the groups and feed them as input to the next convolution layers groups, (see Fig. 2). The process of enhancement starts from Group1 (G1) and Group2 (G2) in Block1 when they both take the preprocessed low light image as an input, then the process continues to all the layers, and groups, and add operations to get the final enhanced image. To describe the structure of the proposed model in detail:-

The first Block (B1) contains three groups G1, G2, and G3, with an add operation, named (resL1). The first Group1 (G1) has three convolution layers with its ReLU activation functions, the first two layers are 3×3 convolution layers and the third is a 2×2 convolution layer. The input of G1 is the preprocessed low-light image, sequentially the input image flow throws the other convolution layers of G1 and the output of G1 will be stored in (resL1) only, which means the connection between layer3 of G1 and layer1 of G2 in the same block (B1) is skipped. The second Group2 (G2) has two convolution layers with ReLU activation functions, the first layer is a 3×3 convolution layer and the other one is a 2×2 convolution layer. The input of G2 is also the preprocessed low-light image, after being processed by the second 2×2 convolution layer of the G2, the output of G2 will be stored in the (resL1) and also fed as input to the third group (G3) without skipping connections. The last Group (G3) has one 2×2 convolution layer with ReLU activation function. The input of this layer is the output of G2 and the output will be stored in (resL1) in the same block (B1). As a result, the resL1 in B1 marge the outputs of G1, G2, and G3 of B1 in order to forward the outputs to the next block in the network.

The second block (B2) also contains three groups G1, G2, and G3, with one add operation, named (resL2). The first Group1 (G1) has three convolution layers with its ReLU activation functions, the first two layers are 3 × 3 convolution layers and the third is a 2 × 2 convolution layer. The input of G1 is the resL1, this means the connection between G1 in B2 and G3 in B1 is skipped. Sequentially the input flow throws the other convolution layers of G1 and the output of G1 will be stored in (resL2) only, which means the connection between layer 3 of G1 and layer 1 of G2 in the same block (B2) is skipped. The second Group2 (G2) has two convolution layers with ReLU activation functions, the first layer is a 3 × 3 convolution layer and the other one is a 2 × 2 convolution layer. The input of G2 is also the resL1, after being processed by the second 2 × 2 convolution layer of the G2, the output of G2 will be stored in (resL2) only, with connection skipping between layer2 in G2 and the layer of G3 in the same block (B2). The last Group (G3) has one 2 × 2 convolution layer with ReLU activation function. The input of this layer is also the resL1 and the output will be stored in (resL2) in the same block (B2). As a result, the resL2 in B2 marge the outputs of G1, G2, and G3 of B2 in order to forward the outputs to the next block in the network.

The third block (B3) contains three groups G1, G2, and G3, with one add operation, named (resL3). The first Group1 (G1) has one 3 × 3 convolution layer with its ReLU activation function. The input of G1 is the resL2 which means there is a connection skipped between G3 in B2 and G1 in B3. The output of G1 will be stored in (resL3) only, and the connection between G1 and G2 in the same block (B3) is skipped. The second Group2 (G2) also has one 3 × 3 convolution layer with its ReLU activation function. The input of G2 is the resL1. The output of G2 will be stored in (resL3) only, and the connection between G2 and G3 in the same block (B3) is skipped. The resL3 in B3 marge the outputs of G1, G2 of B3, and resL2 of B2. In order to forward the outputs to the last group in the network (G3 of B3). The last Group (G3) has three convolution layers with ReLU activation functions. The input of the first 3 × 3 convolution layer and the second 2 × 2 convolution layer is the resL3, with skipping the connection between these two layers. The last layer takes the output of the previous layer and returns the final enhanced image. The process of feeding the residual blocks output as inputs to the convolution layers blocks with skip connection between layers and groups represents the residual learning in the proposed model and shows the reuse of features in the model between layers and residual blocks as well. In order to ? the process of enhancement of the low-light image (see algorithm 2) where (3 × 3 × 16) Convolution layer described the size of the kernel and the number of filters used for each Convolution layer.

Algorithm (2) of the proposed model

Input: low light noisy image
Output: enhanced image

Begin

1. Feature Extraction:

Group 1:
Layer 1: Apply (3×3×16) Convolution with ReLU activation to the input.
Layer2: Apply (3×3×32) Convolution with ReLU activation to Layer1 output.
Layer 3: Apply (2×2×64) Convolution with ReLU activation to Layer 2 output.
Group 2:
Apply (3×3×32) Convolution with ReLU activation to the input.
Apply (2×2×64) Convolution with ReLU activation to previous convolution output.
Group 3:
Apply (2×2×64) Convolution with ReLU activation to the output of group 2.

2. Combine Features:

Combine groups Outputs:
Add outputs of group 1, group 2, and group 3 to create `add operation (1)`.

3. Residual Learning:

Residual Block 1:
Apply (3×3×64) Convolution with ReLU activation to `add operation (1)`.
Apply (3×3×32) Convolution with ReLU activation to previous convolution output.
Apply (2×2×16) Convolution with ReLU activation to previous convolution output.
Residual Block 2:
Apply (3×3×32) Convolution with ReLU activation to `add operation (1)`.
Apply (2×2×16) Convolution with ReLU activation to previous convolution output.
Residual Block 3:
Apply (2×2×16) Convolution with d ReLU activation to `add operation (1)`.

4. Combine Residual Outputs:

Add outputs Residual Block 1, Residual Block 2, and Residual Block 3 to create `add operation (2)`.

5. Feature Refinement:

Layer 4: Apply (3×3×16) Convolution with ReLU activation to `add operation (2)`.
Layer 5: Apply (3×3×16) Convolution with ReLU activation to `add operation (1)`.

6. Combine Refinement Outputs:

Add the outputs of Layer 4, Layer 5, and ` add operation (2)` to create `add operation (3)`.
7. Final Enhancement:

Output Layer:
Apply (3×3×16) Convolution with ReLU activation to `add operation (3)`.
Apply (2×2×16) Convolution with ReLU activation to previous convolution output.
Apply the final (3×3×3) Convolution with ReLU activation to previous convolution output to produce the enhanced image.

End

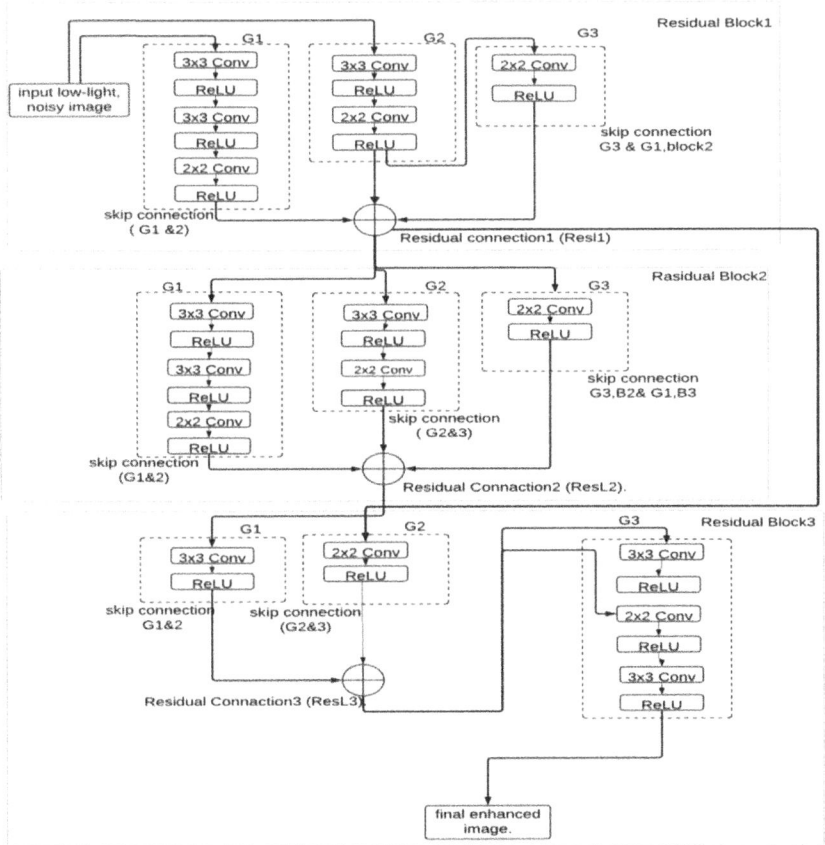

Fig. 2. The flowchart of the proposed model

5   Experiments Results

The proposed model was evaluated through experiments performed on a system including Intel(R) Core (TM) i7-8550U CPU @ 1.80 GHz, 8.00 GB RAM, and we used Jupyter notebook of Anaconda platform for training the proposed model with ADAM optimizer for training parameters optimization. The training epochs were 55 epochs with eight steps per epoch depending on the size of the training dataset and the improvement of the visual evaluation of the test outcomes.

5.1   Datasets

For training the proposed model the LOL dataset [28] (a more popular low-light dataset) is used for training which includes 485 paired low-light and normal-light images. In order to control the lighting of images that the model will train on and specify the suitable noise type. The normal-light images are used as ground truth images and produce the low-light image through the preprocessing phase. To verify the effectiveness of the proposed algorithm, four datasets are used for testing: DICM [29] with 40 images, MEF [30] with 17 images, NPE [31] with 50, and LOL [28] with 15 test images.

5.2   Comparison with State-of-the-Art Algorithms

The proposed algorithm is compared with two groups of deep algorithms in order to verify the effectiveness of the proposed algorithm. The first group used the LOL [28] dataset for testing, the algorithms of this group are KinD++ [32], URetinex-Net [33], DCC-Net [34], and LLIE [35]. The second group uses DICM [29], MEF [30], and NPE [31] datasets for testing, the algorithms of this group are RetinexNet [28], MBLLEN [36], EnlightenGAN [37], RUAS [38], Zero-DCE [39], SCI medium [10], and LLE-NET [40].

Qualitative Comparison
For the subjective visual evaluation, Fig. 3 below represents various indoor and outdoor images from different datasets (LOL, DICM, MEF, and NPE) with the results of implementing the proposed algorithm, in the LOL dataset the selected images include indoor images that have multi-shades and different spectrum colour images to show the model restoring colour ability with lighting enhancement, while for DICM dataset, the selected images include outdoor images with dark parts (the house in first image and the road in second image) the proposed model enhanced their lighting with restoring the details of dark parts as clear as possible. In the third dataset (MEF) the first image is indoor with dark parts (the desktop and shelves) image also the model restored the details for dark parts and enhanced the lighting. While the second image is an outdoor coloured image with details, the enhanced image shows the model's ability to restore colour, details, and lighting. For the NPE dataset, the selected images include both outdoor and indoor scenes, characterized by dark areas and predominantly dark colour tones. The enhanced results on the NPE dataset demonstrate the model's capability to effectively handle dark colours, restoring them with improved detail and accurate lighting correction. The results indicate producing enhanced light images with more natural colour while preserving the details of the images and visual image quality. As a result, the proposed method demonstrates in terms of subjective visual evaluation that, first, it is more reliable with the enhancement of low-light images from different low-light environments without over-exposure, over-something, under-exposure, or colour distortion. Secondly, results in a good restoration of images in extremely dark regions and better recovery of image details. Third, the proposed method can correctly enhance the image brightness with good generalization.

Quantitative Comparison
In terms of objective comparison, three objective metrics have been used to evaluate the proposed method and compare it with other methods quantitively. The metrics that have been used are peak signal-to-noise ratio (PSNR), structural similarity index (SSIM) [41], and natural image quality evaluator (NIQE) [42]. The Image quality improves with increasing SSIM and PSNR values, whereas lower NIQE values suggest better quality.

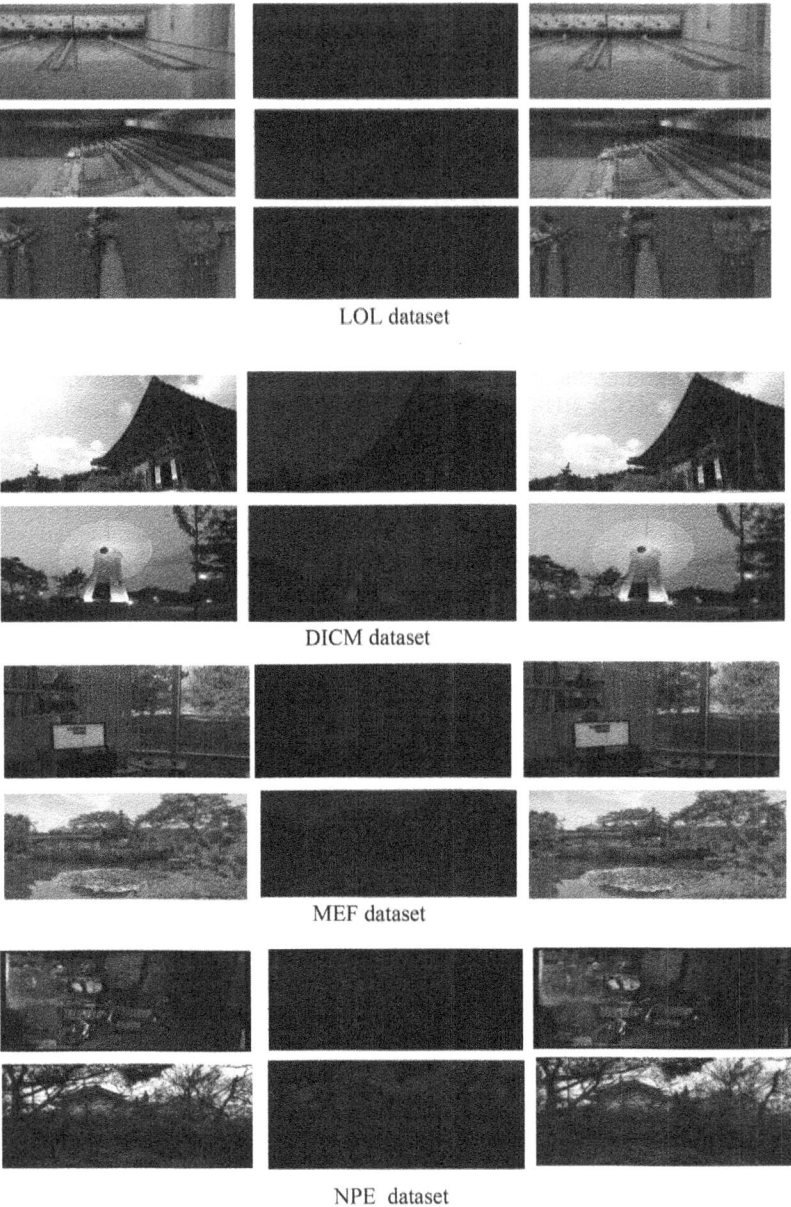

LOL dataset

DICM dataset

MEF dataset

NPE dataset

(a)Ground truth   (b)Low-light image   (c)Enhanced image

Fig. 3. Visual low light image enhancement on LOL, DICM, MEF, and NPE datasets.

Table 1 displays the quantitative comparison between the proposed algorithm and state-of-the-art algorithms on DICM [29], MEF [30], and NPE [31] datasets. For the sample (↑) means higher values give better results, and (↓) means lower values give better results.

As shown in Table 1 the best image enhancement results are presented by the proposed algorithm in PSNR for the three datasets where in the DICM dataset = 33.71, MEF = 33.47, and NPE = 34.86 which means PSNR achieved the best results for all three datasets. The second metric is SSIM, our proposed algorithm achieved high similarity values for the three datasets compared with other algorithms where in the DICME dataset = 0.94, MEF = 0.95, and NPE = 0.91. The last metric is the NIQE metric as compared with all datasets it gives the best results for MEF = 3.18 and NPE = 3.13 while for DICM the EnlightenGAN approach is superior to the proposed method in NIQE metric which gives 3.48 while the proposed algorithm in NIQE for DICM give 3.79.

Table 1. The quantitative results (PSNR, SSIM, and NIQE) of the proposed algorithm and other state-of-the-art algorithms. Bold shows the best outcomes.

Dataset	Method	PSNR ↑	SSIM ↑	NIQE ↓
DICM [29]	MBLLEN	18.22	0.72	4.20
MEF [30]		16.17	0.59	4.73
NPE [31]		19.51	0.74	4.54
DICM [29]	RUAS	10.74	0.60	4.78
MEF [30]		12.01	0.57	3.69
NPE [31]		10.33	0.60	5.68
DICM [29]	EnlightenGAN	13.28	0.60	**3.48**
MEF [30]		12.65	0.43	3.22
NPE [31]		12.63	0.65	4.11
DICM [29]	Zero-DCE	14.58	0.63	3.60
MEF [30]		13.69	0.44	3.22
NPE [31]		13.86	0.65	4.11
DICM [29]	SCI-medium	9.45	0.51	3.79
MEF [30]		10.22	0.39	3.44
NPE [31]		9.02	0.50	3.44
DICM [29]	LLE-NET	14.16	0.63	3.69
MEF [30]		14.01	0.48	3.38
NPE [31]		14.17	0.54	3.32
DICM [29]	Proposed Method	**33.71**	**0.94**	3.79
MEF [30]		**33.47**	**0.95**	**3.18**
NPE [31]		**34.86**	**0.91**	**3.31**

The same matrices PSNR, SSIM, and NIQE were used to compute the quantitative comparison between the proposed algorithm and other state-of-the-art algorithms on the LOL [28] dataset as shown in Table 2, the result also indicates that the proposed method produced better quality enhanced images than other algorithms. For PSNR the proposed method result is 33.73 which is higher than all compered methods. The SSIM metric for the proposed method is 0.96 and the NIQE result for the proposed algorithm is close to the LLIE and URetinex-Net results but it is also better than both of them, which was = 3.22.

Table 2. The quantitative results (PSNR, SSIM, and NIQE) of the proposed algorithm and other state-of-the-art algorithms on the LOL dataset. Bold shows the best outcomes.

Method	PSNR ↑	SSIM ↑	NIQE ↓
KinD++	21.80	0.82	4.01
URetinex-Net	21.33	0.83	3.54
DCC-Net	22.98	0.84	3.67
LLIE	24.31	0.85	3.52
Proposed Method	33.73	0.96	3.22

6 Conclusion

The proposed method addresses the low light image problem by using the CNN model and residual learning with skip connections. The structure of the proposed method relies on two phases. First, the preprocessing phase is to prepare the input image, and the second phase is to use the CNN model to enhance the input image. The model architecture contains three blocks, each block has three groups of convolution layers with ReLU activation function and one residual block. The input image goes through several layers then is saved in residual blocks in order to forward the data to other groups in the network by skipping some connections to apply the residual learning, where the residual connections are employed to improve the efficiency of image enhancement by reducing the loss of details during implementing the CNN network. The qualitative and quantitative experiment results indicated excellent improvement in the visual quality of the lighting image, also after comparing the proposed method with other state-of-the-art methods the results show that the proposed method gives more effective outcomes on four separate datasets using three measures.

References

1. Litjens, G., et al.: A survey on deep learning in medical image analysis. Med. Image Anal. **42**, 60–88 (2017). https://doi.org/10.1016/j.media.2017.07.005
2. Badue, C., et al.: Self-driving cars: a survey. Expert Syst. Appl. **165**, 113816 (2021). https://doi.org/10.1016/j.eswa.2020.113816

3. Masi, I., Wu, Y., Hassner, T., Natarajan, P.: Deep face recognition: a survey. In: 2018 31st SIBGRAPI Conference on Graphics, Patterns and Images (SIBGRAPI). IEEE, Parana (2018). https://doi.org/10.1109/sibgrapi.2018.00067

4. Zhao, Z.-Q., Zheng, P., Xu, S.-T., Wu, X.: Object detection with deep learning: a review. IEEE Trans. Neural Netw. Learn. Syst. **30**(11), 3212–3232 (2019). https://doi.org/10.1109/tnnls.2018.2876865

5. Wei, C., Wang, W., Yang, W., Liu, J.: Deep Retinex Decomposition for Low-Light Enhancement (2018). arXiv: arXiv:1808.04560. Accessed: 17 Sep. 2024

6. Guo, J., Ma, J., García-Fernández, Á.F., Zhang, Y., Liang, H.: A survey on image enhancement for Low-light images. Heliyon **9**(4) (2023)

7. Ali, H.H., Naif, J.R., Humood, W.R.: A new smart home intruder detection system based on deep learning. Al-Mustansiriyah J. Sci. **34**(2), 60–69 (2023)

8. Al-Tai, M.H., Nema, B.M., Al-Sherbaz, A.: Deep learning for fake news detection: literature review. Al-Mustansiriyah J. Sci. **34**(2), 70–81 (2023)

9. Salman, S., Soud, J.H.: Deep learning machine using hierarchical cluster features. Al-Mustansiriyah J. Sci. **29**(3), 82–93 (2018)

10. Ren, W., et al.: Low-light image enhancement via a deep hybrid network. IEEE Trans. Image Process. **28**(9), 4364–4375 (2019)

11. Shen, L., Yue, Z., Feng, F., Chen, Q., Liu, S., Ma, J.: MSR-net: Low-light Image Enhancement Using Deep Convolutional Network (2017). arXiv: arXiv:1711.02488. Accessed: 17 Sep. 2024

12. Loh, Y.P., Liang, X., Chan, C.S.: Low-light image enhancement using gaussian process for features retrieval. Signal Process. Image Commun. **74**, 175–190 (2019)

13. He, W., et al.: Low-light image enhancement combined with attention map and u-net network. presented at the 2020 IEEE 3rd International Conference on Information Systems and Computer Aided Education (ICISCAE), pp. 397–401. IEEE (2020)

14. Shashipreeth, R.B., Minu, R., Priya, S.S.: Low light image enhancement using DCE-net aided by pack and unpack operations. presented at the 2021 6th International Conference on Communication and Electronics Systems (ICCES), pp. 1124–1127. IEEE (2021)

15. Zhang, M., Zhang, Y., Jiang, Z., Lv, X., Guo, C.: Low-illumination image enhancement in the space environment based on the DC-WGAN algorithm. Sensors **21**(1), 286 (2021)

16. Wang, M., Li, J., Zhang, C.: Low-light image enhancement by deep learning network for improved illumination map. Comput. Vis. Image Underst. **232**, 103681 (2023). https://doi.org/10.1016/j.cviu.2023.103681

17. Yuan, N., et al.: Low-light image enhancement by combining transformer and convolutional neural network. Mathematics **11**(7), 1657 (2023). https://doi.org/10.3390/math11071657

18. Xu, G., Wang, X., Wu, X., Leng, X., Xu, Y.: Development of Skip Connection in Deep Neural Networks for Computer Vision and Medical Image Analysis: A Survey. ArXiv Prepr. ArXiv240501725 (2024)

19. Alaraimi, S., Okedu, K.E., Tianfield, H., Holden, R., Uthmani, O.: Transfer learning networks with skip connections for classification of brain tumors. Int. J. Imaging Syst. Technol. **31**(3), 1564–1582 (2021)

20. Singh, O., Sengar, S.S.: BetterNet: An Efficient CNN Architecture with Residual Learning and Attention for Precision Polyp Segmentation (2024). arXiv: arXiv:2405.04288. Accessed: 17 Sep. 2024

21. Shafiq, M., Gu, Z.: Deep residual learning for image recognition: a survey. Appl. Sci. **12**(18), 8972 (2022). https://doi.org/10.3390/app12188972

22. Li, N., Gong, X.: An image preprocessing model of coal and gangue in high dust and low light conditions based on the joint enhancement algorithm. Comput. Intell. Neurosci. **2021**(1), 2436486 (2021)

23. Li, Z., Jia, Z., Yang, J., Kasabov, N.: Low illumination video image enhancement. IEEE Photonics J. **12**(4), 1–13 (2020)
24. Liu, S., Long, W., He, L., Li, Y., Ding, W.: Retinex-based fast algorithm for low-light image enhancement. Entropy **23**(6), 746 (2021). https://doi.org/10.3390/e23060746
25. Alqadi, Z.: Salt and pepper noise: effects and removal. Int. J. Electr. Eng. Inform. **2**(07) (2018)
26. Ibrahim, H., Neo, K.C., Teoh, S.H., Ng, T.F., Chieh, D.C.J., Hassan, N.N.: Impulse noise model and its variations. Int. J. Comput. Electr. Eng. **4**(5), 647 (2012)
27. Talebi, H., Milanfar, P.: Learning to resize images for computer vision tasks. presented at the Proceedings of the IEEE/CVF international conference on computer vision, pp. 497–506 (2021)
28. Wei, C., Wang, W., Yang, W., Liu, J.: Deep retinex decomposition for low-light enhancement. ArXiv Prepr. ArXiv180804560 (2018)
29. Lee, C., Lee, C., Kim, C.-S.: Contrast enhancement based on layered difference representation of 2D histograms. IEEE Trans. Image Process. **22**(12), 5372–5384 (2013)
30. Ma, K., Zeng, K., Wang, Z.: Perceptual quality assessment for multi-exposure image fusion. IEEE Trans. Image Process. **24**(11), 3345–3356 (2015)
31. Wang, S., Zheng, J., Hu, H.-M., Li, B.: Naturalness preserved enhancement algorithm for non-uniform illumination images. IEEE Trans. Image Process. **22**(9), 3538–3548 (2013)
32. Zhang, Y., Guo, X., Ma, J., Liu, W., Zhang, J.: Beyond brightening low-light images. Int. J. Comput. Vis. **129**, 1013–1037 (2021)
33. Wu, W., et al.: Uretinex-net: retinex-based deep unfolding network for low-light image enhancement. presented at the Proceedings of the IEEE/CVF conference on computer vision and pattern recognition, pp. 5901–5910 (2022)
34. Zhang, Z., et al.: Deep color consistent network for low-light image enhancement. presented at the Proceedings of the IEEE/CVF conference on computer vision and pattern recognition, pp. 1899–1908 (2022)
35. Matsui, T., Ikehara, M.: Low-light image enhancement using a simple network structure. IEEE Access (2023)
36. Lv, F., Lu, F., Wu, J., Lim, C.: MBLLEN: Low-light image/video enhancement using cnns. presented at the BMVC, p. 4. Northumbria University (2018)
37. Jiang, Y., et al.: Deep light enhancement without paired supervision. HttpsOrg101109TIP **30**, 2340–2349 (2021)
38. Liu, R., Ma, L., Zhang, J., Fan, X., Luo, Z.: Retinex-inspired unrolling with cooperative prior architecture search for low-light image enhancement. presented at the Proceedings of the IEEE/CVF conference on computer vision and pattern recognition, pp. 10561–10570 (2021)
39. Zhang, S., Tang, G., Liu, X., Luo, S., Wang, D.: Retinex based low-light image enhancement using guided filtering and variational framework. Optoelectron. Lett. **14**(2), 156–160 (2018)
40. Cao, X., Yu, J.: LLE-NET: a low-light image enhancement algorithm based on curve estimation. Mathematics **12**(8), 1228 (2024)
41. Wang, Z., Bovik, A.C., Sheikh, H.R., Simoncelli, E.P.: Image quality assessment: from error visibility to structural similarity. IEEE Trans. Image Proc. **13**(4), 600–612 (2004)
42. Mittal, A., Soundararajan, R., Bovik, A.C.: Making a 'completely blind' image quality analyzer. IEEE Signal Process. Lett. **20**(3), 209–212 (2012)

Hybrid Model for Hospital Services Quality Prediction Based on Patient Viewpoint

Mohammed K. Al-khafaji[1](✉) ⓘ and Eman S. Al-Shamery[2] ⓘ

[1] Software Department, Information Technology College, University of Babylon, Hilla, Iraq
Mohammedkodayera.sw@student.uobabylon.edu.iq
[2] Information Security Department, Information Technology College, University of Babylon, Hilla, Iraq
emanalshamery@itnet.uobabylon.edu.iq

Abstract. Health services are vital in people's lives, and it's important to evaluate their quality from the patient's perspective as they are the primary beneficiaries. However, due to the extensive range of medical services, this leads to data scattering during data collection because patients are unable to access all services. This paper presents a study that aims to predict the quality of missing services and offer optimal recommendations to patients. The study involved four Iraqi hospitals, the methods of collecting the samples differed, some were manual via paper, and others were electronic, via the website and social media. To obtain the most precise results, the study employed k-means clustering and hybrid collaborative filtering. The accuracy (Acc) achieved was 97.5%, and the F1-measure (F1) was 97.64%. The proposed model was compared to traditional methods, demonstrating its success in predicting missing services and providing suitable recommendations for the patient's needs.

Keywords: Prediction · Recommendation · Collaborative Filtering · Matrix Factorization · K-Means Clustering · Hospital Service Quality

1 Introduction

Healthcare institutions are critical as they directly impact human life and well-being [1]. Therefore, many countries and organizations strive for continuous development in these institutions. Hospitals provide essential services that play a decisive role in saving people's lives. It is imperative to measure the Quality of Services (QoS) that hospitals provide based on patient experience to study the level of healthcare and understand patient preferences [2] and [3]. Patients expect to receive the best care when going to healthcare centres. Also, patients anticipate high-level interactions with healthcare staff such as doctors, nurses, and others [4]. Analyzing patient interaction data with healthcare institutions is crucial, as it provides a fertile environment for studying a large amount of data [5].

As stated, due to the wide range of hospital services, patients are unable to access all services, resulting in scattered and incomplete data [6]. Therefore, this problem

S. O. Al-Mamory et al. (Eds.): 3INC 2024, CCIS 2329, pp. 133–147, 2025.
https://doi.org/10.1007/978-3-031-81065-7_9

requires careful handling. This paper proposes a framework to address the problem of data sparsity and recommend the best services for patients, machine learning techniques and collaborative filtering methods have been developed as a solution [7]. The proposed framework employs clustering methods to set users into groups, then uses the similarity between users to fill in part of the missing information [8], and finally performs Matrix Factorization (MF) to uncover additional features and complete the data [9]. This process is important for ensuring that patients have access to accurate and complete information about all hospital services.

Collaborative filtering methods have gained great importance, especially in recommendation systems, because of their ability to provide recommendations to service users by studying the similarities between users [10–12], and [13]. On the other hand, it is possible to benefit greatly from collaborative filtering methods to predict the level of QoS and to fill out the scattered data when collecting a sample to study the QoS, as it is possible to benefit greatly from communication networks between users and to study their preferences [14]. The following statement clarifies the essential tasks of collaborative filtering, as depicted in Fig. 1.

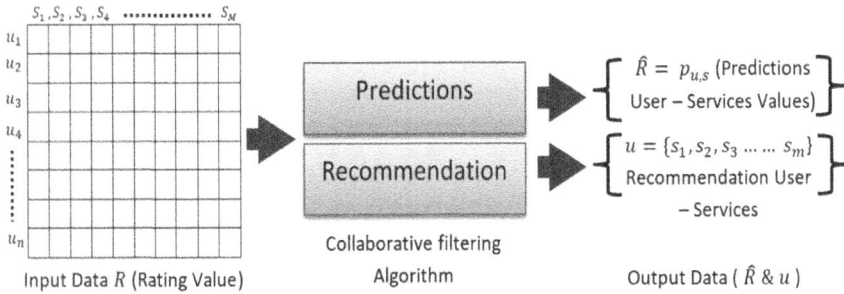

Fig. 1. The essential tasks of collaborative filtering

Evaluating the QoS from the user's viewpoint is crucial because the user is the main recipient of the service [15] and [16]. From this important standpoint, QoS was studied in four Iraqi hospitals in different geographical areas, namely (Al-Hillah General Teaching Hospital in Babylon (H1), Al-Kafeel Hospital in Karbala (H2), Al-Yarmouk Hospital in Baghdad (H3), and Diwaniyah Women's and Children's Hospital in Diwaniyah (H4)). The study included multiple dimensions of quality that are compatible with the service reality provided by service hospitals in Iraq. The service evaluation questionnaire was designed, which is available in both electronic and paper formats and the data was enriched by individuals' feedback on the services via social media platforms. Evaluating the level of services from the user's point of view has many incentives such as creating an interactive environment between hospitals and service recipients, and following up on reactions to the service procedures that the patient receives. On the other hand, this is reflected in hospitals to provide the best services, create a competitive environment between hospitals, improve their service procedures, and redistribute their resources to provide the best service. Therefore, evaluating the level of services benefits for the service recipient in the end [17].

After a general introduction, the paper covers related works, a review of hospital services and collaborative filtering methods, the framework of the proposed model, experimental results, and the conclusion.

2 Related Work

User-based analyses have garnered significant attention and have been explored by numerous researchers across various fields, particularly in the realm of service quality forecasting and recommendation systems [18]. Recommendation systems in the healthcare field encounter significant challenges due to the abundance and complexity of unorganized data [19], making it difficult to make informed decisions about recommending the QoS [20].

Chinnasamy et al. conducted a study using deep learning and collaborative filtering to offer medical recommendations to patients. They monitored individuals' health statuses through social media and provided personalized recommendations, diagnoses, and treatments. The study evaluated the results using direct error, accuracy, precision, recall, and F-measure, comparing them to traditional methods [20].

Fareed et al. proposed a collaborative filtering framework based on social networks to provide more accurate recommendations. The proposed system operates on user-based recommendations. It utilizes movie ratings and social interactions between users. By analyzing user similarity and weights, the system generates recommendations. The results demonstrated that this approach outperformed traditional methods, providing accurate and diverse recommendations [13].

In healthcare, a content-based multi-criteria collaborative filtering system was introduced by Shambour et al. to help patients find the right doctors for their health conditions. The system used the doctor's reputation and content information to improve the accuracy of recommendations. The results demonstrated the system's ability to predict and provide suitable patient recommendations, despite the scattered data, compared to item-based collaborative filtering algorithms [21].

Recommendation systems are precise and complex, requiring a thorough understanding of the user's behaviour. Yannam et al. introduced a group recommendation system as an alternative to traditional individual systems. This system relies on descriptive data such as watching movies with family or going on trips with friends. The paper predicts group classification using multi-criteria perceptron and matrix factorization. The proposed system consists of two stages. The first stage involves learning from the interaction between the group and the elements using the dot product. The second stage involves the interaction between the groups and the elements using data for the groups and data for the elements. These two stages are combined to make final predictions. The paper concluded that using metadata reduces the impact of cold starts [22].

The vast amount of electronic health records poses a challenge for specialists when making patient-centred decisions. This emphasizes the need for health systems that rely on precise recommendations for patients, particularly in the realm of medications. Sae-Ang et al. introduced a medication recommendation system tailored for elderly individuals with conditions such as high blood pressure, diabetes, heart disease, and other comorbidities. The processing involved traditional learning systems and collaborative filtering systems. The findings indicated that the model's performance was inferior to that of traditional collaborative filtering. The study concluded that numerous issues in healthcare need to be addressed to ensure accurate results [23].

In previous studies, it was observed that they all focused on collaborative filtering without incorporating other machine-learning techniques. Additionally, many studies were restricted to small sample sizes and limited datasets. This paper introduces a hybrid model that first employs the clustering method, followed by hybrid collaborative filtering using similarity methods and a factorization matrix. This approach yielded valuable results and provided recommendations tailored to the needs of patients.

3   Hospital Services Quality and Collaborative Filtering

3.1   QoS in Healthcare

Quality of Service (QoS) is a general term that refers to the level of service expected by service recipients. Service quality calculations vary from one service to another, and one needs quality criteria to measure the level of service [24]. Nowadays, improving health services quality is a big problem for all countries in the world. The countries seek through their various policies to develop economic and strategic plans to raise the service level and improve health status. The concept of quality and control of quality has become one of the topics that are most discussed and most interesting by researchers, administrators, consumers, and service funders [25]. Despite the many measures and efforts made to improve the QoS, it remains open always to question [26].

Healthcare comprises a variety of medical procedures and practices and is carried out by a range of professionals including doctors, dentists, nurses, and service workers. The specific resources available may vary between hospitals. Different criteria were used to measure hospital service quality. The SERVQUAL questionnaire is one such measure, which includes empathy, tangibility, responsiveness, reliability, and assurance [27, 28], and [29]. Another method is the Hospital Consumer Assessment of Healthcare Providers and Systems (HCAHPS). It relies on standards such as communication between healthcare staff and the patient regarding medications, maintaining a calm environment, cleanliness, and other protocols [30].

3.2   Memory-Based Collaborative Approach

Collaborative filtering based on memory, also known as neighbourhood-based or user-item filtering, is a straightforward and intuitive technique [13]. It assumes that users who have shared interests in the past will have similar preferences in the future. Ratings of items are determined by analyzing the ratings of similar users or items [12]. Equation 1 demonstrates a method for measuring user similarity, known as the cosine similarity approach. This approach has many benefits, including simplicity, transparency, and the ability to uncover unexpected and enjoyable items [31].

$$SIM_{uv} = \frac{\sum_{i \in I}(s_{ui} - \bar{s}_u)(s_{vi} - \bar{s}_v)}{\sqrt{\sum((s_{ui} - \bar{s}_u)^2}\sqrt{\sum(s_{vi} - \bar{s}_v)^2}} \tag{1}$$

In healthcare, a patient's interaction with a particular service can be used to recommend that service to another patient with similar interests. Conversely, a similar service with which the patient has interacted can also be recommended. Figure 2 shows the memory-based collaborative approach.

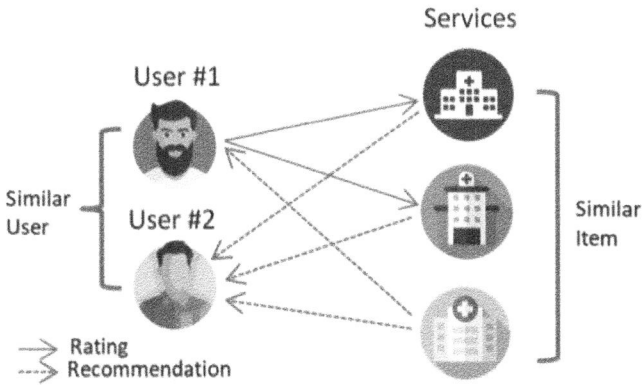

Fig. 2. The memory-based collaborative filtering

3.3 Model-Based Collaborative Approach

This is an approach that uses artificial intelligence techniques to analyze user behaviour. It is considered an advanced and more complex model than the memory-based collaborative approach [32]. The model-based approach does not depend on the user's preferences directly only but rather analyzes the user's behaviour and reactions to the service [33], for example, the user's expressions or comments about the service. Therefore, it provides greater accuracy than the memory model and provides more data about the service's evaluations, but it has complexities in interpreting the user's behaviour, and all intelligence techniques can be used in this approach [32].

3.4 Matrix Factorization

Collaborative filtering is a crucial technique that involves decomposing the evaluation matrix into two matrices with a lower rank [34]. The aim is to solve the problem of limited user ratings for services. Due to the small number of preferences, these are treated linearly using specific parameters [33]. Essentially, this method is based on the idea that users' ratings are sparse and that by decomposing the matrix, it is possible to infer the missing ratings. For instance, R is a representation of the preference matrix M X N. Here, M represents the user of services and N represents the services. $\hat{R}$ is matrix factorization by decomposing R into two lower rank matrices U^T and V. Here U^T is M X D and V is D X N, where D is specific coefficients.

4   The Proposed Model

The proposed methodology comprises three stages. The first stage involves defining the Quality of Service (QoS), collecting data, and preprocessing it. The second stage employs the k-mean clustering and collaborative filtering approach, which includes user similarities and matrix factorization. Lastly, the QoS prediction is made, recommendations for users, and the results are evaluated. Figure 3 illustrates the proposed methodology.

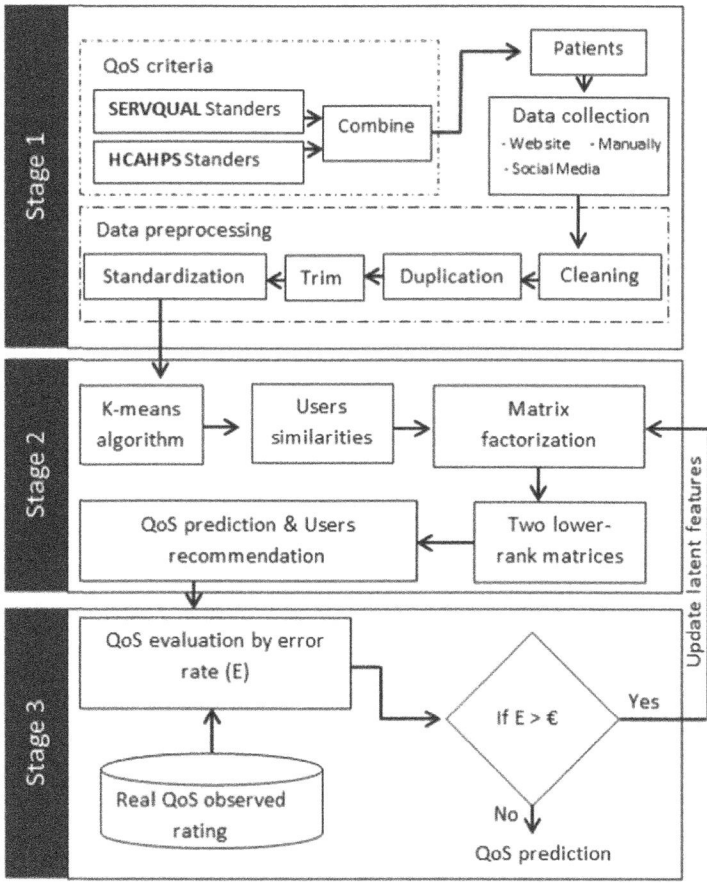

Fig. 3. The framework of the proposed model

4.1   Quality of Service (QoS) Criteria and Data Collection

Numerous studies have been conducted to establish the standards for quality medical services. Popular approaches for setting such standards are the SERVQUAL and HCAHPS, two methods for evaluating service quality and patient experience. Criteria were adopted in this study for hospitals based on numerous studies. These standards include empathy, tangibility, responsiveness, reliability, assurance, and communication among healthcare staff and patients. Other requirements include medication communication, maintaining a clean and quiet environment, and post-discharge follow-up. The sample was collected in two directions. The first direction is through a questionnaire consisting of more than 9 questions representing quality standards, such as some questions: M1: Cleanliness in general (patient rooms and bathrooms); M2: The nurses communicate with the patient. M3: The doctor communicates with the patient; M4: The staff communicate with the patient (explaining medications and how to use them) and promptly assist; M5: Communication about medicines, and explaining how to use medicines after going home by hospital staff; M6: The staff explain the health care method and what the patient should do after going home; M7: Quiet in the hospital near the patient and the areas surrounding the patient; M8: The cost of treatment in terms of the price of treatment and availability of medications; and M9: Do you recommend patients to go to the hospital? Four hospitals were chosen in central Iraq, and the sample was collected at different times. At each time t, more than 50 questionnaires were collected for each hospital, representing the patient's viewpoint of the services provided. This means that the sample was more than 200 questionnaires at each time. For three times, the total sample dataset was more than 690 patients' viewpoints. The second approach is to gather samples from social networking sites to observe people's responses to the service provided by hospitals and analyze it. The four hospitals were chosen because they are all in central Iraq and the experiment can be expanded to include all areas of Iraq. The methods of collecting the sample differed, some were manual, via paper, directly with the patient, and others were electronic, via the website and social media.

4.2   Collaborative Filtering Model

The first step of the model is data preprocessing is a crucial step that needs to be completed before analyzing and feeding data into a model. During this process, the data is cleaned and standardized. It has been observed that some patients do not answer all questions, some choose more than one answer, and others give biased answers. This step helps to ensure that only high-quality data is used in the analysis. After data collection and preprocessing, the proposed model consists of two main steps. These steps aim to predict the quality of missing services and recommend the best services to users. This is illustrated in Fig. 4.

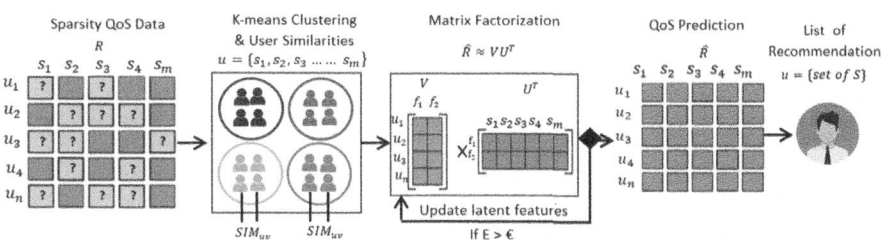

Fig. 4. Prediction and recommendation collaborative filtering model

Assuming there is a set of users (patients) $U = \{u_1, u_2, u_3, \ldots, u_N\}$, a set of services $S = \{s_1, s_2, s_3, \ldots, s_M\}$, where each $u = \{s_1, s_2, s_3 \ldots \ldots, s_M\}$.

To understand user behaviour, users were grouped using the K-means algorithm to study user preferences and group them into specific clusters, the optimal k of k-mean was determined by using the elbow method. Then similarity techniques were applied to find the closest users. This paper employed the concepts of similarity between users to handle some missing data, where cosine distance measures are used as in Eq. 2.

$$sim_{x,y} = cos\left(\overrightarrow{U_x}, \overrightarrow{U_y}\right) = \frac{\overrightarrow{U_x}, \overrightarrow{U_y}}{\overrightarrow{U_{x2}} X \overrightarrow{U_{y2}}} \tag{2}$$

where $sim_{x,y}$, U_x and U_u is representing the degree of similarity between users x and y. $\overrightarrow{U_x}$ and $\overrightarrow{U_y}$ is representing ratings vectors for x and y.

Service missing values are predicted for a user based on the similarity of user ratings to other users, as in the expression in Eq. 3.

$$\hat{v}_{x,i} = \bar{v}_x + \frac{\sum_{z \in N_x} sim_{x,z}\left(v_{z,i} - \bar{v}_z\right)}{\sum_{z \in N_x} |sim_{x,z}|} \tag{3}$$

where N_x is representing a group of users similar to the user z.

Each user is treated as a vector of the services that were assessed, after finding similar users, the missing information from the user (u_1) is filled in by the user (u_4) with the minimum cosine value, as in Fig. 5.

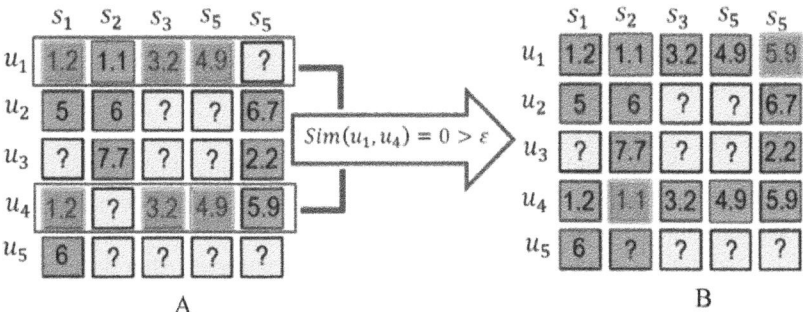

Fig. 5. A: Original data, B: Prediction missing value

The Matrix Factorization (MF) technique is a popular technique for collaborative filtering. The idea behind MF is to decompose the users-services matrix into two lower-rank matrices that are present in Fig. 6.

The first matrix represents the users-features (V), and the second matrix represents the services-features (U). The users-services matrix is then reconstructed by taking the dot product of these two matrices. Equation 4 represents the resulting matrix is without missing values and its value was predicted by decomposing the original matrix into two lower-rank matrices and reconstructing these matrices.

$$\hat{R} \approx VU^T \tag{4}$$

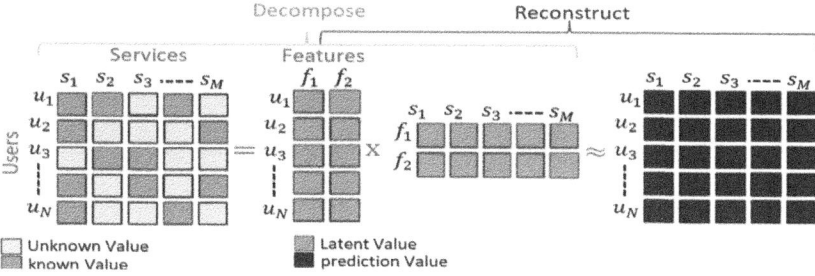

Fig. 6. Matrix factorization (MF), decompose and reconstruct techniques

In this prediction model, it may encounter bias from some user evaluations. Some always evaluate services highly and others always evaluate services low. To avoid this bias from users, as expressed in Eq. 5.

$$\hat{R}_{ij} = V_{ik} U_{kj}^T + b_i + b_j \qquad (5)$$

where k where $k < \; < i, j$ is the latent factor size.

The model is trained by minimizing the squared error between the expected value and the true value. The objective function is defined as in Eq. 6.

$$e_{ij}^2 = \left\| R_{ij} - \hat{R}_{ij} \right\|^2 + \gamma \left(\|V\|_k^2 + \|U\|_k^2 + b_u^2 + b_i^2 \right) \qquad (6)$$

where e is the squared error between the expected value and the true value, γ denotes the regularization score. The regularizing expression $\gamma(\| V \|_F^2 + \|U\|_F^2 + b_u^2 + b_i^2)$ is used to handle over-fitting by penalizing the magnitude of the parameters.

Equations 7 and 8 To minimize the squared error, by minimizing the gradient error, for both U and V.

$$\frac{\partial}{\partial V_{ik}} e_{ij}^2 = -2 \left(R_{ij} - \hat{R}_{ij} \right) (V_{ik}) = -e_{ij}^2 V_{ik} \qquad (7)$$

$$\frac{\partial}{\partial U_{kj}} e_{ij}^2 = -2 \left(R_{ij} - \hat{R}_{ij} \right) (U_{kj}) = -e_{ij}^2 U_{kj} \qquad (8)$$

Through the gradient descent expression, each matrix is adjusted to minimize the error level, as in Eqs. 9 and 10.

$$\hat{V}_{ik} = V_{ik} + \alpha \frac{\partial}{\partial V_{ik}} e_{ij}^2 = V_{ik} + e_{ij}^2 V_{ik} \qquad (9)$$

$$\hat{U}_{ki} = U_{kj} + \alpha \frac{\partial}{\partial U_{kj}} e_{ij}^2 = U_{kj} + e_{ij}^2 U_{kj} \qquad (10)$$

By calculating the square of the total error as Eq. 11, Eqs. 9 and 10 are repeated to obtain the lowest percentage error between the expected value and the true value.

$$E = \sum_{Rij, Vik, Ukj} e_{ij} = \sum_{Rij, Vik, Ukj} \left(R_{ij} - \hat{R}_{ij} \right)^2 \qquad (11)$$

Algorithm 1 summarizes the prediction and recommendation steps:

Algorithm 1 : Prediction And Recommendation Steps
Input R is QoS Matrix data with high sparsity
Output $\hat{R}$ is regular data without sparsity (prediction QoS unrated)
Output services recommendation to users

1	*let $R_{U,S}$ where U is users, S is services*
2	*K= k- **Means** technique to clusters Users based on desistance*
3	*For each i $\in U$, where $U \in K$*
4	*For each j $\in U$*
5	*D=Calculation similarity Sim (U_i, U_j)*
6	*If $(D > \epsilon)$ then $\hat{v}_{i,s}$ is calculated according to Equation 3*
7	*End-for*
8	*End-for*
9	*$R_{U,S}$ decompose for tow matrices:*
10	*$V_{U,k}$ is matrix for Users-Feature, where k is latent feature*
11	*$U_{k,S}$ is matrix for Feature-Services*
12	*$\hat{R}_{U,S} \approx V_{U,k} * U_{k,S}^T b_u + b_s$*
13	*To calculate E the error rate as in the equation 11.*
14	*If E $>\epsilon$ then*
15	*Minimize the E by equation 5 to 11*
16	*Else*
17	*Return $\hat{R}_{U,S}$ & Best recommendations for the user Based on D*

5   Results and Discussion

In the data collection stage, for the sample to be consistent, the study ensured that half consisted of males and females of different ages, as shown in Fig. 7.

The data is passed to be preprocessed to clean the data and take the most appropriate sample to obtain accurate results. Figure 8 shows the data after preprocessing and different methods of collecting data. The total number of the sample was 580, distributed as follows: H1 became 144, H2 became 146, H3 became 141, and H4 became 149.

After the data preprocessing, there was a high degree of scattered data. Not all service users (patients) responded to all the questions about different aspects of the hospital's services. It was necessary to address this scattered data and prediction in the missing data.

In Fig. 9 - A, we can observe the amount of missing data for each measure at every time point. It is clear from Fig. 9 - B that the percentage of missing data is significantly lower than before processing. This was achieved by clustering users based on their preferences and the similarity between service users to find similar users and process some of the missing data.

The first stage of predicting missing services helped to predict a portion of the data and achieved excellent results in reducing the percentage of missing evaluations.

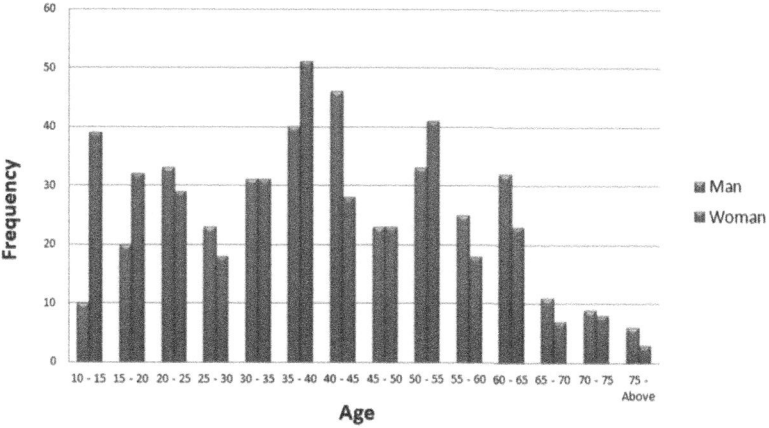

Fig. 7. Overview of data collection

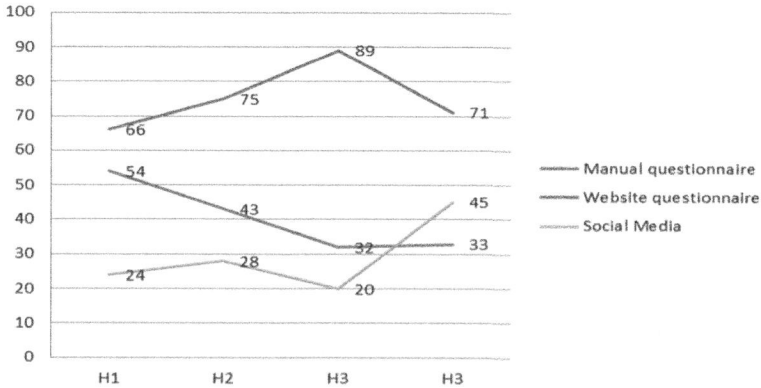

Fig. 8. The data after preprocessing

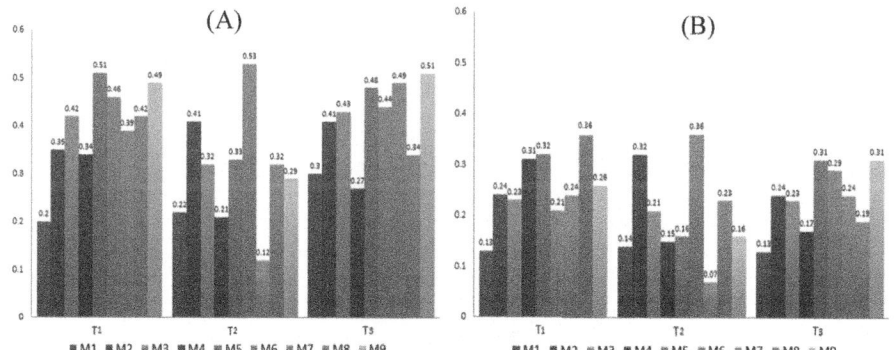

Fig. 9. A: The missing data before similarity, B: The missing data after similarity

After using the matrix factorization and decomposing the main matrix into two lower-rank matrices based on their latent features, a matrix containing high-quality data was extracted. This matrix didn't have any missing data but had a high error rate. The error rate was gradually reduced by updating the coefficients in the matrix factorization until it reached the lowest possible error rate. Table 1 shows the gradual decrease of the error after several iterations of updating the parameters in the matrix factorization, where the Accuracy (Acc), Error Rate (Err), Precision (Pre), Recall (Rec), and F1-measure (F1) were calculated in each iteration.

Table 1. The gradual decrease of the error for several iterations

No Iteration	Err (%)	Acc (%)	Pre (%)	Rec (%)	F1 (%)
Iteration 1	50.1	48.9	47.8	48.9	48.34
Iteration 2	43.2	56.8	51.5	56.8	54.02
Iteration 3	38	62	63.1	62	62.54
Iteration 4	29.7	70.3	72.1	70.3	71.18
Iteration 5	21.3	78.7	74.6	78.7	76.59
Iteration 6	17.5	82.5	83.9	82.5	83.19
Iteration 7	9.6	90.4	91.8	90.4	91.09
Iteration 8	5.2	94.6	94.3	94.6	94.44
Iteration 9	3	97	79.1	97	87.14
Iteration 10	2.5	97.5	97.8	97.5	97.64

According to Fig. 10, the proposed model outperforms traditional collaborative filtering models. The comparison was made based on where the Accuracy (Acc), Error Rate (Err), Precision (Pre), Recall (Rec), and F1-measure (F1).

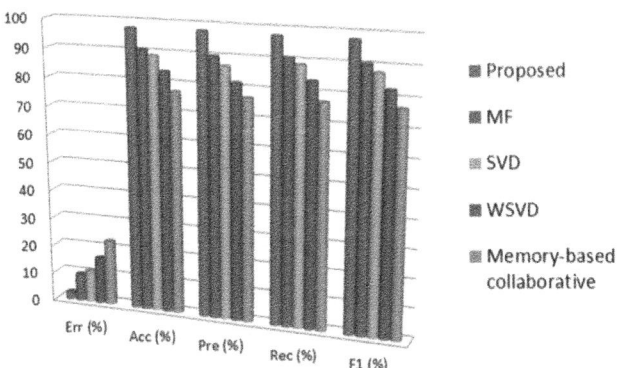

Fig. 10. The results evaluation of the proposed method against the existing method

Through the sample collected and processed and the prediction of the QoS for each hospital, Fig. 11 shows the level of services provided by hospitals according to the point of view of the service beneficiaries.

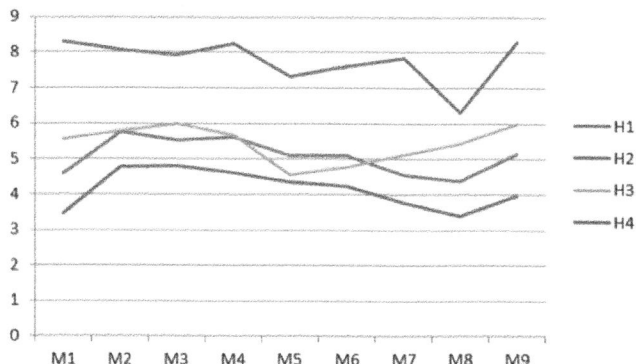

Fig. 11. The level of services provided by hospitals (H1, H2, H3, H4)

6   Conclusion

The perspective of the user is crucial in healthcare, as it provides valuable insight into the quality of services received by the patient. It also creates a competitive environment among hospitals to offer the best services and attract patients. One major challenge in this field is the scattered nature of data collection, as not all patients can evaluate all services. This study aimed to address this issue by developing techniques to predict the quality of missing services and recommendations for best services to patients. The methods used included clustering and hybrid collaborative filtering. The hybrid collaborative filtering method combined memory-based approaches, such as user k-means clustering and similarity between patients, and model-based approaches, such as matrix factorization. The sample has been collected from different geographical areas in Iraq, namely (Al-Hillah General Teaching Hospital in Babylon (H1), Al-Kafeel Hospital in Karbala (H2), Al-Yarmouk Hospital in Baghdad (H3), and Diwaniyah Women's and Children's Hospital in Diwaniyah (H4)). The model achieved a high accuracy rate of 97.5% in predicting service quality compared to observed evaluations. Additionally, the results revealed disparities in service levels and patient satisfaction.

In future work, the model can be improved by applying it to larger and more diverse samples from hospitals in various countries and geographical regions. Additionally, developing a user-friendly interface, interactive questionnaires, and indirect patient behaviour monitoring to obtain high-quality data.

References

1. Grynko, T., Shevchenko, T., Pavlov, R., Shevchenko, V., Pawliszczy, D.: The impact of collaboration strategy in the field of innovation on the effectiveness of organizational structure of healthcare institutions (2020)

2. Catherine, A.T., Towfek, S.K., Abdelhamid, A.A.: An overview of the evolution and impact of chatbots in modern healthcare services. Mesopotamian J. Artif. Intell. Healthc. **2023**, 71–75 (2023)

3. Khalsan, M., et al.: A novel fuzzy classifier model for cancer classification using gene expression data. IEEE Access (2023)

4. Zaid, A.A., et al.: The impact of Total quality management and perceived service quality on patient satisfaction and behavior intention in Palestinian healthcare organizations. Technol. Reports Kansai Univ. **62**(03), 221–232 (2020)

5. Ravikumar, R., et al.: The impact of big data quality analytics on knowledge management in healthcare institutions: lessons learned from big data's application within the healthcare sector. South East. Eur. J. Public Heal. (2023)

6. Fei, L., Lu, J., Feng, Y.: An extended best-worst multi-criteria decision-making method by belief functions and its applications in hospital service evaluation. Comput. Ind. Eng. **142**, 106355 (2020)

7. Kong, L., et al.: Time-aware missing healthcare data prediction based on ARIMA model. IEEE/ACM Trans. Comput. Biol. Bioinforma. (2022)

8. Chen, J., Wang, X., Zhao, S., Qian, F., Zhang, Y.: Deep attention user-based collaborative filtering for recommendation. Neurocomputing **383**, 57–68 (2020)

9. Liu, H., et al.: EDMF: efficient deep matrix factorization with review feature learning for industrial recommender system. IEEE Trans. Ind. Informatics **18**(7), 4361–4371 (2021)

10. Martins, G.B., Papa, J.P., Adeli, H.: Deep learning techniques for recommender systems based on collaborative filtering. Expert. Syst. **37**(6), e12647 (2020)

11. Srifi, M., Oussous, A., Ait Lahcen, A., Mouline, S.: Recommender systems based on collaborative filtering using review texts—a survey. Information **11**(6), 317 (2020)

12. Alharbe, N., Rakrouki, M.A., Aljohani, A.: A collaborative filtering recommendation algorithm based on embedding representation. Expert Syst. Appl. **215**, 119380 (2023)

13. Fareed, A., Hassan, S., Belhaouari, S.B., Halim, Z.: A collaborative filtering recommendation framework utilizing social networks. Mach. Learn. with Appl. **14**, 100495 (2023)

14. Duan, R., Jiang, C., Jain, H.K.: Combining review-based collaborative filtering and matrix factorization: A solution to rating's sparsity problem. Decis. Support. Syst. **156**, 113748 (2022)

15. Al-Neyadi, H.S., Abdallah, S., Malik, M.: Measuring patient's satisfaction of healthcare services in the UAE hospitals: using SERVQUAL. Int. J. Healthc. Manag. **11**(2), 96–105 (2018)

16. Al-Jubory, D.H., Al-Shamery, E.S.: Improving the forecasting of covid-19 cases based on embedding re-weighted and commitment features. Webology (ISSN: 1735–188X) **18**(1) (2021)

17. Bhojak, N.P., Modi, A., Patel, J.D., Patel, M.: Measuring patient satisfaction in emergency department: an empirical test using structural equation modeling. Int. J. Healthc. Manag. **16**(3), 412–426 (2023)

18. Ko, H., Lee, S., Park, Y., Choi, A.: A survey of recommendation systems: recommendation models, techniques, and application fields. Electronics **11**(1), 141 (2022)

19. Khalsan, M., et al.: A survey of machine learning approaches applied to gene expression analysis for cancer prediction. IEEE Access **10**, 27522–27534 (2022)

20. Chinnasamy, P., et al.: Health recommendation system using deep learning-based collaborative filtering. Heliyon **9**(12) (2023)

21. Shambour, Q.Y., Al-Zyoud, M.M., Hussein, A.H., Kharma, Q.M.: A doctor recommender system based on collaborative and content filtering. Int. J. Electr. Comput. Eng. **13**(1) (2023)

22. Yannam, V.R., Kumar, J., Babu, K.S., Sahoo, B.: Improving group recommendation using deep collaborative filtering approach. Int. J. Inf. Technol. **15**(3), 1489–1497 (2023)

23. Sae-Ang, A., et al.: Drug recommendation from diagnosis codes: classification vs. collaborative filtering approaches. Int. J. Environ. Res. Public Health **20**(1), 309 (2022)
24. Gonu, E., Agyei, P.M., Richard, O.K., Asare-Larbi, M.: Customer orientation, service quality and customer satisfaction interplay in the banking sector: An emerging market perspective. Cogent Bus. Manag. **10**(1), 2163797 (2023)
25. Salih Al-Shamery, E.: A fuzzy assessment model for hospitals services quality based on patient experience. Karbala Int. J. Mod. Sci. **6**(3), 10 (2020)
26. Francis, R.: Report of the Mid Staffordshire NHS Foundation Trust public inquiry: executive summary, vol. 947. The Stationery Office (2013)
27. Parasuraman, A., Zeithaml, V.A., Berry, L.L.: A conceptual model of service quality and its implications for future research. J. Mark. **49**(4), 41–50 (1985)
28. Aghamolaei, T., et al.: Service quality assessment of a referral hospital in Southern Iran with SERVQUAL technique: patients' perspective. BMC Health Serv. Res. **14**(1), 322 (2014)
29. Kalaja, R., Myshketa, R., Scalera, F.: Service quality assessment in health care sector: the case of Durres public hospital. Procedia-Social Behav. Sci. **235**, 557–565 (2016)
30. Tefera, L., Lehrman, W.G., Conway, P.: Measurement of the patient experience: clarifying facts, myths, and approaches. JAMA **315**(20), 2167–2168 (2016)
31. Aditya, P.H., Budi, I., Munajat, Q.: A comparative analysis of memory-based and model-based collaborative filtering on the implementation of recommender system for E-commerce in Indonesia: A case study PT X. In: 2016 International Conference on Advanced Computer Science and Information Systems (ICACSIS), pp. 303–308. IEEE (2016)
32. Pujahari, A., Sisodia, D.S.: Model-based collaborative filtering for recommender systems: An empirical survey. In: 2020 First International Conference on Power, Control and Computing Technologies (ICPC2T), pp. 443–447. IEEE (2020)
33. Do, M.-P.T., Nguyen, D.V., Nguyen, L.: Model-based approach for collaborative filtering. In: 6th International conference on information technology for education, pp. 217–228 (2010)
34. Mnih, A., Salakhutdinov, R.R.: Probabilistic matrix factorization. Adv. Neural Inf. Process. Syst. **20** (2007)

Security and Privacy

Advanced Text Vectorization and Deep Learning Models for Enhanced Fake News Detection on Social Media

Mustafa Abdul-Razzaq Kareem[(✉)] and Amer Abdulmajeed Abdulrahman

Deptartment of Computer Science, College of Science, University of Baghdad, Baghdad, Iraq
{mostafa.abd2201m,amer.abdulrahman}@sc.uobaghdad.edu.iq

Abstract. Within the context of addressing misinformation on social media platforms, the identification of fake news emerges as a crucial obstacle. Nowadays, organizations across many sectors are struggling to find efficient ways to detect online phoney news. Identifying false material online can be mentally stimulating, often crafted to mislead visitors. Deep learning enables algorithms for fake news detection more accurately than other machine learning. These algorithms are characterized by high accuracy and the use of neural networks that allow them to effectively detect fake news. This work outlines an approach that improves upon previous works utilizing the Truth Seeker 2023 dataset. Another part of the methodology is to use natural language processing algorithms to clean the tweets and use neural network architectures to identify subtle signs of false leads. The Multilayer Perceptron (MLP) model consist of densely connected hidden layers with specific activation functions. To convert textual information into numerical characteristics, such as Count Vectorizer and Term Frequency-Inverse Document Frequency TF-IDF, the most proficient text vectorization methods were adopted. Our model achieves an exceptional accuracy above 99% by conducting thorough experimentation and optimization, which is a significant improvement compared to previous studies' highest accuracy of 96%. We demonstrate our method's unmatched accuracy in identifying fake news reports by utilizing deep learning and the comprehensive features of the Truth Seeker 2023 dataset. Our research sets a new standard for spotting fake news. It shows how advanced technologies may reinforce social media platforms against misleading information, creating a more dependable digital environment for people worldwide.

Keywords: Fake News Detection · Machine Learning · Deep Learning · Binary Text Classification · Term Frequency-Inverse Document Frequency · Natural language processing

1 Introduction

Social media has significantly transformed the sharing and consumption of knowledge in recent years. Social media platforms like Facebook, Twitter (now X), and Instagram provide immediate access to a diverse range of news items. Although the swift dissemination of information enables worldwide contact, it has unintentionally fuelled the proliferation

© The Author(s), under exclusive license to Springer Nature Switzerland AG 2025
S. O. Al-Mamory et al. (Eds.): 3INC 2024, CCIS 2329, pp. 151–171, 2025.
https://doi.org/10.1007/978-3-031-81065-7_10

of misinformation. Multiple definitions exist for the term "Fake News." According to the Collins English Dictionary, fake news is defined as deceptive and sensational material that is not true. Originally, people used the phrase to refer to deliberately and provably untrue news items intended to deceive readers. However, it has gradually evolved to encompass any type of incorrect or misleading material disseminated through digital media [1]. This comprehensive comprehension emphasizes the difficulty of discerning and countering false information, which can closely mimic authentic news. The peril of exposure to deceptive or inaccurate information matches the ease of obtaining news via social media. This situation is especially concerning because consumers frequently consume and place trust in unconfirmed news, which can result in substantial societal damage. The intricate characteristics of counterfeit news further complicate the task of identifying it, as it closely mimics authentic news. Without intervention, the spread of false information can quickly increase, eroding the confidence of the public, disrupting democratic systems, and endangering social unity [2].

Social media has emerged as a powerful tool for disseminating both accurate information and false information. The worldwide user population of social media platforms has experienced a yearly growth rate of 9.9%, resulting in an average of 13 new users joining every second. In 2021, there were roughly 4.5 billion active social media users globally, with a notable majority among younger age groups. Approximately 90% of young people, aged 18 to 29, frequently use these platforms [1, 3].

Forecasts suggest that the worldwide social media user base will surpass six billion by 2027, continuing the current rapid expansion. In January 2023, almost 59% of the global population utilized social media, dedicating an average of 151 min per day to these platforms. This is a significant rise compared to previous years [4]. This phenomenon highlights the significant impact of social media in modern culture. All of the platforms, including Facebook, Instagram, WhatsApp, X, and so on, are highly active, with millions to billions of active customers. X, in particular, plays a vital role in the instant dissemination of information that can include truth and lies. As of mid-2021, X had 206 million daily active users, meaning that its role in disseminating information is critical [3]. The universality of social media use, especially in the youthful population, underlines the need to tackle misinformation with even more vigour. Fake news has repercussions on all fronts, as will be evidenced next, including misinformation of the public on various issues. Fake news overload has the potential and ability to influence people's thoughts, influence electoral processes, cause social unrest, and even negatively impact citizens' health. During events such as COVID-19, fake news about treatments, vaccines, and general health measures caused confusion and a hostile response from health practitioners. Similarly, the spread of fake news during the leadership contest may lead to the subversion of democratic processes and even the outcome of the respective polls. One of the consequences of not doing anything is that fake news spreads rampantly and can be devastating to individuals, organizations, and institutions, as well as the general public, so there is a need to come up with efficient ways of detecting fake news [5].

A difficult task is to identify misinformation concerning the events that have occurred recently. One of the major challenges to telling the truth about these events is the absence of a systemic understanding and recording of them. To address this problem, we have proposed a novel approach that combines conventional Machine Learning concepts with state-of-the-art Deep Learning techniques. To extract features, this study employs Term Frequency-Inverse Document Frequency (TF-IDF) and a Deep Neural Network (DNN) with several fully connected layers and Leaky ReLU activation functions. The goal of this method is to increase the level of identification in cases where it is either impossible or desirable to gather a great deal of information quickly.

A constraint of inherent nature highly relevant to the detection of false information is the absence of a full dataset that adequately covers the many fields with a high incidence of false news. Given the vast array of cases, languages, and presentation modes used in producing false news, it is challenging to set adherence standards for identifying misleading material. The Canadian Institute for Cybersecurity created the Truth-Seeker dataset to address this issue [6], This is a huge dataset that contains more than 134,000 labels from 2009 to 2022, making it a close representation of real-life data.

The framework adopted in this study involves complex preprocessing and state-of-the-art feature extraction techniques in order to capture the nuances of misleading information. To overcome the various and ever-changing aspects of false information, techniques like natural language processing and deep learning models are included in our approach. Such integrations are designed for improving the detection reliability and the means of its implementation in various situations.

The work's originality lies in the development of a new methodology that integrates existing methodologies to improve previous studies' outcomes. The newly created 'The Truth-Seeker' dataset and proposed approach to integrating TF-IDF and deep neural networks, as well as modifications to the preprocessing pipeline, improve its performance in detecting fake news. These findings not only enhance the performance measures compared to previous works on the same dataset but also significantly enrich the scientific study of fake news identification. Presented below is a concise overview of the research framework:

- This study begins with a review of the literature on identifying fake information and its challenges.
- The second section comprehensively explains the investigation's technique, including the data preprocessing procedures and models employed.
- The third section showcases the results of our research and delves into their implications.
- The fourth section concludes the research by summarizing our findings and suggesting directions for further investigation.

2   Related Work

Researchers have suggested several ways to detect and expose social media misinformation. We'll examine some of these works:

Dadkhah et al. [6] curated novel datasets, dubbed "Truth-Seeker," comprising over 180,000 labelled tweets from 2009 to 2022. These labels were meticulously assigned through a classification process using Amazon Mechanical Turk, resulting in two categorization schemes: one with five labels and another with three. Rigorous validation stages were employed to ensure the dataset's accuracy as a ground-truth standard. Following this, the author conducted an extensive evaluation utilizing a variety of machine learning and deep learning algorithms, including adaptations of BERT-based models and six distinct machine learning models (DT, RF, KNN, BN, AB, and LR). The goal was to determine which versions yielded the most favourable outcome metrics in detecting genuine and false tweets across both categorization schemes. Results revealed that the RF algorithm attained the utmost level of accuracy at 70%, while the AdaBoost algorithm yielded the lowest accuracy rate of 59%. Among the deep learning models, the BERTWEET model attained the highest accuracy of 96%. However, it's important to note that the "unknown" category within the dataset may introduce potential misrepresentations in tweet classifications.

This study by Sharrab et al. [7] aims to improve text data forensics in social media by utilizing the "CIC Truth Seeker Dataset 2023" and harnessing deep neural networks' analytical skills. The researchers examined the appropriateness of Deep Neural Networks, specifically Long Short-Term Memory and Feed-forward Neural Networks, for identifying questionable content. Both models achieved a 96% precision rate in the initial evaluations.

Dirjen et al. [8] introduced a hoax detection method that relies on feed-forward and backpropagation neural networks. They employed two vectorization techniques during the development process: TF-IDF and Word2Vec. They specifically engineered the model to autonomously acquire characteristics to distinguish between genuine and deceptive news articles. The neural network incorporates multiple hidden layers to achieve this. Twitter data is used in this study. A total of 50,646 tweets were collected, with 25,021 classified as hoaxes and 25,624 classified as non-hoaxes. TF-IDF gave the neural network 78.76% accuracy.

Abdulrahman and Baykara [9] utilized four conventional techniques to obtain text characteristics: TF-IDF, Count Vector, character level vector, and N-Gram vector. Additionally, ten distinct classifiers from machine and deep learning were employed to classify the fake news dataset. The findings have shown that it is possible to categorize fabricated news articles with written content, specifically by utilizing CNN. By using various classifiers, this study achieved 81–100% accuracy.

R. K. Kaliyar. [10] recommend a Kaggle dataset with real and fake news. They use ML, NLP, and deep learning to process the dataset. They also studied feature extraction benefits. TF-IDF and n-gram features were retrieved and added to our model. They also explored how word embedding and word2vec affect DNNs. The Naive Bayes classifier was 90% accurate.

Ajao et al. [11] present a framework that utilizes a combination of convolutional neural networks and long-short-term recurrent neural network models to identify and categorize fake news messages in a Twitter posts dataset where the researchers labelled approximately 5,800 tweets as either rumour or non-rumour, concentrating on five specific rumour stories in the dataset. Utilizing this deep learning methodology results in an accuracy rate of 82%.

Sachithanandam et al. [12] aim to categorize the reviews of specific restaurants on the Internet using various machine and deep learning methods and summarize the results. The findings demonstrate that deep learning techniques are significantly more effective in detecting fraudulent reviews. To be more precise, the integration of BERT and a 4-layered Feed Forward network resulted in a detection accuracy of 96% for identifying fake reviews. The authors employ the "restaurant review" dataset, initially developed by a group of students to study false review identification, which consists of 260 samples that are evenly distributed between fake and authentic evaluations.

Buzea et al. [13] compare a convolutional neural network, a recurrent neural network with long short-term memory and gated recurrent unit cells, and a Bidirectional Encoder Representations from the Transformers (BERT) model, specifically RoBERT, which is a pre-trained Romanian BERT model. Deep learning architectures are contrasted with the outcomes obtained from two traditional classification algorithms: Naïve Bayes and Support Vector Machine. Their proposed methodology is based on a Romanian news corpus of 25,841 authentic news articles and 13,064 fabricated news articles. The convolutional neural network achieved the highest result, almost 98.20%, exceeding standard categorization and BERT models.

The article by Ajao et al. [14] gathers 1356 news instances from diverse people through Twitter and media sites like PolitiFact. It then generates multiple datasets for both genuine and fabricated news stories. They have compared advanced techniques, which include convolutional neural networks, long short-term memory ensemble methods, as well as attention processes. Out of all the architectures we analyzed, the CNN architecture had the lowest level of accuracy. With the comparison of the simple CNN architecture, it can be seen that LSTM and bidirectional LSTM architecture showed significantly better performance. An ensemble network comprising a CNN, bidirectional LSTM, and attention mechanism achieved the best accuracy of 88.78%.

This work [15] aims to address the problem of identifying a fake news story through the use of deep learning techniques. Meaning, all the feedforward network architectures CNN and LSTM were trained using datasets that encompassed the complete text and the headline text of news articles. Both the models are effective for this task, but the CNN model provides a phenomenal accuracy of 97% on complete text data and a good accuracy of 93% on title texts.

This system [16] introduces data preparation approach for improving the machine learning method used to identify fake news by focusing on the missing values problem. Most of the time, they employ imputation techniques that include the most frequently occurring value for a categorical variable and, for a numerical one, the mean of the column. Feature extraction is carried out using TF-IDF vectorization in an attempt to enhance the relevancy of information retrieved from the networks. When this preprocessing technique is used with the MLP classifier, the results obtained are high, and it stands way above the baseline models to the tune of 15% or more.

3 Advanced Machine Learning

Machine learning itself can be further divided into the comparatively narrower branch called deep learning DL which is almost exclusively associated with Artificial Neural Networks ANNs. Dechter adopted the ML in 1986 while Aizenberg et al. adopted the ANN in 2000. Since then, DL has invented many architectures, such as, deep neural networks, deep belief networks, recurrent and convolutional neural networks, etc. Many spheres use (DL) extensively; in view of effectiveness, it often surpasses the traditional ML algorithms and experts. Deep Neural Network (DNN) is a type of Artificial Neural

Network (ANN) which is composed of many layers; where the output of one layer serves as the input of another layer. We have input layer, output layer, and there are several hidden layers in between and all those layers use the same activation function. As DL utilizes the feature selection in which algorithms aim to recover the necessary features from an input, hence the importance of the deep learning technology, to enhance the capability of analyzing big data and the advancement of AI technology [17].

4   A Proposed Approach

This paper highlights a robust model for distinguishing the news broadcasts as either erroneous or truthful with the help of a combination of NLP approaches embedded with a DNN model. The methodology has five primary phases: Data Description, Data Cleaning, Data Transformation and Feature Selection, Model Building, and Prediction. Figure 1 depicts these stages in order.

1. Dataset

The study uses Truth-Seeker Dataset [6], consisting of a large collection of Twitter news items. The research employs this dataset that consists of samples of real and fake news articles labelled in advance.

2. Data preprocessing:

The study used Truth-Seeker dataset, with over 134,000 tweets labelled and collected between 2009 and 2022. The dataset required pre-processing in order to rid it of noise and other features that are irrelevant in a study of this sort and the text data went through tokenization, stop word removal, stemming, and normalization.

3. Data Splitting

The dataset of the study was split into training, validation, and a hold out or testing set. In more detail, it was decided to allocate 70% of data for training, and the rest, 30%, was used for testing the results. In order to prevent other sets from influencing the testing result, the holdout set was constantly kept apart from the training and validation set; also, the 5 folds cross validation technique was applied in the training stage. The method involves a division of the training data into five sets where the model is successively trained with four sets and validated with the fifth set. Applying this method ensures that such performance is not a result of random training and testing and that it is fairly consistent regardless of the segment chosen from the overall data.

4. Holdout Dataset

The holdout dataset, which makes 30% of the total sample, consists of nearly 40,200 items. This dataset was only used to for testing of the model and hence was not utilized for either training or tuning of the specific model parameters. The generalizing capability of the model was further assessed using another set of measures including accuracy, precision, recall and F1 score on this dataset.

1. Feature Extraction

Feature extraction is the process of converting the preprocessed text into numerical form which is more understandable for the model. This study utilizes two fundamental methodologies:

- The process of feature extraction entails transforming the preprocessed text into a numerical format that the model can comprehend and process. This study utilizes two fundamental methodologies:
- Count Vectorizer: Transforms the text into a matrix where each row represents a document and each column represents the count of a specific token.
- Term Frequency-Inverse Document Frequency (TF-IDF) is a technique that adjusts the raw frequency of words by accounting for their inverse document frequency. This approach assigns greater emphasis to keywords that are unique or different within the dataset.
- **The model's architecture:**

  The proposed model is a deep neural network built with Keras and consists of:

- Input Layer: Receives the TF-IDF features with a dimension of 40,511.
- Hidden Layers: Nine fully connected layers with Leaky ReLU activation functions.
- Output Layer: A single unit with a sigmoid activation function for binary classification.
- Hyperparameters:

  - Learning Rate: 0.001
  - Batch Size: 64
  - Epochs: 100
  - Optimizer: Adam with a learning rate of 0.001

- **Experimental Procedure**
- Data Splitting: The dataset is split into training and testing sets using a 70/30 ratio.
- Training: The model is trained on the training set with the specified hyperparameters, using binary cross-entropy as the loss function and accuracy as the evaluation metric.
- Evaluation: The model's performance is evaluated on the testing set. Metrics reported include:

  - Accuracy: The proportion of correctly classified instances.
  - Precision, Recall, F1-Score: Computed using classification _ report.
  - Confusion Matrix: Visualized using matplotlib to assess the model's classification performance.

- **tools and libraries**
  The experiments are conducted using Python in conjunction with the following libraries:

  - Pandas/Numpy: For data manipulation and numerical operations.
  - NLTK: For text processing and stop words removal.
  - Scikit-Learn: For vectorization, model evaluation, and data splitting.

- Keras/TensorFlow: For building and training the neural network.
- Matplotlib: For visualization of the confusion matrix.

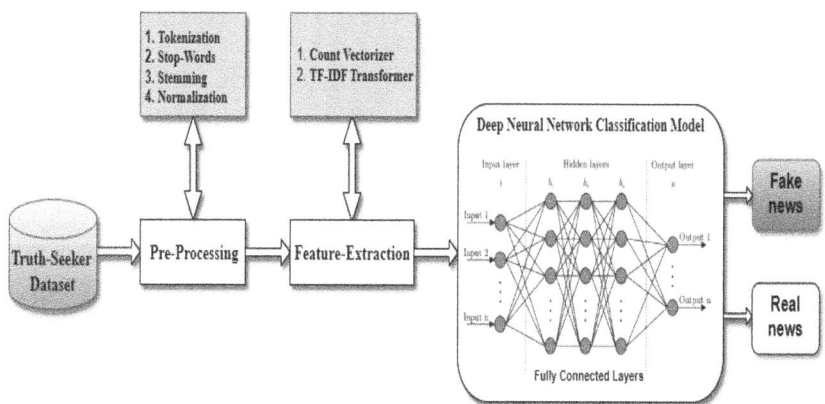

Fig. 1. Proposed Pipeline for Classifying News.

4.1 Dataset Description

This study is mainly based on a thorough and inclusive dataset; to achieve this, the Truth-Seeker Dataset 2023 [6] was utilized; it is a standardized dataset developed to examine the integrity of news items shared on social media platforms. With almost 134,000 categorized tweets, this dataset is one of the largest in its category. The dataset underwent a meticulous evaluation process, including a three-factor active learning verification method that involved 456 distinct and highly skilled Amazon Mechanical Turk workers to annotate each tweet. Furthermore, the dataset contains three additional social media metrics: the bot score, credibility score, and impact score, which aid in examining Twitter users' patterns and characteristics. The Truth-Seeker dataset was generated by extracting data from tweets related to genuine and deceptive news sourced from the PolitiFact dataset in English. Amazon Mechanical Turk primarily serves as the primary method for crowdsourcing to gather consensus on the veracity of a tweet. As a result, a highly comprehensive ground truth database has been created to spot bogus news on the X platform [7].

4.2 Preprocessing Stage

Data preparation can be defined as the systematic extraction of meaningful insights from unstructured textual data. This data frequently includes a variety of contaminants, such as HTML elements, individual characters, ads, non-English characters, numerical numbers, or apostrophes [18] transforming textual data into human language is extremely difficult and falls under NLP. AI's NLP branch focuses on computer-human language interaction

[19]. Its fundamental purpose is to help machines understand, interpret, and produce meaningful human language. Multiple approaches exist to transform disorganized data into structured data suitable for machine processing. This work utilized fundamental Natural Language Processing (NLP) techniques, including tokenization, stop word removal, stemming, and normalization algorithms, to purify the dataset. Structured and relevant content can increase machine learning algorithms' efficiency and comprehensibility [9, 20].

4.2.1 Stemming

Stemming is the procedure of eliminating affixes, prefixes, suffixes, and prepositions to obtain the fundamental form of words. Through the indexing procedure, finding the essential word from the term allows for determining the frequency of the term's occurrence in each document. For instance, stemming reduces the terms "used," "uses," and "useful" to their base word "use" [21].The stemming algorithm varies between different languages. This paper utilized the Port Stemmer algorithm because of its exceptional accuracy. Martin Porter is the creator of the widely employed Porter stemmer, a popular algorithm for stemming.

4.2.2 Stop Word Filtering

The stop words in the English language are used to fill up the frame of the sentences by means of which rarely the intent information of a person can be conveyed. Therefore, when it comes to text analysis, the words like: and, the, is, in, among others, are useless. Therefore, in the trials, it was considered that it is necessary to remove stop words in order to minimize their influence and enhance objects' identification. Thus, excluding those terms, we can focus on the bigger constituents of a text, which increases the effectiveness of our text analysis and categorization techniques. For instance, if we are to apply stop words on the statement "The cat is on the mat," the outcome would be "cat mat," which retains the core meaning while stripping off the words which are not significant at all. Stripping out such friendly flab means that only the primary characteristics can be taught to the models, which must increase the ability of the algorithm to analyze the real patterns in the dataset. This stage is important on building more accurate and reliable machine learning models on a dynamic training dataset [22].

4.2.3 Normalization

The formalization of text removes dates, whitespaces, abbreviations, acronyms, and diacritics and standardizes classification criteria. Normalization includes converting the text to lower case, stripping out the symbols, handling URLs and mentions, and deleting spaces. It is essential to preprocess the data and get rid of the components that are not meaningful before analyzing and constructing classifiers [23]. Applying this cleaning procedure enhances the quality of data. The first Data purification benefits the initial functions of natural language processing, as it enhances the textual data and prevents statistical analysis. Preprocessing techniques eliminate irrelevant features and leave only those terms that have some significance [24].

4.2.4 Tokenization

This is a process of dividing text into tokens, which are the individual workable elements of a text. Machine learning models can then analyze the text using its most important features. In terms of cleaning and preprocessing the tokens, excluding stop words and applying stemming is quite useful. The goal is to segment the text into words as much as possible, ensuring precision in the subsequent stages. One of the initial steps of text preprocessing is tokenization, a set of actions that help prepare the raw text for further analysis and analytical modelling. The foremost method of tokenization is to segment a text into meaningful pieces. Tokens tag and indicate these components. One of them is dividing a large message into words or phrases. The primary function can determine how to classify the input text into tokens based on our criteria [25].

4.3 Feature Extraction

Reducing a large number of variables into a wide range of options requires a significant amount of computer power and memory. Moreover, classification algorithms may provide a high capacity for increasing the accuracy of classification among new samples of the training data while failing to generalize new samples. In order to resolve these issues, we use the feature extraction method at the system design level. Feature extraction relates to how the original variables are grouped together in order to lower the dimensionality of the data but keep as much of the fundamental information about it as possible. Its option is beneficial because it eliminates overfitting, resulting in a simpler model that also increases the model's computational efficiency and performance. Feature extraction converts the data into an easier, more understandable, and more recognizable format, which improves model training and the ability to recognize previously unseen data [26]. For feature extraction in the context of text processing, the Count Vectorizer and Term Frequency-Inverse Document Frequency TF-IDF Transformer are used in this study. The Count Vectorizer transforms text documents into a matrix that indicates the frequency of each word in the documents. Then the TF-IDF Transformer, which we have also discussed, converts this matrix to a TF-IDF representation, showing how important the particular word is in the whole database. The subsequent section focuses on the description of the Count Vectorizer and TF-IDF transformer.

Count Vectorizer: Enumerate Text processing uses a vectorizer, one of the most important operations, which transforms a set of documents into a matrix containing the frequency of each word, also known as the "bag of words". The Count Vectorizer function estimates the frequency of a word in the given document and builds a vector with a size equal to the number of words in the vocabulary. When a word appears in a document, the vector denotes its position as 1. For instance, when a word appears repeatedly in a document, its frequency level increases. Additionally, there are new words that the dictionary automatically means when it does not already contain them [27].

Term Frequency-Inverse Document Frequency (TF-IDF): TF-IDF is a usual method for extracting features from the text data. TF-IDF is an effective machine learning tool because it can measure the value of the terms in the text relative to a collection of documents, where compressed data must be relevant and accurate. This study used the

TF-IDF vectorizer to measure word components based on the scores received. Recall that the Frequency found the quantity of how often a term was used in the document, while the Inverse Document Frequency reduces the importance of pervasive words. TF-IDF quantifies the importance and curiosity of the words. The process involves tokenizing the entire document, acquiring the vocabulary, calculating the inverse document frequency weightings, and enabling the encoding of new documents [28]. TF-IDF assigns values to words using the following formula [29]:

$$\mathbf{Tf(t, d)} = \frac{\textbf{term t count in d}}{\textbf{count of term } \mathbf{T_d}} \tag{1}$$

$$\mathbf{IDf(i)} = \log_2 \frac{N}{N_i} \tag{2}$$

$$\mathbf{TF-IDF} = \mathbf{TF_i} * \left(\mathbf{log_2}\left(\frac{N}{N_i}\right)\right) \tag{3}$$

where TF stands for term frequency, t represents a specific term, and d refers to a document.

t count in document d: The number of times the term appears in the document d.
Total term count in document d: The total number of words or terms.
N represents the overall quantity of papers inside a collection of documents.
Ni represents the frequency at which the word "I" appears inside a specific set of publications.

Using Count Vectorizer and TF-IDF Transformer provides a concise yet comprehensive approach for extracting characteristics from textual input. The Count Vectorizer method records the occurrence rate of terms within documents, whereas the TF-IDF Transformer method evaluates their importance throughout the entire dataset. This combination achieves a compromise between preserving crucial information and reducing dimensionality, thereby improving the performance and generalization ability of the text categorization model and frequently enhancing the performance of machine learning models when applied to textual data, Figs. 2 and 3 detail the count vectorizer and TF-IDF operations [30].

5 Building Proposed Model

The DNNs classification model is constructed using the Keras Sequential API, allowing for the sequential stacking of layers. The neural network architecture consisted of 11 dense (ultimately linked) layers; each neuron in a layer is coupled to every neuron in the previous layer. The dataset was divided into 70% training and 30% testing sets. The model underwent 100 training rounds, known as epochs, with a batch size of 64. It utilized stochastic gradient descent optimization with the Adam optimizer. This process enables the model to understand the underlying patterns and relationships in the training data.

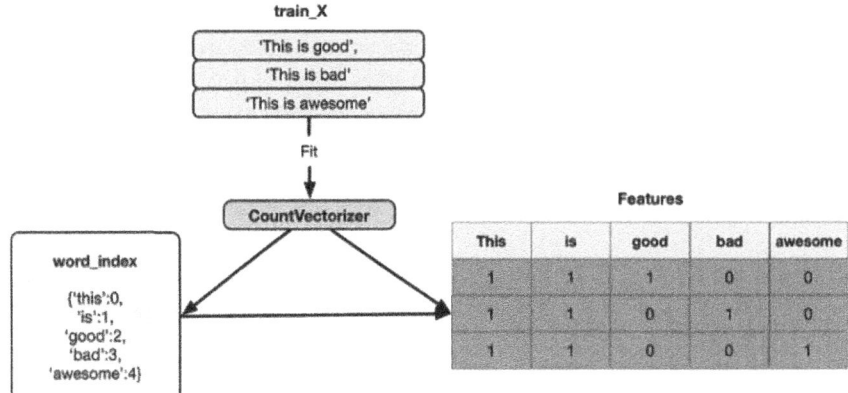

Fig. 2. Count vectorizer work.

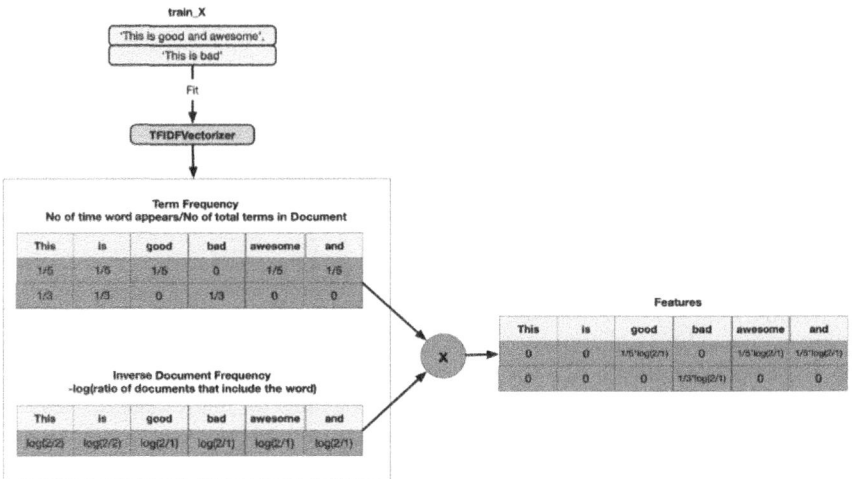

Fig. 3. Performing TF-IDF calculations.

5.1   Proposed Neural Network Architecture

The neural network architecture comprises eleven levels, including an input layer, nine hidden layers, and an output layer. The dense layers analyze the input data and extract features. In contrast, the Leaky ReLU activation layers guarantee that the gradient flows effectively and introduces non-linearity, hence improving the ability of the network to learn intricate patterns and make precise predictions.

The architecture commences with an input layer that handles the TF-IDF matrix derived from the tweets in the Truth-Seeker dataset [6]. Each of the 40,511 input dimensions corresponds to a word feature. The input layer utilizes the rectified linear unit (ReLU) activation function to incorporate non-linearity and facilitate feature translation.

After the input layer, we apply the Leaky ReLU activation function with a slope of 0.3 after every dense layer. This helps to handle inactive neurons, enhance pattern identification, ensure efficient gradient propagation, and reduce the occurrence of the vanishing gradient problem. The hidden layers are organized in the following manner:

- The first hidden layer has 32 ReLU-activated neurons, followed by a Leaky ReLU layer.
- The next concealed layer with 32 neurons with ReLU, followed by a Leaky ReLU layer.
- The third hidden layer has 64 ReLU-activated neurons, followed by a Leaky ReLU layer.
- The fourth hidden layer with 64 ReLU-activated neurons, A Leaky ReLU layer follows.
- The main equation for all hidden layers is:

For every hidden layer i (where $i = 1, 2, ...,11$):

$$h_i = \text{Leaky ReLU } (\text{ReLU}(W_i \cdot h_{i-1} + b_i)) \tag{4}$$

h_{i-1} Is the preceding layer output (or the input x if $i = 1$).
W_i Represents the weight matrix for the i-th layer.
bias vector b_i Represents the bias for the i-th layer.

$$\text{ReLU}(z) = \max(0, z) \tag{5}$$

$$\text{Leaky ReLU}(z) = \begin{cases} \alpha z \text{ if } z < 0 \\ z \quad \text{ if } z \geq 0 \end{cases} \tag{6}$$

α is a small constant that determines the negative slope for the z values. The α value is set to 0.3.

The activation function gets input **z**. Multiplying each input by weight and adding the bias term yields the neural network variable z. as seen in Fig. 5. A neuron is mathematically:

$$z = \sum_{i=1}^{m} (x_i \cdot w_i) + b \tag{7}$$

where **z** is the pre-activation value, while x_i Is neuron input. w_i The weights match the input features. **b** denotes the bias equation. **m** is the input feature count.

Finally, the sigmoid function activates a single neuron in the output layer. This neuron produces a value ranging from 0 to 1, which indicates the probability of a tweet being false (closer to 1) or true (near 0), as shown in the following equation.

$$y = \sigma(W_{out} \cdot h_{11} + b_{out}) \tag{8}$$

where W_{out} refers to the weight matrix used in the output layer

b_{out} is the bias vector for the output layer.
σ is the sigmoid function denoting with the following equation:

$$\sigma(z) = \frac{1}{1 + e^{-z}} \tag{9}$$

where $\sigma(z)$: Output of the Sigmoid function, between 0 and 1.

z: The input to the Sigmoid function, it is usually calculated using Eq. 7.
e: Euler's number is about 2.71828.

Every model layer performs data processing and transformation, allowing it to differentiate between tweets containing fake news and those containing actual news. During the training process, the model fine-tunes its parameters to decrease the inaccuracy of its predictions and optimize its performance in classifying data. Figure 4 depicts the structure of the hidden layers.

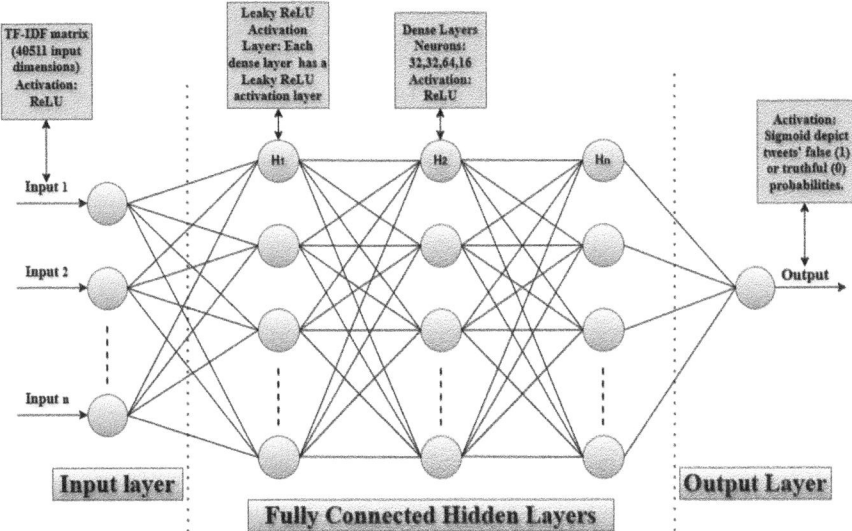

Fig. 4. Model architecture.

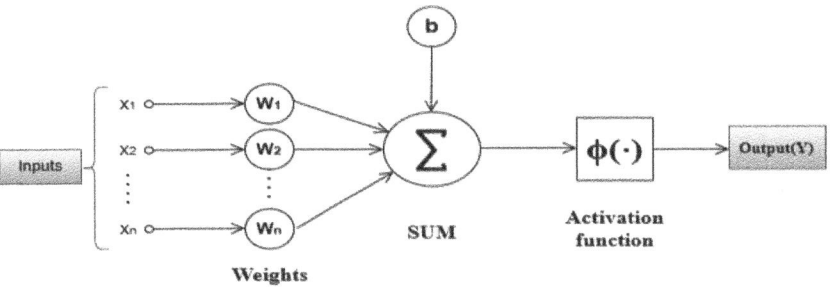

Fig. 5. Functioning of a single neuron.

5.2   Compilation and Training of the Model

With a learning rate of 0.001, the Adam optimizer compiled the model using binary cross-entropy as the loss function. This loss function selection is suitable for jobs involving binary classification. Each of the 100 epochs, or training cycles, processed 64 data points. To avoid overfitting, we tested model performance and optimized parameters using the validation set during training.

5.3   Evaluation Metrics of the Classification Model's Performance.

The present study utilized four measures in order to evaluate the progress of categorization performance. Accuracy, recall, F1-measure, and precision are frequently used metrics in the field of text classification. Dimensions were derived using the confusion matrix, which is a crucial resource for evaluating binary classification models [31].The confusion matrix graphically represents the anticipated class in the rows and the true class in the respective columns. The present study categorizes true news as positive, and fraudulent news as negative. Thus, True Positives (TP) are news items that are correctly identified as true. False Positives (FP) refer to cases when historically inaccurate news is erroneously classified as true. True Negatives (TN) refer to instances when news materials that are truly false are accurately identified as false. False Negatives (FN) is defined as the erroneous prediction that genuine news is false. These metrics, obtained from the confusion matrix, are essential for assessing the model's performance and comprehending its capacity to accurately categorize and distinguish between authentic and fabricated news pieces [32], as outlined below:

5.3.1   Precision

Also known as positive predictive value, is the ratio of accurately identified positive tweets to the number of optimistic predictions [33] The Following equation determines:

$$Precision = \frac{TP}{TP + FP} \qquad (10)$$

5.3.2   Recall

Classifier analysis measures the model's ability to identify all positive cases in the dataset using recall, also known as sensitivity or actual positive rate. Previously, it referred to the accuracy of the system's input classification [34]. It computes using the formula:

$$Recall = \frac{TP}{TP + FN} \qquad (11)$$

5.3.3   F1 Score

Serves as a metric to assess a classification model's performance; it is the harmonic mean of recall and Precision. It determines each classifier's ultimate performance measure value [35] We can calculate the F1 score using the following formula:

$$F1 = 2 \cdot \frac{\textbf{\textit{Precision}} \times \textbf{\textit{Recall}}}{\textbf{\textit{Precision}} + \textbf{\textit{Recall}}} \tag{12}$$

5.3.4 Accuracy

Is defined as the ratio of the total number of predictions made to the number of correct predictions (which includes both true positives and true negatives) [36]. To determine the accuracy, we can use the following formula:

$$Accuracy = \frac{\textbf{\textit{Correct predictions}}}{\textbf{\textit{All predication}}} \tag{13}$$

6 Result and Discussion

In this work, a new Deep Neural Network (DNN) model is introduced, designed exclusively for the purpose of classifying textual data. The primary goal of this model is to effectively identify false news using the Truth-Seeker dataset. This dataset comprises more than 134,000 annotated tweets gathered from 2009 to 2022, classified into two categories: genuine and fraudulent. The objective is to thoroughly assess the model's performance on previously unseen data. The proposed model consists of eleven layers, all of which are connected and linked to each other through feedforward layer connections. This architecture maintains a relatively small mode, allowing for the capture of complex patterns in the data. The training of the model was done for a hundred epochs with batch size equated to 64 and used the Adam optimizer that adjusts the learning rate during training. The high agreement between the training loss equal to 0.0025 and validation loss equal to 0.0024 demonstrated a reasonable sensitivity to overfitting, showing that the model would prove adept at dealing with new data.

The performance of the model was assessed with the classic measures of accuracy, precision, recall, and F1 values. Table 1 reveals that the DNN model achieved an impressive 99% in all R, A, P, and F1 measures for both classes, demonstrating its balance and precision in classification. The aforementioned result has further highlighted the effectiveness of the structures and preprocessing methodologies in handling the challenges posed by textual data categorization.

For the purpose of further strengthening and confidence in the model, a methodical 5-fold cross validation was used. The dataset was split into five such sets, out of which the model was trained on four sets and tested on the fifth set. The above stated procedure was repeated for each fold thereby providing a comprehensive result that minimizes bias and increases the credibility of the results. The results of cross validation are presented in Table 2 where we can see that overall accuracy, precision, recall, and F1 score stand and have the level of 99% for all the folds. The consistency observed is evidence that its generalization capability is excellent and remains active throughout parts of the given dataset.

Table 1. Model Classification Performance.

Evaluation Metrics	Class 1 (False)	Class 0 (True)	Overall
Precision	99%	99%	99%
Recall	99%	99%	99%
F1-Score	99%	99%	99%
Accuracy	-	-	99%

Table 2. 5-Fold Cross-Validation Results.

Fold	Accuracy (%)	Precision (%)	Recall (%)	F1-Score (%)
Fold 1	99	99	99	99
Fold 2	99	99	99	99
Fold 3	99	99	99	99
Fold 4	99	99	99	99
Fold 5	99	99	99	99
Average	**99**	**99**	**99**	**99**

Table 3. Model Confusion Matrix

Actual\Predicted	True (0)	Fake (1)
True (0)	20504	26
Fake (1)	15	19715

Table 3 contains the confusion matrix which can explain more about the model such as ability to classify between real and fake labels.

According to Table 3, the False Positive and False Negative values are very low; the model has just 26 wrong classifications of positive instances and 15 wrong classifications of negative instances out of a dataset over 40,000 in size. The enhanced degree of accuracy displayed in the model goes a long way in supporting its ability to distinguish between correct and incorrect data.

A comparative analysis was conducted to assess the efficacy of our proposed model by comparing it to two recent studies that also used the Truth-Seeker dataset: one published by Sharrab et al. and the other published by Dadkhah et al.

Sharrab et al. [7]. Investigated the effectiveness of Deep Neural Networks, specifically Long Short-Term Memory (LSTM) and Feed Forward Neural Networks (FFNN), in categorizing textual material into multiple groups. Their analysis then determined a precision rate of 96% and a model accuracy of 96%. Also, Dadkhah et al. [6]. Used standard non-generative machine-learning methods and BERT-based models on the Truth-Seeker set. The BERTWEET model had the best accuracy, at 96%.

Figure 6 provides a graphic comparison between the results of these investigations and our proposed deep neural network (DNN) model. The findings of the study show that overall, for all the evaluation metrics, namely precision, recall, F1-score, and accuracy, the model has been enhanced by a whopping 99% improvement. Although the 3% increase may appear small, it corresponds to a significant improvement in the realm of classification jobs, especially considering the intricate and nuanced nature of the textual material under analysis.

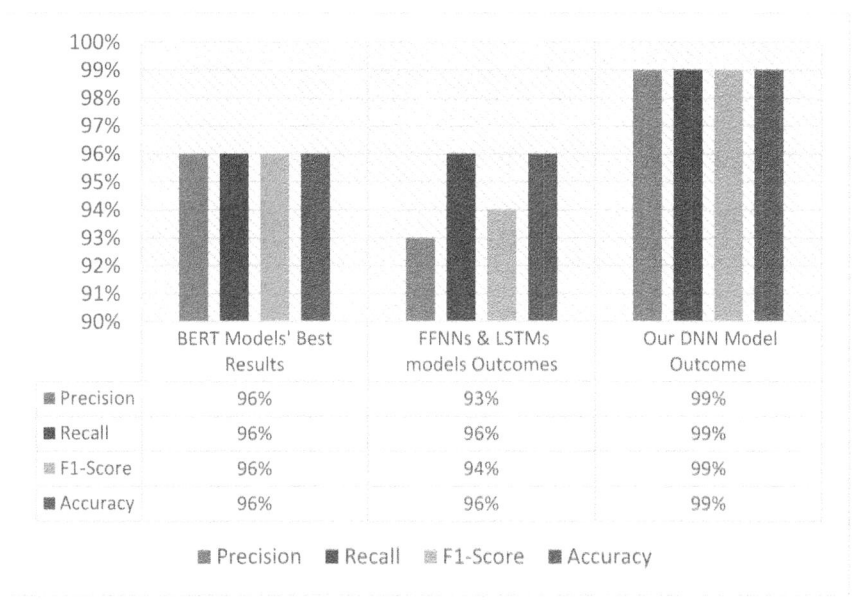

Fig. 6. Comparison with Two Studies on the Truth-Seeker Dataset.

The bar chart in Fig. 6 clearly demonstrates the exceptional performance of our Deep Neural Network (DNN) model in comparison to the models employed in the cited studies. Although Sharrab et al. and Dadkhah et al. both had impressive outcomes, notably with precision and accuracy figures reaching as high as 96%, our model's unwavering 99% performance across all measures underscores its resilience and dependability. The significant enhancement in precision and recall is particularly remarkable, as it demonstrates the improved capability of our model to correctly detect both true and false occurrences with a reduced number of errors.

7   Conclusion

This study showcases the efficacy of sophisticated techniques in building a Deep Neural Network (DNN) model for binary classification tasks, particularly in identifying fraudulent news on social media. By applying the dataset called Truth-seeker, which is one of the most extensive benchmark datasets in the field, we were able to enhance the model's ability to detect more complex patterns and provide highly accurate predictions. The data has been compiled by the Canadian Institute for Cybersecurity and contains over 180,000 labels ranging from 2009 to 2022. It has also been verified rigorously through an active learning process based on three factors. In preliminary investigations featuring this data, the best achieved accuracy was at 96%. One of them was done by the author of this dataset who used several modifications of BERT in his experiment. In another study, two models were used, which are FFNN and LSTM. In comparison with the others, our model achieved a remarkably high overall accuracy of 99% for this dataset, thus setting the new benchmark for the methodology proposed in this study.

Its results can be traced back to the accuracy which the model possesses, hailing from its precisely created 11 layers neuron network aiming at distinguishing between fabricated news and real news. By applying tokenization, stop word removal, stemming and normalization and applying feature extraction with Count Vectorizer and TF-IDF, the input data was kept clean and possessed meaningful insights. In case of the Truth-seeker dataset, the careful operation to preprocess the data, careful adjustment of the hyperparameters, and careful addition of statistical cues all helped to increase the performance of the network, which was even better than the best predecessors.

The results clearly show that careful feature selection, feature extraction algorithms, and neural network design are necessary for achieving meaningful results in binary classification tasks. Future studies can apply these approaches to virtually any binary classification problem. The concepts laid out in this research are generalizable to various types of data and situations.

Despite the approach's success, there have been instances mistakenly classifying authentic news as false, and vice versa. These events suggest that further research is required in some subjects. To avoid such errors, more research should be done to review other feature extraction methods, enhanced model structure and design, or better machine learning algorithms. Furthermore, it is important to fine-tune these approaches and analyze their adaptability to various datasets. This is important in the sense that the model should work and be flexible in many scenarios, hence enhancing its usefulness in a host of classification scenarios.

References

1. Aïmeur, E., Amri, S., Brassard, G.: Fake news, disinformation and misinformation in social media: a review. Soc. Netw. Anal. Min. (2023). https://doi.org/10.1007/s13278-023-01028-5
2. Ozbay, F.A., Alatas, B.: Fake news detection within online social media using supervised artificial intelligence algorithms. Phys. A: Stat. Mech. Appl. **540**, 123174 (2020). https://doi.org/10.1016/j.physa.2019.123174
3. Koul, Y., Mamgain, K., Gupta, A.: Lifetime of tweets: a statistical analysis. Soc. Netw. Anal. Min. (2022). https://doi.org/10.1007/s13278-022-00926-4
4. Stacy, J.D.: Most popular social networks worldwide as of October 2023, ranked by number of monthly active users. https://www.statista.com/statistics/272014/global-social-networks-ranked-by-number-of-users/
5. Rabani, S.T., Khan, Q.R., Ud Din Khanday, A.M.: Detection of suicidal ideation on Twitter using machine learning & ensemble approaches. Baghdad Sci. J. **17**(4), 1328–1339 (2020). https://doi.org/10.21123/bsj.2020.17.4.1328

6. Dadkhah, C., et al.: TruthSeeker: The Largest Social Media Ground-Truth Dataset Truth-Seeker: The Largest Social Media Ground-Truth Dataset for Real/Fake Content for Real/Fake Content TruthSeeker: The Largest Social Media Ground-Truth Dataset for Real/Fake Content (2023). https://doi.org/10.36227/techrxiv.22795130.v1

7. Sharrab, Y., Al-Fraihat, D., Alsmirat, M.: EasyChair Preprint Deep Neural Networks in Social Media Forensics: Unveiling Suspicious Patterns and Advancing Investigations on Twitter Deep Neural Networks in Social Media Forensics: Unveiling Suspicious Patterns and Advancing Investigations on Twitter (2023)

8. Dirjen, S.K., et al.: Terakreditasi SINTA peringkat 2 hoax detection on twitter using feed-forward and back-propagation neural networks method. masa berlaku mulai **1**(3), 648–654 (2017)

9. Abdulrahman, A., Baykara, M.: Fake news detection using machine learning and deep learning algorithms. In: 3rd International Conference on Advanced Science and Engineering, ICOASE 2020, Institute of Electrical and Electronics Engineers Inc., pp. 18–23 (2020). https://doi.org/10.1109/ICOASE51841.2020.9436605

10. Galgotias University. School of Computing Science and Engineering, Institute of Electrical and Electronics Engineers. Uttar Pradesh Section, and Institute of Electrical and Electronics Engineers. In: 2018 4th International Conference on Computing Communication and Automation (ICCCA)

11. Ajao, O., Bhowmik, D., Zargari, S.: Fake news identification on Twitter with hybrid CNN and RNN models. In: ACM International Conference Proceeding Series, Association for Computing Machinery, pp. 226–230 (2018). https://doi.org/10.1145/3217804.3217917

12. Sachithanandam, B., Namin, A.S., Abri, F.: The performance of machine and deep learning algorithms in detecting fake reviews. In: Proceedings – 2023 IEEE International Conference on Big Data, BigData 2023, Institute of Electrical and Electronics Engineers Inc., pp. 2499–2507 (2023). https://doi.org/10.1109/BigData59044.2023.10386101

13. Buzea, M.C., Trausan-Matu, S., Rebedea, T.: Automatic fake news detection for romanian online news. Information **13**(3), 151 (2022). https://doi.org/10.3390/info13030151

14. Kumar, S., Asthana, R., Upadhyay, S., Upreti, N., Akbar, M.: Fake news detection using deep learning models: a novel approach. Trans. Emerg. Telecommun. Technol. (2020). https://doi.org/10.1002/ett.3767

15. IEEE Joint 19th International Symposium on Computational Intelligence and Informatics and 7th International Conference on Recent Achievements in Mechatronics, Automation, Computer Sciences and Robotics : proceedings : 14–16 Nov 2019, Szeged, Hungary. IEEE (2019)

16. Kotteti, C.M.M., Dong, X., Li, N., Qian, L.: Fake news detection enhancement with data imputation. In: 2018 IEEE 16th International Conference on Dependable, Autonomic and Secure Computing, 16th International Conference on Pervasive Intelligence and Computing, 4th International Conference on Big Data Intelligence and Computing and Cyber Science and Technology Congress(DASC/PiCom/DataCom/CyberSciTech), IEEE, pp. 187–192 (2018). https://doi.org/10.1109/DASC/PiCom/DataCom/CyberSciTec.2018.00042

17. Kumar, N., Raubal, M.: Applications of deep learning in congestion detection, prediction and alleviation: a survey. Transport. Res. Part C: Emerg. Technol. **133**, 103432 (2021). https://doi.org/10.1016/j.trc.2021.103432

18. Abdulrahman, A.A., Ibrahem, M.K.: Intrusion detection system using data stream classification. Iraqi J. Sci. **62**(1), 319–328 (2021). https://doi.org/10.24996/ijs.2021.62.1.30

19. Alfarhany, A.A.-R., Abdullah, N.A.Z.: Iraqi sentiment and emotion analysis using deep learning. J. Eng. **29**(09), 150–165 (2023). https://doi.org/10.31026/j.eng.2023.09.11

20. Mohammed, Z.K., Abdullah, N.A.Z.: Survey for arabic part of speech tagging based on machine learning. Iraqi J. Sci. **63**(6), 2676–2685 (2022). https://doi.org/10.24996/ijs.2022.63.6.33

21. Aninditya, A., Hasibuan, M.A., Sutoyo, E.: Text mining approach using TF-IDF and naive bayes for classification of exam questions based on cognitive level of bloom's taxonomy. In: Proceedings – 2019 IEEE International Conference on Internet of Things and Intelligence System, IoTaIS 2019, Institute of Electrical and Electronics Engineers Inc., pp. 112–117 (2019). https://doi.org/10.1109/IoTaIS47347.2019.8980428
22. Jiang, T., Li, J.P., Haq, A.U., Saboor, A., Ali, A.: A novel stacking approach for accurate detection of fake news. IEEE Access **9**, 22626–22639 (2021). https://doi.org/10.1109/ACCESS.2021.3056079
23. Alkhair, M., Meftouh, K., Smaïli, K., Othman, N.: An arabic corpus of fake news: collection, analysis and classification. In: Smaïli, K. (ed.) Arabic Language Processing: From Theory to Practice: 7th International Conference, ICALP 2019, Nancy, France, October 16–17, 2019, Proceedings, pp. 292–302. Springer International Publishing, Cham (2019). https://doi.org/10.1007/978-3-030-32959-4_21
24. Saadi, M.Q., Dhannoon, B.N.: Arabic cyberbullying detection using support vector machine with cuckoo search. Iraqi J. Sci. (2023). https://doi.org/10.24996/ijs.2023.64.10.37
25. Abdullah, N.A.Z., Jaboory, N.T.: Arabic keywords extraction using conventional neural network. Iraqi J. Sci. **63**(1), 283–293 (2022). https://doi.org/10.24996/ijs.2022.63.1.28
26. Mridha, M.F., Keya, A.J., Hamid, M.A., Monowar, M.M., Rahman, M.S.: A comprehensive review on fake news detection with deep learning. IEEE Access **9**, 156151–156170 (2021). https://doi.org/10.1109/ACCESS.2021.3129329
27. Fadel, F.H., Behadili, S.F.: A comparative study for supervised learning algorithms to analyze sentiment tweets. Iraqi J. Sci. **63**(6), 2712–2724 (2022). https://doi.org/10.24996/ijs.2022.63.6.36
28. Varshney, C.J., Sharma, A.. Yadav, D.P.: Sentiment analysis using ensemble classification technique. In: 2020 IEEE Students' Conference on Engineering and Systems, SCES 2020, Institute of Electrical and Electronics Engineers Inc. (2020). https://doi.org/10.1109/SCES50439.2020.9236754
29. Hera, S.Y., Amjad, M.: Prediction of explicit features for recommendation system using user reviews. Iraqi J. Sci. **63**(11), 5015–5023 (2022). https://doi.org/10.24996/ijs.2022.63.11.36
30. Khan, M.Y., Qayoom, A., Nizami, M.S., Siddiqui, M.S., Wasi, S., Raazi, S.M.K.U.R.: Automzated prediction of good dictionary examples (GDEX): a comprehensive experiment with distant supervision, machine learning, and word embedding-based deep learning techniques. Complexity (2021). https://doi.org/10.1155/2021/2553199
31. Nasser, E.S., Dawood, F.A.A.: Diagnosis and classification of type ii diabetes based on multilayer neural network. Iraqi J. Sci. **62**(10), 3744–3758 (2021). https://doi.org/10.24996/ijs.2021.62.10.33
32. Khan, J.Y., Khondaker, M., Afroz, S., Uddin, G., Iqbal, A.: A benchmark study of machine learning models for online fake news detection. Mach. Learn. Appl. **4**, 100032 (2021). https://doi.org/10.1016/j.mlwa.2021.100032
33. Thaher, T., Saheb, M., Turabieh, H., Chantar, H.: Intelligent detection of false information in arabic tweets utilizing hybrid harris hawks based feature selection and machine learning models. Symmetry **13**(4), 556 (2021). https://doi.org/10.3390/sym13040556
34. Sabbeh, S.F., Baatwah, S.: Arabic news credibility on twitter: An enhanced model using hybrid features (2018). www.jatit.org
35. Zaxo, Z.: Duhok Polytechnic University, IEEE Computational Intelligence Society. Iraq Chapter., IEEE Communications Society. Iraq Chapter, Institute of Electrical and Electronics Engineers. Iraq Section., and Institute of Electrical and Electronics Engineers. In: 2019 International Conference on Advanced Science and Engineering : 2–4 April 2019
36. Verma, P.K., Agrawal, P., Amorim, I., Prodan, R.: WELFake: word embedding over linguistic features for fake news detection. IEEE Trans. Comput. Soc. Syst. **8**(4), 881–893 (2021). https://doi.org/10.1109/TCSS.2021.3068519

Utilizing Graph Neural Networks for the Detection of Fake News Through Analysis of Relationships Among Various Social Media Entities

Alaa Safaa Mahdi$^{(\boxtimes)}$ (ID) and Narjis Mezaal Shati (ID)

Department of Computer Science, College of Sciences, Mustansiriyah University, Baghdad, Iraq
{alaa.safaa,dr.narjis.m.sh}@uomustansiriyah.edu.iq

Abstract. Social media platforms have become increasingly popular for news consumption, due to their speed, low cost, and accessibility. However, these platforms facilitated the widespread propagation of fake news, making it essential to ensure users received accurate information. Traditional methods are generally unsuccessful, false news is imitated by real news to mislead users. This highlighted the necessity to discover more advanced detection techniques. This research focused on using Graph Neural Networks (GNNs) to enhance fake news detection by incorporating social context into the detection process. Entities such as news, authors, publishers, users, article titles, and tweet_IDs are represented as nodes within a graph structure, with relationships between these entities transformed into numerical representations using techniques such as TF-IDF. The experiments are presented on three real-world datasets, which achieved significant improvements over traditional baseline methods. Finally, the suggested approach achieved accuracies of 0.95 on the BuzzFeed dataset, 0.87 on the PolitiFact dataset, and 0.91 on the Gossipcop dataset. These results performed its effectiveness in detecting fake news.

Keywords: Fake news detection · Graph Neural Networks · GNN · Propagation Graphs · Social Media

1 Introduction

Nowadays, posting and sharing information on social media platforms is very easy. Users can access a significant amount of data. Social media platforms are regarded as the main source of news and information, causing an increasing number of people to rely on social media platforms instead of traditional media sources like newspapers and television for their information needs [1].

The World Health Organization announced on February 2nd ?year that the COVID-19 pandemic was an "infodemic", due to the overwhelming amount of information, which is sometimes real and sometimes fake. Therefore, there are many challenges in dealing with social media, since it is difficult to distinguish between fake and real information.

© The Author(s), under exclusive license to Springer Nature Switzerland AG 2025
S. O. Al-Mamory et al. (Eds.): 3INC 2024, CCIS 2329, pp. 172–185, 2025.
https://doi.org/10.1007/978-3-031-81065-7_11

As a result, the European Commission addressed these concerns in its 2018 report, "Fake News and Disinformation Online", as part of the Eurobarometer initiative [2]. Another example, during the 2016 US presidential election, Clinton supporters were influenced by conventional news from known left-leaning or centrist sources. On the other hand, Trump supporters were affected by the influence of well-known spreaders of false news. These instances highlighted the serious effects of false information across various fields [3]. Therefore, preventing the spread of false information on social media is essential.

The two primary categories for detecting fake news approaches can be classified into content-based and context-based approaches. A content-based approach analyzed sentences and other news item components to identify and understand semantic linkages. However, false information frequently mimicked real news, making it difficult to differentiate between them. This highlighted the difficulties of using a content-based approach [4]. Therefore, it is essential to analyze other features derived from the social component of articles [5].

Rather than focusing solely on article content, context-based approaches analyzed social media relationships and network dynamics to identify patterns that might be related to the propagation of false information [6]. Recent methods, Graph Neural Networks (GNNs) have been developed to identify fake information on social media platforms. Despite the challenges caused by the requirement: reliable, annotated datasets and the dynamic nature of social network operations. Graph neural networks (GNNs) exhibited a great deal of potential, for processing graph-structured data efficiently. GNNs are useful methods to mitigate the negative impacts of incorrect information and uphold the integrity of the Internet exchange of information [7]. This study aimed to enhance the detection of false news by employing the GNNs model that captured the relationships among news, authors, users, and publishers. Additionally, it combined the relationship between tweet_IDs and article titles. GNNs utilized relational data effectively from BuzzFeed, Gossipcop, and PolitiFact datasets.

2 Related Works

The detection of fake news has received interesting attention in recent years. Despite numerous studies exploring various methods, GNN performed an effective rule in identifying fake news. Several related works in this domain have been highlighted:

In 2019, the authors introduced TriFN, a tri-relationship embedding framework that concurrently models publisher-news relations and user-news interactions. TriFN achieved a recall of 0.89 on both the Politifact and BuzzFeed datasets. Further research is needed on early detection of evolving fake news and psychological feature extraction [8].

In 2020, the authors trained powerful Graph Neural Network (GNN) classifiers using text features extracted with the BERT transformer-based language model and user features. The result recorded an accuracy of 0.88 on the Twitter15 dataset, their best-performing model (GCN text only). They identified the need for improved generalization, better regularization, and updated user features to address dataset limitations [9].

In 2020, the authors suggested a Structure-aware Multi-Head Attention Network (SMAN), integrated news content, and user-publisher relations to optimize false news detection. The results achieved approximately 0.95 accuracy on the Weibo dataset and 0.91 accuracy on the Twitter15 and Twitter16 datasets [10].

In 2021, the authors proposed a propagation-based method using GNNs to differentiate fake and real news from the propagation pattern using limited social context features. The results obtained an accuracy of 0.81 on the PolitiFact dataset and 0.84 on the GossipCop dataset. Features extraction was emphasized to mitigate the catastrophic forgetting [11].

In 2021, the authors introduced SCARLET, an attention-based explainable graph neural network model designed to predict whether a node is likely to spread false information. For the model to learn node embedding, it first assigned important scores based on trust and then proportionally aggregated the credibility features of its neighbourhood. The results recorded an accuracy greater than 0.87 in detecting fake information [12].

In 2021, the authors presented a graph-based method using a summarization technique that depended on internal information for detecting false news. This technique calculated the contextual information reflection rate of sentences and then created a graph to present the relationships between all sentences using an attention mechanism. The results achieved a high accuracy of 0.91 [13].

In 2022, the authors utilized the hybrid approach on the graph neural network to analyze the social context of false news identification. This model combined bi-directional encoder representations from the transformers model with a graph neural network for news propagation for news content to enable text feature learning. As a result, this approach achieved an F1-score of 0.91on the Politifact dataset and an F1-score of 0.93 on the Gossipcop dataset [14].

In 2023, the authors suggested a unified graph-based model called GETRAL for detecting false news to improve representation learning complex semantic structures, used to explore intricate semantic adversarial contrastive learning. By using the PolitiFact dataset, the model obtained an F1-Micro score of 0.69, and an F1-Macro score of 0.80 on the Snopes dataset [15].

In 2024, the authors introduced a propagation-based technique by utilizing positive similarity and information on news-sharing to identify false news. This approach used a Graph Transition Network (GTN) to address the dissemination of comparable stances, which are common features in the spread of false news due to confirmation bias achieving accuracy values of 0.79 on the FibVid dataset and 0.79 and 0.86 on a custom dataset [16].

3   Using a GNN Model for Detecting Fake News

Graph Neural Networks (GNNs) are recent and powerful techniques in detecting fake news. The basic steps of this technique are clarified in Fig. 1.

3.1   Data Preparation

Data preparation is an essential and complex phase of building precise and reliable false news detection systems. Datasets consisted of BuzzFeed, Gossipicop, and PolitiFact.

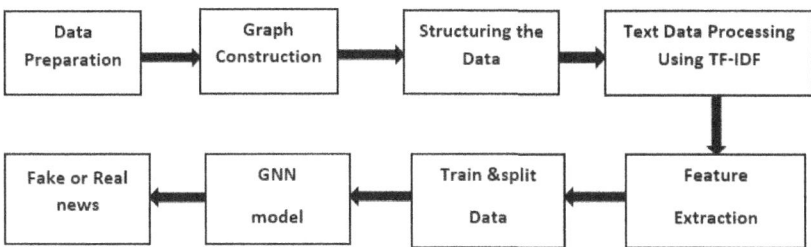

Fig. 1. Architecture of a GNN Model for Fake News Detection: From Data Preparation to Classification

- **BuzzFeed Dataset:** It contained articles from nine news outlies shared on Facebook, including those from the week before the 2016 US presidential election. Journalists from BuzzFeed have fact-checked every article referenced in the dataset [17].
- **Gossipcop Dataset:** It included tweet_IDs and titles from various articles. This information facilitated the analysis of the posted news on social media platforms.
- **PolitiFact Dataset:** It contained tweet_IDs and article titles, that are used to analyze the spread of false and political information.

3.2 Text Data Processing Using TF-IDF

Raw text data is sometimes inconsistent, incorrect, or inappropriate. Preprocessing these data is a useful technique for addressing these challenges. As part of preprocessing data, this technique eliminated any stop words and special characters from the text contents after crawling every piece of the available news. In addition, it removed all non-alpha data [18], which is the TF-IDF (Term Frequency and Inverse Document Frequency) scale measures semantic similarity for text clustering. It is a metric used in Information Retrieval (IR) and Machine learning. The term frequency is modified based on the document's length. Every appearance is assigned a value of (1), and the total number of words in the text is divided by the absence of any appearances (0) [19].

3.3 Feature Extraction

Selection of the best features of the data to train a model is known as feature extraction. These features can be extracted using various techniques to simplify data and focus on the significant features [20]. Subsequently, the data is divided into test and training sets, so that can determine the performance of the model.

3.4 Evaluate the Model

This study employed evaluation metrics to assess model performance, focusing on enhancing predictive power before deployment on unseen data. These metrics are based on the confusion matrix, which represented the classifier's performance on the test set. The prediction result consisted of four possible outcomes: True Positive (TP), True Negative (TN), False Positive (FP), and False Negative (FN). The FP and FN outcomes are also known as Type I and Type II errors, respectively, as shown in Fig. 2.

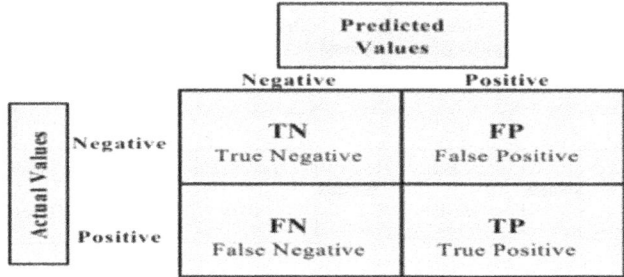

Fig. 2. Shows evaluate the Model [21].

A. **Accuracy**

It is the ratio of accurately classified cases to total cases [22]:

$$Accuracy = \frac{\#TP + \#TN}{\#FP + \#FN + \#TP + \#TN} \tag{1}$$

B. **Precision**

Precision is an important indicator of a model's performance, to determine the prediction quality. It is defined as the number of true positives divided by the total number of positive predictions. It is essential in scenarios where the cost of a false positive is high:

$$Precision = \frac{\#TP}{\#TP + \#FP} \tag{2}$$

C. **Recall**

The recall is the true positive rate, measured by how often the model correctly predicted "yes" with the actual label as "yes". Both precision and recall are used together to assess model performance, especially in situations with class imbalance:

$$Recall = \frac{\#TP}{\#FN + \#TP} \tag{3}$$

D. **F1-Score**

The F1-score is the harmonic mean of recall and precision, ranging from 0 to 1 (1 as the best possible score and 0 as the worst). It is primarily used to compare the performances of the two classifiers. A model with a higher F1 score performed better if one classifier registered high recall and the other with high precision [22].

$$F_1 = 2x \frac{\#Precision \; x \; \#Recall}{\#Precision + \#Recall} \tag{4}$$

4   Methodology

The methodology for detecting fake news utilized complex network relationships within social media platforms, leveraging a Graph Neural Network (GNN)model. This approach involved defining entities, establishing relationships among them, and converting textual data into numerical representation. By analyzing these structured relationships and features through the GNN model, the proposed methodology aimed to enhance both the accuracy and robustness of fake news detection, the proposed model can enhance both the accuracy and robustness of fake news detection, as illustrated in Fig. 3.

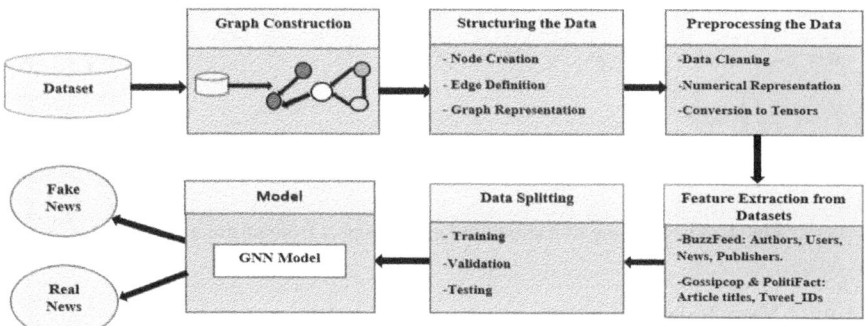

Fig. 3. Illustrates the proposed methodology for fake news detection using the GNN model.

4.1 Dataset Overview

This study utilized three datasets for fake news detection: BuzzFeed, GossipCop, and PolitiFact. BuzzFeed dataset included users, publishers, authors, and news, labelled as fake or real. In contrast, the Gossipcop and PolitiFact datasets consisted of article titles and tweet_IDs, with articles also labelled as fake or real.

4.2 Graph Construction

For machine learning applications. Creating graphs is an essential step in the data analysis process, by converting unstructured data into a structured graphical dataset, this method made it possible to train models more effectively by highlighting the relationships between social media interactions. A graph structure example presenting nodes and edges is shown in Fig. 4.

– BuzzFeed Dataset

The relationships between all the components in the BuzzFeed dataset can be shown using a graph structure, as can be described:

– News-User Relationship

The relationship between news items and users can display the news-user relationship dataset. This included likes, comments, shares, and other forms of interaction. Through an analysis of these exchanges, trends that point to the spread of false information are identified, such as posts shared mostly by untrusted persons.

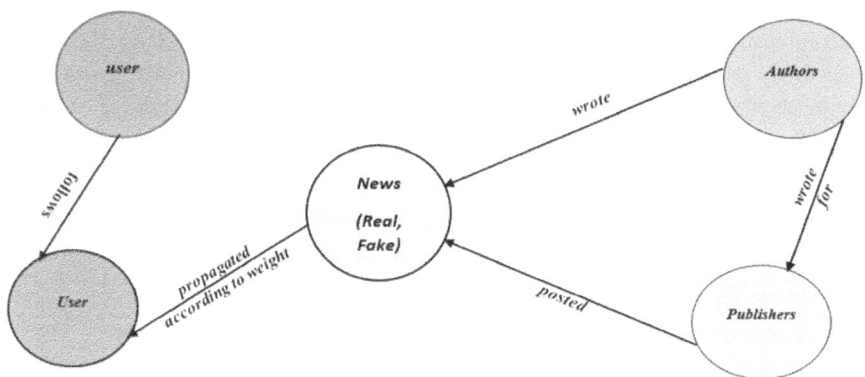

Fig. 4. The building of a structured graph dataset from unstructured data

- Author-News Relationship

The author-news relationship consisted of details about the articles written by authors. The analysis of authors' history and writing patterns can determine their credibility. Authors with a history of producing misleading content can be marked for more severe examination, as their news is more likely to be inaccurate.

- Publisher-News Relationship

This dataset links to the news articles published. It is crucial to identify the overall credibility of the content based on the publisher's reputation. Publishers with a history of disseminating false information can be highlighted, and their content can be given additional attention during the verification process.

- Publisher-Author Relationship

This dataset captured the connection between news publishers and authors. It included information on which authors are associated with publishers. These relationships facilitated the identification of potential biases or tendencies in news reporting. For instance, a publisher known for partisan views may have authors who frequently contributed to fake news.

– Gossipicop Dataset

For the Gossipcop dataset, the graph structure can be formed based on the relationships between them, as can be shown:

Titles and tweet_IDs: Nodes represented titles articles and tweet_IDs, with edges indicating the association between a tweet and its corresponding title. This created a graph where: Each tweet_IDs is linked to the title of the news item, which is referred to.

– PolitiFact Dataset

The PolitiFact dataset can be structured similarly to the GossipCop dataset, which is based on the relationships between tweet IDs and titles of the news items.

4.3   Structuring the Data

To organize these datasets into a structured graph format, the following items must be included:

- **Node Creation:** Identifying and creating nodes for each unique entity (e.g., users, publishers, authors, news articles, tweet_IDs, titles).
- **Edge Definition:** Defined the relationships between nodes by creating edges (e.g., user-news interactions, publisher-news associations, author-news contributions, and tweet-title links).
- **Graph Representation:** Represented these nodes and edges in a graph database or data structure that supported graph-based queries and analysis.

Converting the BuzzFeed, GossipCop, and PolitiFact datasets into structured graph datasets, can enhance the inherent relationships. As well as improving the performance of machine learning models in detecting false news. This method allowed the comprehension of the interactions and dissemination of news inside social media networks.

4.4   Preprocessing the Data

Preprocessing is essential for preparing raw data for graph-based machine learning models. It comprised of several key steps:

- **Data Cleaning:** This step refined textual data to eliminate irrelevant information. It included:

  - **Tokenization:** Splitting text into individual tokens, like phrases or words.
  - **Stopword Removal:** Eliminating common, non-essential words.
  - **Normalization:** Converting text to lowercase and applying stemming or lemmatization.
  - **Special Character Removal:** Replacing or removing characters that are not alphanumeric.

- **Numerical Representation:** Cleaned textual data is converted into numerical vectors using techniques such as TF-IDF.
- **Conversion to Tensors:** Numerical vectors are transformed into tensors compatible with machine learning frameworks like PyTorch for integration with graph neural networks (GNNs).

These preprocessing steps can enhance the performance and accuracy of graph-based machine learning models for applications of fake news detection.

4.5   Feature Extraction from Datasets

For feature extraction, the BuzzFeed dataset involved extracting entities such as authors, users, news articles, and publishers, along with their interrelationships. In contrast, the PolitiFact and GossipCop datasets focused on extracting attributes like article titles and tweet_IDs to analyze social media platforms.

4.6 Data Splitting

Data splitting is the division of the dataset into distinct subsections for training, validation, and testing. The training set is used to train the model. Subsequently, using the validation set can improve the model's performance during training. The test set is used to evaluate the final performance of the model on unseen data.

4.7 Steps to Build a GNN Model for Fake News Detection

A. **Input Layer**
– Node Features: Initialized attributes for nodes using data from the dataset, such as news articles, tweet_IDs, publishers, authors, and users. These features captured crucial information needed to identify fake news.
– Edge Index: Defined the relationships between nodes.
B. Hidden Layers
– Message Passing:

Aggregation: Collected information from neighbouring nodes to update each node's feature representation.
Transformation: Apply linear transformations and activation functions (e.g., ReLU) to the aggregated features to enhance and model complex relationships.

C. **Dense Layers**
– Fully Connected Layers: Connected each node to every neuron in the subsequent layers to process, learn high-level representations, and capture intricate patterns.
D. **Output Layer**
– Sigmoid Activation Function: Converted final node representations into probability scores (0 to 1), indicating whether news is fake (scores > 0.5) or real (scores < 0.5). Finally, following these steps, the GNN model can process graph-structured data, to accurately classify news as fake or real through enhanced features and relationship analysis.

5 Results

The performance of the proposed model is evaluated on the BuzzFeed, PolitiFact, and GossipCop datasets using precision, recall, F1-score, and accuracy. The results are summarized in Table 1.

Table 1. Evaluation Metrics for the Proposed Model in Fake News Detection

Dataset	precision	recall	F1-score	accuracy
BuzzFeed	0.90	**1.00**	0.95	**0.95**
PolitiFact	0.86	**0.93**	0.89	**0.87**
Gossipcop	0.86	**0.96**	0.91	**0.91**

- **BuzzFeed Dataset:** The model achieved an accuracy of 95%, a precision of 0.90, a recall of 1.00, and an F1-score of 0.95. These results presented the high efficiency of the model in detecting fake news.
- **PolitiFact Dataset:** with an accuracy of 87, a precision of 0.86, a recall of 0.93, and an F1-score of 0.89. This indicated a balanced performance with strong recall and a lower accuracy.
- **GossipCop Dataset:** With an accuracy of 91%, a precision of 0.86, a recall of 0.96, and an F1-score of 0.91, the model showed robust performance in identifying true positives. Although precision is slightly lower, the high recall and balanced F1-score reflected the effective performance of the overall identification of the truest positives. All these datasets showed excellent overall performance of the classifier. Both the accuracy and the F1-score showed a well-balanced performance with a small variance among the dataset.

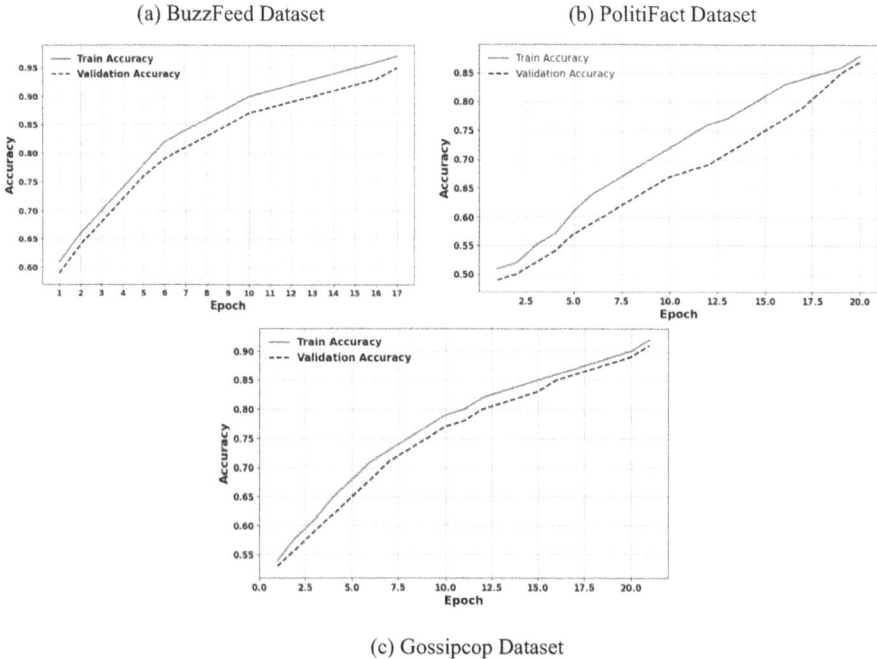

(a) BuzzFeed Dataset   (b) PolitiFact Dataset

(c) Gossipcop Dataset

Fig. 5. Training and Validation Accuracy Over Epochs for the Three Datasets: (a) BuzzFeed Dataset; (b) PolitiFact Dataset and (c) Gossipcop Dataset.

Figure 5, clarified the progression of training and validation accuracies of the proposed model across epochs for the BuzzFeed, PolitiFact, and GossipCop datasets, reflecting the model's effective learning capability and its ability to enhance performance over time:

(a) **BuzzFeed Dataset:** Training accuracy improved from 0.61 to 0.97, while validation accuracy increased from 0.59 to 0.95.

(b) **PolitiFact Dataset:** Training accuracy raised from 0.51 to 0.88, while validation accuracy improved from 0.49 to 0.87.

(c) **GossipCop Dataset:** Training accuracy increased from 0.54 to 0.92, while validation accuracy enhanced from 0.53 to 0.91.

These results across all three datasets reflected the model's robustness and effectiveness in fake news detection.

6 Discussion

The field of fake news detection has experienced significant advancements, particularly with the use of Graph Neural Networks (GNNs). This study offered a comparative analysis of the current and past methods in similarities, differences, innovative features, performance metrics, and overall, that highlighted both progress and areas of improvement, as can be shown in Table 2:

- **Similarities:** Both current and previous studies focused on employing GNNs to capture complex data relationships, emphasizing the signature of social context and user interactions. High recall performance, ensuring that most of the true positives are detected.
- **Differences:** The current study showed notable advancements in dataset performance. On the BuzzFeed dataset, the current model achieved a precision of 0.90, a recall of 1.00, an F1-score of 0.95, and an accuracy of 0.95, outperforming previous models in recall and balance. For the PolitiFact dataset, the model's precision of 0.86, recall of 0.93, F1-score of 0.89, and accuracy of 0.87 are comparable to models like TriFN, though with a slight edge in the recall. On the GossipCop dataset, the model achieved stronger performance with a precision of 0.86, a re-call of 0.96, an F1-score of 0.91, and an accuracy of 0.91, exceeding previous propagation-based methods.
- **Innovative Features:** The current study combined content and context features using GNNs, incorporating advancements like the TF-IDF vectorizer, enhancing feature extraction and performance.
- **Performance Metrics.** On the GossipCop dataset, the proposed model performed better than previous approaches, with a higher total accuracy, and F1 rating. This performed a better balance between recall and accuracy.
- **Overall:** The proposed research has advanced feature extraction to detect false news. Improving F1-score, recall, precision, and accuracy across various datasets, indicating progress in detecting fake news.

Table 2. Comparison between the current work and previous work

Research	Methods	Dataset	results
[8]	TriFN	the Politifact and BuzzFeed datasets	Recall: 0.89 on both datasets
[9]	GNN	Twitter15/16	Accuracy: 0.88
[10]	SMAN	Weibo and Twitter15 and Twitter16 datasets	accuracy:0.95 on Weibo accuracy:0.91 on the Twitter15 and Twitter16 datasets
[11]	GNN	PolitiFact and the GossipCop dataset	accuracy:0.81 on PolitiFact accuracy:0.84 on GossipCop datasets
[12]	SCARLET	Network dataset	accuracy: over 0.87
[13]	graph-based + Summarization	HDSF dataset	accuracy:0.91 on HDSF and accuracy:0.88 on Cross Validation datasets
[14]	GNN	PolitiFact and the Gossipcop dataset	F1-score:0.91 on the PolitiFact F1-score:0.93 on the Gossipcop datasets
[15]	GETRAL	Snopes dataset and PolitiFact dataset	F1-Macro score: 0.80 on Snopes F1-Micro score: 0.69 on PolitiFact datasets
[16]	GTN	Custom dataset and FibVid dataset	accuracy:0.86 on the custom accuracy:0.79 on the FibVid datasets
Current model	GNN	BuzzFeed, PolitiFact, and Gossipcop datasets	recall of 1.00 on BuzzFeed recall:0.93 on PolitiFact recall:0.96 on Gossipcop datasets

7   Conclusion and Future Directions

The aim of this research is to determine the importance of relationships between news, users, publishers, and authors. In addition, accomplishment of the connections between tweet_IDs and headline articles on social networking platforms, for identifying false information. This approach collected data effectively from diverse sources of information, including users and news items, and analyzed the relationships between various datasets. It achieved significant rules with real-world fake news datasets. The results suggested that these relationships contributed to strong detection performance, especially if the news arrived early.

GNNs can manage interactions and complex relationships within the news network. As a result, it can provide a reliable and efficient framework for detecting false news.

Additionally, to counteract the rapid dissemination of false information on social media platforms, future directions in this domain will focus on exploring useful features and models designed for early identification. Continuous progress in deep learning and data analysis techniques is expected to enhance the ability to limit the spread of fake news. This study highlighted the promising potential of combining advanced machine learning methods with a comprehensive understanding of the social context to develop more accurate fake news detection systems.

Acknowledgments. For their assistance with this study, the authors would like to thank Mustansiriyah Universityin Bagdad, Iraq (https://www.uomustansiriyah.edu.iq/).

References

1. Al-Tai, M.H., Nema, B.M., Al-Sherbaz, A.: Deep learning for fake news detection: literature review. Al-Mustansiriyah J. Sci. **34**(2), 70–81 (2023). https://doi.org/10.23851/mjs.v34i2. 1292
2. Liao, H., Liu, Q., Shu, K.: Fake News Detection through Graph Comment Advanced Learning (2020). arXiv Prepr. arXiv2011.01579
3. Monti, F., Frasca, F., Eynard, D., Mannion, D., Bronstein, M.M.: Fake News Detection on Social Media using Geometric Deep Learning, pp. 1–15 (2019). http://arxiv.org/abs/1902. 06673
4. Shu, K., Mahudeswaran, D., Wang, S., Liu, H.: Hierarchical propagation networks for fake news detection: Investigation and exploitation. In: Proceedings of the international AAAI conference on web and social media, pp. 626–637 (2020). https://doi.org/10.1609/icwsm. v14i1.7329
5. Pierri, F., Ceri, S.: False news on social media: a data-driven survey. SIGMOD Rec. **48**(2), 18–32 (2019). https://doi.org/10.1145/3377330.3377334
6. Zhang, X., Ghorbani, A.A.: An overview of online fake news: Characterization, detection, and discussion. Inf. Process. Manag. **57**(2), 102025 (2020). https://doi.org/10.1016/j.ipm.2019. 03.004
7. Vosoughi, S., Roy, D., Aral, S.: The spread of true and false news online. Science **359**(6380), 1146–1151 (2018). https://doi.org/10.1126/science.aap9559
8. Shu, K., Wang, S., Liu, H.: Beyond news contents: The role of social context for fake news detection. In: Proceedings of the twelfth ACM international conference on web search and data mining, pp. 312–320 (2019). https://doi.org/10.1145/3289600.3290994
9. Autef, A., Matton, A., Romain, M.: Fake news detection using machine learning on the graphs-final report (2020). arXiv Prepr. arXiv2007.03316
10. Yuan, C., Ma, Q., Zhou, W., Han, J., Hu, S.: Early detection of fake news by utilizing the credibility of news, publishers, and users based on weakly supervised learning. In: COLING 2020 – 28th Int. Conf. Comput. Linguist. Proc. Conf., no. August 2022, pp. 5444–5454 (2020). https://doi.org/10.18653/v1/2020.coling-main.475
11. Han, Y., Karunasekera, S., Leckie, C.: Graph neural networks with continual learning for fake news detection from social media (2020). arXiv Prepr. arXiv2007.03316
12. Rath, B., Morales, X., Srivastava, J.: SCARLET: explainable attention based graph neural network for fake news spreader prediction. In: Karlapalem, K., et al. (eds.) Advances in Knowledge Discovery and Data Mining: 25th Pacific-Asia Conference, PAKDD 2021, Virtual Event, May 11–14, 2021, Proceedings, Part I, pp. 714–727. Springer International Publishing, Cham (2021). https://doi.org/10.1007/978-3-030-75762-5_56

13. Kim, G., Ko, Y.: Graph-based fake news detection using a summarization technique. In: Proceedings of the 16th Conference of the European Chapter of the Association for Computational Linguistics: Main Volume, pp. 3276–3280 (2021). https://doi.org/10.18653/v1/2021.eacl-main.287

14. Saikia, P., Gundale, K., Jain, A., Jadeja, D., Patel, H., Roy, M. Modelling social context for fake news detection: a graph neural network based approach. In: 2022 International Joint Conference on Neural Networks (IJCNN), IEEE, pp. 1–8 (2022). https://doi.org/10.1109/IJCNN55064.2022.9892311

15. Soga, K., Yoshida, S., Muneyasu, M.: Graph-based interpretability for fake news detection through topic-and propagation-aware visualization. Computation **12**(4), 82 (2024). https://doi.org/10.3390/computation12040082

16. Soga, K., Yoshida, S., Muneyasu, M.: Exploiting stance similarity and graph neural networks for fake news detection. Pattern Recognit. Lett. **177**, 26–32 (2024). https://doi.org/10.1016/j.patrec.2023.11.019

17. Joshi, S., Shojael, H.: Detecting social media fake news using graph machine learning with Amazon Neptune ML. AWS Machine Learning Blog (2022). https://aws.amazon.com/blogs/machine-learning/detect-social-media-fake-news-using-graph-machine-learning-with-amazon-neptune-ml/

18. Mahmud, F.B., Rayhan, M. M. S., Shuvo, M. H., Sadia, I., . Morol, M.K.: A comparative analysis of Graph Neural Networks and commonly used machine learning algorithms on fake news detection. In: 2022 7th International Conference on Data Science and Machine Learning Applications (CDMA), IEEE, pp. 97–102 (2022). https://doi.org/10.48550/arXiv.2203.14132

19. Salman, Z.A.-W.: Text summarizing and clustering using data mining technique. Al-Mustansiriyah J. Sci. **34**(1), 58–64 (2023). https://doi.org/10.23851/mjs.v34i1.1195

20. Roshan, R., Bhacho, I.A., Zai, S.: Comparative analysis of TF–IDF and hashing vectorizer for fake news detection in sindhi: a machine learning and deep learning approach. Eng. Proc. (2023). https://doi.org/10.3390/engproc2023046005

21. Feng, Y.: Misreporting and fake news detection techniques on the social media platform. Highlights Sci. Eng. Technol. **12**, 142–152 (2022). https://doi.org/10.54097/hset.v12i.1417

22. Weli, Z.N.S.: Covid-19 prediction model using data mining algorithms. Al-Mustansiriyah J. Sci. **33**(1), 45–50 (2022). https://mjs.uomustansiriyah.edu.iq/index.php/MJS/article/view/1076

Classification of Internet of Things Cybersecurity Attacks Using a Hybrid Deep Learning Approach

Eman Karkawi Kareem[1] ⓘ and Mehdi Ebady Manaa[2,3](✉) ⓘ

[1] Department of Information Networks, College of IT, University of Babylon, Babylon, Iraq
emankarkawik.net@student.uobabylon.edu.iq
[2] Intelligent Medical Systems Department, College of Sciences, Al-Mustaqbal University,
51001 Babylon, Iraq
mahdi.ebadi@uomus.edu.iq
[3] College of Information Technology, University of Babylon, Babylon, Iraq

Abstract. IoT devices play an integral part of our digital life today, yet pose significant security risks. These risks allow attackers to carry out various cyberattacks, mainly distributed denial of service (DDoS) attacks. To address these challenges, this paper proposes a hybrid deep learning approach that uses deep neural networks (DNNs) and long short-term memory (LSTM) networks to classify IoT cybersecurity attacks. The binary classification technique of LSTM is applied, whereby the models indicated sufficient results in terms of accuracy and performance, with the LSTM model showing an accuracy of 0.999 and the DNN model showing an accuracy of 0.999. To enhance detection capabilities, we used a comprehensive approach that includes 15 different attack categories. Although the DNN model equals the LSTM model with an accuracy of 0.95 in some scenarios, the hybrid model, which integrates the DNN feature outputs and the LSTM-derived features, showed an overall accuracy of 95.36. We further conducted extensive tests on the Edge-IIoT dataset to validate the effectiveness of our hybrid model. The proposed solution effectively exploits the strengths of the DNN and LSTM architectures, providing a robust framework for detecting and classifying DDoS attacks within IoT networks. These results contribute to a promising approach to mitigate the risks associated with IoT vulnerabilities.

Keywords: Internet of Things · Cybersecurity Attacks · DDoS Attacks · Edge-IIoT dataset · IoT Security · IoT Attacks

1 Introduction

The Internet of Things (IoT) is transforming our lifestyle by integrating intelligent devices that can make decisions, thereby contributing to the growth and strength of the global economy [1]. Protecting the IoT system from harmful attacks is an exceedingly challenging task. Denial of Service (DoS) and Distributed Denial of Service (DDoS) attacks are widely recognized as common hostile assaults. These attacks provide substantial security hazards to all networks, especially IoT devices with restricted resources

S. O. Al-Mamory et al. (Eds.): 3INC 2024, CCIS 2329, pp. 186–200, 2025.
https://doi.org/10.1007/978-3-031-81065-7_12

[2, 3]. Despite the widespread use of the Internet of Things in industrial environments, current intrusion detection systems face challenges, especially with unbalanced sampling, which may affect their ability to detect critical attacks, thereby increasing the likelihood that essential attacks of the network will not be detected [4, 5]. IoT applications expose the limitations of traditional cloud computing, which has led to the adoption of fog computing to improve performance by processing data closer to IoT nodes. This paper focuses on addressing the challenge of distributed denial of service (DDoS) attacks within the context of the Industrial Internet of Things (IIoT) [6, 7]. Service availability is crucial for computer networks, as they face an increasing danger of DDoS attacks every year. Machine learning (ML) is a highly effective method for detecting DDoS assaults. It consistently achieves good outcomes when dealing with already-known attacks [8]. DDoS attacks exploit vulnerabilities in IoT networks by flooding them with excessive traffic, making target devices inaccessible to regular network traffic. An HTTP flood is a type of cyber-attack that involves overwhelming a website or server with many HTTP requests to disrupt its normal functioning. DDoS attacks involve inundating a specific server with many HTTP queries to overpower and hinder it. Automated port scanning is used to scan networked IoT devices [9]. The objective is to ascertain the status of each port, whether it is active, inactive, or secured. OS Fingerprinting is a technique used to determine a computer's operating system. Once the operating system has been identified, a threat can exploit its weaknesses. Various cyberattacks target vulnerabilities in IoT systems, putting their security and integrity at risk. These attacks include DNS spoofing, ARP and XSS spoofing, SQL injection, and ransomware [10].

The main goals of this study are to accomplish the following objectives by conducting a thorough assessment of the pertinent literature: Deep learning can be employed to establish a resilient IoT network capable of effectively preventing DoS assaults. Perform an investigation on deep learning techniques to reduce the impact of DDoS attacks. By employing deep learning algorithms to merge the LSTM model with the DNN model, an effective hybrid model is created to detect distributed denial-of-service assaults.

2 Related Works

Related works applied deep learning to the Edge IIoT dataset using binary and 15 categories. Use M.A. Ferrag's (2022) data set for centralized intrusion detection, using four classifiers: RF, SVM, KNN, and DNN across binary classifications, 6 categories, and 15 categories [11].

Tareq et al. (2022) [12] A proposed model for detecting cyber-attacks through a multiclass classification approach. The evaluation commenced by assessing the performance of the Edge-IIoT dataset. Comparative analysis was conducted to discern various cyber-attacks. The highest accuracy obtained was 94.94% achieved training and validation accuracies; it could be observed that, after 34 epochs, the Edge-IIoT dataset used the Inception Time algorithm.

Alashhab et al. (2022) [13] proposed a deep learning model that uses LSTM activation to detect various types of DDoS attacks in IoT networks. The experiment outcomes depict its single-class accuracy measurement, which indicates 98.88% accuracy in the model. The model has been evaluated and verified using the Edge IIoT dataset, which includes cybersecurity attacks.

Javeed et al. (2023) [14] suggested that IDS TBPTT be used to handle long network data sequences. Provide an attack scenario and deployment architecture for the proposed IDS in the harsh SA environment. The proposed IDS achieved a validation loss of 0.0032% and validation ACC of 99.82% on the CIC-IDS2018 dataset (for ten-class only) and validation ACC and validation loss of 99.55% (for nine-class only) and 0.0028%, respectively, with the ToN-IoT dataset, while it achieved 98.32% validation ACC (for eight- classes only) and 0.0023 under the Edge-IIoT dataset, respectively.

Ding et al. (2023) [15] introduced DeepAK-IoT, an alternative deep learning model for IoT cyberattack detection. A powerful alternative model for addressing cyber threats in IoT networks, DeepAK-IoT, was evaluated in terms of accuracy and generalization ability over three well-known public datasets, TON-IoT, Edge-IIoT, and UNSW-NB15. With an accuracy of 90.57% for TON-IoT, 94.96% for Edge-IIoT dataset, and 98.41% for UNSW-NB15, DeepAK-IoT was proven to be a potent alternative model for handling cyber threats.

Rahman et al. (2023) [16] proposed a Federated Learning (FL) method for detecting intrusions in IoT networks, achieving up to 94% accuracy and 93% F1-score with RNN and CNN approaches on the Edge-IIoT dataset. Jadhav et al. (2023) [17] introduced a hybrid RNN-LSTM model for intrusion detection, outperforming traditional classifiers with 83.29% and 68.59% accuracy on the KDD Cup 99 and NSLKDD datasets, respectively.

3 Methodology

3.1 Dataset Description

The study utilizes a comprehensive real-world dataset, Edge-IIoT dataset, designed for IoT cybersecurity. This collection includes data from various IoT applications and devices [18]. It captures 14 types of attacks classified into five threat categories, such as denial of service and distributed denial of service attacks. The dataset contains 20,952,648 records, with 11,223,940 normal attack cases and 9,728,708 attack cases. 80% of the 1,927,304 processed samples were used for training and 20% for testing, ensuring consistent ratios of categories across 15 categories [19, 20] (Table 1).

Table 1. The Edge-IIoT dataset contains a comprehensive collection of records, encompassing various categories and a total count of numbers.

IoT traffic	Attack Type	Data Number
Normal	Normal	1,615,643
Attack	DdoS (UDP, ICMP, TCP)	288,066
	SQL Injection & Others	201,267
	Scanning & Fingerprint	23,565
	Other Attacks	73,661

3.2   Proposed System

A hybrid DNN-LSTM model was used on the Edge-IIoT dataset to distinguish the attack from normal traffic. The data was pre-processed; 80% of it was used for training and 20% for testing, and then the system was evaluated.

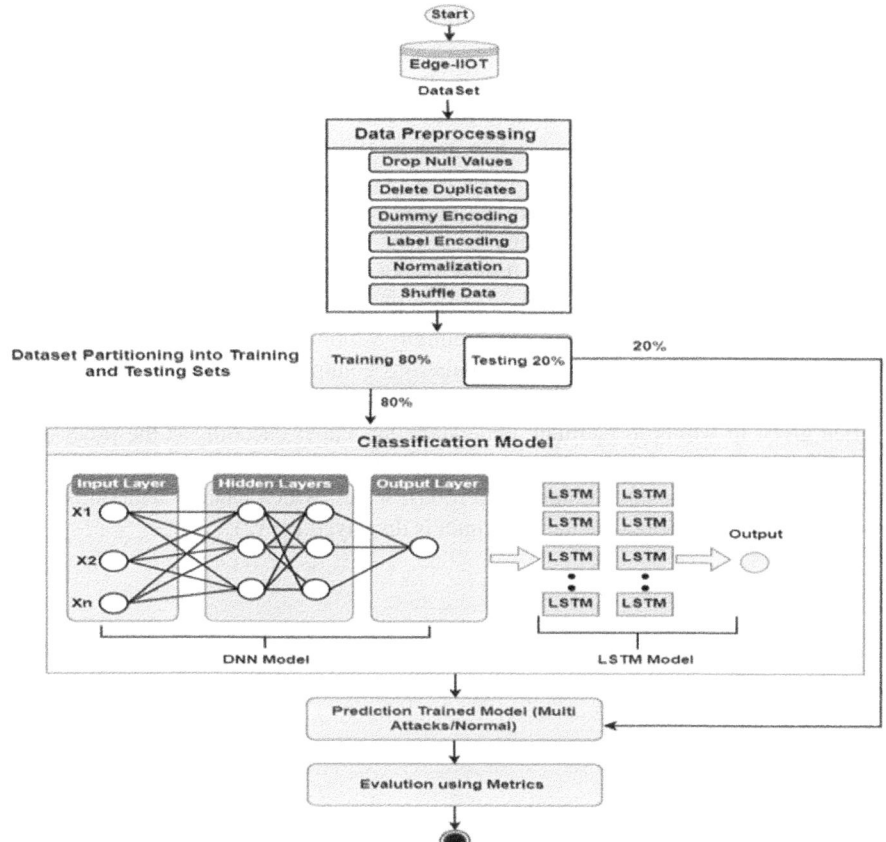

Fig. 1. Proposed System of Enhanced Hybrid Deep Learning Model for IOT Security Attack Classification.

3.3 Dataset Preprocessing

The data of Edge-IIoT undergoes preprocessing to ensure its compatibility with deep learning algorithms, and the raw data is purified for careful analysis. These algorithms can be implemented, and we can select the one that yields superior outcomes. This paper employs the following preprocessing techniques:

- Drop Null Value: Missing values can indicate incomplete data. Missing input values cannot be compared, categorized, or used with mathematical methods. Hence, many data mining methods cannot handle them. Before doing data mining, missing values must be fixed. Discarding the sample is the easiest way to fix missing values. This strategy works well if a dataset has few missing values.
- Delete duplicates: Eliminating duplicate rows, empty columns, and incorrect feature columns is a part of cleaning the data before analysis, which helps to ensure the dataset is reliable and of high quality.
- Dummy Encoding: The categorical data encoding technique converts a categorical variable into a group of numerical variables and introduces (n − 1) dummy variables, where n is the number of classes of the dummy variable.
- Label Encoder: The dataset contains numerous columns with several labels. These symbols can be expressed as either numerical numbers or words. However, they are often given in words to facilitate understanding. Label encoding is the process of machines converting labels into a numerical format to enhance their readability.
- Normalization: This study employed a robust scaler, which handles data outliers to scale features. The robust scaler's formula is displayed in (12)

$$x_{scaled} = \frac{(x - Q2(x))}{(Q3(x) - Q1(x))} \tag{1}$$

The scaled and normalized value of a characteristic x is represented by scale, the data point is x, the median (Q2) is the second quartile, the first quartile is Q1, and the third quartile is Q3.

3.4 Hybrid (DNN-LSTM) Model

The model comprises two components: DNN and LSTM. The DNN and LSTM models consist of 6 layers connected by a reshape layer. The outcomes of the model produced by the DNN serve as inputs to the LSTM model, resulting in the generation of new attributes, as illustrated in Table 2 below.

Table 2. Hybrid (DNN-LSTM) Model.

DNN Model	Layer type	Output Shape	Param
	flatten (Flatten)	(None, 92)	0
	dense (Dense)	(None, 256)	23808
	dropout (Dropout)	(None, 256)	0
	dense_1 (Dense)	(None, 128)	32896
	dropout_1 (Dropout)	(None, 128)	0
	dense_2 (Dense)	(None, 15)	1935
LSTM Model	reshape (Reshape)	(None, 15, 1)	0
	input_1 (Input Layer)	[(None, 15,1)]	0
	lstm (LSTM)	(None, 15, 200)	161600
	lstm_1 (LSTM)	(None, 100)	120400
	dropout (Dropout)	(None, 100)	0
	dense (Dense)	(None, 50)	5050
	dense_1 (Dense)	(None, 15)	765
Total prams			346,454
Trainable prams			346,454
Non-trainable prams			0

And algorithm (1) illustrates hybrid classification model.

Algorithm 1: The Hybrid Classification Model

Input: dataset after preprocessing
Output: 15 Class
Begin
1. **FUNCTION build_model_dnn (num_classes, input_shape):**
      input layer = Input (shape=input_ shape)
      x = Flatten () (input_ layer)
      x = Dense (256, activation='relu', kernel initializer=glorot_uniform(seed=0))(x)
      x = Dropout(0.3)(x)
      x = Dense (128, activation='relu', kernel initializer=glorot_uniform(seed=0))(x)
      x = Dropout (0.3) (x)
      dnn_output = Dense (num_classes, activation='softmax', kernel_initializer=glorot_uniform(seed=0))(x)
      dnn_model = Model (inputs=input _layer, outputs=dnn_output)
    RETURN dnn_model
2. **FUNCTION build_model_lstm (num_classes, input_shape):**
      Input_ layer = Input(shape=input_shape)
      x = LSTM (units=200, return sequences=True, activation='tanh')(input_ layer)
      x = LSTM (units=100, return_ sequences=False, activation='tanh')(x)
      x = Dropout(0.3)(x)
      x = Dense (50, activation='relu')(x)
      lstm_output = Dense (num_classes, activation='softmax')(x)
      lstm_model = Model (inputs=input_ layer, outputs=lstm_output)
    RETURN lstm_model
3. **FUNCTION build_hybrid_model (num_classes, input_shape):**
      dnn_model = build_model_dnn(num_classes, input_shape)
      dnn_output_shape = dnn_model. Output_ shape [-1]
      lstm_input_shape = (dnn_output_shape, 1)
      lstm_model = build_model_lstm (num_classes, lstm_input_shape)
      combined input = Input(shape=input_shape)
      dnn_output = dnn_model(combined_input)
      dnn_output = Reshape ((dnn_output_shape, 1))(dnn_output)
      lstm_output = lstm_model(dnn_output)
      hybrid_model = Model (inputs=combined_input, outputs=lstm_output)
    RETURN hybrid_model
4. num_classes = 15
5. input_shape = (92, 1)
6. hybrid_model = build_hybrid_model (num_classes, input_shape)
End

All three models share the same parameters, which include a parameter checkpoint. It focuses on the significance of Vall_Loss. Each time it drops, it archives the previous model and generates a new one. The model is stored based on the best results determined by the Vall_Loss and the early_stopping parameters. During the execution of a model, if it achieves less accuracy, it tracks the validation loss and evaluates the loss percentage. Whenever the model diminishes, it stays stationary—continuity at a specific place. When the value of Vall_Loss decreases, it indicates a higher level of accuracy. If the rate of reduction in early stopping persists, the model will halt. Regarding the parameter lr_reduce, when the accuracy reaches a particular level and then improves, lr_reduce decreases the value of Vall_Loss. The lower the learning percentage, the higher the accuracy.

4   Results and Discussion

The assessment was performed on a Windows 11 Pro machine with an Intel Core i7 (8th Gen) CPU, Nvidia GPU 6 GB, 16 GB of RAM, and a 256 GB solid-state drive (SSD) using Python in ANACONDA with Jupyter notebooks.

4.1   Preprocessing

The Edge-IIoT data set in Sect. 3.3. The data preparation approach encompasses various techniques, including data cleansing, categorical data encoding, and data scaling. Data is cleansed by examining for the presence of null values. If null values are found, they are substituted with the mean for numeric attributes and the most frequent value for categorical attributes. Upon data processing, the count significantly decreased from 2,219,200 to 1,927,304. Subsequently, the reprocessed data was subjected to rigorous testing using deep learning algorithms: Deep Neural Network (DNN) and Long Short-Term Memory (LSTM), as illustrated in Table 3 below.

Table 3.   The dataset was obtained after processing the Edge-IIoT data.

IoT traffic	Attack Type	Data Number
Normal	Normal	1380858
Attack	DDoS (UDP, ICMP, TCP, HTTP)	287,771
	SQL Injection	50,826
	Password	49,933
	Vulnerability Scanner	50,026
	Uploading	36,915
	Backdoor	24,026
	Port Scanning	19,983
	XSS	15,066
	Ransomware	9,689
	Fingerprinting	853
	MITM	358

4.2 Results of Deep Learning Algorithms

Figure 2 indicates deep learning techniques, specifically deep neural networks (DNN) and long short-term memory (LSTM). The Edge-IIoT dataset was tested with the following results: The DNN model attained an accuracy of 0.999, while the LSTM model earned an accuracy of 0.999.

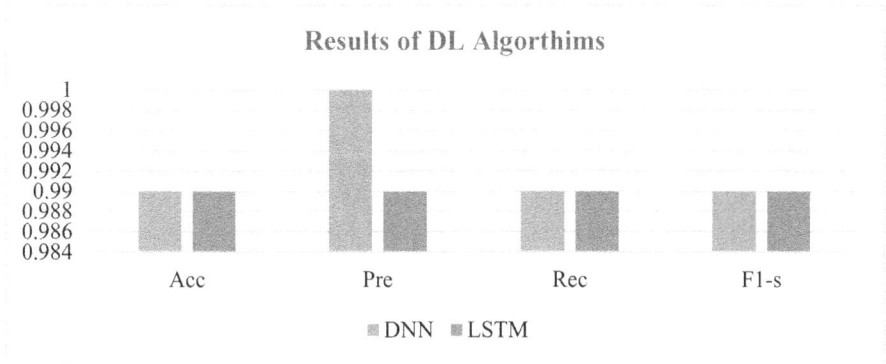

Fig. 2. Results of DNN and LSTM deep learning

Table 4 presents the accuracy, precision, recall, and F1_score of the classification binary outcomes achieved by Deep Learning in both the verification and testing stages. The vast amount of data influences the quality and precision of the DNN and LSTM models in the training phase.

Table 4. Result in Deep Learning.

Algo	Acc	Pre	Rec	F1-s
DNN	0.999	1.0	0.999	0.999
LSTM	0.999	0.999	0.999	0.999

The confusion matrix depicts the efficacy of the Edge-IIoT dataset model on a dataset consisting of two classes. Figure 3 and Fig. 4. By employing sophisticated deep learning techniques, specifically the Long Short-Term Memory (LSTM) and Deep Neural Network (DNN) algorithms, it was determined that the LSTM approach reached a remarkable accuracy of 0.999. In contrast, the DNN algorithm produced an accuracy of 0.999. The results indicate that deep learning algorithms are highly efficient and superior in identifying DDoS attacks using epoch 20 and batch size 512. Figure 2 and Table 4 display the reports for the LSTM and DNN algorithms, including metrics such as accuracy, precision, recall, f1-score, and support.

The results of 2 Classes of confusion matrix are shown in Fig. 5, which shows the performance of the hybrid model in binary classification. It achieved an accuracy rate

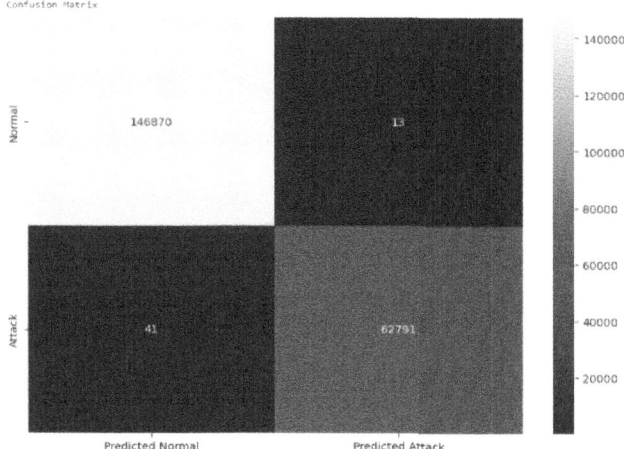

Fig. 3. Confusion matrix 2-Class (LSTM)

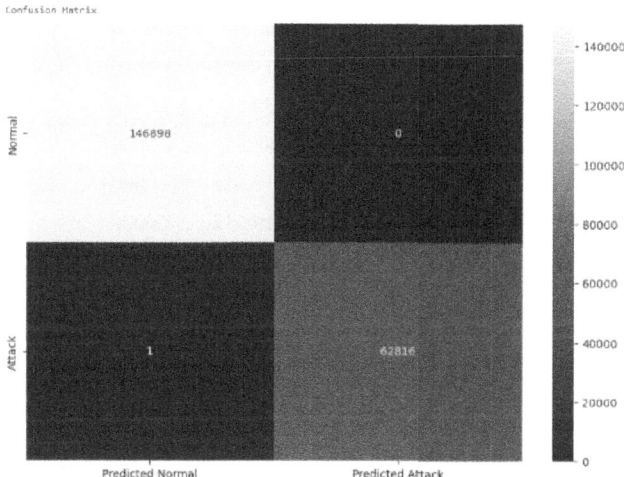

Fig. 4. Confusion matrix 2-Class (DNN)

of 100%, as shown in the classification report in Fig. 6, which includes metrics such as precision, recall, f1 score, and support. In the training phase, the number of epochs is shown in Table 6, and the parameters used in this proposal are shown in Table 7.

Model binary.

The model was set to run for 20 epochs but terminated at the 13th epoch due to early stopping. This decision was made because the model's accuracy remained constant during all execution phases. The confusion matrix displays the performance of the deep learning models on a dataset consisting of 15 different classes. Figure 7 and Fig. 9

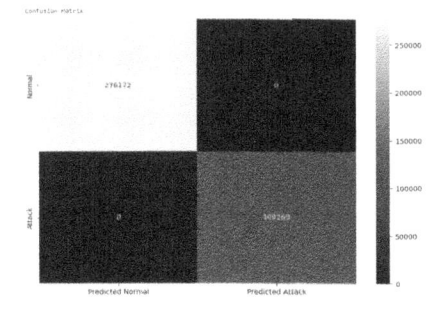

True Positives (TP): 109289
True Negatives (TN): 276172
False Positives (FP): 0
False Negatives (FN): 0

Classification Report
                  precision   recall f1-score   support

         Normal   1.00   1.00   1.00   276172
         Attack   1.00   1.00   1.00   109289

       accuracy   1.00   385461
      macro avg   1.00   1.00   1.00   385461
   weighted avg   1.00   1.00   1.00   385461

Fig. 5. Confusion matrix Hybrid (DNN-LSTM

Fig. 6. Classification Report for binary classes

Table 5. The train phase Hybrid Model (2-class DNN-LSTM)

N	Epoch	Time(second)	Accuracy	Loss	Val_accuracy	Val_loss
0	1	42	0.9979	0.0040	1.0000	3.3799e-08
1	2	35	1.0000	1.9673e-08	1.0000	0.0000e+00
2	3	35	1.0000	5.1230e-10	1.0000	0.0000e +00
3	4	35	1.0000	1.8788e-11	1.0000	0.0000e +00
4	5	35	1.0000	3.4019e-12	1.0000	0.0000e+00
5	6	35	1.0000	3.4019e-12	1.0000	0.0000e +00
6	7	34	1.0000	9.2779e-13	1.0000	0.0000e +00
7	8	34	1.0000	2.3195e-13	1.0000	0.0000e +00
8	9	34	1.0000	6.1853e-13	1.0000	0.0000e+00
9	10	34	1.0000	1.5463e-13	1.0000	0.0000e +00

By employing sophisticated techniques in deep learning, specifically LSTM and DNN algorithms, it was determined that the DNN algorithm achieved an accuracy of 0.95, and the LSTM algorithm achieved an accuracy of 0.95. Consequently, the DNN and LSTM were selected for implementation in the proposed hybrid model for detecting DDoS attacks. Deep learning techniques for a 15-class problem and Figs. 8 and 10 presented classification reports for DNN and LSTM algorithms, as well as accuracy, recall, precision, and fi-score.

Table 6. Hyperparameters used in our proposed System.

Hyper parameter	Value
Number of epoch	20(2-Class)
	70(15-Class)
Batch size	512
Learning rate	0.001
Callbacks	checkpoint, early_stopping, lr_reduce
Activation function	Relu, sigmoid, tanh, softmax
Normalization function	MinMaxScaler
Loss function	categorical_crossentropy
num_classes	Binary,multi-class

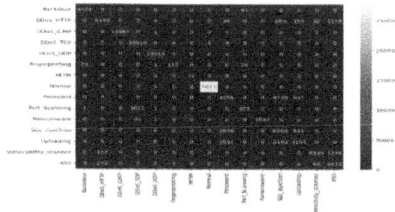

Fig. 7. The confusion matrix (LSTM)

```
Classification Report
                        precision   recall  f1-score   support

              Backdoor       0.99     0.98      0.99      4805
             DDoS_HTTP       0.96     0.83      0.89      9841
             DDoS_ICMP       1.00     1.00      1.00     13588
              DDoS_TCP       0.77     1.00      0.87     10012
              DDoS_UDP       1.00     1.00      1.00     24313
         Fingerprinting       1.00     0.67      0.80       171
                  MITM       1.00     1.00      1.00        71
                Normal       1.00     1.00      1.00    276172
              Password       0.54     0.44      0.48      9987
          Port_Scanning       0.90     0.24      0.38      3997
            Ransomware       1.00     0.98      0.99      1938
         SQL_injection       0.48     0.66      0.56     10165
             Uploading       0.69     0.57      0.62      7383
  Vulnerability_scanner       0.99     0.85      0.92     10005
                   XSS       0.52     0.89      0.65      3013

              accuracy                          0.95    385461
             macro avg       0.86     0.81      0.81    385461
          weighted avg       0.96     0.95      0.95    385461
```

Fig. 8. Classification Report (LSTM)

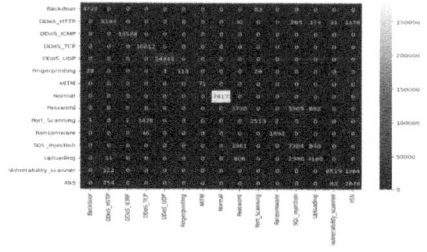

Fig. 9. The confusion matrix (DNN)

```
Classification Report
                        precision   recall  f1-score   support

              Backdoor       0.99     0.98      0.99      4805
             DDoS_HTTP       0.95     0.83      0.89      9841
             DDoS_ICMP       1.00     1.00      1.00     13588
              DDoS_TCP       0.87     1.00      0.93     10012
              DDoS_UDP       1.00     1.00      1.00     24313
         Fingerprinting       1.00     0.66      0.80       171
                  MITM       1.00     1.00      1.00        71
                Normal       1.00     1.00      1.00    276172
              Password       0.57     0.37      0.45      9987
          Port_Scanning       0.96     0.63      0.76      3997
            Ransomware       1.00     0.98      0.99      1938
         SQL_injection       0.48     0.72      0.58     10165
             Uploading       0.69     0.57      0.62      7383
  Vulnerability_scanner       0.99     0.85      0.91     10005
                   XSS       0.51     0.89      0.65      3013

              accuracy                          0.95    385461
             macro avg       0.87     0.83      0.84    385461
          weighted avg       0.96     0.95      0.95    385461
```

Fig. 10. Classification Report (DNN)

4.3 Hybrid (DNN-LSTM) Model

Two models, LSTM and DNN, discussed earlier in Sect. 3.4, were combined. Based on the inputs of the DNN model, the model was evaluated and achieved an accuracy of

95.36 after fusion. Once these features are identified, they are fed into the LSTM model as inputs. The LSTM model then extracts new features and performs classification, as shown by the confusion matrix in Fig. 11 and the number of the first (13) epochs in Table 8.

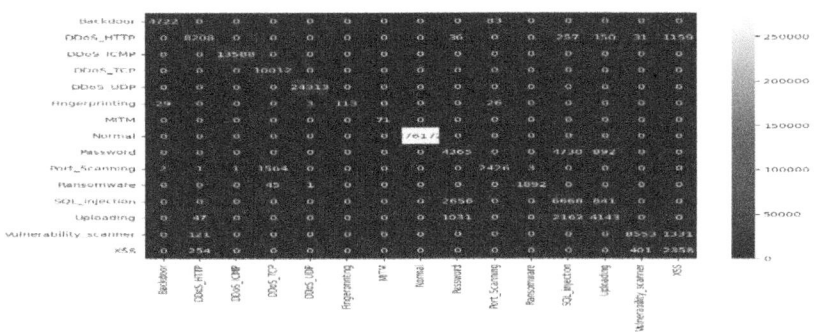

Fig. 11. Confusion matrix Hybrid (DNN-LSTM) Model.

Table 7. The train phase Hybrid Model (15-Class, DNN-LSTM)

No	Epoch	Time(second)	Accuracy	loss	val_accuracy	val_loss
0	1	46	0.7790	0.6777	0.8044	0.4778
1	2	41	0.8169	0.4553	0.8408	0.4091
2	3	41	0.9131	0.1977	0.9350	0.1351
3	4	41	0.9334	0.1354	0.9342	0.1312
4	5	41	0.9342	0.1328	0.9357	0.1292
5	6	41	0.9344	0.1317	0.9357	0.1289
6	7	44	0.9348	0.1309	0.9352	0.1286
7	8	43	0.9347	0.1306	0.9356	0.1287
8	9	41	0.9347	0.1299	0.9353	0.1274
9	10	41	0.9348	0.1291	0.9358	0.1281
10	11	42	0.9350	0.1290	0.9356	0.1278
11	12	42	0.9349	0.1289	0.9359	0.1271
12	13	42	0.9352	0.1286	0.9358	0.1272

Table 8. Shows the main comparison between different approaches in the related works of the Edge-IioT cyberattack dataset.

Ref	Method	Data set	Class	Accuracy
[11]	DNN	Edge-IIoT	2-class	99.99%
			15-class	94.67%
[13]	RNN-LSTM	Edge-IIoT	(single-class only)	98.88%
[14]	a hybrid model BiGRU, LSTM, and softmax	Edge-IIoT	(8-Class only)	98%
[15]	Deepak-IoT	Edge-IIoT	15-Class	94.96%
[17]	RNN-LSTM	KDD Cup 99; NSLKDD	2-Class	83.29% 68.59%
The proposed system	LSTM	Edge-IIoT	2-Class	99.99%
			15-Class	0.95%
The proposed system	DNN	Edge-IIoT	2-Class	99.99%
			15-Class	0.95%
The proposed system	Hybrid (DNN-LSTM)	Edge-IIoT	2-Class	100%
			15-Class	95.36%

5   Conclusion and Future Work

In this paper, we proposed a hybrid model that combines DNN and LSTM models to classify and detect cybersecurity attacks on the Internet of Things. The Edge-IIoT dataset, which consists of Edge IoT Big data, was used. It is the largest dataset of about 2,219,200 records and is suitable for deep learning techniques using the binary class of deep learning algorithms for the LSTM and DNN and the hybrid model (DNN-LSTM). Note that the results were high for deep learning algorithms, where the accuracy was 0.999 in binary classification for attack and normal type. Fifteen distinct classes were used for the exact data for the same LSTM and DNN algorithms and were evaluated. The results were 0.95, which is a potential solution for detecting distributed denial of service attacks for LSTM or DNN. The hybrid model combines the LSTM and DNN models, using the data entering the DNN and the inputs from this output to the LSTM algorithm. This process generates new outputs that achieved an accuracy of 95.36%. Future work will include experimenting with a dataset specific to a DDoS attack, linking the environment in real-time, and working on deep learning algorithms (2-Class, 15-Class). We will use a hybrid model and conduct real-world attacks to evaluate the effectiveness of the model in detecting attacks.

References

1. Vishwakarma, R., Jain, A.K.: A survey of DDoS attacking techniques and defence mechanisms in the IoT network. Telecommun. Syst. **73**(1), 3–25 (2020)

2. Salim, M.M., Rathore, S., Park, J.H.: Distributed denial of service attacks and its defenses in IoT: a survey. J. Supercomput. **76**, 5320–5363 (2020)
3. Hassan, K.F., Manaa, M.E.: Detection and mitigation of DDoS attacks in internet of things using a fog computing hybrid approach. Bull. Electr. Eng. Inf. **11**(3), 1604–1613 (2022)
4. Wehbi, K., Hong, L., Al-salah, T., Bhutta, A.A.: A Survey on Machine Learning based Detection on DDoS Attacks for IoT systems. In: 2019 SoutheastCon, IEEE, pp. 1–6 (2019)
5. S. Ullah, S., Boulila, W., Koubaa, A., Ahmad, J.: MAGRU-IDS: a multi-head attention-based gated recurrent unit for intrusion detection in IIoT networks. IEEE Access (2023)
6. Atlam, H.F., Walters, R.J., Wills, G.B.: Fog computing and the internet of things: a review. Big Data Cogn. Comput. **2**(2), 10 (2018)
7. Chaudhary, S., Mishra, P.K.: DDoS attacks in industrial IoT: a survey. Comput. Networks 110015 (2023)
8. Najafimehr, M., Zarifzadeh, S., Mostafavi, S.: A hybrid machine learning approach for detecting unprecedented DDoS attacks. J. Supercomput. **78**(6), 8106–8136 (2022)
9. Sasi, T., Lashkari, A.H., Lu, R., Xiong, P., Iqbal, S.: A comprehensive survey on IoT attacks: taxonomy, detection mechanisms and challenges. J. Inf. Intell. (2023)
10. Siwakoti, Y.R., Bhurtel, M., Rawat, D.B., Oest, A., Johnson, R.C.: Advances in IoT security: vulnerabilities, enabled criminal services, attacks, and countermeasures. IEEE Internet Things J. **10**(13), 11224–11239 (2023)
11. Ferrag, M.A., Friha, O., Hamouda, D., Maglaras, L., Janicke, H.: Edge-IIoTset: a new comprehensive realistic cyber security dataset of IoT and IIoT applications for centralized and federated learning. IEEE Access **10**, 40281–40306 (2022)
12. Tareq, I., Elbagoury, B.M., El-Regaily, S., El-Horbaty, E.-S.M.: Analysis of Ton-IoT, UNW-NB15, and edge-IIoT datasets using DL in cybersecurity for IoT. Appl. Sci. **12**(19), 9572 (2022)
13. Alashhab, A.A., Zahid, M.S.M., Muneer, A., Abdullahi, M.: Low-rate DDoS attack detection using deep learning for SDN-enabled IoT networks. Int. J. Adv. Comput. Sci. Appl. **13**(11) (2022)
14. Javeed, D., Gao, T., Saeed, M.S., Kumar, P.: An intrusion detection system for edge-envisioned smart agriculture in extreme environment. IEEE Internet Things J. (2023)
15. Ding, W., Abdel-Basset, M., Mohamed, R.: DeepAK-IoT: an effective deep learning model for cyberattack detection in IoT networks. Inf. Sci. (N Y) **634**, 157–171 (2023)
16. Rahman, A., et al.: Federated Llearning-based AI approaches in smart healthcare: concepts, taxonomies, challenges and open issues. Cluster Comput. **26**(4), 2271–2311 (2023)
17. Jadhav, K.P., Arjariya, T., Gangwar, M.: Intrusion detection system using recurrent neural network-long short-term memory. Int. J. Intell. Syst. Appl. Eng. **11**(5s), 563–573 (2023)
18. Ferrag, M.A.: Edge-IIoTset Cyber Security Dataset of IoT & IIoT. Accessed on Feb. Accessed on 15 Sep. 2024. https://www.kaggle.com/datasets/mohamedamineferrag/edgeiiotset-cyber-security-dataset-of-IoT-IIoT
19. Ferrag, M.A., Friha, O., Maglaras, L., Janicke, H., Shu, L.: Federated deep learning for cyber security in the internet of things: concepts, applications, and experimental analysis. IEEE Access **9**, 138509–138542 (2021)
20. Laiq, F., Al-Obeidat, F., Amin, A., Moreira, F.: DDoS attack detection in Edge-IIoT using ensemble learning. In: 2023 7th Cyber Security in Networking Conference (CSNet), Montreal, QC, Canada, pp. 204–207 (2023). https://doi.org/10.1109/CSNet59123.2023.10339784

Hybrid Multimodal Biometric Identification System: Integrating Face and Palmprint Traits Through Feature-Level Fusion

Ola Najah Kadhim[1,2]([✉]) [iD] and Mohamad Hasan Abdulameer[3] [iD]

[1] Department of Computer Science, Faculty of Computer Science and Mathematics, University of Kufa, Najaf, Iraq
[2] Technical Institute of Al-Mussaib, Al-Furat Al-Awsat Technical University, Najaf, Iraq
Ola.najah@atu.edu.iq
[3] Department of Computer Science, Faculty of Education for Girls, University of Kufa, Najaf, Iraq
mohammed.almayali@uokufa.edu.iq

Abstract. Global information security demands sophisticated solutions, with multimodal biometric systems enhancing recognition accuracy and overcoming single-mode system limitations. Unimodal biometric systems face challenges like forgery, user variability, and data security, which cannot be easily mitigated. Multimodal biometric systems offer enhanced security and robustness, addressing these limitations effectively. This project aims to develop a multimodal biometric identification system that fuses face and palmprint features at the feature level. It uses Convolutional Neural Networks to extract features from face and palmprint data. These feature vectors are integrated through feature-level fusion to improve identification effectiveness. The merged vector is then classified using a Support Vector Machine. The proposed multimodal system, evaluated using the real MULB dataset, significantly improves accuracy, recall, precision, equal error (ERR), false acceptance, and false rejection rates. The accuracy rates for individual palmprint and face systems are 97.30% and 98.97%, respectively, with EERs of 0.0162 and 0.0143. While the multimodal system achieves an improved accuracy rate of 99.28% and a low EER of 0.0095.

Keywords: Multimodal Biometric · Feature Level Fusion · Deep Learning

1 Introduction

Today, security is one of the most essential factors, especially with companies embracing the new world of technology with computers and the Internet. The more traditional and current measures of security features, including passwords and PINs, present several risks and challenges, such as the loss of such passwords, forgetting PINs and hacking. This has spurred the use of biometric systems that check for physiological and behavioural characteristics of the users to offer enhanced and more secure identification [1]. Biometric systems employ different characteristics peculiar to each individual, including

S. O. Al-Mamory et al. (Eds.): 3INC 2024, CCIS 2329, pp. 201–212, 2025.
https://doi.org/10.1007/978-3-031-81065-7_13

fingerprints, facial form, iris and voice. These systems pose numerous advantages over conventional methods of authentications, as they promise to display enhancements in security, simplicity, and the possibility of forgery. The biometric features are unique to the person; thus, an illegitimate person can't imitate the biometric characteristics. Therefore, the increased use of biometrics has been incorporated into different security uses, from using biometrics to unlocking a mobile device or gaining access to a sensitive area [2]. Even though unimodal biometric systems where identification is done using one or more biometric measurements for identification purposes have shown to work, it has not been without its drawbacks, which have been noted as follows. Several challenges in single-mode systems include noise in the sensed data, lack of universality, and spoofing attacks. To address these issues, multimodal biometric systems in the development process combine several biometric traits to provide maximal security and minimal false rates [3]. A multibiometric system is an amalgamation of multiple factors where two or more biometric factors like fingerprints, face, iris, palm, and voice are combined and used for identification and authentication. These systems with many attributes proved to possess higher accuracy, adaptability for changes, and better defence against spoofing than standard adaptive systems using only a single attribute. It is also essential to distinguish that multimodal biometric systems can work at different fusion stages: the sensor level, feature level, score level and decision level; all these approaches possess specific advantages and disadvantages [4]. Feature-level fusion is a highly beneficial technique employed in multi-biometric systems. Before classification, it combines the feature vectors acquired from multiple traits into a unified fused feature vector. This method preserves all the information in the separate feature sets so that the feature representation of the biometric data becomes complete and more discriminative. Biometric feature-level fusion has substantial potential to enhance the biometric system's performance since the fusion method takes the best qualities of each modality while addressing their shortcomings [5].

The suggested multimodal face-palmprint system is incorporated through feature-level fusion, which will use a Convolutional Neural network (CNN) for extracting features and a Support Vector Machine (SVM) with the One versus One (OvO) approach for classification. This approach combines the features of deep learning methods and machine learning methods so that the developed biometric identification system is stable, accurate, and reliable. The proposed system shows substantial enhancements in terms of security and reliability over the traditional unimodal biometric system, thus being a more secure solution for biometric authentication. The subsequent content might delineate the paper's contributions: (1) Developing a framework that combines face and palm attributes at the feature level for multimodal biometrics. (2) comparing the kind of recognition provided by biometric systems based on a single biometric with those based on many biometric systems. (3) training a model with a deep-learning approach to extract critical features from the face and palm. (4) feature-level fusion can improve the decision-making process when identifying humans.

2 Related Works

Multiple biometric systems with several identification techniques have become the focus of academic research and investigations. This section highlights multimodal biometric systems reflecting on several traditional and deep machine learning approaches. Mazen Selim et al. proposed multi-modal biometric human identification using face and iris recognition techniques [6]. It utilized 2D wavelet transform and 2D Gabor filters for feature extraction, which employed features-level fusion. Lastly, a deep-belief network was used in the identification, and it was found that with the SDUML-HMT dataset, 99% accuracy was possible. Milind Rane and Umesh Bhadade [7] implemented a multi-modal biometric recognition technique through face and palmprint biometrics. Two t-norms combined matching scores: The Frank t-norm and the Yager t-norm. The feature extraction methods encompass the Gabor transform, Radon transform, Radon-Gabor, Ridgelet, FPLBP, and TPLBP, with the Pearson correlation coefficient used for classification. The process achieved 99.7% accuracy on a chimeric dataset. Despite the system's high accuracy, it used a chimeric dataset, not the actual dataset. Annie Joseph et al. [8] introduced a multi-modal biometric recognition system based on fingerprint and face characteristics. It used CNN for face recognition, oriented FAST and rotated BRIEF (ORB), and hamming distance for fingerprint recognition, with the scores fused at score level fusion. It achieved an accuracy of 96.54% on a chimeric dataset from the UCI machine learning repository dataset. The use of imbalanced datasets can impact the generalization and robustness of the proposed method, potentially leading to biased results.

Yang Wang et al. [9] suggested a multi-modal biometric identification system that integrates finger vein and facial images, utilizing deep learning models like AlexNet and VGG-19. Feature extraction and features-level fusion techniques achieved identification accuracies ranging from 98.84% to 99.98% across chimeric datasets, including SDUMLA-FV, FV-USM, and CASIA-WebFace. Zahraa Talal and Ahmed M. Alkababji [10] designed a multi-modal biometric system that integrates face and palmprint traits. It utilizes a new 2-D circular wavelet filter based on HAAR filters for extracting features from face datasets and employs contourlet transformation for palmprint datasets. Additionally, a model is utilized to train and evaluate the system. The results of the approach indicate an accuracy of 99.3% when utilizing feature-level fusion. C Sapna Kumari et al. [11] suggested a multi-modal biometric system merging iris and facial modalities. It employs SWT and LBP algorithms for feature extraction and PCA for dimensionality reduction. The classification process utilizes the Euclidean distance classifier, achieving a recognition rate of 99.42% on chimeric datasets through effective feature-level fusion. The scalability of larger datasets or real-time applications must be addressed thoroughly.

3 Methodology

The proposed multimodal identification system combines a CNN and an SVM classifier. The system employs feature-level fusion to merge the characteristics of two traits. The suggested system is efficient in accurately identifying persons. Figure 1 illustrates the primary phases of the proposed system. The face-palm multimodal identification system has four phases: preprocessing, feature extraction, feature level fusion, and classification; these are shown in the subsequent sections:

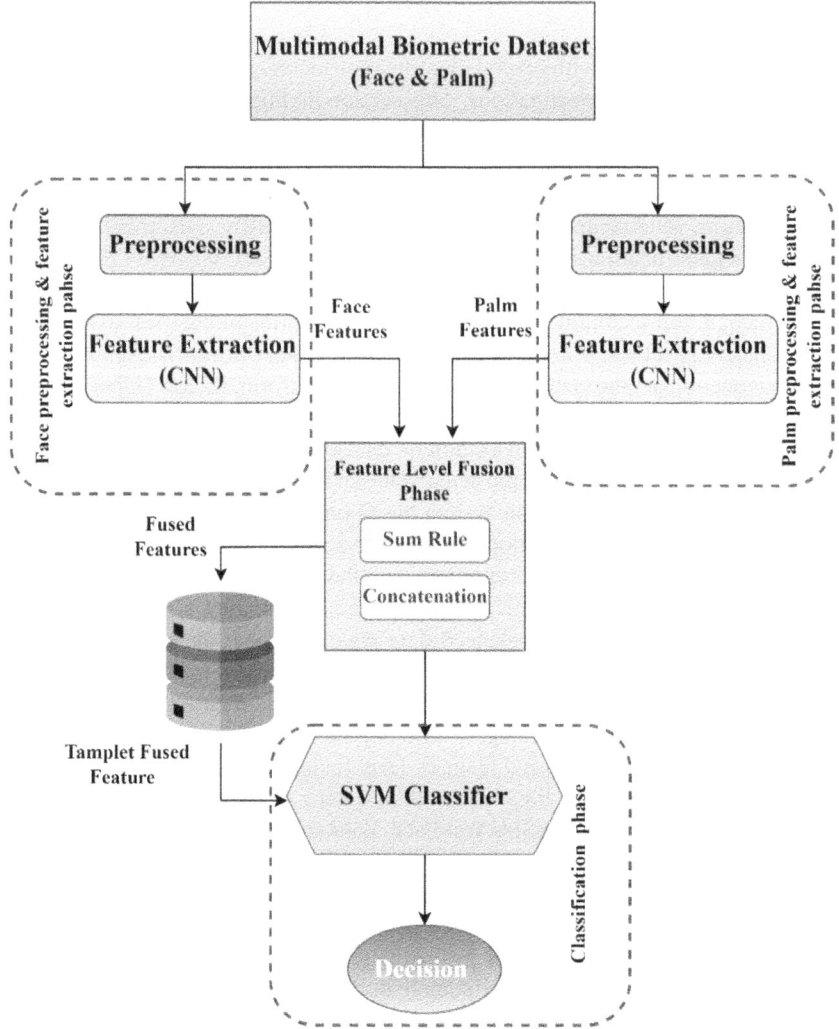

Fig. 1. The face-palm multimodal identification system block diagram.

3.1 Data Preprocessing

The suggested system's initial phase is preprocessing, an essential phase that intends to simplify and prepare the input images for the subsequent phases. In the face preprocessing phase, face detection is a necessary portion of this stage and substantially impacts the final results. The Multi-task cascaded Convolutional Neural Network (MTCNN) [12] utilizes a cascade architecture to detect faces, separated into three phases (Proposal-Net, Refine-Net, and Output-Net). This technique uses a deep convolutional neural network to recognize and align facial features. The systematic approach ensures accurate and consistent facial identification at different scales. We start by enlarging the size of the original image to multiple sizes and constructing an image pyramid. Together with the networks, this pyramid helps select faces with high precision regarding the pyramid levels. Subsequently, we rescale all images to the suitable dimensions, apply facial section cropping for all images we have, and convert all incoming images to the grayscale format. The series of operations involved in facial image preprocessing is illustrated in Fig. 2.

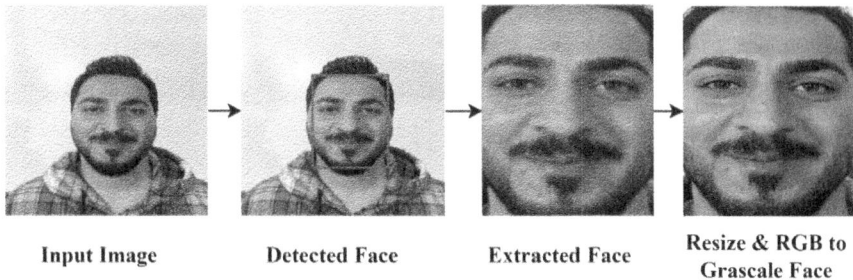

| Input Image | Detected Face | Extracted Face | Resize & RGB to Grascale Face |

Fig. 2. Face Preprocessing Steps

The preprocessing part for palmprint is the most vital because the sizes of images have to be changed, the original image converted to grayscale, further cropping and region of interest (ROI) to extract. One of their core components must be considered as it dramatically impacts the overall results. The methodology described in [13] defining the region of interest involves mathematical computation to arrive at an ROI in the form of a square with an area of 192*192 pixels. Figure 3 illustrates the various preprocessing stages. The steps in [13] are: (1) Applying a Gaussian smoothing to the input image. (2) Converting the smoothed image into a binary image using a specified threshold value, denoted as 'T'. (3) Using boundary tracking to determine the boundaries within the binary image. (4) Identifying the points between fingers establishes the border image's two-dimensional ROI pattern. (5) Finally, the ROI is extracted.

3.2 Features Extraction

During the second stage of the proposed system, the feature is extracted. It involves extracting significant features from each face and palmprint trait using a highly efficient CNN model. The study employed a CNN model of 10 layers, comprising three convolutional and max-pooling layers, one flattening layer, one fully connected layer (FC), and a dropout layer. Figure 3 shows a visual representation. The architectural sequence begins with a convolutional operation in the initial layer.

The process involves convolution layers with a Rectifier Linear Unit (ReLU) activation function, Max-Pooling reducing the feature image dimensions to 100×100 pixels, 50×50 pixels, and 25×25 pixels. A flattening layer transforms the feature map into a vectorized representation, and a fully connected layer is added to reduce complexity. A dropout layer is incorporated to mitigate overfitting. The model is optimized using the

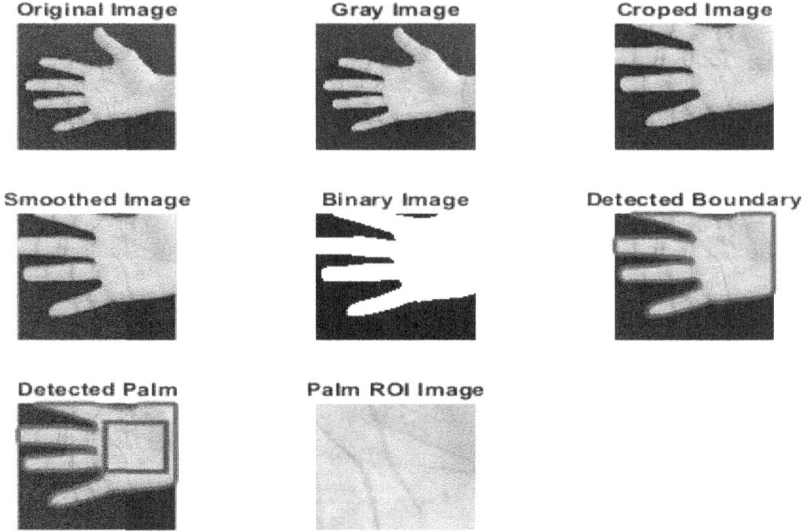

Fig. 3. Palmprint preprocessing steps.

Adam optimizer technique and trained using the loss function (categorical cross-entropy) (Fig. 4).

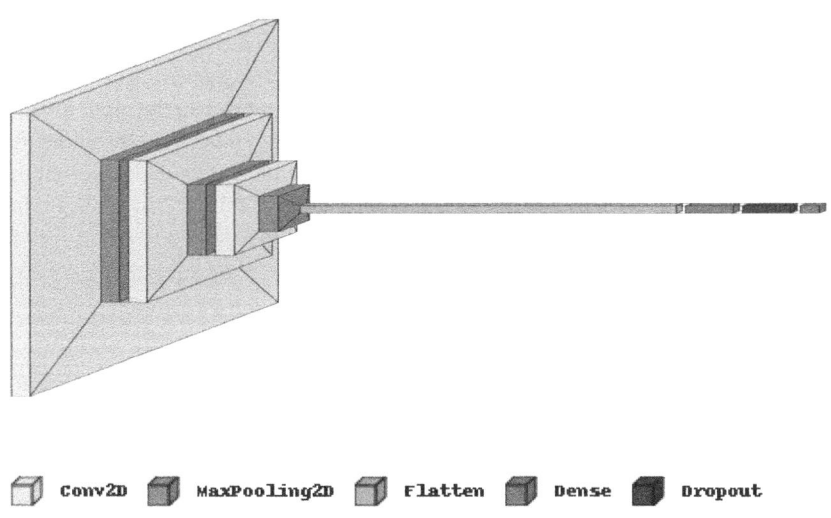

Fig. 4. The structure of CNN

3.3 Feature Level Fusion

Fusion refers to the process of integrating characteristics acquired from several modalities. The features of the two distinct traits are joined to generate new characteristics that precisely depict the user. The model develops the ability to identify and efficiently employ these merged features in the fusion technique. The aggregation stage combines the feature vectors gained from the fully linked layers of the two models into a single integrated vector. We utilize two fusion strategies, the sum and concatenation rules (Con.), as described in Eqs. (1) and (2).

$$F_{fused} = F_{face}^{(i)} + F_{palm}^{(i)} \tag{1}$$

$$F_{fused} = \begin{bmatrix} F_{face}^{(i)} \\ F_{palm}^{(i)} \end{bmatrix} \tag{2}$$

where $F_{face}^{(i)}$ and $F_{palm}^{(i)}$ represent the features vectors from face and palmprint traits for samples (i), respectively.

3.4 Classification Process

The resulting fused feature vector is classified using the SVM classifier after the fusion process in the proposed face-palmprint multimodal system. SVM is a powerful classifier that seeks to identify the ideal hyperplane that maximizes the separation between various classes. In a multi-class classification problem, the OvO strategy involves training a separate SVM classifier for each pair of classes as: (1) Each classifier distinguishes between a pair of classes. (2) During classification, each classifier votes for one of the two classes it was trained on. (3) The final class is determined by the class that receives the most votes.

4 Experimental Results

The proposed multimodal identification approach uses Google Colab with an Nvidia Tesla K80 GPU. Face photos are pre-processed in Google Colab, while MATLAB v18.a processes and extracts regions of interest from iris images. The MULB dataset is partitioned into training (70%), validation (10%), and testing (20%) subsets to evaluate the system's effectiveness.

4.1 Dataset Description

The MULB dataset, described in [14] owned by the authors, is a thorough compilation of an individual's facial, palmprint, and iris characteristics, making it a real multimodal dataset. This work's suggested multimodal biometric identification method exclusively employs the facial and palmprint characteristics extracted from the MULB dataset. The unique attributes of the MULB dataset are presented in Table 1. The writers used the micro iPhone 14 Pro Max camera to record each trait's data aspect meticulously. The

MULB dataset, which consists of data collected from staff and students et al.-Furat Al-Awsat Technical University in Kufa, Iraq, is accessible online for academic and research purposes without charge at https://www.kaggle.com/datasets/olankadhim/multimodal-biometric-dataset-mulb.

Table 1. Characteristics of MULB dataset.

Characteristics	Details
Traits	3
Trait types	Face, hand, iris
Colour image	Yes
Total number of distinct individuals	176
Image number per individual	20
Age	17–54
Gender	118 males, 58 females
Number of images in total	20*3*176 = 10,560
Format of image	jpg
Environments	Face: emotions, possess and accessories. Hand: varying perspectives and illumination. Iris: diverse illumination and viewpoints

4.2 Evaluation Metrics

The proposed system is assessed using several metrics, which are presented below:

1. Accuracy (Acc) is a quantitative measure that calculates the proportion of predicted occurrences to the total number of instances in a dataset, as determined in (3) [13].

$$Acc = \frac{(T_{pos} + T_{neg})}{(T_{pos} + T_{neg} + F_{pos} + F_{neg})} \tag{3}$$

2. Precision (Pre) is a measure that calculates the ratio of correctly forecast positive cases to the overall number of instances predictable as positive by the model, as determined in (4) [13].

$$Pre = \frac{T_{pos}}{(T_{pos} + F_{pos})} \tag{4}$$

3. Recall (Rec) is a quantitative measure that evaluates the accuracy of a model in correctly identifying positive events by comparing it to the actual positive events, as determined in [9].

$$\text{Rec} = \frac{T_{pos}}{(T_{pos} + F_{neg})} \tag{5}$$

4. The F1 Score is computed using the harmonic mean of precision and recall. The harmonic mean provides equal importance to both precision and recall, as determined in (6) [13].

$$F1_{score} = 2 * \frac{(\text{Pre} * \text{Rec})}{(\text{Pre} + \text{Rec})} \tag{6}$$

5. False Acceptance Rate (FAR): the probability of the wrong person being given access to someone not in the biometric dataset or not authorized to be around. Computed in (7) [15].

$$\text{FAR} = \frac{F_{pos}}{(F_{pos} + T_{neg})} \tag{7}$$

6. The False Rejection Rate (FRR) quantifies the likelihood of a system inaccurately denying contact to an unregistered or unauthorized user. It is computed in (8) [15].

$$\text{FRR} = \frac{F_{neg}}{(T_{pos} + F_{neg})} \tag{8}$$

7. The Equal Error Rate (EER) is the threshold at which the False Acceptance Rate (FAR) is equal to the False Rejection Rate (FRR), as determined in (9) [15].

$$\text{ERR} = \frac{\text{FAR} + \text{FRR}}{2} \tag{9}$$

where Tpos indicates the model correctly predicted a "positive" result, Tneg means the model accurately predicted a "negative" result. Fpos signifies the model incorrectly predicted a "positive" result when it should have been "negative," and Fneg indicates the model incorrectly predicted a "negative" result when it should have been "positive."

4.3 Results Analysis

Table 2 displays the identification performance results for both the unimodal and multimodal models. These results were obtained from the tests that were conducted. The findings suggest that the multimodal biometric model achieved superior results to the single modal biometric system in evaluation measures. This highlights that multimodal biometrics, in its fundamental state, provides a highly efficient method for improving the evaluation metrics of a biometric system.

From Table 2, the proposed multimodal identification with the concatenation fusion method outperforms the sum rule fusion method. Table 3 displays the error rate values of the proposed system when analyzing error rate results, including FAR, FRR, and ERR. The proposed multimodal system exhibited decreased error rates compared to the unimodal biometrics system. EER is commonly employed to assess the total efficacy of a biometric system. Smaller ERR numbers specify superior complete performance.

Table 2. The outcomes of unimodal and multimodal systems' performance

Models	Traits	Techniques	Fusion	Acc	Pre	Rec	F1-score
Unimodal	Face	CNN + SVM	–	97.30%	97.20%	97.30%	98.14%
	Palm	CNN + SVM	–	98.72%	98.94%	98.72%	98.70%
Multimodal	Face-Palm	CNN + SVM	Sum	99%	99.17%	99%	98.99%
			Con.	**99.28%**	**99.40%**	**99.28%**	**99.28%**

Table 3. The outcomes of unimodal and multimodal systems' performance with FAR, FRR and ERR.

Models	Traits	Techniques	Fusion	FAR	FRR	ERR
Unimodal	Face	CNN + SVM	–	0.0098	0.0227	0.0162
	Palm	CNN + SVM	–	0.0201	0.0085	0.0143
Multimodal	Face-Palm	CNN + SVM	Sum	0.0049	0.0142	0.0095
			Con.	**0.0048**	**0.0142**	**0.0095**

5 Comparative Study

The proposed multimodal system (face-palm) based on feature-level fusion was compared with previous relevant works. Due to the restricted accessibility of the multimodal datasets, the real multimodal dataset (MULB) was applied to the models of three relevant works for comparison, as shown in Table 4. It presents a comparative analysis of several state-of-the-art multimodal biometric identification systems, highlighting different techniques, datasets, and fusion methods and their accuracy.

Table 4. Comparative results of different relevant works with proposed multimodal system

Ref.	Techniques	Dataset	Fusion	Acc
[16] (2023)	Modified VGG16	Paper dataset: KVKR (face, fingerprint)	Score-level	99.65%
		Our dataset: MULB (face, palm)		**99.52%**

(*continued*)

Table 4. (*continued*)

Ref.	Techniques	Dataset	Fusion	Acc
[7] (2020)	Gabor transform, Radon transform, Radon-Gabor, and TPLBP (Three-Patch Local Binary Pattern). Pearson correlation coefficient for classification	Paper dataset: Chimeric dataset Face 94 dataset for a face. IITD dataset for palm	Score-level	99.7%
		Our dataset: MULB (face, palm)		**99.75%**
[8] (2021)	CNN modal, SoftMax classifier for the face ORB algorithm, Hamming distance for fingerprint	Paper dataset: Chimeric dataset from UCI machine learning repository dataset	Score-level	95.94%
		Our dataset: MULB (face, palmprint)		**96.11%**
Proposed system	CNN + SVM	MULB (face, palm)	Feature-level	99.28%

6 Conclusion

A successful multimodal biometric system incorporating facial and palmprint identification has been successfully implemented. This approach enhances security and dependability by combining complementary information from both features. Utilizing an SVM classifier ensures resilient and precise identification. The hybrid approach effectively mitigates the limitations of unimodal systems. The feature-level fusion results in a more robust system, improving recognition performance and security compared to using face or palmprint traits alone. Experiments with a real dataset show the multimodal system's superior performance compared to unimodal systems. The face recognition system achieves an accuracy rate of 97.30%, while the palm recognition system achieves 98.72%. The multimodal system reaches an accuracy rate of 99.28%. The EER for the face and palmprint systems are 0.0098 and 0.0201, respectively, whereas the multimodal system achieves a superior EER of 0.0048. The results indicate that multimodal systems outperform unimodal systems regarding accuracy, security, and reliability. The study demonstrates the potential of hybrid multimodal systems in real-world biometric applications, offering a practical solution for more secure and reliable identification. In the future, with the scarcity and inaccessibility of multi-modal datasets, we aim to apply our approach to a different dataset once it becomes accessible.

References

1. Daas, S., Yahi, A., Bakir, T., Sedhane, M., Boughazi, M., Bourennane, E.-B.: Multimodal biometric recognition systems using deep learning based on the finger vein and finger knuckle

print fusion. IET Image Proc. **14**(15), 3859–3868 (2021). https://doi.org/10.1049/iet-ipr.2020.0491

2. Jain, A.K., Ross, A.A., Nandakumar, K.: Introduction to Biometrics: A Textbook. Springer, US (2011)
3. Al-Mahafzah, H., AbuKhalil, T., Alksasbeh, M., Alqaralleh, B.: Multi-modal palm-print and hand-vein biometric recognition at sensor level fusion. Int. J. Electr. Comput. Eng. **13**(2), 1954–1963 (2023). https://doi.org/10.11591/ijece.v12i5
4. Ahmad, M.I., Woo, W.L., Dlay, S.: Non-stationary feature fusion of face and palmprint multimodal biometrics. Neurocomputing **177**, 49–61 (2016). https://doi.org/10.1016/j.neucom.2015.11.003
5. Rasool, R.A.: Feature-level vs. score-level fusion in the human identification system. In: Applied Computational Intelligence and Soft Computing, vol. 2021, pp. 1–10 (2021). https://doi.org/10.1155/2021/6621772
6. Selim, M.M., Mahmoud, R.O., Muhi, O.A.: A feature level fusion of multimodal biometric authentication system. J. Converg. Inf. Technol. **13**(1), 1–11 (2018)
7. Rane, M.E., Bhadade, U.S.: Multimodal score level fusion for recognition using face and palmprint. Int. J. Electr. Eng. Educ. **57**(1), 1–19 (2020). https://doi.org/10.1177/0020720920929662
8. Joseph, A.A., et al.: Person verification based on multimodal biometric recognition. Pertanika J. Sci. Technology. **30**(1), 161–183 (2021). https://doi.org/10.47836/pjst.30.1.09
9. Wang, Y., Shi, D., Zhou, W.: Convolutional neural network approach based on multimodal biometric system with fusion of face and finger vein features. Sensors **22**(16), 1–15 (2022). https://doi.org/10.3390/s22166039
10. Talal, Z., Alkababji, A.M.: Face-palm print recognition system based on 2d circular wavelet Filter and contourlet transformation. J. Optim. Decis. Mak. **2**(2), 247–252 (2023)
11. Kumari, C., Nagapushpa, K., Jayalaxmi, H., Asha, C., Harakannanavar, S., Jakati, J.: Experimental Analysis of face and Iris biometric traits based on the fusion approach. Indian J. Sci. Technol. **16**(31), 2388–2397 (2023). https://doi.org/10.17485/IJST/v16i31.314
12. Zhang, K., Zhang, Z., Li, Z., Qiao, Y.: Joint face detection and alignment using multitask cascaded convolutional networks. IEEE Signal Process. Lett. **23**(10), 1499–1503 (2016). https://doi.org/10.1109/LSP.2016.2603342
13. Bachay, F.M., Abdulameer, M.H.: Hybrid deep learning model based on autoencoder and CNN for palmprint authentication. Int. J. Intell. Eng. Syst. **15**(3), 488–499 (2022). https://doi.org/10.22266/ijies2022.0630.41
14. Kadhim, O.N., Abdulameer, M.H.: A multimodal biometric database and case study for face recognition based deep learning. Bull. Electr. Eng. Inf. **13**(1), 677–685 (2024). https://doi.org/10.11591/eei.v13i1.660510.11591/eei.v13i1.6605
15. Aung, H.M.L., Pluempitiwiriyawej, C., Hamamoto, K., Wangsiripitak, S.: Multimodal biometrics recognition using a deep convolutional neural network with transfer learning in surveillance videos. Computation **10**(127), 1–15 (2022). https://doi.org/10.3390/computation10070127
16. K. Shinde, K., Kayte, C.: Multimodal deep learning based score level fusion using face and fingerprint. In: Proceedings 1st International Conference on Advances in Computer Vision and Artificial Intelligence Technologies (ACVAIT 2022), pp. 140–152 (2023). https://doi.org/10.2991/978-94-6463-196-8_13

Improving Machine Learning-Based Intrusion Detection Systems: A Comparative Study on NSL-KDD Dataset

Zahraa H. Salim[(✉)] and Safwan O. Hasoon

Department of Software, College of Computer Science and Mathematics, University of Mosul, Mosul, Iraq
zahraa.22csp6@student.uomosul.edu.iq,
dr.safwan1971@uomosul.edu.iq

Abstract. The potential for crimes and attacks poses a potential threat to real-world personal computer networks, presenting risks such as service outages, data breaches, and financial losses. Due to the failure of traditional methods to remain aware of the rapidly changing nature of risks, traditional intrusion detection systems (IDS) typically have high false positive rates and reduce detection accuracy. The use of meta-learning (ML) can advance the development of discontinuity identification frameworks by using their ability to distinguish between examples and ways of eliminating information. This paper explores the application of meta-learning in intrusion detection using the NSL_KDD dataset. By leveraging meta-learning techniques, the study aims to enhance the performance of traditional IDS. Different machine learning algorithms are evaluated and compared. The results demonstrate the effectiveness of the proposed approach, displaying improved accuracy and reduced false positive rates. Using Grid search CV contributes to optimizing the hyper parameters of the models, further improving their performance. Overall, this research highlights the potential of meta-learning in enhancing intrusion detection systems and provides valuable insights for selecting appropriate algorithms and configurations to improve network security.

Keywords: Intrusion Detection Systems · Meta-Learning · NSL-KDD Dataset · Grid search CV

1 Introduction

At present, crime and interruptions represent a tireless danger to PC organizations, possibly bringing about help disturbances, information breaks, and financial misfortunes. Because of their powerlessness to stay aware of evolving dangers, customary rule-based interruption identification frameworks (IDS) much of the time produce bogus advantages and have unfortunate recognition exactness. Thus, the interest in progressively mind-boggling and canny interruption location strategies is rising [1].

ML has turned into a significant device for various organizations, one of which is network security. Because ML algorithms are so good at deriving patterns and behaviours

© The Author(s), under exclusive license to Springer Nature Switzerland AG 2025
S. O. Al-Mamory et al. (Eds.): 3INC 2024, CCIS 2329, pp. 213–229, 2025.
https://doi.org/10.1007/978-3-031-81065-7_14

from data, they may detect abnormalities and intrusions that traditional IDS might miss. The objective is to improve intrusion detection systems' accuracy and effectiveness by using ML algorithms, which will fortify organization security overall [2].

To ensure the pertinence and rightness of the training data, data preparation is a fundamental stage in any AI framework. Preprocessing with regard of intrusion detection involves eliminating commotion and pointless data from datasets like NSL-KDD. This eliminates properties that are not helpful for intrusion detection, yielding a more targeted and valid feature set. Then, to pick the most chosen, the most discriminatory and informative features, attribute selection methods are utilized, which bring down the dimensionality of the data and then improve the performance of machine learning algorithms [1].

Several ML classifiers are utilized in this research to classify network traffic data as normal or as a threat. The effectiveness of the system is entirely determined by measures like discovery proficiency and precision among classifiers. How we might interpret ML-based intrusion detection frameworks is progressed by this comparative study, which helps with deciding the best exact and powerful intrusion detection recognition model for the NSL-KDD dataset [3].

Utilizing AI methods and datasets, for example, NSL-KDD, a definitive objective is to make keen and strong (IDS) that can rapidly recognize and mitigate network breaches. Considering the arising risks, our research adds to the continuous endeavours to further develop network security.

2 Related Works

Zhou et al. (2019): Used ensemble learning, and utilized datasets like NSL-KDD, AWID, and CIC-IDS2017 utilizing C4.5, irregular Endlessly Backwoods Dad, individually. They further developed attack acknowledgment by utilizing outfit strategies and casting ballot components after dimensionality decreased using CFS-BA. The review caused notice of the requirement for better huge-scope information on the board and rare peril location [4].

Gao et al. (2019) presented a technique focusing on adaptive ensemble learning (IDS) and achieved an accuracy speedup of 85.2% on the NSL-KDD dataset. They understood the value of improving preprocessing, highlighted the design, and used decision trees, random forests, KNN, DNN, and Adaboost to achieve the best accuracy. The study lacked data preprocessing to achieve a better result [5].

Xu et al. (2020), proposed FC-Net, which achieved accuracy rates of 94.64% and 97.87% on datasets such as CICIDS2017 and ISC2012. Although accuracy was good, they noted that the use of DNNs limited the ability to effectively deal with conflicting data, which affected reaction time [6].

Su et al. (2020) achieved an accuracy rate of 84.25% for DNN-based intrusion detection on NSL-KDD data by using bidirectional LSTM and attention processes. Nevertheless, they had difficulties in accurately identifying U2R class assaults [7].

Maniriho et al. (2020): Used the NSL-KDD and UNSW-B15 datasets and investigated single ML classifiers and ensemble approaches. High-dimensionality data difficulties were disregarded [8].

ElDahshan et al. (2022): suggested a meta-heuristic approach, with accuracy rates of 98.93% and 99.63%. While they acknowledged problems in managing new attack types and small datasets, they emphasized data pretreatment and creative techniques [9].

Sohail et al. (2023): INFUSE was first presented, which achieved accuracy rates of 91.6% and 85.6% on the NSL-KDD dataset. They emphasized the necessity of more studies using a variety of datasets [10].

Jose & Jose (2023): Using deep learning methods by using CIC-IDS2017, they were able to get accuracy rates of 94.61%, 97.67%, and 98.61%. They lacked varied datasets and data preparation necessary for deep learning [11].

Thockchom et al. (2023): Using a variety of datasets, investigated ensemble learning and achieved accuracy rates of 99.84%, 93.88%, and 99.80%. They underlined the difficulty of countering emerging threats and the requirement for sophisticated data processing techniques [12].

Al-Momani et al. (2023): Using UNSW-B15 data, ensemble learning was used and achieved an accuracy rate of 97.95%. However, diverse real-world situations were required for evaluation, and using a single dataset to represent many threat types is a limitation of the research [13].

While each study presents valuable insights and advancements in intrusion detection, common themes include the need for improved data preprocessing, handling of emerging threats, and broader dataset utilization. Addressing these areas could enhance the effectiveness and applicability of intrusion detection methods. Table 1 shows summary of the studies and their drawbacks.

Table 1. Summary of The Studies and Their Drawbacks.

Author(s)	Technique	Datasets Used	Accuracy Rates	Drawbacks	Differentiation
Zhou et al. (2019)	Ensemble Learning, C4.5, Random Forest, Bagging	NSL-KDD, AWID, CIC-IDS2017	Not specified	Limited scope of datasets, dimensionality reduction might lose important features	Notable use of ensemble methods and dimensionality reduction; lacks newer advancements in deep learning
Gao et al. (2019)	Adaptive Ensemble Learning	NSL-KDD	85.20%	Lack of thorough data preprocessing, over-reliance on ensemble methods	Broad approach with diverse classifiers; could benefit from improved preprocessing strategies
Xu et al. (2020)	FC-Net (DNN-based)	CICIDS2017, ISC2012	94.64%, 97.87%	DNNs struggle with conflicting data, affecting response time	High accuracy with FC-Net; needs better handling of data conflicts and diverse attack scenarios

(*continued*)

Table 1. (*continued*)

Author(s)	Technique	Datasets Used	Accuracy Rates	Drawbacks	Differentiation
Su et al. (2020)	DNN with Bidirectional LSTM and Attention	NSL-KDD	84.25%	Difficulty in identifying U2R class attacks, limited dataset representation	Advanced use of bidirectional LSTM and attention mechanisms; needs better U2R detection
Maniriho et al. (2020)	Single ML Classifiers and Ensemble Approaches	NSL-KDD, UNSW-B15	Not specified	Ignored high-dimensionality data challenges, limited dataset coverage	Explored various classifiers and ensembles; addressing high-dimensionality issues could improve robustness
ElDahshan et al. (2022)	Meta-Heuristic Approach	Not specified	98.93%, 99.63%	Issues with new attack types and small datasets	High accuracy with meta-heuristics; needs better management of new attack types and larger datasets
Sohail et al. (2023)	INFUSE	NSL-KDD	91.6%, 85.6%	Limited dataset variety, lack of diverse testing	Emphasis on INFUSE; incorporating more datasets could improve robustness
Jose & Jose (2023)	Deep Learning	CIC-IDS2017	94.61%, 97.67%, 98.61%	Limited to CIC-IDS2017, inadequate data preparation	High accuracy with deep learning; needs broader dataset diversity and better data preparation
Thockchom et al. (2023)	Ensemble Learning	Various datasets	99.84%, 93.88%, 99.80%	Challenges with emerging threats, need for sophisticated data processing	High accuracy across datasets; addressing emerging threats and improving data processing techniques
Al-Momani et al. (2023)	Ensemble Learning	UNSW-B15	97.95%	Limited to UNSW-B15 dataset, needs diverse real-world evaluations	Effective use of ensemble learning; needs more diverse datasets and real-world evaluations
Zhou et al. (2019)	Ensemble Learning, C4.5, Random Forest, Bagging	NSL-KDD, AWID, CIC-IDS2017	Not specified	Limited scope of datasets, dimensionality reduction might lose important features	Notable use of ensemble methods and dimensionality reduction; lacks newer advancements in deep learning

(*continued*)

Table 1. (*continued*)

Author(s)	Technique	Datasets Used	Accuracy Rates	Drawbacks	Differentiation
Gao et al. (2019)	Adaptive Ensemble Learning	NSL-KDD	85.20%	Lack of thorough data preprocessing, over-reliance on ensemble methods	Broad approach with diverse classifiers; could benefit from improved preprocessing strategies
Xu et al. (2020)	FC-Net (DNN-based)	CICIDS2017, ISC2012	94.64%, 97.87%	DNNs struggle with conflicting data, affecting response time	High accuracy with FC-Net; needs better handling of data conflicts and diverse attack scenarios

3 Methodology

The methodology of the proposed system is shown in (Fig. 1), the steps of which will be explained sequentially.

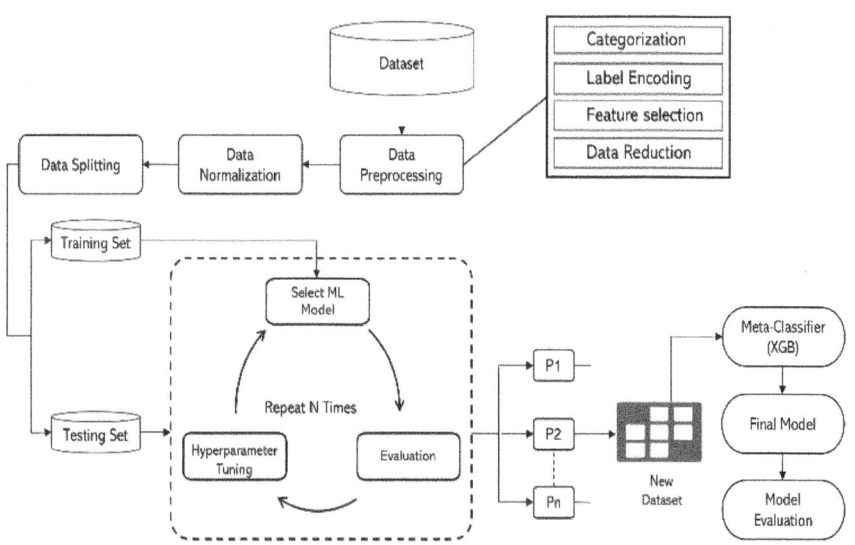

Fig. 1. Proposed Diagram for Intrusion Detection System

An essential dataset widely utilized for anomaly detection techniques since 1999 is the Knowledge Discovery and Data Mining (KDD"99) dataset. However, it has been noted that the results of using this dataset for anomaly detection were unsatisfactory. Consequently, researchers sought a better solution, leading to the development of a new dataset known as NSL-KDD. This dataset is comprised of selected records from the original KDD dataset. The training set consists of 125,973 samples, while the test set consists of 22,544 samples, with each sample containing 41 attributes representing either attacks or normal behaviour. The attacks in this dataset are categorized into four types: denial of service (DoS), root-to-local (R2L), user-to-root (U2R), and probe attacks. DoS attacks involve the restriction of processing resources' time to prevent illegitimate users from accessing them. R2L attacks occur when attackers prevent access from remote systems and are categorized as both network-based and host-based (NIDS). U2R attacks involve attempting to gain a user's password to access the system legitimately and retrieve data. Finally, probe attacks involve the examination of a network to collect information and potentially make penetrations in the future [1]. Table 2 represents a description of the dataset.

Table 2. Summary of the Datasets

Dataset	NSL_KDD
No. of Record	148,517
No. of Attribute	41
No. of Attribute after preprocessing	13
No. of Attack	4
Classes	2
Normal	77,054
Anomaly	71,463

The paper employs NSL-KDD dataset which, despite being popular in the field of network intrusion detection, is more than a decade old. Using the KDD Cup 99 dataset, the dataset has been criticized as having some drawbacks, which include outdated attack patterns and imbalanced classes. The rationale for selecting this data should be provided as well as the argument why this is still more appropriate than using more recent and diverse data. The authors should explain why they selected NSL-KDD dataset and how the limitations of the dataset were dealt with in the paper. This discussion is important for the identification of the conditions under which the results can be applied to the modern situations.

3.1   Dataset Preprocessing

Table 3 explains the steps of preprocessing activities, including their objectives and activities.

After completing the pre-processing and selecting the best features, the dataset, which contains 41 features, was reduced to 31 features, which are considered among the most relevant features and have the greatest impact on the classification process, which leads to reducing the complexity present in the data and making it more powerful and efficient. Arranging priorities has a significant impact. It is based on the ability to

Table 3. Summary of Preprocessing Steps for the Dataset

Preprocessing Step	Description
Attack Type Simplification	For binary classification uniformity, entries in the attack type column are categorized into "normal" and anything else considered "attack"
Label Encoding	To convert the categorical features to numeric for labels (service, flag, protocol type, and attack_type) for additional analysis, Label Encoding was used to transform them
Feature Selection: by absolute correlation matrix	To cut down on dimensionality and noise, a correlation matrix was created, and the ten features that were least connected with the type of assault were chosen
Feature Selection: by Standard Deviation	To find features with less variability, the five features with the least variance were chosen after the standard deviation for each feature was computed
Feature Elimination	To increase the efficiency and accuracy of the model, features found using the correlation matrix and standard deviation were integrated and eliminated from the dataset
Dataset Reduction	Features of the dataset that were designated for removal were removed, creating a dataset containing the most highly correlated features suitable for further analysis

separate between different types of attacks by identifying the characteristics that are most closely related to the variable "attack_type", which produces a model that can perform better by focusing on the best and most prominent features that are deeply related to the target.

3.2 Initial and Final Features

The Initial dataset, which had 31 characteristics after preprocessing, was sorted into its best properties using Data analysis by histogram and Heatmap. A selection of 13 characteristics was chosen through analysis using the algorithm of Random Forest, (see Fig. 2), taking into account both their significance to the study's purpose and its target variable as well as their association with one another. In order to minimize duplication and multicollinearity, this procedure required finding the characteristics that showed the greatest correlations with the target variable or with each other. This subset of characteristics was chosen because it was thought to include the most useful information for the analysis or modelling work at hand. This reduced the number of dimensions and computing complexity in the data representation, making it more effective and efficient.

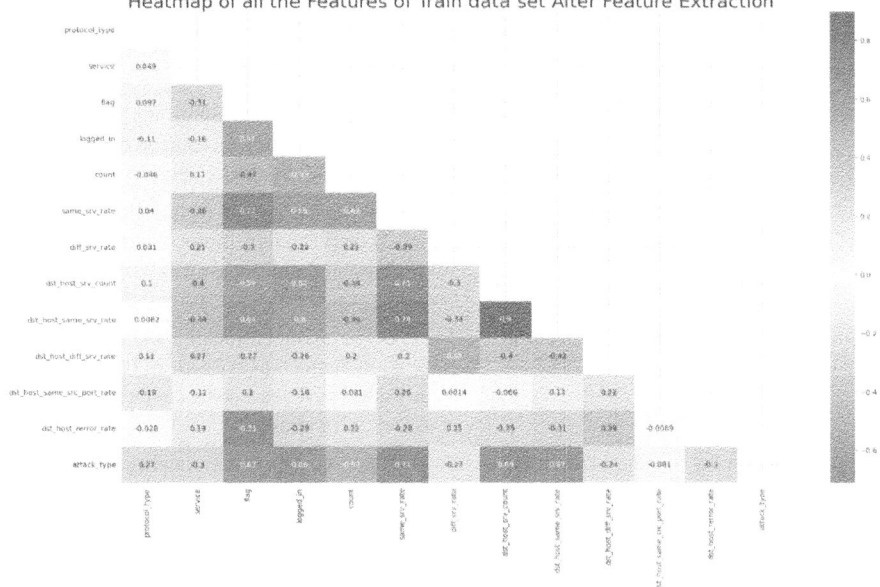

Fig. 2. The Final Features

In order to reduce dimensionality and computational complexity and identify the most significant features that contribute to the predictive job, feature selection is an essential stage in the construction of successful machine learning models. In this instance, it is likely that the features that have been picked have been chosen for their prospective predictive power as well as their association with the target variable (attack_type).

In order to reduce dimensionality and computational complexity and identify the most significant features that contribute to the predictive job, feature selection is an essential stage in the construction of successful machine learning models.

The prioritization of variables that significantly impact the ability to differentiate between various attack types is shown by the feature selection process, which is based on correlation with the target variable (attack_type). It may be possible for the model to perform better in terms of discrimination and classification by concentrating on these highly associated features.

3.3 Dataset Normalization

The given code scales the features between the range of 0 and 1, utilizing Min-Max scaling, a normalization approach. By ensuring consistency in feature scales, this procedure assists with improving convergence when training the model. Before transforming the training and testing data, the scaler is fitted to the training data (X_train) to ascertain the minimum and maximum values for each feature. Min-max scaling improves the comparability of features by standardizing the feature range, which eventually boosts the effectiveness of machine learning models.

3.4 Dataset Splitting

At this stage of the proposed work design steps, the generated data is divided by 70% for training data, which is 103,960 samples, and test data is divided by 30%, which is 44,555 samples.

3.5 Select Machine Learning Model

In this paper the different ML algorithms used for intrusion detection systems are explained below:

1- Logistic Regression: A linear classification approach that uses one or more predictor variables to represent the probability of a binary result. It functions best when there is a linear relationship between the target variable and the characteristics [14].

2- Naive Bayes: An algorithm for probabilistic classification based on the independence of features and the Bayes theorem. It performs very well with high-dimensional data and is especially useful for text classification [15].

3- AdaBoost Classifier: A technique for ensemble learning that builds a strong classifier by combining several weak classifiers. It concentrates more on the challenging cases while gradually fixing the flaws of the earlier models [16].

4- Gradient Boosting Classifier: An additional ensemble technique that adds weak learners one after the other, fixing each other's mistakes, until a strong classifier is created. It is renowned for having a strong predictive capacity and handling heterogeneous features with ease [17].

5- Linear Discriminant Analysis (LDA): An algorithm for classification that determines which linear feature combinations work best to divide data into distinct classes. When the classes are well-separated and the requirements of normality and equal covariance matrices are met, it is especially helpful [18].

6- Quadratic Discriminant Analysis (QDA): QDA does not presume equal covariance matrices across classes, in contrast to LDA. Although it is more versatile, accurate estimation of the additional factors takes more data [19].

7- Random Forest: An ensemble learning technique that constructs several decision trees during training and produces the mean prediction (regression) or the mode of the classes (classification) for each unique tree [20].

8- LightGBM: a gradient-boosting framework with learning algorithms based on trees. When compared to other boosting algorithms, it has faster training times and is built for efficiency. It also handles large datasets effectively [21].

Specifically, machine learning methods chosen which are Logistic Regression, Naive Bayes, AdaBoost, Gradient Boosting, LDA, QDA, Random Forest, LightGBM are categorized on the basis of approach that would help in solving the classification problem with reference to characteristics of data and its complexity. Logistic Regression is preferred due to its simplicity and interpretability in linear problems while Naive Bayes is preferred despite its independence assumption especially with high-dimensional feature space, large text datasets. AdaBoost and Gradient Boosting are selected because they employ ensemble methods that learn from and build upon previous mistakes to improve the model fitness to the data while Gradient Boosting is capable of providing a strong solution for large datasets. LDA and QDA provide discriminative power where in LDA the covariance of the classes is assumed to be equal whereas in QDA the covariance is allowed to vary. This means that Random Forest resulted in the making of a collection of decision trees that provided better robustness and accuracy as compared to a single decision tree, while LightGBM is preferred due to its applicability and capability to handle big data results. The assumptions and characteristics influencing each method's effectiveness shape the authors' decision on which method to use when addressing particular issues.

3.6 Hyperparameter Tuning

A hyperparameter tuning method called GridSearchCV is used to determine the optimal hyperparameters for machine learning models. To ascertain which combination of hyperparameters produces the highest performance, it carefully searches through a pre-defined network of hyperparameters and applies cross-validation to each possible combination. By adjusting several parameters, including learning rate, regularization strength, and tree depth, the performance of the models is improved.

Each set of hyperparameters is systematically evaluated by the GridSearchCV algorithm, which assigns a score to each one depending on a predefined evaluation criterion such as accuracy, precision, or F1 score. The set of hyperparameters that performs best is then selected. GridSearchCV helps reduce the time cost and resources used for data preparation, thus improving process efficiency and final model quality, and ensures successful model generalization to new data by automating validation and parameter adjustment processes. Table 4 shows the best-tuning parameters.

Table 4. Best Tuning Parameters

Algorithm	Parameters		
Logistic Regression	C: 0.01	Penalty: 11	Solver: Saga
Random Forest	N-estimation: 100	Min amples_split: 1	Min samples_leaf: 2
Gaussian Naive Bayes	Var Smoothing: 1		
AdaBoost	N-estimation: 50	Learning Rate: 1	Algorithm: SAMME.R
Gradient Boosting Classifier	N-estimation: 100	min samples split: 2	min samples leaf: 4
	max depth: 4	learning rate: 0.5	
Linear Discriminant Analysis	Solver: Svd	Shrinkage: None	N-components: None
Quadratic Discriminant Analysis	reg param: 0		
LightGBM	Subsample: 0.9	N-estimators: 200	Max_depth: 10
	Learning_rate: 0.2	Colsampl_ bytree: 1.0	

Class designation		Actual class	
		True (1)	False (0)
Predicted class	Positive (1)	TP	FP
	Negative (0)	FN	TN

Fig. 3. Binary Classification Confusion Matrix

3.7 Testing

When training a classifier, the assessment scale is crucial to getting the best classifier possible. So, selecting the right rating scale is crucial for differentiating and getting the best classifier. In order to enhance the generative classifier, this section has thoroughly analyzed pertinent assessment metrics that are intended to act as discriminators. Generally speaking, precision is a measure that many generative classifiers employ to identify the best solution while training [22]. Accuracy has various drawbacks, including being less informative, less discriminatory, and biased against data from the dominant class. Other measurements that are explicitly intended to define the ideal solution are briefly included in this paragraph as well. Also mentioned are these alternate measures' drawbacks [22].

Confusion matrix for a binary classifier (Fig. 3). Actual values are marked True (1) and False (0), and are predicted as Positive (1) and Negative (0). Estimates of the possibilities of classification models are derived from the expressions TP, TN, FP, FN, which exist in the confusion matrix [23].

- True Positive (TP) – The type of data that is relevant when considering the disarray framework is the true positive point because in this case, positive result is actually typical and so is whatever transpires.
- FP (False positive) – When the data of interest in the L(disarray) is a positive value, if a positive value is typical and what occurred is negative. The mistake that is made in this situation is referred to a sort 1 mistake. I've seen something very similar to that vitriolic talent in the form of awful premonition.
- FN (False Negative) It is the bogus negative when A normal result of data of interest and what actually occurred is positive result in the disarray lattice. This case is of the kind 2 and they are as dangerous as kind 1 mistakes which are a major source of trouble.
- TN (True Negative) Valid Negative, if indeed the result of the analysis of the data of interest in the specified disarray framework results to an adverse result which is normal, then the TN equivalent will have occurred (Table 5).

Table 5. The elements of the evaluation process (variables, definitions, and equations)

Variable	Definition	Equation
Accuracy	the percentage of accurately anticipated data from tests is easily determined by dividing all accurate forecasts by all predictions	$Accuracy = \frac{Tp+TN}{TP+TN+FP+FN}$
Precision	the proportion of outstanding instances among all anticipated ones from a specific class	$Precision = \frac{TP}{TP+FP}$
Recall	the ratio of the total number of occurrences to the proportion of instances that were supposed to be members of a class	$Recall = \frac{TP}{TP+FN}$
F1-Score	The phrase is used to describe a test's accuracy. The maximum F1-score is 1, which denotes outstanding recall and precision, while the lowest F1-score is 0	$F1 - Score = 2 \times \frac{percision \times recall}{Percison+recall}$

4 Results

4.1 Before Tuning

The models were assessed using a range of measures as shown in Table 6, including accuracy, precision, recall, F1 Score, and ROC AUC. RF and LightGBM stood out as the best, exhibiting consistently excellent results on all measures. With RF marginally outperforming LightGBM in all measures, these models showed remarkable predictive potential. Though they performed marginally better than the top two models overall, the AdaBoost, LR, and LDA all trailed closely behind. The AdaBoost Classifier exhibited momentous accuracy and review, delivering it fitting for use where diminishing misleading up-sides and bogus negatives is basic. Then again, the NB model performed less well than the others, showing lower scores for all standards.

4.2 After Tuning

In the wake of tuning the models, critical improvements were seen across different execution measurements as displayed in Table 7.

RF Tuned and LightGBM Tuned kept up with elevated degrees of accuracy, Precision, Recall, F1 score, and ROC AUC, demonstrating fruitful streamlining of their hyperparameters. AdaBoost Tuned additionally shows reliable execution enhancements, exhibiting the viability of boundary tuning. Algorithm Tuning showed upgrades in all measurements, demonstrating further developed model execution following hyperparameter changes. QDA-Tuned and LDA-Tuned both showed peripheral upgrades after tuning, proposing that boundary stream-lining be added to their improved exhibition. While NB

Table 6. Model Results Metrics Before Tuning

Model	Train Acc.	Acc.	Precision	Recall	F1 Score	ROC AUC
NB	0.85320	0.8529	0.8368	0.8874	0.8613	0.85
LDA	0.91319	0.9151	0.9019	0.9369	0.9191	0.91
LR	0.91453	0.9172	0.9034	0.9395	0.9211	0.91
QDA	0.91929	0.9209	0.9125	0.9359	0.9241	0.92
AdaBoost	0.94825	0.9504	0.9432	0.9616	0.9523	0.95
GBoost	0.97214	0.9737	0.9705	0.9785	0.9745	0.97
LightGBM	0.98851	0.9876	0.9876	0.9884	0.9880	0.98
RF	0.99606	0.9902	0.9910	0.9897	0.9903	0.99

Table 7. Model Results Metrics After Tuning

Model	Train Acc.	Acc.	Precision	Recall	F1 Score	ROC AUC
RF -Tuned	0.9960	0.9901	0.9910	0.9897	0.9903	0.9983
LightGBM-Tuned	0.9939	0.9901	0.9906	0.9901	0.9904	0.9995
GBoost-Tuned	0.9903	0.9882	0.9884	0.9887	0.9885	0.9991
AdaBoost-Tuned	0.9482	0.9504	0.9432	0.9616	0.9523	0.9924
LR-Tuned	0.9187	0.9211	0.9072	0.9432	0.9248	0.9651
QDA-Tuned	0.9192	0.9209	0.9125	0.9359	0.9241	0.9739
LDA-Tuned	0.9131	0.9151	0.9019	0.9369	0.9191	0.9631
NB-Tuned	0.8608	0.8611	0.8283	0.9209	0.8722	0.9487

Tuned showed humble increases in all measures. As demonstrated in (Fig. 4). Generally speaking, the tuning system successfully upgraded the models' hyperparameters, leading to improved predictive accuracy and performance across the board.

5 Meta Learning Results

The forecasting process is divided into two stages in this study. Using data, the many machine learning methods discussed above train models to predict the future. The first predictions were provided by algorithms.

The declarative learning model for the second stage is XGBoost. The basic "stack" model, XGBoost, acts as a control and coordination mechanism. The predictions of the first stage algorithms serve as input for training XGBoost. To get more accurate final predictions, XGBoost learns how to combine the predictions of different algorithms. This makes it possible to improve the performance of the final model by taking advantage of

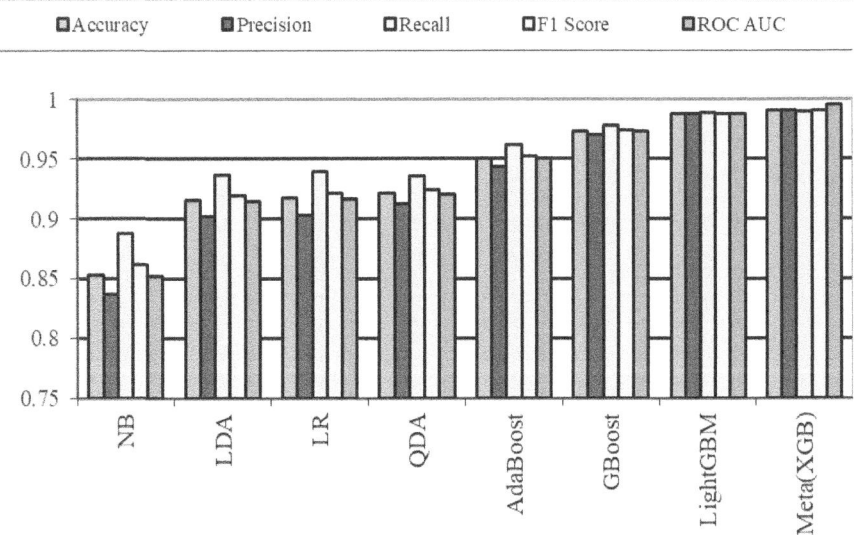

Fig. 4. A graphic illustration of performance metrics for all ML algorithms

the power and diversity of different algorithms at the initial stage. This tactic makes it possible to improve model performance and prediction accuracy.

A critical improvement in implementation measures between Meta Classifier and Meta Classifier with adjustment by results is shown in Table 8. The test accuracy showed a significant improvement, with the Tuned Meta Classifier obtaining an accuracy of 99.03% instead of the Meta Classifier's 99.01% accuracy. Improvements were also found in, precision, recall, F1 score, and ROC AUC, with the Tuned Meta Classifier showing higher qualities in each of these classifications. Taking everything into account, these findings demonstrate how changing hyperparameters can improve model performance and improve prediction accuracy.

Table 8. Meta-Learning Metrics After Tuning

Model	Train Acc.	Test Acc.	Precision	Recall	F1 Score	ROC AUC
Meta Classifier	0.996	0.990	0.991	0.989	0.990	0.995
Meta Classifier Tuning	0.996	0.990	0.991	0.989	0.990	0.995

6   Related Works Comparison

Using two-way LSTM with attention, Su et al. (2020) achieved an accuracy of 84.25% in the comparative examination of related works. INFUSE was introduced by Sohail et al. (2023), who reported an accuracy of 91.60%, demonstrating the diversity of methods used. The current study is noteworthy for its use of Meta Learning, which produced an impressive accuracy of 99.5652% as shown in Table 8. This comparison shows the diversity of algorithms used to solve the problem using the same data set as well as the differences in performance between different methods as shown in (Fig. 5) (Table 9).

Table 9. Related Works Comparison

#	Researchers	Algorithm	Accuracy
1	Su et al. (2020)	Bidirectional LSTM with Attention	84.25%
2	Sohail et al. (2023)	INFUSE	91.60%
3	Present Study	Meta-Learning(XGBoost)	99.56%

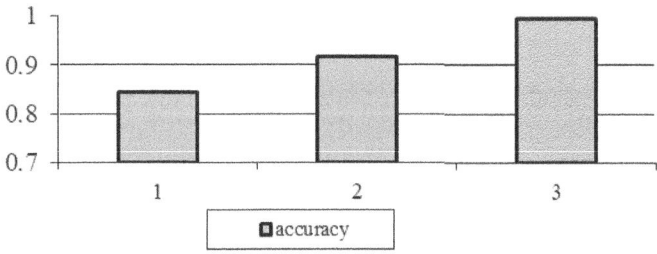

Fig.5. Percentages of accuracy for related works comparison

7   Conclusions

This study finishes by featuring the viability of Meta-learning strategies in improving the abilities of intrusion recognition frameworks. Much headway has been made in the improvement of clever and vigorous Intrusion Detection Systems (IDS) that can quickly identify and mitigate network intrusions by utilizing machine learning (ML) techniques and datasets like NSL-KDD. Across various classifiers, critical additions in anticipated exactness and execution have been made via cautious feature selection, data preparation, and model tuning. The outcomes underline how critical hyperparameter optimization is for upgrading gauge precision and model execution. Meta Classifier with Tuning shows enhancements in accuracy, Precision, Recall, F1 score, and ROC AUC making it a particularly encouraging strategy. These findings highlight how model performance may be optimized and network security can be improved in the face of new threats by adjusting hyperparameters. This paper is solely dedicated to the binary classification without explaining why this type of classification was used and not the multi-class classification. It was suggested that there should be considered the use of the multi-class classification approach that is capable of providing more detailed insight into the problem since it is based on a differentiation of more than two classes. It could provide more details and thus give a better understanding of the problem and the relations in question. Lack of discussion on this aspect, or even a suggestion for future work is a lost opportunity to consider the possibilities of the broader classification approach.

References

1. Mohammed, B., Gbashi, E.: Intrusion Detection system for NSL-KDD dataset based on deep learning and recursive feature elimination. Eng. Technol. J. **39**(7), 1069–1079 (2021). https://doi.org/10.30684/etj.v39i7.1695
2. Surya, L.: International engineering journal for research & development. Int. Eng. J. Res. Dev. December 2019 (2020)
3. Almomani, O., et al.: Machine Learning Classifiers for Network Intrusion Detection System: Comparative Study (2021).https://doi.org/10.1109/ICIT52682.2021.9491770
4. Xu, C., Shen, J., Du, X.: A method of few-shot network intrusion detection based on meta-learning framework. IEEE Trans. Inf. Forensics Secur. **15**(c), 3540–3552 (2020). https://doi.org/10.1109/TIFS.2020.2991876
5. Gao, X., Shan, C., Hu, C., Niu, Z., Liu, Z.: An adaptive ensemble machine learning model for intrusion detection. IEEE Access **7**, 82512–82521 (2019). https://doi.org/10.1109/ACCESS.2019.2923640
6. Vujović, Ž: Classification model evaluation metrics. Int. J. Adv. Comput. Sci. Appl. **12**(6), 599–606 (2021). https://doi.org/10.14569/IJACSA.2021.0120670
7. Sohail, A., Ayisha, B., Hameed, I., Zafar, M.M., Khan, A.: Deep neural networks based meta-learning for network intrusion detection (2023). http://arxiv.org/abs/2302.09394
8. Maniriho, P., Mahoro, L.J., Niyigaba, E., Bizimana, Z., Ahmad, T.: Detecting intrusions in computer network traffic with machine learning approaches. Int. J. Intell. Eng. Syst. **13**(3), 433–445 (2020). https://doi.org/10.22266/IJIES2020.0630.39
9. Rahme, J., Masimukku, B., Daclin, N., Zacharewicz, G.: Improving ERPs integration in organization: an EOS-based GreneOS implementation. Computers **11**(12), 1–14 (2022). https://doi.org/10.3390/computers11120171
10. B. Sachin Sukhadeo, B., et al.: International journal of intelligent systems and applications in engineering MLIDS: a machine learning-based intrusion detection system using the NSLKDD data. Orig. Res. Pap. Int. J. Intell. Syst. Appl. Eng. IJISAE **2024**(4s), 167–179 (2024). www.ijisae.org
11. Jose, J., Jose, D.V.: Deep learning algorithms for intrusion detection systems in internet of things using CIC-IDS 2017 dataset. Int. J. Electr. Comput. Eng. **13**(1), 1134–1141 (2023). https://doi.org/10.11591/ijece.v13i1.pp1134-1141
12. Su, T., Sun, H., Zhu, J., Wang, S., Li, Y.: BAT: deep learning methods on network intrusion detection using NSL-KDD dataset. IEEE Access **8**, 29575–29585 (2020). https://doi.org/10.1109/ACCESS.2020.2972627
13. Almomani, A., et al.: Ensemble-based approach for efficient intrusion detection in network traffic. Intell. Autom. Soft Comput. **37**(2), 2499–2517 (2023). https://doi.org/10.32604/iasc.2023.039687
14. Kaplow, L., Shavell, S.: Speech and language processing. Fairn. versus Welf. vii–viii (2022). https://doi.org/10.4159/9780674039315-001
15. Berrar, D.: Bayes' theorem and naive Bayes classifier. Encycl. Bioinforma. Comput. Biol. ABC Bioinforma. **1–3**(September), 403–412 (2018). https://doi.org/10.1016/B978-0-12-809633-8.20473-1
16. de Zarzà, I., de Curtò, J., Hernández-Orallo, E., Calafate, C.T.: Cascading and ensemble techniques in deep learning. Electron. **12**(15), 1–18 (2023). https://doi.org/10.3390/electronics12153354

17. Shrivastav, L.K., Kumar, R.: An ensemble of random forest gradient boosting machine and deep learning methods for stock price prediction. J. Inf. Technol. Res. **15**(1), 1–19 (2021). https://doi.org/10.4018/jitr.2022010102

18. Zhang, T., et al.: Improving convection trigger functions in deep convective parameterization schemes using machine learning. J. Adv. Model. Earth Syst. **13**(5), 1–19 (2021). https://doi.org/10.1029/2020MS002365

19. Song, F., Mei, D., Li, H.: Feature selection based on linear discriminant analysis, vol. 1 (2010). https://doi.org/10.1109/ISDEA.2010.311

20. Li, Q., Shao, J.: Sparse quadratic discriminant analysis for high dimensional data. Stat. Sin. **25** (2015). https://doi.org/10.5705/ss.2013.150

21. D. Kocev, D., Vens, C., Struyf, J., Džeroski, S.: Ensembles of multi-objective decision trees. Lecture Notes Computer Science (including Subseries Lecture Notes Artificial Intelligent Lect. Notes Bioinformatics), vol. 4701 LNAI, no. August, pp. 624–631, 2007, https://doi.org/10.1007/978-3-540-74958-5_61

22. M. R. Machado, M.R., Karray, S., De Sousa, I.T.: LightGBM: an effective decision tree gradient boosting method to predict customer loyalty in the finance industry. In: 14th International Conference Computer Science Education ICCSE 2019, no. Nips, pp. 1111–1116 (2019). https://doi.org/10.1109/ICCSE.2019.8845529

23. Sári, D., Ferroudj, A., Abdalla, N., El-Ramady, H., Dobránszki, J., Prokisch, J.: Nano-management approaches for salt tolerance in plants under field and in vitro conditions. Agronomy **13**(11) (2023). https://doi.org/10.3390/agronomy13112695

24. Dipto, I.C., Rahman, M.A., Islam, T., Rahman, H.M.M.: Prediction of accident severity using artificial neural network: a comparison of analytical capabilities between Python and R. J. Data Anal. Inf. Process. **08**(03), 134–157 (2020). https://doi.org/10.4236/jdaip.2020.83008

Enhancing Penetration Testing: Leveraging Machine Learning for Ethical Hacking

Mohannad Hossain Hadi[(✉)] [iD] and Karim Hashim Al-Saedi[iD]

Department of Computer Science, College of Science, Mustansiriyah University, Baghdad, Iraq
{muhanad.hussein,dr.karim}@uomustansiriyah.edu.iq

Abstract. As the digital landscape evolves, so does the complexity of cyber threats, making traditional cybersecurity methods, such as penetration testing, less effective against sophisticated attacks. This study introduces the NextGen-PenTest model, a pioneering approach that integrates machine learning techniques with traditional penetration testing tools to enhance the detection, analysis, and prioritization of network vulnerabilities. Using a Random Forest Classifier, the model processes network-scan data and known vulnerabilities to predict the likelihood of successful exploits, thereby enabling a more efficient and targeted approach to cybersecurity. Our comprehensive evaluation in a simulated network environment, mirroring real-world infrastructure, demonstrated significant improvements with an accuracy of 0.93, precision of 0.89, recall of 0.93, and F1-score of 0.91. The NextGen-PenTest model not only optimizes penetration testing processes, but also adapts to emerging threats, offering a robust framework for proactive cyber defence. This advancement represents a shift from reactive to predictive security measures, ensuring that cybersecurity practices keep pace with the evolving threat landscapes.

Keywords: Cybersecurity · Ethical Hacking · Machine Learning · Penetration Testing · Network Security · Nmap · Metasploit Framework

1 Introduction

In the contemporary world, where everything is interconnected through the Internet, it is crucial to ensure cybersecurity. The more complex the network structures in organizations, the higher the importance of elaborate protective measures. Ethical hacking, also known as penetration testing, remains an integral part of cybersecurity measures because it offers a valuable way of identifying possible weaknesses in an organization's systems [1]. Penetration testing is an intentional and well-planned real-world attack on the information technology systems of an organization that aims to identify the vulnerabilities of computing systems, networks, and applications, based on practical rather than theoretical situations. This security practice is typically formulated with a proactive intent, the role of which is to identify vulnerabilities and threats before they can be turned into risks and ultimately lead to data leaks.

Penetration testing involves the use of automated tools and several other methods to test the security of a system. However, scalability, speed, and precision are challenges, particularly under complex network conditions. Budgeting, time constraints, and the general objectives of penetration testing can be crucial determinants of the type and efficiency of penetration-testing strategies [2]. Moreover, the choice of specific tools and procedures typically depends on trial and error or the expertise of cybersecurity personnel, which can result in suboptimal resource utilization and potential security gaps.

Recognizing the limitations of traditional methods, there is growing interest in leveraging Artificial Intelligence (AI) and Machine Learning (ML) to enhance the capabilities of cybersecurity tools [3]. AI and ML technologies are buzzwords for the new world and can bring a revolution in different fields, such as cybersecurity, where they can lead to more effective, efficient, and proactive security.

In this study, the NextGen-PenTest model was proposed as a new penetration testing tool built on the Metasploit framework and machine learning technologies. NextGen-PenTest represents a significant evolution in cybersecurity practices, combining traditional network scanning and vulnerability assessment with the predictive analytics of machine learning. The tool starts with extensive network scanning through Nmap to detect hosts that are ON, various open ports, and the services running on them. This creates an array of correlations between the initial data and vulnerabilities listed in the CVE database, and is connected to the corresponding exploits in the metasploit framework.

The RandomForestClassifier forms the core of the NextGen-PenTest model, which is among the most accurate and efficient algorithms for handling large datasets [4]. This model was specifically and carefully calibrated using historical data to predict how readily specific identified vulnerabilities could be exploited. Furthermore, unlike the traditional approach to identifying vulnerable targets, the model also ranks these targets, meaning that in addition to its ability to identify potential targets for exploitation, it also considers the likelihood and consequences of exploitation given feedback from previous outcomes. This practice of intelligent prioritization enables cybersecurity professionals to target specific threats that are likely to cause significant damage. Thus, their response strategies and management methods are timely, efficient, and effective.

The integration of machine learning with conventional penetration testing tools highlights a new approach geared toward modern cyber threats that is more intelligent, preemptive, and dynamic. This paper presents the role, approach, and practical efficiency of the NextGen-PenTest model and its ability to redefine the essence of penetration testing and enhance network protection in the era of digitalization.

In the domain of cybersecurity, various studies have focused on efforts aimed at improving the predictions of vulnerability exploitation through the creation of new tools using a machine learning approach. A concise overview of these efforts is provided below:

The pioneering Expected Exploitability (EE) model was introduced by Suciu et al. (2021), after which it was continuously refined and adjusted based on the data acquired from various sources to predict the evolution of vulnerabilities. Compared to static models, this approach is much evolutionary in the sense that it provides an improved prediction window with newer data, and when it comes to it, is a better approach toward a more dynamic approach to protect against cyber threats [5]. Hoque et al. (2021) proposed a unique prediction model that can minimize class imbalance in vulnerability data by applying a new cost function and using vectors trained specifically for that purpose. This model bears a marked improvement in the efficiency of determining exploited vulnerabilities with higher sensitivity and better accuracy than previous models across the broad landscape of cybersecurity [6]. Jacobs et al. (2023) developed the Exploit Prediction Scoring System (EPSS) that implements data from multiple sources and experts. This model, tested against a large dataset of vulnerability features, is a magnitude better in terms of predictive accuracy and operational utility than prior models, and enables organizations to better prioritize those vulnerabilities [7]. Eskandari et al. (2023) focused on the challenge of high-dimensional and imbalanced datasets prevalent in cybersecurity databases such as the NVD. Their OutCenTR model applies a novel feature reduction technique to enhance the performance of baseline outlier detection models, thereby significantly improving the detection of potential exploits [8]. Charmanas et al. (2023) proposed a topic-based machine learning approach that involves text mining to evaluate and predict the exploitability of vulnerabilities. This framework offers a novel way of not only analyzing which vulnerabilities are likely to be exploited but also facilitates the planning of cybersecurity threat management based on the language patterns within vulnerability descriptions [9].

The implications of these contributions are to continue enhancing the competencies for accurate forecasting of cybersecurity models and from mere reactive towards proactive measures to guard the networked systems from new forms of threats. These methods are efficient not only in filling gaps in the existing methodologies but also in contributing to the original and objective baselines for the accuracy and flexibility of exploit-prediction technologies.

The remainder of this paper is organized as follows. In Sect. 2, the materials and methods employed in this study are detailed, including the computational resources, software tools, and machine learning methodologies. Section 3 outlines the proposed NextGen-PenTest model and describes its components, including Nmap, Metasploit, database, and machine learning techniques used. The experimental results are presented and a discussion of the results is presented in Sect. 4. Finally, Sect. 5 concludes the paper.

2　Materials and Methods

This section elaborates on the computational resources, software tools, experimental setup, and machine learning methodologies utilized in the development and evaluation of the proposed model.

2.1　Software and Platforms

Programming Languages and Libraries: Python 3.8 is utilized for scripting and automation because of its wide support for statistical and machine learning libraries.

- TensorFlow 2.4: Employed to develop and train deep learning models.
- scikit-learn 0.24: Used for classical machine learning models, data preprocessing, and model evaluation tasks.

Penetration Testing Tools:

- Metasploit Framework 6.1.14: Integrated for managing and executing exploitation modules.
- Nmap 7.80: Used to conduct initial network scans and service detection.

2.2 Simulated Environment

A simulated network environment mimicking a real-world corporate network with 1,000 devices is distributed as follows:

- 300 Windows devices: Various versions and configurations to simulate typical enterprise desktops and servers.
- 300 Linux devices: Multiple distributions to represent backend servers, web applications, and database servers.
- 200 IoT devices: Simulating the connected devices commonly found in modern office environments.
- 100 MacOS devices: Representing workstations used in creative and administrative functions.
- 100 Network devices: Including routers and printers to complete the network ecosystem.

Each device type was assigned a realistic set of vulnerabilities from the CVE database based on its operating system and known exploits associated with the service versions detected by Nmap, as listed in Table (1).

Table 1. Assigned Vulnerabilities by Device Type

Device Type	Quantity	Assigned Vulnerabilities
Windows	300	CVE-2020-0601, CVE-2020-1472, CVE-2019-0708
Linux	300	CVE-2021-3156, CVE-2021-33909, CVE-2019-10149
IoT	200	CVE-2020-28553, CVE-2019-12525, CVE-2018-0296
MacOS	100	CVE-2020-9854, CVE-2020-9945, CVE-2021-30713
Network	100	CVE-2020-35782, CVE-2021-20090, CVE-2019-15271

2.3 Data Preprocessing

The transformation of raw data from the network scans and identification of vulnerabilities for creating an overall suitable format for machine learning include some crucial steps known as preprocessing. First, during *the Data Transformation* step, numerical values are assigned to scanned port numbers, and during Data Preprocessing, service types such as HTTP, FTP, or SSH are converted to categorical data using one-hot or label encoding. Furthermore, every CVEs (Common Vulnerabilities and Exposures) is in binary form to determine whether it is present in the dataset. The next critical stage is *Data Cleaning*, wherein records with missing attributes, such as service type or port number, are removed or, in some cases, reconstructed through statistical estimation. Information that was not used in the analysis was excluded to ensure that the dataset was concise and relevant.

Feature Scaling and Normalization are then used to ensure that numerical values, such as ports, and the success rate of exploits are at the same scale to enhance the efficiency of the machine learning algorithms. Normalization can also be used to achieve a more standardized exposure in terms of the Gaussian distribution and improve the accord in the dataset. Finally, *Dataset Construction* involves compiling the features derived from the scan results, CVE details, and historical exploitation outcomes into a comprehensive dataset. Each record is labelled as a successful (1) or unsuccessful (0) exploit, based on historical outcomes. These labels form the basis for the target variable in supervised learning models, allowing them to learn from past data to effectively predict future vulnerabilities, as shown in Table 2 below.

Table 2. Example Structured Dataset Format

IP Address	Port	Service Type	CVE Identifier	Exploit Used	Label
IP1	P1	S1	CVE1	M1	1
IP2	P2	S2	CVE2	M2	0
IP3	P3	S3	CVE3	M3	1

This structured dataset is now ready for the subsequent machine-learning model training phase. It combines the numerical and categorical data necessary for predicting the likelihood of successful exploits, thereby facilitating an effective and robust training process for a machine learning model.

2.4 Model Training

The random forest classifier was trained using the training data. The classifier creates multiple decision trees, each trained on a random subset of the training data, and aggregates their predictions to form the final output.

The dataset was split into training and testing sets, typically using a 70–30 split. This ensures that the model has sufficient data for learning, while reserving a portion for evaluating its performance.

The features (input variables) and targets (output variables) were separated. These features include port numbers, service types, CVE indicators, and historical success rates, and the target is the success label (1 for successful and 0 for unsuccessful). The model training involved configuring several hyperparameters: the number of trees in the forest was set to 100 to ensure a good balance between the training performance and model complexity, and the maximum depth of each tree was limited to prevent overfitting with a typical setting of 10 levels.

The model performance was assessed using a suite of metrics to ensure its capacity to accurately predict successful exploits. The key metrics used are listed in Table 3 below.

Table 3. Performance Metrics [10]

Metric	Formulae
Accuracy	(TP + TN) / (TP + TN + FP + FN)
Precision	TP / (TP + FP)
Recall	TP / (TP + FN)
F1-score	2 / ((1/Precision) + (1/Recall))

- True positives (TP): instances in which the model correctly predicted the positive class.
- True Negatives (TN): Instances where the model correctly predicts the negative class.
- False Positives (FP): Instances where the model incorrectly predicted the positive class.
- False Negatives (FN): Instances where the model incorrectly predicts the negative class.

2.5 Proposed Model

The NextGen-PenTest model is initiated with Nmap scan, which infiltrates the network architecture to identify connected nodes, open ports, and available services. This first step serves as the foundation for all further investigations, resulting in an extensive list of all IP addresses observed, the services that these IP addresses use (HTTP, SSH, etc.), open ports, and versions of services for every discovered host. After this important information acquisition step, the raw unanalyzed data were entered into the Metasploit framework for further analysis.

During the integration phase with Metasploit, the services identified along with the identified version are mapped to the large database included in Metasploit, which contains information on vulnerabilities, along with CVE identifiers. In this manner, this precise process helps to identify a list of vulnerabilities that can be exploited according to the currently offered metasploit framework modules for specific vulnerabilities. This vital step not only identifies potential security breaches, but also aligns them with actionable responses. The subsequent phase parses the raw scanning data and vulnerabilities that were found and their conversion into a format suitable for machine learning analysis. This comprises the typecasting of ports into numerical forms, the encoding of services into categorical forms, and the encoding of CVEs into binary forms. In addition, noise or invalid features were removed or imputed, and features with numerical values were normalized or scaled up for the best performance of the machine learning algorithm during the training process.

For training, the model ingests a dataset composed of features derived from the scan results, CVE specifics, and historical data of the exploitation results. Each instance in this dataset was categorized as either a successful exploit (1) or not (0). A Random Forest classifier was used because of its spectacular results across different inputs, with the added advantage of handling overfitting problems. This historical dataset was used to train the model and confirm cross-validation, in addition to hyperparameter optimization for predictive accuracy. The effectiveness of the model was meticulously evaluated through a battery of metrics—accuracy, precision, recall, and F1 score— to ensure that it can predict exploitation success with high reliability.

In its operational phase, NextGen-PenTest leverages new scan data to offer real-time exploitability predictions. It interfaces with Metasploit via an API, which orchestrates the flow of data and facilitates the implementation of recommended exploits based on the model's predictions, NextGen-PenTest selects the Metasploit module most likely to succeed for each identified vulnerability. This strategy ensures that penetration testing efforts are concentrated on the most pressing vulnerabilities, as shown in Fig. 1. The feedback loop was integral to the operational framework of the model. Both successful and unsuccessful exploitation attempts were recorded and reincorporated into the training model, permitting continuous learning and adaptation to the shifting dynamics of the network security. Regular incremental training sessions are scheduled to maintain the acuity of the model, thereby securing its long-term applicability and effectiveness as new threats and patterns unfold in network environments.

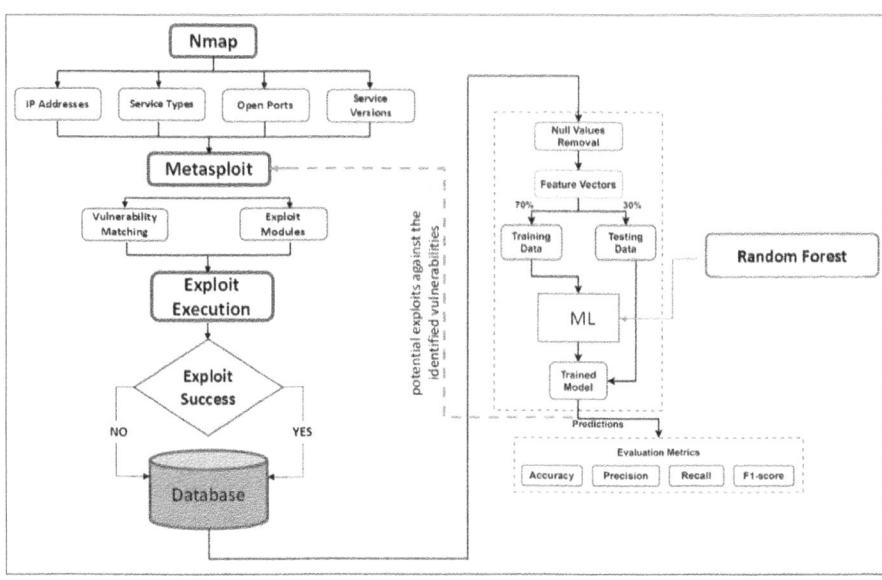

Fig. 1. Proposed Model Architecture

2.5.1 Nmap

Nmap is an open-source tool used for network exploration and security auditing. It helps users discover hosts on a network, identify their services, and detect vulnerabilities. Nmap is popular among network administrators, security professionals, and penetration testers for gathering network information, identifying potential vulnerabilities, and detecting malicious activities [11, 12].

Nmap can identify the operating system of a host, which aids in pinpointing specific vulnerabilities. Nmap's powerful scripting engine allows the creation of custom scripts for tailored tasks, enhancing its suitability for network exploration and scanning. When integrated with other tools like OpenVAS, Nessus, and Metasploit, Nmap provides a comprehensive examination of network vulnerabilities, making it essential for penetration testing [13–15].

Algorithm 1 below delineates a two-tier classification scan strategy using Nmap, focusing on scanning, probing, and identifying open ports and services. This detailed approach helps security practitioners prepare comprehensive reports, aiding in the next level of vulnerability assessment.

Algorithm 1: Nmap Network Scanning

Begin
1. **Initialize Nmap Scanner**:
    - Input: Target IP address or hostname.
    - Instantiate the NmapScanner class with the target.
2. **Execute Full Port Scan with Service Detection**:
    - Utilize the PortScanner module from the Nmap library.
    - Scan parameters:
        - Scan all 65,535 ports using -p-.
        - Enable service and version detection with -sV.
        - Set the scan speed using -T4 for aggressive timing.
    - Execute scan on the target.
    - Output: Retrieve all hosts and a detailed dictionary of open ports along with service information.
3. **Retrieve Scan Results**:
    - For each host in the scan results:
        - Enumerate open ports.
        - For each open port, extract:
            - Service name and version, if available.
            - Additional information like service state (open/closed), protocol, and service extras.
4. **Compile and Format Results**:
    - Prepare a structured report of all detected services and corresponding ports.
    - Include additional details such as the host's IP address, scan time, and the number of open ports.
5. **Return Detailed Scan Report**:
    - Return the comprehensive report containing all pertinent data gathered during the scan.

End

2.5.2 Metasploit

Metasploit frameworks can be described as frameworks for the development of tools and exploits. It is used by network security professionals for penetration tests, system administrators for patch roll-out verifications, and product vendors for regression testing and is utilized by security researchers across the globe. The metasploit framework has numerous modules for performing different types of attacks against different types of devices and servers: (1) an exploit module, which is a module designed to perform particular attacks; (2) a payload module, which is a module for collecting data and information from the target; (3) an auxiliary module for scanning the target; and (4) an encoder module, which is specially used to bypass antiviruses and firewalls [16].

Algorithm 2 delineates a methodical approach designed to automate the process of detecting vulnerabilities in network services and attempting their exploitation to assess the robustness of network defences. This algorithm leverages generic exploitation techniques to simulate attacks based on the information gathered from service scans.

Algorithm 2: Automated CVE Detection and Exploitation

Begin

1. **Initialize the Scanner**:
   - Input: Target IP address or hostname.
   - Establish parameters for the network scan, focusing on identifying open ports and services running on the target.

2. **Perform Service Detection**:
   - Conduct a detailed scan using customized scripts to determine the operating system, service names, and versions on all open ports.
   - Output: List of services with their respective versions detected on each port.

3. **CVE Lookup and Compilation**:
   - For each detected service and version, consult an internal or online CVE database to fetch relevant CVE entries that could affect the identified services.
   - Compile a list of actionable CVEs for each service.

4. **Vulnerability Exploitation Simulation**:
   - For each service associated with one or more CVEs:
     - Simulate exploitation attempts using generic attack vectors tailored to the service and version.
     - Record the results of these simulations, noting any successful exploitation which indicates a vulnerability.

5. **Generate Report**:
   - Compile a detailed report of the scanning and exploitation results.
   - Include information on detected services, CVEs associated with these services, and outcomes of the exploitation simulations.

6. **Return Comprehensive Assessment**:
   - Output the final report, providing insights into potential vulnerabilities and the security posture of the network.

End

2.5.3 Database

In the dynamics of securing a network, systemized mining and indexing of the exploitation results are essential for evaluating the effectiveness of defence procedures. The details of each attempt made for an exploit are recorded, including issues such as target details, the services that were exploited, specific vulnerabilities, and the results of such exploits. To achieve this, a proper database management system is required to maintain the important data, most of which are highly sensitive and must be retrieved and updated quickly.

Algorithm 3 delineates a structured approach to automate the process of storing and managing exploitation results using a database. This algorithm leverages the capabilities of a relational database, specifically SQLite, to create a structured and efficient environment to handle large volumes of security-related data.

Algorithm 3: Automated Storage of Exploitation Results

Begin
1. **Initialize Database Connection**:
    - Input: Database file name (default is "exploitation_results.db").
    - Establish a connection to the SQLite database.
    - Create a table named exploitation_results if it does not already exist. This table will store fields such as target IP, service name, service version, port number, list of CVEs, and the exploitation result.
2. **Storing Exploitation Results**:
    - Input: Exploitation data including target, service name, service version, port, list of CVEs, and the exploitation outcome.
    - For each set of exploitation details:
        - Insert the data into the exploitation_results table using a parameterized SQL query to prevent SQL injection.
        - Commit the transaction to ensure that the data is saved securely in the database.
3. **Data Integrity and Security**:
    - Ensure that each transaction is handled correctly to maintain data integrity.
    - Use secure practices to protect the database against unauthorized access and SQL injection attacks.
4. **Closing Database Connection**:
    - Properly close the database connection after all operations are completed to free up resources and prevent data leaks.
5. **Return Confirmation**:
    - Output a confirmation message indicating the successful storage of exploitation results.
End

2.5.4 Machine Learning

In cybersecurity, employing an approach that uses machine learning techniques to forecast and analyze the results of exploitation is a revolutionary way to strengthen network security. The possibility of using machine learning is in the exploitation history, which allows the identification of vulnerabilities that can be successfully exploited.

Algorithm 4 delineates the comprehensive process for employing machine learning models to analyze the exploitation data stored in a database. The algorithm demonstrates the workflow from data loading and preprocessing to training and evaluating a machine learning model, specifically a Random Forest Classifier, which is well regarded for its efficacy in classification tasks involving complex datasets.

Algorithm 4: Machine Learning Analysis of Exploitation Data

Begin

1. Initialize Database Connection:
- Input: Database file name (default: "exploitation_results.db").
- Establish connection to SQLite database.
- Create a cursor for executing SQL commands.

2. Load Exploitation Data:
- Execute SQL query to retrieve relevant exploitation data from the database.
- Store retrieved data in a pandas DataFrame with columns: target, service name, service version, port, list of CVEs, exploitation results.

3. Preprocess Data:
- Convert categorical data to numerical format using Label Encoding.
- Separate DataFrame into feature vectors (X) and target labels (y)
  X includes service details and CVE lists
  y contains exploitation outcomes

4. Split Data for Training and Testing:
- Divide data into training and testing sets using stratified split.
- Allocate 70% of data for training and 30% for testing.

5. Train Machine Learning Model:
- Instantiate RandomForestClassifier.
- Train model on training data.
- Predict exploitation outcomes on test set.

6. Evaluate Model Performance:
- Calculate model accuracy by comparing predicted outcomes with actual test set results.
- Output model's accuracy as a measure of predictive performance.

7. Close Database Connection:
- Close database connection to ensure data integrity and release resources.

8. Return Trained Model and Performance Metrics:
- Output trained RandomForestClassifier model and its accuracy metric.
- Model categorizes exploitation outcomes into classes:
  Class 0: Not Exploitable
  Class 1: Exploitable

End

---

3 Results

The implementation of the NextGen-PenTest model involves detailed Nmap scans across various device types within a simulated network environment designed to mirror a real-world corporate network. This environment included 1,000 devices, distributed across Windows, Linux, IoT, MacOS, and network devices. Each device type was scanned to identify open ports and running services, which were then analyzed for potential vulnerabilities. Here, we provide a detailed account of the scan results for each device type. The corresponding vulnerabilities matched with the exploits are detailed in the associated tables, which illustrate the application of the model in various scenarios.

1- Figure 3 shows an excerpt from the scan results for a representative Windows server with details on services such as Microsoft RPC, NetBIOS, Microsoft DS, and Terminal Services. Critical vulnerabilities found on ports like 135, 139, 445, and 3389 were matched with relevant exploits, which are documented in Table 4.

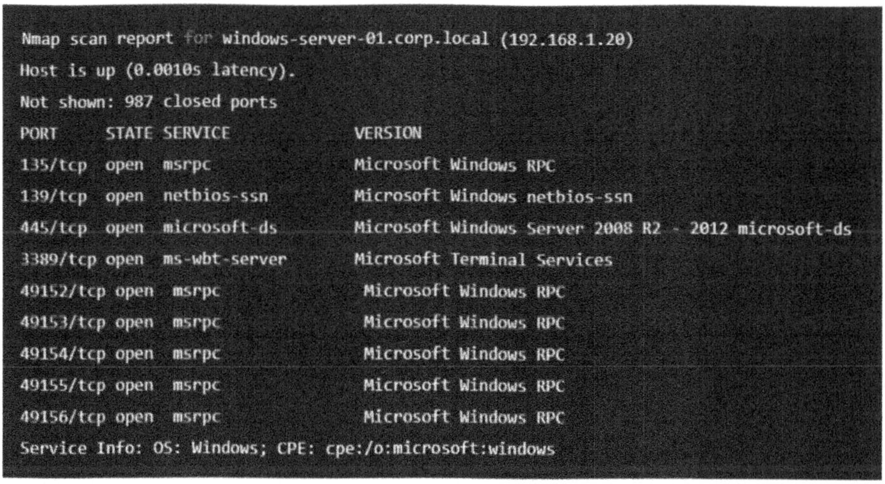

```
Nmap scan report for windows-server-01.corp.local (192.168.1.20)
Host is up (0.0010s latency).
Not shown: 987 closed ports
PORT       STATE SERVICE           VERSION
135/tcp  open  msrpc              Microsoft Windows RPC
139/tcp  open  netbios-ssn        Microsoft Windows netbios-ssn
445/tcp  open  microsoft-ds       Microsoft Windows Server 2008 R2 - 2012 microsoft-ds
3389/tcp open  ms-wbt-server      Microsoft Terminal Services
49152/tcp open  msrpc             Microsoft Windows RPC
49153/tcp open  msrpc             Microsoft Windows RPC
49154/tcp open  msrpc             Microsoft Windows RPC
49155/tcp open  msrpc             Microsoft Windows RPC
49156/tcp open  msrpc             Microsoft Windows RPC
Service Info: OS: Windows; CPE: cpe:/o:microsoft:windows
```

Fig. 3. Windows Server Scan Results

Table 4. Matched Vulnerabilities and Exploits for Windows Devices

CVE ID	Vulnerability Description	Metasploit Module
CVE-2020–0601	Windows CryptoAPI Spoofing Vulnerability	exploit/windows/cryptoapi/spoofing
CVE-2020–1472	Netlogon Elevation of Privilege Vulnerability	exploit/windows/netlogon/zerologon
CVE-2019–0708	Remote Desktop Services Remote Code Execution Vulnerability	exploit/windows/rdp/bluekeep_rce

2- Figure 4 shows an excerpt from the scan results for the Linux Server Scan Results, detailing services such as SSH, SMTP, HTTP, and MySQL. This scan captured essential security risks, with vulnerabilities such as the Sudo Buffer Overflow and Linux Kernel Filesystem Layer Local Privilege Escalation successfully exploited, as listed in Table 5.

3- Figure 5 displays an excerpt from the scanning results for an IoT device, detailing the vulnerabilities in HTTP and HTTPS services administered via lighttpd on ports 80 and 443. The identified critical vulnerabilities and their corresponding exploits are presented in Table 6.

```
Nmap scan report for linux-server-01.corp.local (192.168.3.20)
Host is up (0.0012s latency).
Not shown: 979 closed ports
PORT      STATE SERVICE      VERSION
22/tcp    open  ssh          OpenSSH 7.4 (protocol 2.0)
25/tcp    open  smtp         Postfix smtpd
80/tcp    open  http         Apache httpd 2.4.29
110/tcp   open  pop3         Dovecot pop3d
143/tcp   open  imap         Dovecot imapd
443/tcp   open  ssl/https    Apache httpd 2.4.29
993/tcp   open  ssl/imap     Dovecot imapd
995/tcp   open  ssl/pop3     Dovecot pop3d
3306/tcp  open  mysql        MySQL 5.7.21
8080/tcp  open  http-proxy   Squid proxy 3.5.27
```

Fig. 4. Linux Server Scan Results

Table 5. Matched Vulnerabilities and Exploits for Linux Devices

CVE ID	Vulnerability Description	Metasploit Module
CVE-2021–3156	Sudo Buffer Overflow Vulnerability	exploit/unix/local/sudo_bof
CVE-2021–33909	Linux Kernel Filesystem Layer Local Privilege Escalation	exploit/linux/local/kernel_fs_leak
CVE-2019–10149	Exim Mail Transfer Agent Remote Command Execution	exploit/unix/smtp/exim_exec

```
Nmap scan report for iot-device-01.corp.local (192.168.5.20)
Host is up (0.0023s latency).
Not shown: 996 closed ports
PORT      STATE SERVICE      VERSION
80/tcp    open  http         lighttpd 1.4.45
443/tcp   open  ssl/https    lighttpd 1.4.45
8080/tcp  open  http-proxy   lighttpd 1.4.45
```

Fig. 5. IoT Device Scan Results

Table 6. Matched Vulnerabilities and Exploits for IoT Devices

CVE ID	Vulnerability Description	Metasploit Module
CVE-2020–28553	Multiple vulnerabilities in various IoT devices	exploit/multi/iot/multiple_vulns
CVE-2019–12525	Remote Code Execution in various IoT routers	exploit/multi/iot/router_rce
CVE-2018–0296	Cisco ASA and Firepower Management Exploits	exploit/multi/network/cisco_asa_firepower

4- Figure 6 outlines an excerpt from the scan results for a MacOS workstation, revealing vulnerabilities in SSH, HTTP, and VNC services. Notable vulnerabilities, such as the Apple TCC Bypass, are detailed with the corresponding exploits documented in Table 7.

```
Nmap scan report for macos-workstation-01.corp.local (192.168.6.220)
Host is up (0.0015s latency).
Not shown: 990 closed ports


PORT     STATE SERVICE VERSION
22/tcp   open  ssh     OpenSSH 7.9 (protocol 2.0)
80/tcp   open  http    Apache httpd 2.4.41
548/tcp  open  afp     Apple AFP
631/tcp  open  ipp     CUPS 2.3.3
5900/tcp open  vnc     VNC (protocol 3.8)
```

Fig. 6. MacOS Workstation Scan Results

5- Figure 7 presents an excerpt from the scanning results for a network router, pinpointing vulnerabilities in its Cisco IOS Telnet and SSL services. Specific vulnerabilities and their associated exploits are listed in Table 8.

Each result acts as a focal point, illustrating the effectiveness of the model in distinct scenarios and providing insights into the extensive testing conducted on different device groups within a simulated network. Table 9 shows a snapshot of the extensive data gathered through our simulation, providing a focused view of the penetration test results. Each row presents a distinct instance in which a specific vulnerability is targeted and

Table 7. Matched Vulnerabilities and Exploits for MacOS Devices

CVE ID	Vulnerability Description	Metasploit Module
CVE-2020–9854	Apple Mail Remote Code Execution	exploit/osx/email/mail_rce
CVE-2020–9945	Apple Kernel Memory Disclosure	exploit/osx/kernel/memory_disclosure
CVE-2021–30713	Apple TCC Bypass Vulnerability	exploit/osx/local/tcc_bypass

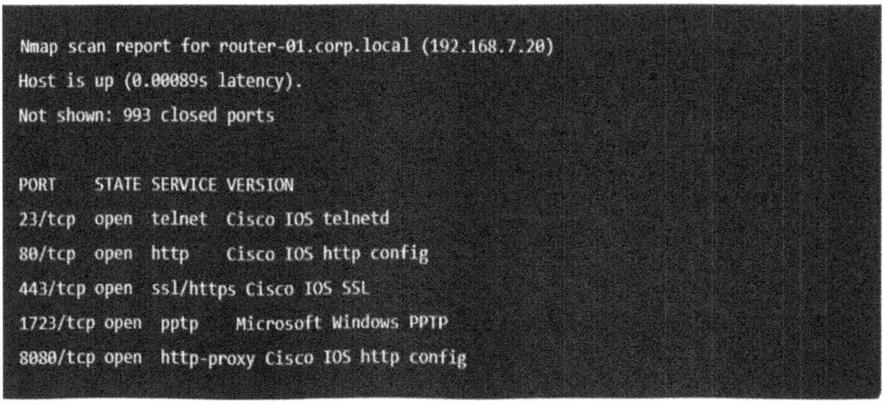

```
Nmap scan report for router-01.corp.local (192.168.7.20)
Host is up (0.00089s latency).
Not shown: 993 closed ports

PORT     STATE SERVICE VERSION
23/tcp   open  telnet  Cisco IOS telnetd
80/tcp   open  http    Cisco IOS http config
443/tcp  open  ssl/https Cisco IOS SSL
1723/tcp open  pptp    Microsoft Windows PPTP
8080/tcp open  http-proxy Cisco IOS http config
```

Fig. 7. Network Router Scan Results

Table 8. Matched Vulnerabilities and Exploits for Network Devices

CVE ID	Vulnerability Description	Metasploit Module
CVE-2020–35782	HP Printer Remote Code Execution	exploit/multi/printer/hp_rce
CVE-2021–20090	Multiple SOHO router vulnerabilities	exploit/multi/router/soho_rce
CVE-2019–15271	Cisco IOS XE Remote Code Execution	exploit/multi/network/cisco_ios_xe_rce

tested against corresponding exploits for various services such as HTTPS, SMB, and RDP. The "Label" column indicates the success or failure of the exploit attempt, where '1' denotes a successful exploit, and '0' represents a failed attempt due to effective defensive measures.

The data gathered from these scans were crucial for training a random forest model, which exhibited a strong performance with an accuracy of 0.93, precision of 0.89, recall

Table 9. Penetration Testing Results

IP Address	Port	Service Type	CVE Identifier	Exploit Used	Label	Outcome Description
192.168.1.20	443	HTTPS	CVE-2020-0601	windows/htt ps/spoofing	1	Successful spoofing of HTTPS traffic, security bypassed.
192.168.1.21	445	SMB	CVE-2020-1472	exploit/wind ows/netlogon /zerologon	1	Successful privilege escalation to domain admin.
192.168.122	3389	RDP	CVE-2019-0708	exploit/wind ows/rdp/blue keep_rce	0	Exploit failed; defensive measures blocked attack.

of 0.93, and an F1-score of 0.91. For this training, the model processed a dataset comprising more than 10,000 instances, each representing a different network scan result. Additionally, 8 features were utilized for the model, including critical data points, such as port numbers, service types, CVE identifiers, and exploit success rates. These metrics not only confirm the model's efficacy but also highlight its significant role in optimizing the penetration testing process across a diverse range of networked devices. This improvement in testing efficiency enhances the cybersecurity stance of the organization, fostering a proactive approach to defending against potential cyber threats.

To contextualize the effectiveness and continuous learning of the proposed model, a comparison with existing methodologies was conducted. The comparison focused on the methodology employed, the reported accuracy of each approach, and their adaptability to continuous learning, which is a critical factor in the ever-evolving cybersecurity landscape. This comparison is presented in Table 10. The high accuracy rate indicates that the model is well-calibrated, and the features selected for training effectively capture the patterns that lead to successful or unsuccessful exploits. Additionally, Random Forest, as an ensemble method, is capable of reducing variance and bias compared to simpler models, which helps achieve higher accuracy.

A high continuous learning capability refers to a model's ability to adapt and improve over time with new data. The NextGen-PenTest model was designed to continually incorporate feedback from new cybersecurity incidents and exploit attempts in its training dataset. This continuous learning approach is crucial in cybersecurity because of the rapidly evolving nature of threats and the constant emergence of new vulnerabilities.

The NextGen PenTest model is the newest and most sophisticated enhancement of the current cybersecurity arsenal, integrating classic penetration testing tools, such as Metasploit and Nmap, and machine learning algorithms to enhance the efficiency of vulnerability analysis. This combination enables a more selective and prioritized approach to network threats, which alters the conventional distribution of resources in IT security operations.

By enabling automated prediction of vulnerability exploitability, the NextGen-PenTest model opens new opportunities for the considered area of analysis by allowing cybersecurity specialists to concentrate on the most possible critical threats, which has a positive impact on the effectiveness of the corresponding response strategies. This

Table 10. Comparison of Different Methodologies

Reference	Methodology	Accuracy (%)	continuous learning
[5]	Expected Exploitability (Dynamic Updates)	86	High
[6]	Novel Cost Function and Custom-Trained Word Vectors	92	Low
[7]	Data-Driven Exploits with Community Insights (XGBoost)	82	Low
[8]	OutCenTR (Semi-Supervised Outlier Detection)	F1: 28.01% (varies by dataset)	Low
[9]	Topic-Based Machine Learning Framework	87	Low
Proposed Model	**RandomForestClassifier on PenTest Data**	**93**	**High**

capability is most important when threats evolve rapidly, and the difference between the quick identification of threats and their neutralization can be a crucial factor in an organization's security.

As evidenced by the practical implementation of the model, it can reduce the time and effort normally used in vulnerability assessments, making a good case for the use of machine learning to enhance security. In addition, this model shows the development of cybersecurity measures that were once mostly focused on detecting threats and acting in response, rather than being preventive in nature.

From a theoretical perspective, this study contributes to the field of cybersecurity by demonstrating how artificial exercises can be combined with widely accepted security approaches to complement and strengthen decision-making practices in the field to improve their effectiveness. The NextGen-PenTest model is a good example of the significant implications of ML applications for cybersecurity frameworks that offer an organized and evidence-based approach to threats. This marks a positive progression in striving to enhance ways of actively preventing and addressing the dangers of cyber threats.

4   Conclusion

This study proposed and tested the NextGen-PenTest model, which is an advanced model that combines or employs machine learning technology and conventional tools such as the Metasploit framework and Nmap. Through the additions of a RandomForest-Classifier, this model enhances the speed and precision of vulnerability assessments, allowing cybersecurity professionals to prioritize critical threats effectively, thereby optimizing resource allocation and reducing mitigation times, thereby optimizing resource allocation and reducing mitigation times.

The approach used in NextGen-PenTest is far better than the usual approaches because it offers automated assessment and vital data-based insights. It is a scalable and extensible model that regularly calibrates predictions with new data to solve new threats in cyberspace. Although promising, the model's performance underscores the need for high-quality, diverse datasets for training, highlighting the ongoing necessity for data refinement.

Further improvements that may be made in the future may add more topological considerations to the model and more complex risk analysis. In doing so, the model can generate even more value by facilitating the creation of significantly better cybersecurity measures that can be learned from past experiences. As cyber threats evolve, the Nextens-PenTest model represents a progressive step toward more sophisticated and effective cybersecurity defences.

Acknowledgement. The Authors would like to thank Mustansiriyah University in Baghdad, Iraq for their support in this work.

Funding. None.

Conflicts of Interest. The authors declare that they have no conflicts of interest.

References

1. Singirikonda, M.: Penetration testing tool guide. J. Cybersecur. **1** (2023)
2. Kongara, D., Krishnama, S.: A process of penetration testing using various tools, vol. 2023, pp. 93–103 (2023)
3. "Impact of Artificial Intelligence and Machine Learning on Cybersecurity," in From 5G to 6G, John Wiley & Sons, Ltd, pp. 159–174 (2023)
4. Abdullah, M.Z., Jassim, A.K., Hummadi, F. N., Al Khalidy, M.M.M.: New strategies for improving network security against cyber attack based on intelligent algorithms. J. Eng. Sustain. Dev. **28**, 342–354 (2024)
5. Suciu, O., et al.: Expected Exploitability: Predicting the Development of Functional Vulnerability Exploits (2021)
6. Hoque, M.S., et al.: An improved vulnerability exploitation prediction model with novel cost function and custom trained word vector embedding. Sensors **21** (2021)
7. Jacobs, J., et al.: Enhancing vulnerability prioritization: data-driven exploit predictions with community-driven insights (2023)
8. Eskandari, H., Bewong, M., Rehman, S.: OutCenTR: a novel semi-supervised framework for predicting exploits of vulnerabilities in high-dimensional datasets (2023)
9. Charmanas, K., Mittas, N., Angelis, L.: Exploitation of vulnerabilities: a topic-based machine learning framework for explaining and predicting exploitation. Information **14**, 403 (2023)
10. Adnan Alnawas, H.A., Al-Jawad, M.: A prediction model based on students' behavior in e-learning environments using data mining techniques (2022)

11. Menaka, S., et al.: Cyber security tool for combat remote work vulnerability. In: 2023 Fifth International Conference on Electrical, Computer and Communication Technologies (ICECCT), pp. 1–4 (2023)
12. Mohammed, F., et al.: Automated Nmap Toolkit. In: 2022 International Conference Advancements Smart, Secure and Intelligent Computing (ASSIC), pp. 1–7 (2022)
13. Rahalkar, S.A.: Introduction to NMAP. Quick Start Guide to Penetration Testing (2018)
14. Mandal, N., Jadhav, S.: A survey on network security tools for open source. In: 2016 IEEE International Conference Current Trends Advances Computer (ICCTAC), pp. 1–6 (2016)
15. Younus, Z.S., Alanezi, M.: A survey on network security monitoring: tools and functionalities. Mustansiriyah J. Pure Appl. Sci. 1, 55–86 (2023)
16. Faturrohman, M.A., et al.: Attack into the server message block (CVE-2020-0796) vulnerabilities in Windows 10 using metasploit framework. JEEMECS (J. Electr. Eng. Mechatron. Comput. Sci.) (2023)

Author Index

S. O. Al-Mamory et al. (Eds.): 3INC 2024, CCIS 2329, p. 249, 2025.
https://doi.org/10.1007/978-3-031-81065-7

The manufacturer's authorised representative in the EU is Springer
Nature Customer Service Centre GmbH, Europaplatz 3, 69115 Heidelberg,
Germany. If you have any concerns regarding our products, please
contact ProductSafety@springernature.com

Printed and bound by CPI Group (UK) Ltd, Croydon, CR0 4YY
24/04/2026
02096367-0009